BRITISH POLICY
IN CHINA
1895–1902

BRITISH POLICY
IN CHINA
1895–1902

L. K. YOUNG

OXFORD
AT THE CLARENDON PRESS
1970

Oxford University Press, Ely House, London W. 1

GLASGOW NEW YORK TORONTO MELBOURNE WELLINGTON
CAPE TOWN SALISBURY IBADAN NAIROBI DAR ES SALAAM LUSAKA ADDIS ABABA
BOMBAY CALCUTTA MADRAS KARACHI LAHORE DACCA
KUALA LUMPUR SINGAPORE HONG KONG TOKYO

PRINTED IN GREAT BRITAIN
AT THE UNIVERSITY PRESS, OXFORD
BY VIVIAN RIDLER
PRINTER TO THE UNIVERSITY

TO
EVELYN BARLOW

ACKNOWLEDGEMENTS

I WISH to acknowledge with grateful thanks the encouragement and helpful advice which has been so freely and generously extended to me by my friends during the preparation of this work. I am particularly indebted to Mr. G. F. Hudson, in whose book-strewn study at Oxford my interest in Sino-British relations first took root; to Professor Brian Harrison, formerly of the University of Hong Kong and now at the University of British Columbia, under whom I had the good fortune to work for a number of years; and to Professor Gerald Graham of King's College, London, who kindly read parts of the manuscript and who has offered so much searching and valuable criticism in the form of gentle advice.

I am grateful to the Most Hon. The Marquess of Salisbury for permission to quote from the papers of his grandfather; and to the Librarian of the University of Birmingham and the Trustees of the Chamberlain Papers for allowing me to use those papers. Crown copyright material in the Public Record Office appears by kind permission of the Controller of Her Majesty's Stationery Office. For their indefatigable help over the years I wish to thank the librarians, archivists, and staff of the Public Record Office, the Bodleian, the British Museum, the University of Birmingham Library, Christ Church Library, the Foreign Office Library, the India Office Library, the Church Missionary Society, the London Missionary Society, and the Society for the Propagation of the Gospel in Foreign Parts.

I should like to express my special debt of gratitude to my wife for her unfailing patience and to my sister who gave so much of her time to the typing and the retyping of a chaotic manuscript and to encouraging me in this work.

L. K. Y.

CONTENTS

LIST OF MAPS

(AT END)

ABBREVIATIONS

Adm.	Admiralty Papers
B.D.	*British Documents on the Origins of the War, 1898–1914*
B.P.P.	British Parliamentary Papers
Cab.	Cabinet Papers
C.O.	Colonial Office Papers
CSPSR	*Chinese Social and Political Science Review*
Customs Treaties	*The Maritime Customs, Treaties, Conventions, etc., between China and Foreign States*
D.D.F.	*Documents diplomatiques français, 1871–1914*
FEQ	*Far Eastern Quarterly*
F.O.	Foreign Office Correspondence:

	F.O. 17/ China	F.O. 46/ Japan	
	27/ France	65/ Russia	
	65/ Germany	5/ United States	

Foreign Relations	*Papers Relating to the Foreign Affairs of the United States*
Grosse Politik	*Die Grosse Politik der europäischen Kabinette, 1871–1914*
HJAS	*Harvard Journal of Asiatic Studies*
I.H.T.	*I-ho-t'uan (tzu-liao ts'ung-k'an)* [Source materials on the Boxers]
JAS	*Journal of Asian Studies*
JRUSI	*Journal of the Royal United Services Institution*
PHR	*Pacific Historical Review*
P.R.O.	Public Record Office Papers:

	P.R.O. 30/33/ Satow	P.R.O. 30/40/ Ardagh

PSQ	*Political Science Quarterly*
S.J.	Satow's Journal: see under 'Satow Papers' in Bibliography
S.P.	Salisbury Papers
tel.	telegram
TRHS	*Transactions of the Royal Historical Society*
T.T.S.L.	*Ta-ch'ing li-ch'ao shih-lu* [Veritable records of the Ch'ing Dynasty]
WHW.	Weihaiwei
W.O.	War Office Papers

I

INTRODUCTION

FOR the whole term of Lord Salisbury's Third Administration (1895–1902) Chinese affairs occupied much of the attention of the British Government. In this period Great Britain did not want an active situation in the Far East. 1895 marked the beginning of a critical period in British foreign policy. The Armenian massacres had reopened the question of Russian activity in the Straits. In Africa, France was moving to an aggressive policy in the Niger region and Anglo-French relations over Egypt were in a serious state. Before the end of the year, Anglo-German relations were to become strained through the Kaiser Wilhelm II's interference in the affairs of the Transvaal and the United States was to assert her growing international outlook over the Venezuelan boundary question. Moreover, these events had to be assessed in relation to the newly formed Franco-Russian alliance of 1894. From 1895 the political thinking of British statesmen pivoted on the central fact that Great Britain had no satisfactory reply to this potentially hostile combination.

The political significance of the Dual Alliance had been clearly perceived by Salisbury as early as June 1892, when the *rapprochement* between the two powers had first become apparent. On the basis of a report by the directors of military and naval intelligence which indicated that the defence of Constantinople against Russian attack could only be made over the ruins of the French fleet at Toulon, Salisbury thought it questionable whether the closure of the Straits by Great Britain could any longer be guaranteed.[1] Consequently, when he left office a few months later he urged Lord Rosebery who succeeded him to maintain the Mediterranean agreements of

---

[1] Memorandum by Salisbury, most confidential, printed for Cabinet, 8 June 1892, with Director of Military Intelligence and Director of Naval Intelligence Report of 18 Mar. 1892 annexed. Salisbury Papers (hereafter cited S.P.).

1887, which formed a minor link with the Triple Alliance powers.[1]

When Salisbury returned to office in 1895, apart from a brief attempt to secure German co-operation over the Armenian question, he adopted a different approach. Throughout his Third Administration Lord Salisbury became increasingly apprehensive of the Kaiser Wilhelm II's large ambitions and of his desire to occupy a decisive role in world affairs. In Salisbury's view, British involvement in the Triple Alliance structure in Europe was too high a price to pay for the doubtful support Germany was likely to offer to Great Britain in defence of her interests overseas. Moreover, from 1895 it became increasingly clear that the expansive tendencies of Russia and France were not turned on Europe, but on the establishment of their positions abroad.

The Far East, in particular, attracted the attention of the two powers. When the real extent of Chinese vulnerability was revealed in the Sino-Japanese war of 1894–5 Russia and France attempted to extend their positions in China. The participation of Germany, Japan, and, to a lesser extent, the United States in this activity resulted in an intense struggle for influence between the powers in the Far East. In this situation, Great Britain was forced on to the defensive, not only to protect her established treaty rights but to preserve the whole basis of her position in China.

Great Britain's Position in the Far East during the Nineteenth Century

Great Britain's principal interest in China during the nineteenth century was trade, and the main aim of her policy there was to bring about a general extension of that trade whilst maintaining for herself the predominant commercial position which she had established in the Far East. This position, secured through two wars with China in 1839–42 and 1856–60, was based on certain established treaty rights. By the Treaty of Nanking, which concluded the first Anglo-Chinese war, Hong Kong was

[1] See Lady Gwendolen Cecil, *Life of Robert, Marquis of Salisbury*, 4 vols. (London, 1921–32), iv. 404–5; Dame Lilian Penson, 'The New Course in British Foreign Policy, 1892–1902', *TRHS* 4th series, 25 (1943), 130.

ceded to Great Britain and trading privileges were secured in the five ports of Canton, Amoy, Foochow, Ningpo, and Shanghai. Conditions were laid down which governed the residential, travel, and extra-territorial rights of British subjects in these treaty ports and a trade tariff was agreed, which was then more precisely defined in the Treaty Tariff and General Regulations of 22 July 1843, and in the Supplementary treaty of Hoomun Chai of 8 October 1843.[1] This position was extended and then consolidated by the Treaty of Tientsin of 1858, which was negotiated during the second Anglo-Chinese war and ratified at the conclusion of the war in 1860. By this treaty additional ports were opened along the China coast and on the Yangtze river. Conditions of trade were improved, the trade tariff was revised, and provision was made for foreigners to travel beyond the treaty ports on a system of passports. In addition, the right of foreign diplomatic residence was established in Peking and arrangements were made for the formation of a Chinese office of foreign affairs, the Tsungli Yamen, through which the foreign powers could deal with China on an official basis.[2]

The lead taken by Great Britain in this activity was accepted and followed by the other foreign powers, for at that time their commercial interests were not as widely extended in the Far East. Thus, at the time of the Nanking treaty settlement the United States and France negotiated separate treaties with China, followed by a number of other powers over the next few years.[3] Subsequently, France participated actively in the war of

---

[1] *China. The Maritime Customs, Treaties, Conventions, etc., between China and Foreign States*, 2 vols., 2nd ed. (Shanghai, 1917), i. 351–6, 383–99; hereafter cited as *Customs Treaties*. British policy during this period is covered in M. Greenberg, *British Trade and the Opening of China, 1800–1842* (Cambridge, 1951); W. C. Costin, *Great Britain and China, 1833–1860* (Oxford, 1937); J. K. Fairbank, *Trade and Diplomacy on the China Coast: the Opening of the Treaty Ports, 1842–1854*, 2 vols. (Cambridge, Mass., 1953); G. H. C. Wong, 'The Ch'i-shan–Elliot negotiations concerning an offshore entrepôt and a revaluation of the abortive Chuenpi Convention', *Monumenta Serica*, 14 (1949–55), 539–73.

[2] *Customs Treaties*, i. 404–21.

[3] Ibid. 677–712, 771–813. For French and American activity at this time see A. Grosse-Aschhoff, *Negotiations between Ch'i-ying and Lagrene, 1844–1846* (New York and Louvain, 1950); J. F. Cady, *The Roots of French Imperialism in Eastern Asia* (New York, 1954), 43–69; E. Swisher, *China's Management of the American Barbarians: A Study of Sino-American Relations, 1841–1861, with Documents* (New Haven, 1953); T. F. Tsiang, 'The Extension of Equal Commercial Privileges to Other Nations than the British after the Treaty of Nanking', *Chinese Social and Political Science Review*, 15 (1931), 422–44; hereafter cited as *CSPSR*.

1856–60 and, to extend their treaty rights, the United States and Russia joined in the Tientsin settlement of 1858.[1]

This participation was welcomed by Great Britain, in that it helped to extend the general position of the foreign powers trading in the east. The only measure which she took to safeguard British interests was to stipulate in the British Supplementary Treaty of 8 October 1843, which was negotiated while the French and American treaties were under consideration, that any privileges granted by China to the subjects of foreign powers should also be extended to British subjects. This principle of most-favoured-nation treatment was rapidly claimed by the other powers who had treaty relations with China. It was written into most other Chinese agreements of the time and reaffirmed in Article 54 of the Treaty of Tientsin of 1858. In effect, it became the keystone of the foreign treaty position in China.[2] In the period after 1895 the safeguard was to be used extensively by Great Britain when China displayed a tendency to grant exclusive and restrictive concessions to the other foreign powers, but at the time of its negotiation this defensive application of the clause was not envisaged by British statesmen. Great Britain's aim, stated by the then British Foreign Minister Lord Clarendon, was simply to ensure that the whole of China should be opened to foreign trade and that all nations should participate in it on an equal footing.[3]

With her control over the existent trade apparently assured, Great Britain's policy in China was then conducted without that sense of overriding urgency which had brought about two wars. In part, this was owing to the reluctance of Lord Palmerston's successors at the Foreign Office to continue an adventurous policy overseas in support of British mercantile ventures; in part, to a greater concentration on European affairs by the Government after 1860. As far as China was concerned, this change became noticeable in the late eighteen-sixties when the Board of Trade submitted a series of reports which drew attention to the real nature and limitations of the commercial

[1] *Customs Treaties*, i. 81–124, 713–35, 814–82.
[2] W. W. Willoughby, *Foreign Rights and Interests in China*, 2 vols. (Baltimore, 1927), i. 35–45; ii. 726–33.
[3] 'Correspondence relative to the Earl of Elgin's Special Missions to China and Japan, 1857–1859', *Accounts and Papers*, Sess. 2, xxxiii. 4–6.

opportunity in China.[1] At the same time, a clearer definition of official attitude was made necessary by the devastating Taiping rebellion which occurred in China in 1851–64. It became clear that, while British commercial interests desired an extension of trade, undue pressure to achieve this could only weaken the existing Manchu Government, aggravate internal discontent in China, and lead to a possible restriction of the existing trade to the detriment of Great Britain's advantageous position. Consequently in the latter part of the nineteenth century, and particularly after the Chefoo Convention of 1876 had placed Great Britain's position on a still firmer basis, British mercantile interests became reconciled to the fact that official policy was directed to the maintenance of Great Britain's commercial preeminence by peaceful means and to the support of Chinese political stability. Within these limits her representatives sought to correct anomalies in the existing treaties so as to consolidate and gradually to extend the commercial position.

There was little in China in the period before the Sino-Japanese war of 1894–5 which led Great Britain to anticipate a threat to her position. During the closing decades of the nineteenth century the British representatives at Peking displayed an easy, even magisterial, attitude over the direction of affairs, confident in Great Britain's control of over 80 per cent of the foreign trade of China.

British influence was paramount at Shanghai, the treaty port at the mouth of the Yangtze river, which by mid-century had replaced Canton as the centre of foreign commercial activity. The rich Yangtze region was generally regarded as an area of special British interest. In the treaty ports British firms dominated over their competitors. Firms such as Jardine, Matheson & Co., Butterfield & Swire, and Dent & Co. controlled the bulk of the import and coastal carrying trade, and if goods were not actually carried in British bottoms more often than not they were conveyed out of Hong Kong in Chinese vessels flying the British flag. The financing of this growing volume of trade was likewise largely served by British interests. The Chartered Bank of India, Australia, and China and the Hongkong and Shanghai Banking Corporation dominated in this field: not

---

[1] N. A. Pelcovits, *Old China Hands and the Foreign Office* (New York, 1948), 53–4, 69–71.

until the eighteen-nineties, with the founding of the Deutsch-Asiatische Bank (1889), the Yokohama Specie Bank (1892), and the redoubtable Russo-Chinese Bank (1895), did British bankers face substantial foreign competition.

Nor was British enterprise confined to a narrow perspective of external commerce. The complex nature of its commitment led to an increasing involvement in every level of the Chinese economy. Although the legal right to establish manufacturing firms was not obtained from China until 1895, British firms were substantially involved in ship-building, engineering, cotton manufacturing, and other activities.

In the south Hong Kong had developed into a thriving entrepôt, through which flowed not only the bulk of the European trade but also that from south-east Asia. The Colony provided a secure point which stabilized the whole of the British position in the Far East and formed a second focus for the extension of British influence. From Hong Kong units of the British Navy patrolled the China coast, engendering mercantile confidence and helping in the eradication of piracy. Successive governors, as the Colonial Office records show, saw their role as something larger than that of mere colonial administration and to an increasing extent they interested themselves in the affairs of southern China.

However, it was in her participation in and control over the Chinese Imperial Maritime Customs that the full extent of Great Britain's commitment in China can be appreciated. The Maritime Customs emerged in Shanghai during the Taiping Rebellion when the breakdown of native authority led the foreign consular officials to assume responsibility for the collection of customs dues. Over the next decade it developed rapidly under the energetic direction of Robert Hart, enforcing the tariff, collecting revenues, and extending its control to the various treaty ports. In its multifarious functions it emerged as the greatest single means by which China modernized herself under the Western impact: it completed the charting of the China coast, installed navigational aids, established a postal system, schools and colleges, published analyses of trade, and sent educational missions abroad. The revenues, honestly collected and scrupulously administered, were returned to the Chinese Government, to play a vital role in propping up the

Imperial finances, paying off indemnities, and providing securities for loans. By the end of the century Hart had achieved a quasi-diplomatic position as unofficial adviser to the Chinese Government. The service employed over 700 foreign employees, the majority of whom were British. Though Hart resisted the assumption, and persisted in regarding himself and his men as servants of the Chinese Government, from the point of view of the foreign powers as well as that of the British Government, the Maritime Customs, and the immense power it wielded, was a particularly British concern.

The Rise of Foreign Competition

During the last few decades of the nineteenth century, several factors did emerge in Far Eastern affairs which threatened the even tenor of British control and indicated the possible rise of foreign competition. In the eighteen-eighties the increased industrial development of the European countries and the United States encouraged them to offer a widespread challenge to Great Britain's domination of the world's trade. This competition was marked by the establishment of tariff walls in the home markets and by a struggle for the control of undeveloped markets abroad. An increased interest was shown in the unappropriated areas of Africa, the Pacific Islands, and the Far East. As the powers could not hope to establish their control in these areas in open commercial competition with Great Britain, they tended to seek a form of exclusive territorial control and to press their mercantile enterprises with diplomatic support. As a result, the principle of equal and open commercial activity which Great Britain sought to maintain throughout the world was steadily undermined by the activities of the other foreign powers.

In China this trend was indirectly encouraged by the establishment of formal diplomatic relations with the Manchu Court after 1860. As their various national aims became more clearly defined there was a natural decline in the co-operative spirit which had marked the activities of the powers in the earlier opening of China. To an increasing extent the various diplomatic representatives at Peking tended to concern themselves with the settlement of specific grievances involving their own nationals, which opened the way for private demands in the matter of compensation. At the same time, the realization of the limited nature of the China trade accentuated the tendency to seek out and to secure individual advantages through diplomatic pressure. While the most-favoured-nation clause ensured that such competitive practices could have no serious effect upon Great Britain's established treaty position, its application tended to reveal the diverging aims of the powers in China.

This aspect of foreign competition became a matter of growing concern in British mercantile circles during the eighteeneighties. In fact, the first loud public outcry in England against the pressure of consular and diplomatic support developed by their foreign competitors, which was rapidly becoming a political issue in the concurrent partition of Africa, arose out of the concern felt in commercial circles for the situation in the Far East in 1884–5.[1] Lord Salisbury, who had just formed his shortlived first ministry, was led to authorize the granting of similar diplomatic support to British merchants, where there was evidence that foreign merchants were being afforded official backing. Thereafter, to the gratification of the China Association, a British mercantile organization which was formed in 1889 to combat this new trend in foreign competition, the assumption at the Foreign Office was that it was legitimate to push British trading interests in China.[2]

A second factor which emerged in Far Eastern affairs at this time was to have a more serious effect on British policy in the period after 1895. The powers, hitherto occupied in China, increasingly turned their attention to the surrounding territories of east Asia. A struggle for the control of China's tributary dependencies developed which defined the distinctive and often conflicting policies and interests of the powers active in those parts.

One such power was the United States, which had in 1853 led the way in the opening of Japan. Although this revival of American interest was not to develop in any significant way before the end of the century, the emergence of Japan did have

[1] R. J. S. Hoffman, *Great Britain and the German Trade Rivalry, 1875–1914* (Philadelphia and London, 1933), 53–5, 172–3. On this situation generally, see Pelcovits, *Old China Hands*, 131–53.

[2] J. A. C. Tilley and S. Gaselee, *The Foreign Office* (London, 1933), 245. On the China Association, see Pelcovits, *Old China Hands*, 157–89.

a more immediate impact. From 1868 Japan embarked on a sustained programme of modernization and political and military reorganization which was to bring her to the level of the great powers by the turn of the century. One of the essentials which faced the Japanese statesmen of the Meiji period was the need to evolve a foreign policy to replace the discarded Tokugawa policy of seclusion. To this end, they applied themselves to the problem of Japan's strategic position in the Far East, and in particular they displayed a close interest in the control of the islands and territories surrounding Japan. Thus in the eighteen-seventies the Liuchiu (Ryukyu) and Bonin islands were taken over, colonization was encouraged in Hokkaido, and serious efforts were made to extend Japanese influence in Formosa and Korea. In particular, the close proximity of Korea made it an area of primary importance in Japanese policy. As Korea was a tributary state of China, a struggle for its control ensued between the two countries which culminated in war in 1894.

Sino-Japanese friction over Korea was complicated further by the growth of Russian territorial interest in this area. Russia, who had a long history of contact with China over a common land frontier, carried her activity in the mid nineteenth century to a new phase. Through the initiative of Count Nikolai Muraviev, governor-general of eastern Siberia, she established settlements in the Ussuri and Amur regions in 1857–9 and founded the port of Vladivostok in 1860.[1] The slow development of this colony soon brought about the realization that effective colonization in the east could only be carried out if an efficient line of communication were established with Russian territories in the west. As the long sea route was impractical, attention turned to the development of overland railway communication. In the eighteen-sixties the piecemeal planning of intra-Siberian lines was begun and by 1875 the concept of a continuous line from the Volga to the Amur had been evolved. A brief interruption then occurred when interest turned to railway construction in the Volga–Ural region at the time of the Russo-Turkish war of 1877–8. But in the following decade the effect of that war, the

[1] A. Malozemoff, *Russian Far Eastern Policy, 1881–1904* (Berkeley and London, 1958), 6–9. Russian diplomatic activity in relation to this expansion is dealt with in M. Mancall, 'Major-General Ignatiev's Mission to Peking, 1859–1860', Harvard University, *Papers on China*, 10 (1956), 55–96.

restriction imposed by the Congress of Berlin on Russian activity in the Middle East, the revelation in 1887 of the secret Austro-German alliance of 1879, and the strong stand taken by Lord Salisbury over Constantinople and the Mediterranean in 1887 led to the limitation of Russian influence in Near Eastern affairs. At the same time difficulties with China over Kuldja, Chinese colonization efforts in Manchuria and the Ussuri region, the opening of Korea to foreign trade and the rapid growth of Japanese influence there aroused Russia's apprehension over the safety of her position in the east. In consequence, the eighteen-eighties were noticeable for a shift in Russian attention from the Near to the Far East. From 1891, when its construction was authorized, the concept of a continuous railway line across Siberia became an important element of Russian policy.[1]

In 1892 the railway project came under the control of Count Sergei Witte, Russian Minister of Finance from 1892 to 1903. Under his forceful direction the Siberian railroad became a dominant factor in Russian policy. To Witte, the railroad was 'one of those world events that usher in new epochs in the history of nations and not infrequently bring about the radical upheaval of established economic relations between states'.[2] The line was to establish Russian communication with the east, while economically it would challenge Great Britain's control of the sea-borne carrier trade. Through economic ties Russia would play a decisive political role in China. This extravagant ambition was made possible in that, as Minister of Finance, Witte had at his disposal the resources of French capital made available by the financial aspect of the Dual Alliance of 1894.

In 1894 plans were drawn up for the construction of the whole line except for the Baikal and Amur sections. The eastern terminus of the line was to be Vladivostok. This port had two serious disadvantages: first, that it was ice-bound for five months of the year; secondly, that to reach it the line would have to take a great sweep around the northern frontier of the Chinese territory of Manchuria. The need to secure a warm-water outlet was considered essential. Although there were

---

[1] Malozemoff, *Russian Policy*, 20–9, 34–9; B. A. Romanov, *Russia in Manchuria, 1892–1906* (Leningrad, 1928, trans. S. W. Jones, Ann Arbor, 1952), 38–44.

[2] Quoted Romanov, *Russia in Manchuria*, 42.

differences of opinion among the Russian planners as to the
exact location of such a port, in general, in the period before
the Sino-Japanese war, official Russian opinion was inclined
toward an extension of the eastern terminus of the railway from
Vladivostok down the Amur coastline to a more favourable
outlet in Korea.[1]

Another European power which developed a territorial interest in the Far East during the latter part of the nineteenth
century was France. France had long been interested in territorial holdings in the east, but these had been lost to her at the
time of the Napoleonic wars. In the early part of the nineteenth
century the French Government made efforts to revive France's
influence overseas by offering support to the Catholic missionary cause. While this measure provided the opening for a
revival of French influence in the east it did little to satisfy
that feeling for a spirited foreign policy which was a legacy of
the Napoleonic era.[2] In 1858 Napoleon III took advantage of
French participation in the second Anglo-Chinese war to intervene in Annam against the exclusionist and anti-missionary
activity of Tu Duc, Emperor of Annam from 1847 to 1883.
Tourane and Saigon were occupied in 1858–9 and a Franco-
Annamese treaty was negotiated in June 1862 by which Annam
ceded her three lower provinces, which were then formed into
French Cochin China.[3]

In the eighteen-sixties France consolidated this position by
extending her influence into Cambodia and Laos. By these
moves she secured control of the outlets of the Mekong and Red
rivers which commanded the trade of the interior of the south-
east Asian mainland and which had a connection with the
interior provinces of China. Not unnaturally, French interest
was aroused by the possibility of reviving the flagging China
trade by tapping the resources of the interior of China along a
route exclusively under French control. Consequently in 1866–8
the Garnier–Lagrée expedition was sent out to explore the
navigability of the Mekong. When Garnier found this route impractical interest turned to the Red river as an alternative route
to the reputedly rich province of Yunnan. Access to China

[1] Ibid. 7–10, 53, 62–3.
[2] Cady, *Roots of French Imperialism*, 17–42, 88–97.
[3] S. H. Roberts, *History of French Colonial Policy*, 2 vols. (London, 1929), ii. 421–2.

along this route was then confirmed by Dupuis, a French merchant stationed in Hankow, who navigated the river from its Yunnan approaches in 1866–72 and in a reverse direction in 1872–3.[1]

The success of these expeditions encouraged a forward move in Indo-China by France for the control of Tonkin, the province which commanded the outlet of the Red river. A treaty was negotiated with the Tonkinese in March 1874 and with the enthusiastic backing of Jules Ferry, then the French premier, the area was brought increasingly under French control until a protectorate was established in August 1883.[2] This led to intermittent war with Annam and with Annam's tributary overlord, China. Despite minor French reverses in this war, which were nevertheless sufficient to bring about Ferry's downfall, by 1885 France was firmly established in an advantageous position on the south-east Asian mainland.

Great Britain's attitude toward these political developments in the east was conditioned by the way in which they affected her existent interests. In general, she welcomed the extension of the China trade to the surrounding territories of east Asia, but she was also determined that these areas should be freely open to commercial enterprise. Consequently she joined in the opening of Japan. Then, with the extension of foreign influence into Korea, she encouraged China to advise her vassal state to frustrate the undue growth of the influence of any one power by allowing equal commercial rights to all the interested foreign powers.[3] After this aim had been secured in the eighteen-eighties official British opinion tended to take a comparatively detached view of the involvement of China, Japan, and Russia in Korean affairs. In the period before 1895, among the three powers involved the only power likely to arouse British apprehension was Russia, but since north-east Asia could not be considered an area of direct British concern Russian activity was largely condoned.

[1] Roberts, *French Colonial Policy*, ii. 422; A. Murphy, *The Ideology of French Imperialism, 1871–1881* (Washington, 1958), 50–9, 60–3.

[2] H. Cordier, *Histoire des relations de la Chine avec les Puissances Occidentales, 1860–1902*, 3 vols. (Paris, 1901–2), ii. 331–92.

[3] E. V. G. Kiernan, *British Diplomacy in China, 1880–1885* (London, 1939), 81–5; M. C. Wright, 'The Adaptability of Ch'ing Diplomacy . . .', *JAS*, 17 (1958), 363–81. British policy in regard to the opening of Japan is dealt with in W. G. Beasley, *Great Britain and the Opening of Japan, 1834–1858* (London, 1951).

The recurrent issue in Anglo-Russian rivalry throughout the nineteenth century lay in the supposed vulnerability of India to Russian attack. Though the possibility was kept alive by voluminous India Office reports of Russian intrigue along the north-west frontier, the almost impenetrable nature of the mountainous terrain allayed any serious fears of a direct invasion by land. British attention was concentrated on preventing a Russian outlet through the Straits, an aspect which took on added importance after the establishment of the short route to India through the Suez Canal in 1869.

During the latter part of the nineteenth century Russian advances in central Asia and the Middle East carried the problem of the defence of India into a new phase. In 1878 and again in 1885 an Anglo-Russian war over Afghanistan seemed imminent, and Great Britain was forced to turn to more active measures and to attempt to arrive at a settlement with Russia on the north-west frontier.[1] In the eighteen-eighties, when overt signs of Russian interference in Korean affairs first became apparent, British attention was more on Russian activity in central Asia than in the Far East. In so far as there was a connection in Chinese affairs, the safety of Kashgaria and Tibet rather than that of Korea exercised the diplomatic ability of the British representatives in Peking. Even the British occupation of Port Hamilton, an island off the Korean coast, in 1885 is to be understood as an aspect of the Afghan crisis of that year.

On the other hand, French activity in the east constituted a more direct threat to British interests in those parts, and thus it received the closer attention of British statesmen. First, the establishment of French territorial holdings on the south-east Asian mainland placed her in competition with Great Britain, who had also established a territorial position there. Secondly, France's interest in tapping the China trade from a southerly direction constituted a possible threat to Great Britain's control of that trade. Finally, as an Imperial concern, the possible establishment of French control along the upper reaches of the

---

[1] C. C. Davies, *The Problem of the North-West Frontier, 1890–1908* (Cambridge, 1932), 1–17, 71–98; W. Habberton, *Anglo-Russian Relations concerning Afghanistan, 1837–1907* (Urbana, 1937), 23–68 *passim*; V. G. Kiernan, 'Kashgar and the Politics of Central Asia, 1868–1878', *The Cambridge Historical Journal*, 11 (1955), 317–42; A. P. Thornton, 'Afghanistan in Anglo-Russian Diplomacy, 1869–1873', ibid. (1954), 204–18.

Mekong river and into the interior provinces of China aroused some apprehension over the safety of India.

Great Britain's territorial position on the south-east Asian mainland was established early in the nineteenth century. By the first Anglo-Burmese war of 1824 the provinces of Arakan and Tenesserim were occupied, and a British residency was established at Ava. After a second war in 1852, Lower Burma was seized; this position was consolidated by further treaties in 1862 and 1867. Thereafter, there were desultory efforts to extend British influence in a northward direction. As with the French, British publicists and travellers were attracted by the prospect of opening up the interior of China with an overland line of communication from the south. In fact the writings of Sprye and Holt Hallet, the British travellers and publicists, preceded Garnier's publications by more than a decade.[1] But while the French turned to the riverine route the British favoured railway schemes. Amongst these, a route between Mandalay and Yunnan was backed by mercantile interests, whilst the Government of India, within whose competence these projects lay, favoured a more westerly link with Yunnan through Bhamo.[2] Partial surveys of this latter route were carried out between 1867 and 1875 until the death of the British consul Margary, who had been sent into Yunnan to negotiate an agreement, brought about a period of official indifference which was not to be revived until French activity in the late eighteeneighties gave the matter a renewed urgency.

In reality, the British Government had little faith in the commercial potentialities of the overland railway connection. As can be seen from the Government of India's preference for the Bhamo route, which was more strategically than commercially attractive, the limited degree of official enthusiasm that was aroused was prompted not by the promise of trading advantages but by an increasing nervousness of French activity in the area. French expeditions into the valley of the Mekong, Franco-Burmese negotiations for a treaty in the eighteen-seventies, and reports of French intrigue in Mandalay indicated the possible

---

[1] W. B. Walsh, 'The Yunnan Myth', *FEQ*, 2 (May 1943), 272–85; H. R. Davies, *Yunnan. The Link between India and the Yangtze* (Cambridge, 1909), 4–17.

[2] Memoranda by Mr. Warner, 'Schemes of railway extension into China' and 'Prospects of trade with Yunnan', S.P. 91/34.

loss of Upper Burma to French enterprise. The consequence of this would be the establishment of a great power on the north-eastern land frontier of India. This possibility assumed a particularly grave aspect in the eighteen-eighties in view of the deterioration of Anglo-French relations as a result of the British occupation of Egypt. In 1885 Great Britain sought to resolve the issue by annexing Upper Burma.

Thereafter, the principal objective of British policy in this area was to oppose any further encroachment by France into the interior. To this end Great Britain favoured the maintenance of Siam as a buffer state between the French and British possessions. Secondly, she sought to effect a clear demarcation of the Burmese frontier. Surveys were carried out along the Salween and Mekong rivers by the British in 1890, which were recognized by Siam in 1893. However, this settlement was disputed by France, who objected to the Siamese claim to the area on the left bank of the Upper Mekong. Two French gunboats were sent to Bangkok in July 1893, and when it was reported that British gunboats had been ordered out of the river, strained relations followed between Great Britain and France which involved for a moment the possibility of war.[1]

However, in the following year, the Siamese crisis was overshadowed by the Sino-Japanese war, which carried the activities of the powers into a new phase.

The Sino-Japanese War

By the summer of 1894 the struggle between China and Japan for a controlling influence in Korean affairs prompted a rising by a nationalistic Korean faction, known as the Tonghaks, which led to hostilities between China and Japan. In the ensuing conflict Japan's overwhelming military and naval superiority resulted in repeated Chinese defeats. Japanese victories at Pingyang (15 September 1894) and on the Yalu (17 September 1894) were followed by the landing of Japanese forces on the Liaotung peninsula, the strategically vital southern part of Manchuria. Port Arthur, the main fortified centre in the area, was taken in November. In January 1895 Japanese military

[1] W. L. Langer, *The Diplomacy of Imperialism, 1890–1902*, 2nd ed. (New York, 1951), 43–5.

forces were landed on the Shantung promontory, capturing Weihaiwei, the only port in northern Chinese waters apart from Port Arthur which had any strategic use. In the face of a mounting Japanese threat towards Peking, the Chinese sued for peace. Fighting then continued sporadically until April, while the two countries negotiated a settlement at Shimonoseki.

The war had not been anticipated by Great Britain and the Government were at a loss for a suitable attitude to adopt. Initially, there was some feeling over the sinking of the *Kowshing*, a Chinese ship sailing under the British flag, which had been sunk by the Japanese whilst transporting Chinese reinforcements to Korea. Concern was also shown over the safety of Shanghai from possible Japanese attack. However, British opinion was soon mollified when Japan gave assurances for the safety of foreign interests in China and also made promises of full reparation over the loss of the *Kowshing*.

Lord Rosebery, who had just taken over an uneasy control of the Government after Gladstone's resignation in March, did not want an active situation in the Far East. As Foreign Secretary during the Siamese crisis of the previous year, he had been made aware of the possible repercussions on British policy of international complications in the east. Rosebery's efforts, therefore, were directed toward a conciliatory move which would restore the situation. After an extended period of preliminary negotiation a British proposal of mediation was circulated to the United States, France, Russia, and Germany on 6 October 1894.[1]

The suggestion was not taken up. In 1894 the attention of the continental powers was concentrated on events in Europe and the Near East and on the political consequences of the Franco-Russian *rapprochement* of that year. Similarly, the United States had yet to develop that interest in Pacific and Far Eastern affairs which was to be aroused by the Spanish–American war of 1898. Russia, whose ambitions were most clearly affected, was then briefly preoccupied with the succession of Tsar Nicholas II. Further, she was undecided on a suitable policy to adopt in relation to the war. As Japan's military successes mounted in the late summer of 1894, Russia could not decide whether to come out strongly against Japan

[1] P. Joseph, *Foreign Diplomacy in China, 1894–1900* (London, 1928), 73.

or to come to an arrangement with her for Japanese agreement to a Russian outlet in Korea for the projected Siberian railway.[1] This indecision marked the reaction of all the powers, who had been taken by surprise by the precipitate development of events.

However, as the war progressed Russian anxiety was aroused by the Japanese occupation of the Liaotung peninsula and Korea. Consequently in February 1895, when it became apparent that the Chinese were suing for peace, Russia took the initiative which had been abandoned by Great Britain after the failure of the overture of 6 October, and came forward with suggestion for the mutual guarantee of Korean independence by the foreign powers.[2] Conversations then followed during February and March between Great Britain, France, Russia, and Germany, which were inconclusive in that the powers delayed a decision in order to ascertain the terms which Japan would demand in the settlement then being negotiated at Shimonoseki. By 4 April these were known. In addition to a claim for a large indemnity and for the opening of further ports in China to foreign trade as well as other commercial concessions, Japan was demanding the independence of Korea and the annexation of Formosa, the Pescadores, and the Liaotung peninsula.[3]

The extensive territorial nature of these demands seriously alarmed Russia. Four days later, on 8 April, she came forward with a suggestion to the powers that they should join in advising Japan that the annexation of the Liaotung peninsula would render Korean independence illusory and constitute a lasting and serious threat to peace in the Far East. This suggestion was accepted by France and Germany.[4]

The British Cabinet met on 8 April and after serious deliberation it was decided that Great Britain should abstain. 'The

[1] Malozemoff, *Russian Policy*, 58–9; Romanov, *Russia in Manchuria*, 53–7, 70; Russian Documents from the *Krasnyi Arkhiv* (Red Archives) are available in translation as follows: Krasnyi Arkhiv L and LI, 1932, covering the efforts by the powers to prevent the war during the period from February to August 1894 in *CSPSR*, 17 (1933), 480–514, 632–70; Krasnyi Arkhiv, LII, 1932, reporting the meetings of the Russian council of ministers in 1894–5 to decide on the policy to be pursued in the Far East, in *CSPSR*, 18 (1934), 236–81.
[2] Malozemoff, *Russian Policy*, 59–60.
[3] Joseph, *Foreign Diplomacy*, 102–3.
[4] Langer, *Diplomacy of Imperialism*, 182.

Japanese conditions', Lord Kimberley, the British Foreign
Secretary, informed Sir Nicholas O'Conor, the British minister
at Peking, 'do not afford grounds for interference on our part.'[1]
On 17 April, the day on which the Sino-Japanese Treaty of
Shimonoseki was signed, Prince Lobanov, the Russian Foreign
Minister, made a further overture for European intervention.
This was backed eagerly by Germany and, rather more reluc-
tantly, by France. On 23 April the British Cabinet met and
reaffirmed its original decision not to intervene.[2]

Several factors influenced Great Britain in this attitude. The
Liaotung peninsula was not an area of direct British concern
and Rosebery was reluctant to interfere because he was convinced that force would have to be used against Japan.[3] He was
supported in this view by his Cabinet, particularly by Sir
William Harcourt, then Chancellor of the Exchequer, who was
strongly opposed to a policy of 'meddling' in what was regarded
by many as a preventative war by Japan against Russian
encroachment in the east.[4] Again, although there was some
concern over the possibly adverse effects of the large indemnity,
Great Britain was drawn by the attractive nature of the commercial advantages in China which Japan had included in the
peace terms, in which she could expect to participate by the
application of the most-favoured-nation clause.[5] Finally, since
the autumn of 1894 there had been a change of feeling in
England toward Japan. This swing in public opinion is particularly noticeable in the attitude of *The Times*, whose editorials
and leaders over the winter of 1894–5 became increasingly
favourable toward Japan. By the spring of 1895 the newspaper
was openly advocating Anglo-Japanese friendship, and on 8
April, the day on which the Cabinet met to consider the Russian

[1] Kimberley to O'Conor, tel. 37, secret, 8 Apr. 1895, F.O. 17/1242.

[2] Memorandum on the Decision of the Cabinet, 23 Apr. 1895, *Kimberley Papers*,
quoted E. Parkin, 'British Policy in the Chinese Question', M.A. thesis, London
University, 68.

[3] I. H. Nish, *The Anglo-Japanese Alliance* (London, 1966), 31.

[4] Parkin, *British Policy*, 78–84.

[5] The Foreign Office correspondence reveals that the Government were not
thinking in terms of a radical change of policy at this time, but rather of the
measures which would have to be adopted in order to regularize Great Britain's
commercial position in view of the new developments. See Memorandum by
Mr. Giffan on 'Commercial Aspects of the Treaty between China and Japan',
17 Apr. 1895; and Board of Trade to Foreign Office, 29 Apr. 1895, F.O. 46/459.

proposal, *The Times* called for a policy of non-interference by Great Britain in the east.[1]

In formulating his policy of non-intervention Rosebery appears to have been influenced by two main considerations. The first was grounded in the favourable feeling which had sprung up towards Japan, which led to a natural reluctance to oppose her in any unnecessary way. The second was rooted in his conviction that Britain should give an example of restraint, rather than join the other powers in the opportunistic free-for-all developing at the time. 'I would have Great Britain hanging like a thundercloud over these filibusters,' he later explained, 'not dispersed in showers all over the Empire.'[2]

However, in abstaining from the Russian proposal Rosebery had misread both the Far Eastern situation and the attitude of the powers. On the evening of 23 April, Russia, France, and Germany acted independently of Great Britain and handed identical notes to Japan advising her to withdraw from the Liaotung peninsula. After some hesitation Japan yielded to these representations and an amended Treaty of Shimonoseki was ratified at Chefoo on 8 May. In this, Japan received a larger indemnity in place of her territorial demands in Manchuria, which was formally retroceded to China on 8 November.[3]

The triple intervention revealed Great Britain's isolation in the east, and the activities of the powers threatened to undermine the British position in China. From 1895 the Government was forced into a searching reappraisal of British policy in China to decide the extent to which it was prepared to act in support of her interests there. The issue for Lord Salisbury and his ministers, was a straightforward one: to defend in an age of competition that which Great Britain had obtained in an age of monopoly.

[1] *The History of The Times, 1785–1984,* 4 vols. (London, 1935–52), iii. 190–2.
[2] Rosebery to Wemyss Reid, 30 Dec. 1897, The Marquess of Crewe, *Lord Rosebery,* 2 vols. (London, 1931), ii. 554.
[3] J. V. A. MacMurray, *Treaties and Agreements with and concerning China, 1894–1919,* 2 vols. (New York, 1921), i. 50–1.

II

LORD SALISBURY AND CHINA

IN 1895 the control of policy rested with Lord Salisbury, who held both the premiership and the seals of the Foreign Office until he relinquished the latter post to Lord Lansdowne in November 1900. Salisbury in 1895 was at the height of his political career and at the head of possibly the most talented and individualistic of any of the British Cabinets of the nineteenth century. But he was sixty-five years of age, in poor health, and too often he found it necessary to take recuperative trips abroad.

Arthur Balfour, who deputized for him at the Foreign Office in his absence, lacked Salisbury's imperturbability and well-known capacity for inaction. The Marquis of Lansdowne, Secretary for War, Lord George Hamilton, Secretary for India, and George Goschen, First Lord of the Admiralty, as well as other members of the Cabinet who were actively and continuously involved in policy decisions because of the responsibilities of their particular offices, also felt the need to act positively in a way which affected Chinese affairs. Sir Michael Hicks Beach, the vigilant Chancellor of the Exchequer, disturbed by the increasing burden of Great Britain's financial commitment, was likewise driven to look for a political solution in the east. This tendency became more marked after the Port Arthur crisis of 1898 when Joseph Chamberlain, the Colonial Secretary, began to interest himself in the Chinese situation. Chamberlain's involvement, and the dynamic suggestion of an Anglo-German alliance which he proposed as a solution, created a virtual dualism in the conduct of British policy in China which can be traced through to 1902.

Among the permanent Foreign Office staff Sir Thomas Sanderson, Permanent Under-Secretary, and Francis Bertie, later Lord Bertie of Thame, exercised a considerable influence over the formulation of Great Britain's Chinese policy. Under

Bertie's control the China Department at the Foreign Office became a centre of feverish activity, which contrasted sharply with the peaceful atmosphere which had prevailed there in the period before the Siamese crisis of 1893. After 1895 memoranda and advice, positively and convincingly phrased, flowed profusely from Bertie's desk in a way which revealed the competence which was later to raise him to an ambassadorship at Paris.

A similar degree of competence was displayed by Great Britain's diplomatic representatives in China. Three different ministers served at Peking between 1895 and 1902 and each possessed qualities which significantly influenced the formulation of British policy. Sir Nicholas O'Conor, appointed Minister to China in 1892, impulsive in action and visionary in outlook, was quick to point to the inevitable political consequences which would result from the Sino-Japanese war. His dispatches, written with an arresting turn of phrase, rapidly aroused the attention as well as the apprehension of the Government. However, the vigorous manner in which he protested to the Chinese Government against any containment of British influence deeply offended the Manchu Court and a request was made that he should be withdrawn. He was transferred to St. Petersburg in 1896 where his contribution was less effective. O'Conor was succeeded at Peking by Major Sir Claude Maxwell MacDonald. MacDonald, who had served in the Egyptian campaigns in the early eighteen-eighties and then in the consular service in Zanzibar and on the Niger Coast, seemed a poor choice for the Peking post and *The Times* spoke out against the appointment.[1] In fact, it was an inspired move by Salisbury. MacDonald showed a tenacity of purpose and a grasp of detail which he used to advantage during the scramble for concessions, while his personal courage and qualities of military leadership inspired confidence during the siege of the legations. Sir Ernest Satow, who moved from Tokyo to change posts with MacDonald after the siege, was a different type of man. Scholarly and reflective by nature, he possessed in abundance the patience and tact which enabled him to negotiate across the conference table during the long months of the post-Boxer settlement.

To a considerable extent the day-to-day conduct of policy

[1] *The Times*, 13 Jan. 1896.

was affected by the lack of a reliable means of communication. The development of telegraphic communications during the last three decades of the nineteenth century brought about a change in the nature of diplomatic activity. The relative freedom of action previously enjoyed by the British representatives in China gave way to greater control by the Government in London. This accelerated the policy-making process and gave the Government a closer understanding of the points at issue while a matter was still in dispute. But in turn it raised fresh problems in that this medium of communication was still technically imperfect. In 1871 a British cable was laid from Singapore to Cape St. James, near Saigon, and from there to Hong Kong. The area to the north of Hong Kong, however, was controlled by the extensive system of the Great Northern Telegraph Company of Denmark. Between 1871 and 1883 this company laid cables between Vladivostok, Japan, and Shanghai and between Shanghai, Amoy, and Hong Kong. The British attempted to compete against this control by laying submarine lines between Hong Kong and Shanghai in 1884 and additional lines on behalf of the Chinese Government between Taku, Chefoo, and Shanghai in 1898–1900.[1] By the end of the century telegraphic communication was the normal procedure, supplemented by fuller written dispatches transmitted by the diplomatic bag. However, breakdown of communication was a frequent occurrence, particularly at the height of the Boxer crisis when an extensive disruption of services resulted. The Foreign Office was then driven to repeat its instructions to Shanghai, Tokyo, and Peking in the hope that at least one of the messages would get through to the British minister.

The cost of telegraphic messages was also a factor to be taken into account. The government rate to north China was 8s. 9d. per word before 1890, and was still 6s. 6d. per word in 1900. The heavy cost of transmission clearly made it impossible for the Government to convey its intentions with sufficient clarity of detail for the guidance of its ministers, just as it was impossible for the British ministers at Peking to report in detail on the finer nuances of the diplomatic attitude which were displayed in the Chinese capital. Meaning was often obscured by the continual attempts at brevity, and Satow's efforts towards

[1] C. S. Goldman (ed.), *The Empire and the Century* (London, 1905), 276–7.

economy during the crucial Boxer negotiations earned him a reprimand from Salisbury.[1]

Nor was accurate information about China easily available. Before the arrival of the British Expeditionary Force in the summer of 1900 five different offices were involved in intelligence work in China. These were the Foreign Office; the Intelligence Division of the War Office; the Intelligence Division of the Admiralty; the Intelligence Branch, Quarter-Master-General's Department, India Office; and the Foreign Department, India Office. There were also various agents who functioned independently. These were the Military Attaché at Peking; the General Officer Commanding, Hong Kong; the Naval Commander-in-Chief, China Station; H.M. Legation at Peking; H.M. consular officers at the treaty ports, as well as occasional military officers who happened to be travelling on leave or on duty. Despite this impressive list the information which was received was generally extremely rudimentary. There was little or no inter-communication between the various offices, nor any unity of administration. When information was received it was often misleading; maps were in short supply. In comparison, Russia had long kept *agents-militaires* in China, with officers serving up to the rank of major-general. By 1900 Germany was following suit and Japan had a wide network which was envied by the other powers.

After the Field Force went out the nucleus of an integrated Intelligence Department was formed by General Gaselee. Control of this unit was given to Major Wingate, who built up an information network in north China and the Yangtze region. Intelligence reports were returned, at first sporadically, then on a weekly basis. By 1902 General Creagh, who took over the command of the British forces in China after Gaselee's departure, proposed the division of the Chinese Empire into three sections for intelligence purposes, broadly covering north China, the Yangtze basin, and south China.[2] The committee

[1] Satow's experience is reflected in his well-known book, *A Guide to Diplomatic Practice*, where he observes that 'telegrams leave no time for reflection' (2nd ed., i. 157) and that the young diplomat 'will be well advised to explain his reasons at length. It is better to spend money on telegrams than to risk the failure of a negotiation' (3rd ed., i. 96). The incident is discussed, below, pp. 341-5.

[2] India Office to Foreign Office, encl. G.O.C. China to India Office, 29 Apr. 1902, F.O. 17/1551.

which was formed to consider the matter felt that the project would be financially too burdensome. Instead it was suggested that use could be made of the newly formed Anglo-Japanese alliance, and that intelligence could be obtained by relying on the extensive Japanese system already in existence.[1] The suggestion revealed the intricate structure of international relationships which had emerged in the Far East by 1902. It indicated, as well, the measures the British Government was driven to contemplate during these years.

Until the Port Arthur crisis of the spring of 1901 emerged as an issue which threatened to split the unity of his Cabinet, Lord Salisbury did not have any special interest in Chinese affairs. Not that he was unaware of the significance of the events which surrounded the Sino-Japanese war, nor that he overlooked the possibly adverse effect on Great Britain's position of the political activities of the powers. In August 1895, within a month of resuming office, he supported Balfour's suggestion of a Committee of Defence to co-ordinate the views of the Cabinet with those of the military and naval advisers of the country. From the start Salisbury envisaged that the scope and activities of the committee would extend beyond questions of home defence. 'It will further include the service of the Mediterranean and the China Seas', he observed, 'in which large questions of policy must necessarily be touched. . . .' Moreover, even at this early stage he was ready to discuss in general terms the numbers and disposition of the ships required in the Far East.

In the China Seas other questions of policy must be dealt with [he added]. Is the British force to be capable of coping in the open sea with the combined forces maintained there by Russia and by France? Or is its duty to keep vessels of the size and numbers required for the purpose of aiding the action of diplomacy in China? Or is it to be so constituted that it will be able to discharge both these functions?[2]

After 1900, when it had become clear that British interests in China were endangered, Salisbury was among the first to discuss specific measures which would commit British resources

---

[1] Memorandum by Campbell of 6 Aug. 1902, F.O. 17/1552.
[2] Minutes on a proposed constitution of a Committee of Defence, Aug.–Dec. 1895, Cab. 1/2/55.

in the east. Also, somewhat sooner than his ministers, he was prepared to contemplate the possibility of an alliance with Japan. But until then he did not admit that there was a need for action, other than to make provision for it in the proposed cabinet committee of defence.

In Salisbury's view the Far East was a convenient area which could absorb the expansive tendencies of the Dual Alliance powers, and the protection of British interests in China was but one aspect of Great Britain's Imperial responsibilities. Yet, possibly to a greater extent than other statesmen of his day, Salisbury was aware of the political consequences which could flow from such expansionist activity. The progression of events in Africa, Persia, and Turkey illustrated the tendency to disintegration which foreign pressure could bring on a weak and defenceless country. 'When a nation dies', Salisbury declared in a speech given in Glasgow in May 1891, 'there is no testamentary distribution of its goods, there is no statute of distribution for what it leaves behind. The disappearance of a nation means a desperate quarrel for what it had possessed.'[1] He believed that the growth of new areas where the great powers fought for influence was one of the greatest threats to peace in his time, and the need for international restraint is a theme on which he dwelt repeatedly in his public speeches in the eighteennineties.

Despite this, for political reasons he was ready to encourage France and Russia to turn to the east after 1895. However, in public, the activity of the two powers was assessed not in political but in commercial terms; and it was in relation to their commercial aspirations that British approval was expressed. From 1895 the limitless extent of the commercial opportunity in China was a recurrent theme in ministerial speeches. At first this was enunciated to reassure mercantile opinion, but later it was adopted as a deliberate aspect of British policy. By dwelling on the commercial aspect Great Britain sought to deny and to refuse to recognize the political nature of foreign activity.

Salisbury was reluctant to abandon this approach even after events in China had assumed an obviously political character.

[1] Quoted Lady Gwendolen Cecil, *Life of Robert, Marquis of Salisbury*, 4 vols. (London, 1921–2), iv. 385.

His apparent failure to recognize this fact and his reluctance to adopt a more positive attitude over the direction of policy aroused exasperation in the country as well as ministerial discontent. By 1898, when many of his colleagues began to think in terms of wide alliances to meet the urgent demands of Great Britain's many responsibilities, the Prime Minister's cautious attitude seemed to verge on timidity or neglect. Nevertheless, the delicate balance which Salisbury sought to maintain between encouragement and restraint, and his persistence in holding to this view, forms the basis of his China policy during these years.

Rather more readily than many of his contemporaries, Salisbury was content to see other powers active in an area over which Great Britain had no special claim. However, he accepted it as one of the responsibilities of office that in tolerating this activity he would maintain Great Britain's existing and clearly established interests in the area intact. This pragmatic approach led him to attempt to isolate differences which arose between Great Britain and the powers, by negotiating limited regional settlements to preserve British interests *in statu quo*. For a statesman apparently so firmly convinced of the adequacy of 'isolation' Salisbury showed a surprising willingness to come to terms with his foreign adversaries in those areas where their interests clashed. China, weakened by the Sino-Japanese war and faced with the urgent need to find the money to pay the war indemnity, was one such area at the end of the nineteenth century.

The Indemnity Loans

The concept of foreign borrowing was not a new one to the harassed statesmen of the Ch'ing dynasty, who had increasingly been made aware of the difficulty of meeting the extraordinary demands of internal rebellion and foreign wars from a fixed Imperial revenue based primarily on the traditional land tax and a rigid salt gabelle.[1] Between 1861 and 1894 about twenty-five minor loans were made by foreign firms and banking interests, amounting to about £12 million. These loans, mostly

---

[1] The grain tribute, likin (internal transit dues), the maritime and native customs revenues, the sale of offices, and other miscellaneous levies helped to make up the revenue.

made to provincial authorities for military purposes, were generally promptly repaid. It could be said that, before the Sino-Japanese war, China had no significant foreign public debt.

From 1894 this pattern changed. Four loans totalling £6,635,000 were made during the war to meet war expenses. After the war, the Japanese indemnity was set at 200 million Kuping taels. Half of this amount was to be paid over a period of six years, in equal annual instalments, and was to carry a 5 per cent interest unless paid by 1898. The port of Weihaiwei was to be occupied by Japan until the debt had been resolved, China being responsible for the cost of the occupation. An additional 30 million Kuping taels was involved in connection with the retrocession of the Liaotung peninsula. China's total obligation amounted to 250 million Kuping taels, or about £38 million.[1]

China resorted to foreign loans to meet this debt. Between 1895 and 1898 she approached the foreign powers for three major and two minor loans amounting to £49·8 million; with the interest involved the total sum came to £54·5 million. The control of the resources which China was forced to pledge as security for these loans was of importance to the powers, and China's creditor nations had a lever by which concessions could be obtained. Thus after 1895 an intense struggle for financial influence developed in China among the foreign powers.

The financial aspect of the struggle was not a matter of serious concern to Great Britain. In the period 1870–1914 Great Britain was predominant in the field of international investment, and London was in effect the financial capital of the world. The British Government, confident that the amount of money involved could not be raised without recourse to the London market, overlooked the possibility of China turning elsewhere for smaller amounts. Moreover, it was slow to realize that the Chinese loans were more political than financial in character, and that they were not to be secured on their own merits but through the exercise of political pressure at Peking. In this respect, British abstention from the triple intervention isolated her diplomatically in the east, while her refusal to

[1] C. M. Hou, *Foreign Investment and Economic Development in China, 1840–1937* (Cambridge, Mass., 1965), 23–4, 236.

participate against Japan also led to an irritating loss of influence over the Manchu Court.[1]

When the loan negotiations opened in April the Hongkong and Shanghai Bank expressed itself willing to find the money in combination with a German syndicate. At the time, the amount rather than the provision of the indemnity was of more concern to the British Government. To keep the indemnity within reasonable limits it tried to prevail upon Japan to accept further commercial advantages rather than additional monetary compensation for the return of the Liaotung peninsula.[2] This lack of vigour in the British approach became more marked when it emerged that the German element in the proposed banking syndicate was not content with the securities offered by the Maritime Customs and contemplated the establishment of an international administration in China to secure the loan. France rapidly responded to the suggestion, and then endeavoured to draw in Russia.[3] Thus within a fortnight of the opening of discussions Great Britain was faced with the possibility of a European settlement which excluded herself.[4]

Even then the British Government did not quite realize the speed with which the loan negotiations were to be conducted. By this time a syndicate of six French banks and four Russian banks was being formed to provide the £16 million being requested. A loan, guaranteed by the Russian Government, was then offered to China.[5]

From a British point of view the unsuccessful negotiations over the first indemnity loan illustrate the difficulties which were to face the Government in the changed condition of Chinese affairs. From the outset the British response was hampered by an understandable official reluctance to provide adequate political backing in a technically private matter. The close cohesion of Russia and France invited caution, and the obvious inclination of Germany to work with them added to an imponderable political situation. Nor could the Government

---

[1] O'Conor to Salisbury, 3 July 1895, S.P. 106/1.
[2] Nish, *Anglo-Japanese Alliance*, 31–2.
[3] Romanov, *Russia in Manchuria*, 65–6.
[4] Memorandum by Sanderson of 7 May 1895, F.O. 17/1252.
[5] The actual amount was 400 million francs, or £15,820,000; Hou, *Foreign Investment*, 46.

foresee the political consequences which were to surround the Franco-Russian loan.

These, however, soon became apparent. While Russia, for reasons which will be discussed later, did not take immediate advantage of the political benefits which accrued to her from this loan, France lost no time in presenting her claims. On 20 June 1895 two Sino-French conventions were negotiated which adjusted the Sino-Annamese border in France's favour and which gave France extensive mining and railway privileges in the southern Chinese provinces of Yunnan, Kwangsi, and Kwangtung. These concessions initiated a new form of foreign activity in China which was opposed to British interests in the east.

Consequently, when Salisbury returned to office in July there was an urgent need for positive measures. Rosebery's aim of having Great Britain hanging like a restraining thundercloud over the powers obviously had little effect. Two new factors were present in the Chinese situation and both needed the unremitting attention of the Government if Great Britain were to maintain her paramount position in the east. The first was the financial competition which was emerging over the Japanese indemnity loans. The second was the struggle over the concessions which China was forced to grant to secure these loans. The country was in a disturbed and vulnerable state and there were clear signs of change and, to some, of impending catastrophe. A degree of political involvement was called for which was entirely at variance with the traditional British policy of laissez-faire commercialism.

However, Salisbury refused to embark on an anticipatory policy in China. At a practical level there was little to drive a man of Salisbury's pragmatic nature to act precipitately. In the first two years after the Sino-Japanese war Great Britain appeared to be holding her own in China. After the first indemnity loan had gone to Russia and France a rough political equilibrium emerged in the financial struggle. Largely because of French resistance to co-operation with Germany, Germany drifted to the side of Great Britain in the competition for the loans. The two powers joined to press the Chinese Government to negotiate loans with their respective nationals which resulted in two minor loans, each for £1 million, being granted in 1895. At the same time an arrangement was made between the Hongkong and Shanghai Bank and the Deutsche-Asiatische Bank for closer co-operation in financial matters, and by which each secured the option of sharing with the other any railway or commercial concessions acquired by either in China. Moreover, by the time the second indemnity loan came up for discussion at the end of 1895, China had become apprehensive over the political nature of the Franco-Russian demands. To strengthen her hold on the situation she turned to the Anglo-German banks for the loan. An Anglo-German loan for £16 million was arranged in 1896.[1]

On the other hand, the concessions obtained by France through the two conventions of 20 June did give Salisbury more cause for concern. For a decade France had sought exclusive advantages in the southern provinces of China contiguous to her possessions in Annam. To counteract her, Great Britain had written safeguards for her interests in the area into the Anglo-Chinese Convention of 1 March 1894 relative to Burma and Tibet.[2] From the British point of view the Sino-French conventions of 20 June violated these agreements, for Article 5 of the second convention stipulated that, in the exploitation of her mines in the provinces of Yunnan, Kwangsi, and Kwangtung, China would address herself in the first instance to French commerce and engineers. Consequently, Salisbury approached China in defence of Great Britain's established treaty rights. These negotiations culminated in the Anglo-Chinese Agreement of 4 February 1897 which re-established the diplomatic basis of Great Britain's position in southern China.[3]

Although it was necessary, this application of the most-favoured-nation clause tended to increase rather than lessen Anglo-French tension. Moreover, there was a wider application of the struggle, which was really an extension of the competition already existing between the two powers in mainland south-east Asia. Anglo-French relations in this area were already bitter after the Siamese crisis of 1893. French gains in south-west China through the conventions of 20 June introduced a new level of competitive activity in the area, in which the initiative

---

[1] For 36 years at 5 per cent, issued at 94. The two minor loans were the Cassel loan (British) and the Nanking loan (German).

[2] *Customs Treaties*, i. 506–8, 520–31.   [3] Ibid. 532–8.

lay with France. It was clearly inadequate for Great Britain to
try to recover the position by merely bringing pressure to bear
on China. Consequently, Salisbury decided to treat that situation as an Imperial rather than a Chinese matter, and to make a
direct approach to France to arrive at an understanding.

The Settlement with France

In August 1895 discussions were initiated with Baron de
Courcel, the French Ambassador in London. If Courcel is to
be believed, as early as 1892, before the Siamese crisis, Salisbury
had expressed himself as personally in favour of an arrangement
that Great Britain and France should bind themselves to each
other not to extend their influence beyond the Mekong. In a
conversation with Kimberley, in the closing days of Rosebery's
administration, the Ambassador stated that Salisbury had then
given an assurance that Britain would not advance beyond the
line of the Upper Mekong.[1] Courcel's recollections may have
been faulty and formed out of his strong desire for closer Anglo-
French relations. In any case, Kimberley chose to assume that
there had been a misunderstanding and that Salisbury would
not have pledged Great Britain to this limitation of her influence. However, in the autumn of 1895 some such arrangement was in Salisbury's mind and, as might be expected,
discussions flowed smoothly with the Anglophile French Ambassador. The discussions ranged widely over the affairs of
Siam, Tunisia, and the Niger; the most important being Siam,
to which the Chinese issue was incidental. An agreement was
then signed on 15 January 1896.[2] In this agreement Salisbury
agreed to the Upper Mekong as the boundary between Burma
and French Indo-China, thereby conceding the territory on the
left bank which had been the cause of Anglo-French friction in
the summer of 1893. In regard to China he secured French
agreement that any commercial or railway concessions obtained
in the south should be common to both powers.
   The settlement was widely condemned in England by the

---

[1] Memorandum by Kimberley of 28 May 1895, Cab. 37/39/33.
[2] J. V. A. MacMurray, *Treaties and Agreements with and concerning China, 1894–
1919*, 2 vols. (New York, 1921), i. 54–5; J. D. Hargreaves, 'Entente manquee;
Anglo-French Relations, 1895–1896', *The Cambridge Historical Journal*, 11 (1953),
65–92.

Liberal opposition for the concessions which had been made to France, particularly on the Siamese boundary issue.[1] The charges were unfair, but the Prime Minister was not in a position to defend himself. He had actually prepared a dispatch for circulation setting out the advantages the agreement gave to Great Britain, which he was advised not to publish in that form for fear of arousing French opinion.[2] In fact, Salisbury's views on the Siamese issue were well thought out and are convincing: they can be examined in the letters he wrote to Chamberlain, during and after the negotiations with Courcel.

In Salisbury's view England could either play the *beau role*, and protest in favour of the integrity of Siam, or the *base role*, and join in its partition before the last stage was reached.[3] France was in full process of absorbing the country, in a way that Rosebery had been unable to prevent. England would not fight for Siam, and had no treaty right to interfere even if inclined to do so, 'and no one believes', he observed to Chamberlain, 'that we could have induced the English nation to go to war in a cause where we had no rights whatever'.[4] The Agreement of 1896 gave Great Britain that right, and effectively controlled France in that area. The argument was put clearly to Chamberlain in the same letter of June 1897:

. . . we induced France to sign a treaty which gives us that right, and which practically makes the conquest of Siam by France impossible. To obtain this advantage, we surrendered a claim to a worthless territory inland, which I greatly doubt that we could have maintained before an arbiter; and which was of no use strategically, commercially, or fiscally. France lost the reversion of Siam, and gained an undisputed entry to a small tract to which she had at all events quite as much right as we had. I do not call this giving France a great deal or anything. . . .[5]

The letters are revealing, not only for the light they shed on

[1] S. L. Gwynn and G. M. Tuckwell, *The Life of the Rt. Hon. Sir Charles W. Dilke*, 2 vols. (London, 1917), ii. 486; *The History of The Times, 1785–1948*, 4 vols. (London, 1935–52), iii. 201–2. For the acclaim with which the agreement was received by the country at large, see Langer, *Diplomacy of Imperialism*, 251–4.
[2] Salisbury to Chamberlain, letter of 7 June 1897, private, Chamberlain Papers 5/7.
[3] Salisbury to Chamberlain, letter of 4 Sept. 1895, Chamberlain Papers 5/7.
[4] Salisbury to Chamberlain, letter of 7 June 1895, private, Chamberlain Papers 5/7.
[5] Loc. cit.

Salisbury's thinking in this controversial issue, but for a closer understanding of the principles which guided his conduct in this type of dispute. In an age when Great Britain and the powers were involved in a scramble for possessions, no British Government could hope to move to war with the support of the country unless England's vital interests were involved or there was a clear infringement of her established treaty rights. The first step for any British Government was to indicate those rights clearly, preferably by agreement, thus removing foreign misunderstanding, and also strengthening the Government's hand. Until then, in view of the competitive spirit of the times, it was well to remember that other powers had as much right as Great Britain to expand into areas where British interests were undefined.

However, too much must not be made of the Anglo-French agreement of 1896. Salisbury would have been the first to admit that at best it was a workable arrangement which effectively removed Siam as a source of disagreement between Great Britain and France and, at the same time, nullified the advantages that France had gained in China through the first indemnity loan. Anglo-French relations in mainland south-east Asia, as elsewhere, were to continue in an uneasy state until the *entente* of 1903–4. Before that the prospect of a durable settlement with France became increasingly remote in view of French activity in Equatorial Africa, where Anglo-French relations were to worsen steadily until the Fashoda crisis of 1898. During these years French activity in southern China was a basic factor influencing Great Britain's attitude in Far Eastern affairs.

In this connection, during the Salisbury–Courcel negotiations of the autumn of 1895 the British Cabinet was led to re-examine the whole extent of Great Britain's interest in the wide area embracing the Bay of Bengal and the South China Sea. At various Cabinet meetings discussion centred on the integrity of the Malay peninsula and on the extent of Great Britain's commercial stake in Siam, the basin of the Mekong, and the prospects of trade into Yunnan.[1] In particular, attention was concentrated on railway construction projects. To offset French advantages the decision was made to sanction the

[1] Cab. 1/2/335.

construction of a commercial railway in this area. This was a departure from the previous approach when, it will be recalled, the Government of India had preferred the more strategic Bhamo route in the west.

Two schemes were considered. (1) The Mandalay–Kunlon scheme; (2) the Burma–Siam–China railway. Little enthusiasm was shown for the Burma–Siam–China (or Sumao) route which would stretch for 703 miles and which existed only in outline 'traced by a magician's wand, unsurveyed and unexplored'.[1] There were also serious strategic objections to a line which would pass through Siam, whose grasp over its northern and eastern territories had been enfeebled by French aggression. Moreover, such a line was impossible without negating the Anglo-French discussions then in progress.

The Mandalay–Kunlon route, however, held out more promise. This was a long-standing project which had been supported by Lord Salisbury when previously in office; at the India Office in 1866 he had authorized a survey of Sprye's route.[2] During his second ministry (1886–92) French activity had led him to call for a report from Holt Hallet, the British publicist and traveller who had succeeded Sprye as the exponent of the Mandalay route. This was submitted on 31 May 1892.[3] Between 1892 and 1894 a favourable survey was made of the route between Mandalay and Kunlon.[4] It was envisaged that the line would run 224 miles up to the Salween, and thence 270 miles to Kunlon. The cost for the two sections was estimated at Rupees 18,298,137 and, to Kunlon, 226 lakhs. It was recognized that there was little likelihood of the line passing through mountainous Yunnan province to tap the rich, fertile, populous Szechuan region, which was then being publicized by Colquhoun as the El Dorado of foreign commercial enterprise in China. However, it was considered that Yunnan was an adequate objective and that the Mandalay–Kunlon line, stemming from the best British port in the Bay of Bengal, provided the most promising approach to the interior.

[1] Cab. 37/40/59.
[2] N. A. Pelcovits, Old China Hands, 121.
[3] Holt Hallet's Report of 31 May 1892 is attached to Lord George Hamilton's Report, secret, of 19 Nov. 1895, S.P. Chronological Series 1896.
[4] Government of Indian Administration, Report on Railways in India, 1894–5, 51–2.

Construction of the line was authorized on 16 October 1895,[1] and in March 1897 work was transferred to the Burma Railways Administration.[2] In 1898–9 an expedition was sent into Yunnan, and further surveys were made which revealed the real difficulties of the project.[3] The line, at one point, was expected to traverse the stupendous Gokteik Canyon, a fissure half a mile wide and 1,000 feet deep. Nor did it emerge as a feasible way of matching French advances along the riverine route: while the British railway would have to cross transverse ranges of mountains, the French could follow the longitudinal valleys.[4] By 1901, after six years of arduous work, less than one hundred miles of the first stretch of the line had been laid and the enterprise, which had failed even to reach the Chinese border, had become a matter of ridicule. As Lord Curzon declared in a speech to the Rangoon Chamber of Commerce in December 1901:

... were a bonfire made tomorrow of the prolific literature to which (the Burma–China railway scheme) has given birth, I do not think any one in the world would be the loser ... the idea that, if it were built, the wealth of Szechuan would stream down a single metre-gauge line, many miles of which would have to scale the mountains by a rack, to Rangoon, while great arterial rivers flow through the heart of the province of Szechuan itself, which are quite competent to convey its trade to and from the sea—is one as it seems to me in the present stage of Central Asian evolution almost of midsummer madness.[5]

Curzon was then merely reflecting a generally accepted point of view, which was more freely expressed after Great Britain had secured a stronger hold on the Yangtze valley in the scramble for concessions. Surveys carried out in 1899–1900 clearly

---

[1] See 'Report of the Liverpool Chamber of Commerce to the Secretary of State for India, 21 October 1901', F.O. 17/1510. On the railway generally, see P. H. Kent, *Railway Enterprise in China* (London, 1907), 177 f.

[2] For Indenture see *Administration Report, 1897–8*, Pt. 2, App. 1.

[3] W. J. Weightman, 'Note on the Reports of the Yunnan Expedition of 1898–1899', 6 Jan. 1900, in Yunan Company to Bertie of 16 Feb. 1900, F.O. 17/1437; Yunan Company to Bertie, 18 Oct. 1902, F.O. 17/1554.

[4] Report of Capt. Peach, D.A.A.G., D.G.M.I., Intelligence Division to Foreign Office, 8 Aug. 1901, F.O. 17/1507.

[5] Office of the Superintendent of Government Printing, India, *Speeches by Lord Curzon of Kedleston*, 4 vols. (Calcutta, 1900–6), ii. 382–5; see also a leader in *The Times* of 12 Dec. 1901.

admitted the obvious fact that the natural route to the interior of China lay along the Yangtze river.[1] Nevertheless, despite its impracticability, the Mandalay–Kunlon railway scheme was pursued during this period as a necessary measure to counteract the spread of French influence in these parts, and to ensure that Great Britain would be in a position to share with equal advantage in the exploitation of Chinese resources in accordance with the Anglo-French agreement of 1896.

The Problem of Russia

The equitable relationship which had been reached with France and the positive measures which were taken over the Burmese railway gave a reassuring impression that Great Britain's commercial interests were being adequately supported in China. Consequently, during the first two years of his Third Administration Salisbury tended to view the Far Eastern situation with equanimity. He was aware that Russia would want to extend herself in the furtherance of her Siberian railway project. But, in his view, she was to be encouraged rather than opposed in this activity. The commercial possibilities of the Siberian railroad aroused Salisbury's enthusiasm, but he was inclined to overlook the political implications which were involved.

By the summer of 1895 Russia had been encouraged, by the revelation of Chinese weakness, to abandon the idea of seeking an outlet for the railway in Korea. Instead, a direct line was to be taken across northern Manchuria to Vladivostok, and from this main trunk branch lines were to be constructed through Manchuria into northern China. This plan received the enthusiastic support of Sergei Witte, who saw it as a means of extending Russian political influence in China.

Witte's aim was to bring about a steady economic penetration of the country which would place Russia in an unshakeable position. To further this aim he secured the support of French capital to establish the Russo-Chinese Bank in 1895. The bank was launched under the auspices of the Russian Government 'to operate, on the broadest principles, in the

[1] Memorandum by Mr. Clive Bigham on the Upper Valley of the Yang-tsze Kiang and the Provinces immediately beyond its northern watershed, 17 Nov. 1900, F.O. 17/1499; Capt. Wingate's Report on Railway Extension from the British Indian Empire into China, Simla 1900. Encl. Intelligence Division to Foreign Office, 24 Apr. 1900, F.O. 17/1438.

lands of eastern Asia', and with the appointed task, as Witte saw it, 'of strengthening Russian economic influence in China to counterbalance the enormous importance that the English had managed to achieve there, thanks chiefly to their having virtually taken over the administration of the maritime customs'.[1] Finally, he sought to disguise Russia's intentions by professing a policy of friendship for China, which was to be based on a secret treaty of alliance against Japan.

The cautious manner in which this project was approached contributed to its defeat. A tentative move was made by Count Cassini, the Russian minister at Peking, early in October 1895.[2] When China proved hesitant, Russia decided to delay extensive negotiations until the pro-Russian Chinese minister, Li Hung-chang, travelled to St. Petersburg in the summer of 1896 to attend the coronation of the Tsar. When Li arrived the Russians discovered that the delay had been expensive. The sense of obligation which China had shown immediately after the triple intervention, which had been so opportunely seized on by France in the presentation of her claims, had been largely dissipated under the aggressive actions of the powers. The Chinese minister was prepared to admit the direct line across Manchuria, but he insisted that the Manchurian branch lines were to be constructed on the standard gauge, as distinct from the Russian broad gauge, by private companies which allowed Chinese participation. Secondly, no ice-free port was designated in the Sino-Russian agreements of June 1896.[3] Actually, Russia's plans were still too tentative to allow her to take a more definite stand. Even with regard to the direct line across Manchuria, proper surveys were made only in the spring of 1897, and a plan of construction was not decided until the spring of 1898. From 1896 to 1898 only ground-levelling operations were carried out in north Manchuria.

[1] Romanov, *Russia in Manchuria*, 68.

[2] S. P. Kuo, *Chinese Reaction to Foreign Encroachment; with special reference to the first Sino-Japanese war and its immediate aftermath*, Columbia University, Ph.D. 1953, University Microfilms Publication 6652 (Ann Arbor, 1954), 187-9.

[3] The full French text of the Sino-Russian Treaty of 22 May/3 June 1896 is given in Romanov, *Russia in Manchuria*, 400-2; the Chinese text in *Tung-hua hsu-lu*, Kuang-hsu 136/8-9. The French text was operative. The companion Agreement between China and the Russo-Chinese Bank for the Chinese Eastern Railway, of 8 Sept. 1896, in accordance with Art. 4 of the Treaty of 3 June 1896 is in MacMurray, *Treaties and Agreements*, i. 74-7.

This delay helps to explain Lord Salisbury's attitude to the growth of Russian influence in the Far East. On 25 October 1895 *The Times* reported the 'Cassini Convention' as a reputedly secret agreement between Russia and China giving Russia the right of anchorage at Port Arthur and the right to carry the Siberian railway across northern Manchuria.[1] Salisbury then remarked to Count Hatzfeldt, the German Ambassador in London, that it would not be unwelcome to him if Russia became more deeply engaged in China, and that Great Britain would raise objections only if Russia claimed an exclusive right of anchorage at Port Arthur.[2] On 9 November, speaking at the Guildhall, he sought to quieten commercial disquiet, which had risen in the City after *The Times* report, by giving assurances that British interests in the east would be adequately protected. The Prime Minister spoke against any 'sensitiveness' in regard to Russian activity and stressed the view that in Asia there was room for all the powers.[3] The Earl of Balfour, Sir Michael Hicks Beach, and other members of the Cabinet reiterated this opinion in public speeches during the succeeding months. In the summer of 1896 Lord Salisbury intimated the same view directly to Tsar Nicholas, when the Tsar visited Balmoral. Salisbury later reported to the Cabinet on his conversation with the Tsar:

I introduced the subject of the extreme East and assured him that England had no desire to hinder the commercial and industrial development of Russia in that quarter, because all that favoured industry created trade, and it was on trade we lived. He accepted these assurances with great apparent satisfaction. He said he should try to carry his railway through Manchuria, but that they had yet no definite project as to its outlet.[4]

At the time, although he had no information on the terms, Salisbury was aware of the secret Sino-Russian negotiations which had been carried out at St. Petersburg earlier that

---

[1] *The Times*, 25 Oct. 1895; *History of The Times*, 198–9. The 'Cassini Convention' in MacMurray, *Treaties*, i. 79–81.

[2] Hadzfeldt to the German Foreign Office, 25 Oct. 1895. Germany, *Die Grosse Politik der europäischen Kabinette, 1871–1914*, 40 vols. in 54 (Berlin, 1922–7), x. 35–6, hereafter cited as *Grosse Politik*.

[3] Joseph, *Foreign Diplomacy*, 156–7.

[4] Cabinet memorandum by Salisbury, very secret, of 27 Sept. 1896, S.P. 89/21.

summer.[1] But neither this information, nor the sensational publication of the reputed terms of the treaty in *The Times* of the previous October, were sufficient to deter him from encouraging Russia to turn to the Far East.

The political objectives which prompted this gesture can easily be summarized. At the end of the nineteenth century, both strategically and in her resources, Russia appeared to be moving into a commanding position in international affairs. Her link with France in the Dual Alliance added to the grave situation.

Over the defence of the frontiers of India the prospect appeared as dismal. Russian railway construction in the area, which gave her the strategic initiative, seemed to jeopardize Great Britain's entire position. The completion of the Trans-Caspian railway, and the shift in Russian attention to the Middle East after the Turkish war of 1878, aroused British anxiety over the possible absorption of Persia and the establishment of Russian influence in the Gulf. The relatively new concept of the railway as a strategic striking force restated the traditional problem in terms of overland encroachment against which the British Navy could make no adequate defence. By 1899, when Lord Curzon became Viceroy of India, the British position had been threatened to such an extent that Curzon felt justified in pressing for the defensive division of Persia into spheres.[2] In his reply, Lord Hamilton, Secretary of State for India, considered even this retrogressive step inadequate.

Your plans [Hamilton wrote] are based on the assumption that . . . we should exercise force to maintain our position in that country. . . . I have felt for a very long time past that we must, so far as Russia is concerned, acknowledge the changed condition that the extension of railroads has made in the relative fighting powers of Great Britain and Russia. . . . I have long felt that any tug of war on land between Russia and England must result to our disadvantage, and it is for that reason that I have always believed, so far as China, Persia and Turkey are concerned, Russian influence must gradually become

[1] Memorandum by Ian Malcolm, M.P., of 10 June 1896, S.P. 129/103. Malcolm had made a visit to St. Petersburg. On the publication of the substance of the treaty, see Langer, *Diplomacy of Imperialism*, 404, n. 37.

[2] The 'Curzon Despatch' of 21 Sept. 1899 is given in G. P. Gooch and H. Temperley (eds.), *British Documents on the Origins of the War, 1898–1914*, 11 vols. in 13 (London, 1926–38), hereafter cited *B.D.*

stronger than our own. . . . I do not believe that we can fight with
Russia on land successfully except in the neighbourhood of our
frontiers in India.[1]

At the end of the nineteenth century this view of the inevitability of Russian dominance over the Asian land mass was
commonly held. Major-General Ardagh, the Director-General
of Military Intelligence, was much preoccupied with this
problem. Even Witte, in his grandiose Siberian project, was
influenced by the similar example of the Canadian Pacific Railway as an instrument of domination over vast spaces. At the
turn of the century the use of railways as a means of building
up a cumulative and inexorable Russian threat on the north-
west frontier of India appeared to diminish Admiral Mahan's
doctrines on the influence of sea power, then much in vogue.
The conflict between sea and land power was taken up by
Mahan himself in 1900 in *The Problem of Asia and its effect upon
International Policies*.[2] Mahan predicted an imperial struggle
across Asia between the thirtieth and fortieth parallels of
latitude, covering India, Persia, and the Yangtze valley. It
could be argued that Sir Halford MacKinder's geopolitical
theories of the 'heartland', which were being formed at this
time, were an outcome of this mood.

The argument was also extended to British thinking in
Chinese affairs. It was to be used with force by Sir Nicolas
O'Conor, British minister at St. Petersburg, to urge the Government to condone Russia's occupation of Port Arthur in the
spring of 1898. With a coterminous land frontier with China of
some three or four thousand miles and the inevitable progress of
development in Siberia, O'Conor argued:

> Every year will see the Russians pressing down south more and
> more till the weight of mass eventually tells and an inevitable
> historical episode will be completed. . . . In proportion as we cross
> them in North China they will harass us in Asia, on the Indian
> Frontier, in the Persian Gulf. If we squeeze them in North China
> they will bite us where they can and the other Powers will be only
> too pleased.[3]

In 1900, when news was received of the spread of the Boxer

[1] Hamilton to Curzon, 2 Nov. 1899, S.P., unclassified.
[2] London, 1900.
[3] O'Conor to Sanderson, 24 Mar. 1898, circulated to the Cabinet, S.P. 129/39.

rising to Manchuria, the reaction of the Director-General of Military Intelligence was similar. With Russia involved in Manchuria, Ardagh stated:

. . . anxiety over her activity in Afganistan, Persia and Turkey will be relieved, and also lessen any chance France may have felt for Russian support. . . . (The Manchurian incidents) tend in a marked degree to dissipate some of the storm clouds which appear to threaten us, and we may contemplate the misfortunes of Russia with serenity, and even thankfulness.[1]

From 1895 an appreciable number in the British Government, some not noticeably Russophile, were content to see Russia extend herself in the Far East, thereby loosening Franco-Russian co-operation in Europe and, in the process, helping to restrain France in Egypt as well as lessening Russian pressure on India and stemming the loss of British influence in the Gulf. In Salisbury's outlook, moreover, there was a further consideration which rose above the narrow political view. During these years, when Great Britain was forced to reassess her international position, he looked forward to the time when Great Britain and Russia could re-establish, as the best hope for peace in Europe, their earlier friendship destroyed by the Crimean war. This feeling is clearly expressed in a letter to his friend, Iwan-Muller, in August 1896:

. . . It may not be possible for England and Russia to return to their old relations. But it is an object to be wished for and approached as opportunity offers. At all events efforts should be made to avoid needless aggravation of the feud between them which Governments and not the nations have made. The French and German *people* both hate us; the Russian people do not. It is not possible to stop the impulse which past mistakes have given. The generation whose political beliefs were moulded by the passions of the Crimean war is only now dying out. We may, without any fault of our own, find ourselves opposed to Russia on this question of that, in consequence of past commitments. All we can do is to try to narrow the chasm that separates us. It is the best chance for something like an equilibrium in Europe.[2]

This was written a few days before he saw the Tsar at Balmoral,

---

[1] Memorandum 60 of 19 July 1900, Ardagh's Memoranda, P.R.O. 30/40/14, Pt. 2, pp. 222–3.

[2] Salisbury to E. B. Iwan-Muller, 31 Aug. 1896, *B.D.* iv. 780, App. IV.

and it is easy to understand why he chose to encourage the
Emperor in his Siberian project in the east. The extent to
which he, and other members of his Government, would allow
this Russian activity to undermine Great Britain's position in
China was a problem which then still lay in the future, not to
emerge until the Port Arthur crisis of 1898.

III

THE THIRD INDEMNITY LOAN
AND THE SEIZURE OF
THE NORTHERN PORTS

WHILE a defence of her established treaty rights and participation in the competition for indemnity loans were necessary aspects of British policy in the post-war period, in themselves they were inadequate to meet the changed situation which was emerging in the Far East. After 1895, both politically and militarily China was in a more vulnerable position than at any other time during the period of Western encroachment. The presence of Japanese occupation forces at Weihaiwei and the movement of foreign warships in northern Chinese waters underlined the military inadequacies of the Chinese Government and heightened speculation as to the political intentions of the powers. A Russian move away from Europe to the east may have been a pleasing prospect in London, but from a Far Eastern perspective her advance was menacing.

Between 1895 and 1898, when the territorial aspect of the scramble for concessions emerged, widespread speculation in the treaty ports about the claims which were likely to be made created an atmosphere which gave little promise of a return to a normal situation. Paradoxically, in the uncertainties of the earlier period, while the aims of the powers and particularly those of Russia were as yet unrevealed, there appeared to be a greater danger of the political disintegration of China, the emergence of 'a vast impending crisis', as Rosebery termed it in 1897, when the powers would be matched against each other in a Greater Eastern question.[1]

In particular, attention centred on the acquisition of coaling ports, both as legitimate footholds for economic expansion and to satisfy the expanding national aspirations of the time. There were difficulties, however, over the precise location of these

[1] Crewe, *Rosebery*, ii. 554.

ports, even if they could be peacefully acquired. Despite the long sweep of the Chinese coastline very few sites satisfied the necessary commercial and naval requirements, which were so admirably provided for Great Britain through her possession of Hong Kong. This obvious shortage of suitable ports introduced a competitive element into the relations between the powers.

Germany led the way in this activity. From 1895 there was a noticeable impetuousness in Germany's Far Eastern policy which stemmed from the general dissatisfaction which she felt for her position in the east. Despite her participation in the triple intervention, the close cohesion of Russia and France had forced her to side with Great Britain, where she found herself defending a policy of free trade although her control over that trade was lamentable. The Kaiser, in particular, yearned for a more adventurous policy and for the establishment of a naval base in the Far East. From mid 1895 various ports along the China coast were considered, even as far south as Amoy, until early in 1897, when a surveying team reported on the obvious superiority of Kiaochow.[1]

Kiaochow and Port Arthur

Kiaochow (Chiao-chou) Bay formed a magnificent harbour, large enough to hold all the fleets of the powers in Chinese waters and was, for all practical purposes, open all the winter through. Anchorage was good, but there were large stretches of shallow water with extensive mud flats to the south and west. The bay was formerly connected by a canal with the Gulf of Pechili to the north. This was partially choked, but capable of being reopened with a little expenditure, allowing the power which held the bay to command the coastal trading route between Peking and Shanghai. Kiaochow itself, which was eventually absorbed by the modern port of Tsingtao, had been one of the most important ports in China during the Mongol dynasty, lying about 300 miles distant from the main road to Peking. The potential resources of the Shantung promontory, on which Kiaochow was situated, appeared equally as attractive. The prevailing view was that of Baron Richthofen, the geographer and traveller, which he published

[1] N. R. Rich, *Friedrich von Holstein*, 2 vols. (Cambridge, 1965), 555–6.

in the *Colonial Zeitung* of 6 January 1898. Richthofen drew attention to the excellence of the coal deposits adjacent to Kiaochow, which he thought the largest in the world, and which allowed the power which possessed Kiaochow to control the coal supply in northern Chinese waters. The territory itself, Richthofen admitted, was already too overcrowded to allow European to compete with Chinese labour, so it was quite out of the question that Shantung would form a German colony in the proper sense of the word. But it did meet Germany's objective of obtaining a *point d'appui* for her trade so as to ensure a share in the industrial development of China. In this respect, he concluded, Kiaochow was the natural outlet for the trade of north China during the winter months, while Tientsin was the most convenient port of access in the summer.[1]

The port did have its advantages, but not as many as Richthofen believed. The Chinese originally had the aim of fortifying Kiaochow, but the project had been abandoned during the war, and defensive measures were then concentrated at Taku, which was closer to Tientsin. From the winter of 1895–6 Russia had begun to winter her Far Eastern fleet there, a move which only caused slight interest among the powers. Japan, who had thought of taking the port herself during the war, had abandoned the idea for fear of being shut in by the enemy's fleet; nor did she expect Russia to take permanent possession of the place because of the lack of internal communications. By 1897 persistent rumours of Russia's intention to occupy the place led the Tsungli Yamen to inform MacDonald that China intended to fortify Kiaochow bay as a naval depot, and the China Association pressed to have Kiaochow made into a treaty port to prevent its acquisition by any one power. However, the British minister at Peking felt that the heavy seas caused by the shallow water in the landlocked bay made it unsuitable as a commercial anchorage, a fact of which the Russians were aware, and with some astuteness he argued that they were much more likely to try to take possession of Port Arthur or Talienwan in south Manchuria, which were more easily connected with their Siberian railway project.[2]

Indications of Germany's increasingly vigorous attitude,

[1] Richthofen's article is to be found in W.O. 106/17.
[2] MacDonald to Salisbury, No. 127 of 8 Sept. 1897, F.O. 17/1313.

which was to precipitate events in China, were also noticeable in her uncompromising stance over the negotiations for the third indemnity loan. Although the actual terms of the peace settlement stipulated that the remaining part of the indemnity should be paid in six equal annual instalments, thus extinguishing the debt by 1901, China was determined to free herself of the debt as soon as possible. The Japanese military occupation of Weihaiwei, which was to continue until the indemnity was paid, was a tangible reminder of China's failure in the war and the cause of much public bitterness during 1895–6. To counteract this, Li Hung-chang decided to negotiate a substantial foreign loan to pay the indemnity off in one amount. A further consideration was that if the debt were paid by May 1898 China would save about £2 million from the estimated cost of the occupation expenses of Weihaiwei and the refund of interest payments under the terms of the peace treaty.[1]

Negotiations for the loan began in February when Li Hung-chang asked the Hongkong and Shanghai Bank, which was working with the Deutsche-Asiatische Bank, to watch for a favourable opportunity to launch a loan of £16 million, at a rate of interest not higher than the previous 5 per cent loan. Discussions which followed over the next three months indicated difficulties over the nature of the loan and over the control of the securities. Initially, Li had it in mind to base the loan on the balance of the Maritime Customs revenue and the land tax, which at that time provided about half the total revenue of the Chinese Government. The German element in the syndicate, however, was in favour of a revision of the tariff, the transfer of the salt and likin taxes to the Maritime Customs administration, and the remodelling of that administration for

---

[1] If China proposed to liquidate the balance of the Japanese indemnity on 8 May 1898, the net payment would be:

	£
Indemnity outstanding	13,708,741
Plus occupation expenses of Weihaiwei to 8 May 1898	82,252
	£13,790,993
Less interest payments made by China to be refunded under the terms of the Japanese Peace Treaty.	. 1,782,136
Leaving	£12,008,857

The Rate of Exchange for indemnity payments were fixed by convention at 3s. 3½d. a Kuping Tael. Figures printed for the use of the Foreign Office, 3 Jan. 1898, F.O. 17/1330.

the better safeguarding of European interests. The inclusion of the Russo-Chinese Bank in the contract for the loan was also suggested, so as to secure the co-operation of the French market. On 2 June Li Hung-chang responded with a definite offer of the security of the customs revenue and a pledge of the general revenue in return for a loan of £16 million at 94 for 50 years at 5 per cent, repayment of the principal to commence at the expiration of ten years' service of the loan. The Chinese Board of Revenue was understandably opposed to any foreign control of the additional security, and as this was made a *sine qua non* by the syndicate, deadlock followed.[1]

Early in November 1897 this financial squabble was momentarily pushed into the background when the murder of two German missionaries in Shantung provided Germany with the opportunity to seize Kiaochow. From the late 1880s Germany had begun to challenge France in her self-appointed role of protector of Catholic missions in China, as far as German nationals were concerned, and she was quick to act. Three German ships of war appeared off Kiaochow and compelled the Chinese to evacuate the town. Over the succeeding weeks peremptory demands were made against the Chinese; a force of marine infantry was sent out, a local German governor was appointed and Germany set about establishing herself in the surrounding area.

Initially, the reaction in England to this German move was surprisingly moderate.[2] Until mid-December there was considerable uncertainty in the Foreign Office as to whether Germany actually intended to retain the port or whether it had been occupied temporarily so as to force a settlement on the Chinese. Consequently, the implications of the move, rather than the occupation itself, were a matter of speculation. As

---

[1] Memorandum by Norton of 1 Jan. 1898, F.O. 17/1356.
[2] *The Times*, 6 Dec. 1897, 11 and 30 Apr. 1898; the *Standard*, 4 Feb. 1898, remarked on the cost of the venture; the *Daily Graphic*, 8 Jan. 1898, took a conciliatory attitude and argued that no harm had been done to British trade, and on 4 Feb. 1898 provided a full report of the occupation in enthusiastic terms; the *Daily News*, 22 Jan. 1898, discussed Kiaochow in relation to German colonial expansion to settle Germany's 'enormous surplus population'; the *Morning Post*, 3 May 1898, drew attention to the German Navy League, founded 30 Apr. 1898, which 'has undoubtedly been consummated in consequence of the successful passage of that measure (the first reading of the Navy Bill) and in recognition of German transmarine enterprise in Shantung'.

Russia had the right of winter anchorage at the port it was felt that Germany's action could not have taken place without collusion between the powers and that Russia would want a port, possibly Talienwan, as a counterpoise. Actually, there had been no previous understanding between the two powers; at least, not in the sense assumed by the Foreign Office. Before acting, the Kaiser had asked the Tsar whether Russia would have any objection to the move, and the Tsar had responded rather naïvely to this personal approach to the effect that as far as he was aware Russia had no special interest in the place, which she only used since 1895–6 as a winter anchorage.[1] The Kaiser then occupied the port much to the consternation of the German Foreign Ministry, which was fearful of the possibly adverse effect the move could have on Russo-German relations.[2] In fact, the German occupation of Kiaochow led to considerable ill feeling between Russia and Germany, a situation of which Great Britain was unaware until the end of December when the Austrian Ambassador in London called on Sir Thomas Sanderson, the Permanent Under-Secretary at the Foreign Office, and told him confidentially that there had been no previous agreement between the two powers.[3]

Meanwhile, in mid-November, British statesmen were preoccupied with the possible consequences of a German settlement with China which could give her an alternative coaling port elsewhere. To a large extent, this feeling was deliberately played on by Germany, who hoped to secure British acquiescence to the occupation of Kiaochow by delicately hinting that Russia preferred her to seek a port further to the south.[4] From a British point of view, this would have raised the delicate issue of a probable confrontation with Germany. This possibility had been contemplated during a scare over harbour seizures the previous winter, when the likelihood of Germany claiming a coaling port in the central China area, either at Foochow, Swatow, or Amoy, had led to a pertinent discussion of the

---

[1] *Grosse Politik*, XIV. i. 69; M. J. Bee, 'The Peterhof Agreement of 1897', *CSPSR* (1936–7), xx. 231.

[2] Rich, *Holstein*, 560–6.

[3] Memorandum by Sanderson of 28 Dec. 1897, Sanderson Papers (F.O. 800/2). German annoyance with Russia is indicated in Spring Rice to Villiers, 20 Nov. 1897, S.P. 122/102.

[4] Rich, *Holstein*, 563.

possible need for a British counterpoise. An unofficial approach to the Admiralty had then elicited the opinion that Great Britain would have to claim a similar port in the Chusan Archipelago, at the mouth of the Yangtze river.[1] The prospect of such a policy of counterpoises was distasteful to Salisbury, although he recognized that if necessary it would have to be followed. Under the circumstances he was not disposed to protest against the German occupation of Kiaochow. 'My inclination', he noted, 'is to think that if they stay where they are they would act as an irritant to Russia but would not hurt us, but that if they go to Foochow we ought to obtain compensation at Chusan.'[2]

A fortnight later the situation took a more serious turn. Admiral Buller, Commander-in-Chief China Station, reported the movement of a substantial number of Russian ships in northern China waters. Although this had been expected, their apparent objective came rather as a surprise. Nine Russian men-of-war were reported to be at the Korean port of Chemulpo (Inchon).[3] The report, which later proved to be unfounded, was to have serious consequences. Salisbury, who was thinking in terms of a Russian claim to a south Manchurian port, reacted sharply. On 7 December he ordered that a British naval force to equal that of the Russians should be sent temporarily to the Korean port. The object of the move was to prevent the Koreans from assuming that Russia had any special rights in the area. 'The sight of the fleet has a great effect', he noted, 'and is of more value than many despatches.'[4] The actual effect, however, was one which should have been anticipated. On 9 December a British naval force was ordered to Chemulpo with instructions that a number of ships equal to those of the Russians should remain at the port for a week or ten days, while the remaining British ships should be sent to Port Hamilton, Nagasaki, or elsewhere. Arrangements were then made for units from Nagasaki and the Chusan anchorage to rendezvous with a main force from Hong Kong.[5] Meanwhile,

[1] Memorandum by Bertie of 18 Nov. 1897, F.O. 17/1330.
[2] Minute on above.
[3] Memorandum by Bertie of 7 Dec. 1897, F.O. 17/1330.
[4] Minute on above.
[5] Memorandum by C. I. Thomas, British ships at Port Arthur, précis, 27 Jan. 1898, S.P. 93/28.

it had emerged that there were in fact only three Russian ships at Chemulpo, and that the nine which had been reported were at Nagasaki, then a normal port of call for foreign ships of war. Salisbury, in a rage with the Admiralty for sending false information, realized that if only three Russian ships were active in the area it put an entirely different complexion on the matter.[1] The arrival of a substantial British squadron, subsequently to be diverted to Port Hamilton, would not impress the Koreans but would convince them that Great Britain was about to reoccupy the port which she had taken in 1885.[2] A hurried order was sent out for the movement of only three British ships, but the new orders were issued too late.

By this time Buller had left Hong Kong and during the following fortnight ten British ships were active in northern Chinese waters. By 29 December, seven were at Chemulpo and two, the *Immortalite* and the *Iphigenia*, had been sent on Buller's authority to Port Arthur. Completely oblivious of the delicate situation he had caused, Buller reported with some satisfaction 'that no foreign power except Russia had had leave to visit Port Arthur, but that the Chinese Government had granted permission for English men of war'.[3]

While it cannot be argued that this British move initiated the general scramble for ports which followed Germany's seizure of Kiaochow, it undoubtedly contributed to the process by removing any hesitation the other powers may have felt up to this time. On 13 December Germany informed China that she intended to remain at Kiaochow. At the same time a substantial Russian naval force was hurriedly sent to Port Arthur, partly out of fear of being anticipated at the port by Great Britain.[4]

Again, in December the uncertain political situation which was created by the occupation of Port Arthur and Kiaochow was aggravated further by a serious turn in the indemnity loan negotiations. After the collapse of discussions in the summer, Li Hung-chang had made fruitless attempts to find the money

---

[1] Memorandum by Bertie of 7 Dec. 1897, F.O. 17/1330.
[2] Loc. cit.
[3] Memorandum by Thomas, S.P. 93/28.
[4] Malozemoff, *Russian Policy*, 98–100. Russia explained to Japan (on 17 Dec.) that the move was to oppose the German occupation of Kiaochow. Nish, *Anglo-Japanese Alliance*, 50.

from private sources. Negotiations were carried out with a syndicate headed by Mr. Ernest Hooley and Major Eustace Jameson, and a preliminary agreement was signed for a loan of £16 million on the security of the Maritime Customs and the salt and likin taxes. However, the whole arrangement fell through when the Hooley–Jameson syndicate failed to produce the £100,000 which was to be deposited as security for the performance of the contract. Li then approached the Anglo-German syndicate for the third time, again offering the salt and likin taxes as security. He was also prepared to consider either the foreign control of those taxes in case of default or the appointment of an official of the Hongkong and Shanghai Bank to administer them.[1]

This reasonable suggestion was unacceptable to Germany, who stipulated for the immediate appointment of two inspectors, one British and one German, for the control of the salt and likin taxes, and for the admission of France to an equal share of the loan. When France expressed her willingness, and asked for the appointment of a French inspector, Germany then pressed for the inclusion of Russia and for the establishment of a financial commission such as had been set up in Egypt.[1]

The negotiations, which by this time had been carried through to mid-December, revealed the essentially political nature of the demands being made over the loan. A few days later the full extent of this activity became apparent. On 22 December the Tsungli Yamen asked Sir Claude MacDonald, the British minister at Peking, to ascertain within the week whether the Anglo-German syndicate would take up the June offer and at the same time informed him that a 4 per cent Russian loan at 93 for £16 million had been arranged on the security of the land tax. For this, Russia was to receive a monopoly of the railways in north China and Manchuria and the Inspector-Generalship of the Maritime Customs.[2] Although it was unlikely that Russia could lend on such favourable terms, the report was given authenticity when it was confirmed by Ewen Cameron, manager of the Hongkong and Shanghai

[1] Memorandum by Norton of 1 Jan. 1898, F.O. 17/1356.
[2] MacDonald to Salisbury, tel. 95 of 22 Dec. 1897, F.O. 17/1314.

Bank in London. Cameron stressed the point that if Russia made the loan she would doubtless insist on terms which would seriously damage British influence and prestige as well as cripple British trade. Russia was clearly set on controlling the Maritime Customs, with France and Germany, who would provide the money for the loan, taking a part. He suggested that the British Government should guarantee the loan, and stated that the Bank felt that it could raise the money even if the Government would consent to give only a partial guarantee of 1 or $1\frac{1}{2}$ per cent interest.[1]

This unfavourable turn in the loan negotiations clearly indicated the political ambitions of the powers, which were simultaneously underlined by the occupation of Port Arthur and Kiaochow. Salisbury agreed that positive action was necessary, and that if nothing could be done the Chinese fiscal administration would probably 'fall into unfriendly hands to the serious detriment of our trade'.[2] He ordered that Cameron's appeal for government help should be sent to Sir Michael Hicks Beach, Chancellor of the Exchequer.

At the same time, Salisbury made an attempt to assess the significance for British policy of the occupation of the northern ports. On 22 December discussions were held with Sir Thomas Sanderson and Sir Francis Bertie, the permanent and assistant under-secretaries at the Foreign Office, who were responsible for Chinese affairs. The following day, Sir Nicholas O'Conor, British Ambassador at St. Petersburg, who had previously been minister at Peking and who was then on leave, was also called in. Salisbury felt that there was an urgent need to obtain competent advice on the different aspects of the problem, and the views of the naval and military authorities were also sought.

These discussions of 22–3 December are important for the understanding which they give of the pattern of British thinking in the winter and spring of 1897–8. It is generally assumed that at the end of March 1898 the British Government moved reluctantly to the idea of occupying Weihaiwei, as a necessary measure to offset the actions of Russia and Germany. In fact, from the beginning the Foreign Office thought in terms of a

[1] Hongkong and Shanghai Bank to Foreign Office, 24 Dec. 1897, F.O. 17/1330.
[2] Minute on above.

counterpoise, even before it had been reliably established that Russia and Germany would remain in occupation of their ports.

The scope of the discussions was defined by Salisbury at a preliminary meeting with Sanderson. In view of the Russian and German actions, he reasoned, it was necessary to decide:

1. Whether this would so modify the strategical situation as to make it necessary for us to occupy some new position and if so where.

2. Whether such a step on our part would be required to maintain what is vaguely called our prestige—that is to say our position as a first-rate Power interested above others in the commerce of those seas.

3. Whether the positions held by Russia and Germany would give them such means of exercising political pressure at Peking as to render some countermove on our part necessary for the preservation of our influence in matters which are important for the protection of our commerce, such as the selection of the Inspector General of Customs.[1]

In general, Salisbury was against taking any territory 'unless Russia and Germany had avowedly annexed some portion of Chinese soil'.[2] Bertie, as well, spoke strongly against any action which would define a British sphere of interest and which would invite the other powers to do as they would with the undefined parts. Great Britain's paramount interest in China, he stressed, was unrestricted trade *everywhere* and she should discourage spheres as long as possible. But he was prepared to defer to the naval and military experts if they thought otherwise. 'A squadron', he concluded whimsically, 'able to deal with a Russian–German–French combination would be our best security.'[3]

O'Conor's opinion went to the other extreme. He pressed that Great Britain should state 'frankly and decidedly in a friendly manner to Russia, Germany and France what Britain's principal interests in China were and where they lay'.[4] He was opposed to the taking of additional territory around Hong Kong, which had been suggested as a possible measure, on the

[1] Memorandum by Sanderson of 23 Dec. 1897, Sanderson Papers, F.O. 800/2.
[2] Minute on Memorandum by Bertie of 23 Dec. 1897, F.O. 17/1330.
[3] Loc. cit.
[4] Memorandum by Sanderson of 23 Dec. 1897, F.O. 17/1330.

grounds that Great Britain could take it at need and that it would not be an adequate counterpoise to German and Russian action in the north. Instead, he pressed strongly that Great Britain should occupy Chusan.[1]

Since 1895 suggestions had been made for the occupation of Chusan, which would have ensured British control over the outlet of the Yangtze. From an official point of view, however, Great Britain was perhaps tied by treaty stipulations which prevented her from freely occupying the island. By the Convention of Bocca Tigris of 4 April 1846, after the first Anglo-Chinese war, Great Britain had stipulated, in evacuating the island, that it should never be ceded to any other foreign power (Art. III) and that she would protect Chusan in the case of attack and return it to China (Art. IV). The island was occupied briefly by French and British troops during the second Anglo-Chinese war. However, Great Britain had consistently taken the stand that these articles of the Convention of 1846 were still operative and had in effect been confirmed in the Treaty of Tientsin of 1858 (Art. LIV). This view, which was presented during the Sino-French war of 1884–5 to oppose a possible French move on the island, was reaffirmed with China as late as November 1895 when rumours were current that Germany wanted it as a coaling station. Consequently, in December 1897, Salisbury had some doubts as to whether Great Britain was free to act on O'Conor's suggestion. The opinion of the law officers was sought; they replied that while there was some doubt about Great Britain's obligation to defend Chusan in case of attack, she could not easily claim the advantages of Art. III of the Convention of 1846 (non-alienation of Chusan) without accepting the burden of Art. IV.[2]

In any case, Salisbury was attracted neither to the idea of occupying Chusan, nor to the further suggestion of seizing additional territories for the protection of Hong Kong, which he felt was best achieved through a Chinese promise of non-alienation. As an adequate counterpoise against the Russian and German moves, he tentatively suggested the establishment of a winter station for the British fleet in the north near Chefoo.[3] A few days later, after the matter had been brought before the

[1] Loc. cit.   [2] Memorandum by Oakes of 23 Dec. 1897, F.O. 17/1330.
[3] Memorandum by Sanderson of 23 Dec. 1897, Sanderson Papers, F.O. 800/2.

Cabinet, Salisbury went a stage further by asking Sir Claude MacDonald at Peking whether he could suggest any small port on the Gulf of Pechili which would be suitable as a make-weight for the German occupation of Kiaochow.[1]

Salisbury's emphasis on German activity indicates the state of his feeling over the northern ports in December 1897. A month earlier he had been relatively unperturbed about the German occupation. By February 1898 the issue was to become a clash of Anglo-Russian interests in the east. During the intervening period there was a feeling of antipathy against Germany, which sprang from a growing awareness of Germany's responsibility for the dangerous situation emerging in China.

This attitude was also shared by Sir Michael Hicks Beach. In replying to Salisbury's query about the Chinese loan negotiations, Hicks Beach dwelt on the political aspects of the matter. He felt that without German assent France and Russia would have had difficulty in finding the £16 million which were required, and that this had probably been obtained. He observed, 'the whole drift of the correspondence looks like a rapprochement of the Three Powers in their Chinese policy, with the intention of leaving us out in the cold'.[2] In his reply of 27 December, Hicks Beach also offered a possible solution to the loan problem which immediately interested Salisbury and led him to call a Cabinet meeting the next day. After surveying the main points of difference between Britain and Russia, Hicks Beach stated:

I thought . . . we might agree to share the loan in some way with Russia, on the basis of a division of spheres of influence in China, and each of us extracting from the Chinese what we wanted within our spheres. Russia acting by land, we by sea, could completely control China, and defy any other to interfere with us. Of course this would be a sharp curve—for we have hitherto rather been acting on the opposite lines. But is it not time, in view of the attitude of Germany, for a new departure, which would, I believe, be very popular here, and must influence other matters nearer home.[3]

[1] Salisbury to MacDonald, No. 75, secret, of 28 Dec. 1897, Cab. 37/46/29 (1898), printed for the use of the Cabinet, 26 Mar. 1898. This is a collection of 245 telegrams relating to the Port Arthur crisis, 28 Dec. 1897–22 Mar. 1898, many of which are missing from the Foreign Office General Correspondence.
[2] Hicks Beach to Salisbury, confidential, of 27 Dec. 1897, S.P. 90/42.
[3] Loc. cit.

Over the actual amount of government support which could be offered in response to Cameron's request Hicks Beach was not so sanguine. The alternatives Cameron had suggested were either a direct loan or a guaranteed loan in which the Government should assume the administration of revenues pledged in case of default, or back the Bank of England in issuing the loan. Hicks Beach preferred a direct rather than a guaranteed loan as either of the latter alternatives presented difficulties: the first for the trouble it could lead to with the other foreign powers, the second because of the Bank's reluctance to act without a clear promise of government support. But for a direct loan, the Chancellor of the Exchequer concluded decisively,

> Parliament would require something much more than a mere retention of our present commercial position; and would want some clear step towards predominance, such as the purchase of the Suez Canal Shares gave us in Egypt.[1]

These suggestions led Lord Salisbury to reassess the situation in a way which brought about significant modifications in his Chinese policy and which led directly to his overture to Russia in January 1898.

Salisbury's Overture to Russia

British attempts to preserve the *status quo* in China through public utterances on the territorial integrity of that country and on the open nature of trade had been unavailing against the obviously exclusive character of the demands being pressed on China through the financial loans. To maintain her position Great Britain had entered into the competition for the control of these loans, and negotiation over these had led her into a situation which jeopardized her international position. This was at variance with Great Britain's real aim. British insistence on the integrity of China was not made out of any altruistic impulse for Chinese welfare but to ensure the free extension of trade. Great Britain had no objection to Russia securing a warm-water port in the Far East. Since the formation of the Dual Alliance this had been regarded as a favourable move. Queen Victoria was decisive on this point. 'H(er) M(ajesty) thinks we ought to help the Russians to get a Port in the north

[1] Loc. cit.

of China',[1] Sir Arthur Bigge, secretary to the Queen, reported. Salisbury's sole concern was that any ports taken by Russia should remain open to British trade. Similarly, the loan was only being fought to prevent a containment of British influence and to protect existing British rights in the event of the loan going to another power.

The trouble with Russia could not have come at a more inconvenient time. In West Africa, the French were about to cross the Niger in an attempt to open a corridor of French territory to the river from Dahomey. From Paris the British Ambassador was shortly to report that French irritability over the Dreyfus case made war likely. Inflammable as it was, the West African campaign was but a feint, masking a still more critical situation brewing over the Nile, where Kitchener was on the march to Khartum, and Marchand on the last stages of his journey overland.[2]

One of the qualities which Salisbury brought to office was the abhorrence of bluff in international affairs. Britain could not meet Russia and France in two areas at once, and to Salisbury there was only one possible course. In January 1898 he approached Russia on the possibility of an agreement to settle their differences. In itself the overture was compatible with Lord Salisbury's belief in the pacific settlement of regional differences by negotiated treaty, and he was encouraged to this move by the suggestion presented by Hicks Beach. Although the overture was not made until 17 January a move toward it was made the preceding 31 December when, in discussing the loan terms with Sir Claude MacDonald at Peking, he tentatively suggested that Russia and Great Britain should share the loan.[3]

Salisbury's unsuccessful January overture to Russia was unhappily a fortnight too late. If it had been acted on when it was first suggested, it would probably have secured a more favourable response. But in the intervening period continuing British demands over the loan negotiations aroused Russian suspicions to an impossible extent.

During the first few days of January 1898, various possibilities

---

[1] Bigge to Eric Barrington, 25 Jan. 1898, S.P. 85/65.
[2] Garvin, *Chamberlain*, iii. 215, 217; M. Perham, *Lugard* (London, 1956), 672.
[3] Salisbury to MacDonald, No. 76, secret, of 31 Dec. 1897, Cab. 37/46/29.

were considered as a way of meeting the need for loan securities and the compensation necessary if Germany remained at Kiaochow. The control of the Customs by an Englishman, adequate control over the revenues, the right of continuing the Burmese railway to the valley of the Yangtze and a first refusal of all concessions in that valley, the extension of Hong Kong's boundaries, the possible acquisition of a port or island, and even a novel demand for the introduction of foreign salt, as well as other demands were considered in turn.[1] Naturally, all of these demands were not eventually made, but they indicate the range of British thinking as the Foreign Office set about trying to find the type of 'Suez Canal Shares' move Hicks Beach had said was needed to satisfy Parliament.

On 5 January China attempted to introduce some order by making a formal request in London for a loan. Great Britain responded with the offer of a direct loan of about £12 million, to pay the remaining indemnity, on the security of the maritime and native customs, the salt and likin taxes, and on the understanding that the revenues pledged were to be audited by an Englishman, and, in default, were to be placed under English control.[2] It was also indicated that additional concessions would be sought although these were not so clearly stipulated.

One of these probable demands, however, immediately aroused Chinese concern when it was made known to them. This was that Talienwan should be made a treaty port. Talienwan (Dairen) was the only port in south Manchuria which gave free access to the north in winter. Soon after occupying Port Arthur in mid-December Russia showed clear signs that she had an interest in the port. However, her ultimate intentions over both ports were as yet unknown, and it was to test these that MacDonald suggested that Great Britain should demand that Talienwan should be made a treaty port. When the suggestion was put in mid-January, the Tsungli Yamen admitted that if the port were opened it would be more secure against annexation, but it became plain to MacDonald that the Chinese ministers were fearful of embroiling themselves with Russia. After pressing them for two days he concluded that they

---

[1] Salisbury to MacDonald, No. 75, secret, of 28 Dec. 1897; No. 5, secret, of 8 Jan. 1898, Cab. 37/46/29.
[2] Salisbury to MacDonald, No. 2, secret, of 5 Jan. 1898, Cab. 37/46/29.

were 'greatly frightened' of Russian threats and that they would probably prefer to let the loan go rather than run the risk of Russian reprisals.[1] The strength of Chinese reluctance surprised MacDonald and convinced him of the need to take Russian opposition into account. Consequently, on the afternoon of 16 January he sent a private telegram to Bertie suggesting that the time had arrived when Great Britain should attempt to arrive at an understanding with Russia along the lines already indicated by Salisbury.[2] By this time, Salisbury had begun to suspect that China was intent on playing off one power against the other, and he decided to act. He instructed O'Conor, who had returned to St. Petersburg, to approach Witte on the possibility of an Anglo-Russian understanding. He wrote:

If practicable ask Monsieur Witte whether it is possible that England and Russia should work together in China. Our objects are not antagonistic in any serious degree: on the other hand we can both of us do each other a great deal of harm if we try. It is better therefore we should come to an understanding. We would go far to further Russian commercial objects in the North, if we could regard her as willing to work with us.[3]

At the same time, he tried to resolve the difficulty over Talienwan. Although he admitted that Great Britain would regret giving up the thought of making it a treaty port, he instructed MacDonald at Peking that if it were impracticable he was not bound to insist on it.[4]

At St. Petersburg, O'Conor first introduced the idea to Count Muraviev, the Russian Foreign Minister, at the weekly reception on 19 January. From the outset the conversation took an unexpected turn. Muraviev approved the idea of an understanding, which to him obviously meant the establishment of a Russian sphere of influence in China. This he proceeded to define to O'Conor as 'all northern China from Tientsin to Peking, Peking to Manchuria'.[5] Three days later, when O'Conor saw Witte, the Russian Finance Minister took

[1] MacDonald to Salisbury, tel. 19 of 16 Jan. 1898, F.O. 17/1340.
[2] MacDonald to Salisbury, tel., private, of 16 Jan. 1898, F.O. 17/1340.
[3] Salisbury to O'Conor, tel. 7, secret, of 17 Jan. 1898, B.D. i. 5.
[4] Salisbury to MacDonald, tel., secret, of 17 Jan. 1898, F.O. 17/1338.
[5] O'Conor to Salisbury, tel. 10, secret, of 20 Jan. 1898, B.D. i. 6.

the same view. Witte stressed that Russia's geographical position would sooner or later secure her political predominance in the north of China and that her true policy was to keep China intact. Later, he drew out a map of China and swept his hand over Chihli, Shansi, Shensi, and Kansu, as territory which sooner or later Russia would absorb. The lower part of China, embracing the Yangtze basin, Witte observed magnanimously, would be outside the area of Russian expansion.[1]

In their response, the Russian ministers had assumed that a policy of spheres of influence was meant, a conclusion that had not been contemplated by Salisbury. Moreover, consistently from his point of view, at the initial meeting, Muraviev complained to O'Conor about the continued presence of British warships at Port Arthur and about the British attitude over Talienwan.[2] Salisbury, on the other hand, had been thinking in terms of a commercial not a political division of interests, which would not restrict existing British rights. Much of the blame for the misunderstanding which arose must be placed on O'Conor. There is no evidence to show that the British minister sought to correct the misapprehension. On the contrary, O'Conor, already personally convinced of the need for spheres, was enthusiastic about the Russian response. He also thought it best in his discussions not to reveal to what extent he was speaking with Salisbury's approval, as the outcome was doubtful until the Tsar approved.[3] Finally, from the beginning O'Conor pressed for an Anglo-Russian understanding which would extend beyond China to other areas where the interests of the two powers clashed.[4]

Since 1895 Salisbury had been anxious for a more amicable relationship with Russia, and he found it difficult not to respond. At the same time he realized the growing divergence in the Russian and British outlook. This he sought to correct in a dispatch on 25 January, drafted by his own hand for O'Conor's guidance. The two empires of China and Turkey, he observed, were so weak that they had to be guided by the advice of foreign powers. In this, England and Russia were opposed,

---

[1] O'Conor to Salisbury, tel. 12, secret, of 23 Jan. 1898, *B.D.* i. 7; O'Conor to Salisbury, No. 38, confidential, of 30 Jan. 1898, *B.D.* i. 8.
[2] O'Conor to Salisbury, tel. 7 of 19 Jan. 1898, Cab. 37/46/29.
[3] O'Conor to Salisbury, 26 Jan. 1898, S.P. 129/34.
[4] O'Conor to Salisbury, tel. 10, secret, of 20 Jan. 1898, *B.D.* i. 6.

neutralizing each other's efforts much more frequently than the
real antagonism of their interests could justify. An understanding would be beneficial, but, he warned:

> We contemplate no infraction of existing rights. We would not
> admit the violation of any existing treaties, or impair the integrity
> of the present empires of either China or Turkey. These two condi-
> tions are vital. We aim at no partition of territory, but only a parti-
> tion of preponderance.[1]

It is clear that in regard to China Salisbury was appealing for
an Anglo-Russian understanding made not in a spirit of grudg-
ing concession but out of a sense of community of task. In this,
a division of labour was possible which allowed preponderance
to each power in a regional sense. This he distinguished for
O'Conor's guidance, in the dispatch of 25 January, as the
valley of the Yellow river and the territory of the north for
Russia, while Great Britain should concern herself in the valley
of the Yangtze.

This idealistic view was misunderstood by O'Conor, who
seized on Salisbury's response as the opportunity for a brilliant
coup de main. From then on, until the discussions petered out in
mid-February, he pressed for an understanding which would
extend to all places, even to Egypt, where British policies
conflicted with those of the Dual Alliance powers. 'We may
find some general phrase to answer our purpose', he reported by
February, 'and get us as far as we can in view of the French
alliance.'[2] Moreover, in O'Conor's view Russian compliance
was to be extorted, and the lever he chose was fashioned out of
Witte's admission of Russian nervousness of an Anglo-Japanese
alliance. 'We have got the Japanese card in our hand and I
think we ought to be slow to play it . . .', he argued, 'the possibility of our alliance with Japan haunts them and helps us.'[3]

However, O'Conor's efforts at St. Petersburg must be seen
in a true perspective. From January 1898 a strong anti-Russian
feeling prevailed in England which held out little promise for
a Russian understanding. Even Hicks Beach, with whom the
idea originated, told the Swansea Chamber of Commerce, on

[1] Salisbury to O'Conor, tel. 22, secret, of 25 Jan. 1898, *B.D.* i. 8.
[2] O'Conor to Salisbury, private, 10 Feb. 1898, S.P. 129/36.
[3] O'Conor to Salisbury, 26 Jan. 1898, S.P. 129/34; also tel. 12, secret, of 23 Jan.
1898, *B.D.* i. 7; 10 Feb. 1898, S.P. 129/36.

the day that Salisbury initiated the overture, that England would maintain the open door in China 'even if necessary at the cost of war'.[1]

The only matter in which Salisbury appeared to meet Russian wishes was in regard to the complaint against British warships at Port Arthur. Salisbury, who had been unaware that there were any British ships at the port, thought that Admiral Buller had been strangely ill-advised in sending them there without authority. For this reason more than any other he ordered the withdrawal of the one ship that was actually still at the port at the time of the Russian complaint.[2] The consequences were unfortunate. The move, which was reported by Reuter, added to the considerable anti-Russian feeling in England.

In fact, there is little evidence, even at an official level, that any real effort was made to improve relations with Russia. This is particularly noticeable in the hard attitude which was maintained over the Chinese loan negotiations.

By the end of January China had still not replied to the British offer of a direct loan of £12 million to pay the remaining indemnity. MacDonald, who was convinced that this hesitation was due to Russian threats, suggested a policy of counter-threats to force Chinese compliance. 'There is no leverage,' he observed, 'where Chinese are concerned, like fear, and we, however willing, must meet threat with threat.'[3] In London, Salisbury was ready to go further to counteract any Russian claims to make the loan. 'If a loan from us, who have four-fifths of the trade,' he stated, 'would disturb the balance of influence, *a fortiori* that effect would be produced by a loan from Russia.' If the loan went to Russia, Great Britain would demand compensations to redress the balance in the form of the freedom of inland navigation, territory for the Burmese railway, and the occupation of Chusan. He stated decisively; 'These things China must grant if she accepts the loan from Russia, and, if she refuses, we shall take them.'[4] Desperate over the accu-

---

[1] Lady Victoria Hicks Beach, *Life of Sir Michael Hicks Beach* (London, 1932), ii. 59.

[2] Memorandum by Thomas, British ships at Port Arthur, 27 Jan. 1898, S.P. 93/28; Salisbury to O'Conor, tel. 13 of 21 Jan. 1898, Cab. 37/46/29.

[3] MacDonald to Salisbury, tel. 27, secret, of 28 Jan. 1898, F.O. 17/1340.

[4] Salisbury to MacDonald, tel. 23 of 28 Jan. 1898, F.O. 17/1338.

mulating political demands from both Great Britain and Russia, China then announced that she would borrow from neither power. Private discussions were then resumed with the Hong Kong and Shanghai Bank, which led to the signing of a preliminary agreement for a loan of £16 million on 19 February.[1]

This attempt by China to lift the loan negotiations out of their political context was unsuccessful. Even before China announced her decision not to make a direct loan, Salisbury declared that if after formally asking for a loan China threw it up in deference to Russian wishes, it would be an affront for which concessions would be necessary.[2] Consequently, Mac-Donald continued his pressure against the Chinese. Between 5 and 14 February he secured Chinese agreement to the opening of the inland waterways to steam navigation, the establishment of a treaty port in Hunan, non-alienation of the Yangtze, and confirmation that the post of Inspector-General of the Customs should remain in British hands. In making these concessions China requested that they should be kept entirely disconnected from the loan negotiations so as to prevent Russian counter-claims.[3]

Little attempt was made to disguise these political concessions from Russia. In fact, when Count Lamsdorff, the Russian Deputy-Minister of Foreign Affairs, pressed O'Conor for a description of the British loan demands, Salisbury sent an extended list which went beyond what MacDonald was negotiating at Peking. Listed amongst these was the provocative demand for the opening of Talienwan as a treaty port.[4] In effect, Salisbury used the Chinese loan negotiations to challenge the Russian assumption that Great Britain was prepared to accept a policy of spheres of influence in China. Understandably, there was a reciprocal hardening in the Russian attitude. In commenting on the British demands, Lamsdorff stressed that Talienwan should be excluded from further discussion, and that Russia would make counter-claims in compensation.[5] As a final move, he suggested that Russia would agree that the loan should go

[1] MacDonald to Salisbury, tel. 45 of 19 Feb. 1898, Cab. 37/46/29.
[2] Salisbury to MacDonald, tel. 25 of 1 Feb. 1898, F.O. 17/1338.
[3] Salisbury to MacDonald, tels. 5 and 14 Feb. 1898, Cab. 37/46/29.
[4] Salisbury to O'Conor, tel. 38 of 10 Feb. 1898, F.O. 65/1557.
[5] O'Conor to Salisbury, tel. 31, secret, of 18 Feb. 1898, Cab. 37/46/29.

to Great Britain if she would agree to a Russian lease, for twenty years, of Port Arthur and Talienwan.[1]

Lamsdorff's suggestion of a 'bargain' brought Great Britain to the final stage of the loan negotiations. Since 1897 she had moved through the various phases of a fluctuating policy of competition, compensation, threats, and demands for concessions for 'affront'. The possibility that Russia should indirectly benefit from the loan drove her to a yet narrower view of the British purpose in China. When O'Conor reported the Russian suggestion of a 'bargain' Salisbury concluded it would be unnecessary to negotiate a settlement with Russia in that the concessions Great Britain sought had already been obtained without the loan. 'We have reached a point at which great care is necessary,' he replied to O'Conor, 'with these things gained it is becoming doubtful whether it is wise for us to offer the loan at all.'[2] He was more explicit in reporting the situation to MacDonald. Because of France, Russia would offer no help to Great Britain to further her Burmese railway schemes so 'we should really gain nothing except liberty to advance £16,000,000. Is that in itself of great value?'[3]

Both MacDonald and O'Conor reacted sharply against this narrow view. The main value of the loan, MacDonald stressed, lay not in the accompanying concessions but in the hold it gave Great Britain on the revenue machinery and the chance it allowed of effecting financial reforms. Both ministers advised that the wiser course would be to accept an arrangement with Russia, particularly as she would get the lease of Port Arthur and Talienwan whether Great Britain opposed it or not. O'Conor, faced with this clear indication of the unsubstantial nature of his efforts towards a Russian understanding, observed gloomily: 'We shall re-enter an era of mutual jealousy and distrust, and as the Siberian railway comes nearer to Peking I fear Russian influence will increase to our detriment.'[4]

Salisbury had already recovered his balance without the admonitions of his ministers. The loan went through, inscribed rather reluctantly by the Bank of England. However, the

[1] O'Conor to Salisbury, tel. 32, secret, of 19 Feb. 1898, Cab. 37/46/29.
[2] Salisbury to O'Conor, tel. 52, secret, of 20 Feb. 1898, Cab. 37/46/29.
[3] Salisbury to MacDonald, tel. 44, secret, of 20 Feb. 1898, F.O. 17/1338.
[4] MacDonald to Salisbury, tel. 33, secret, of 22 Feb. 1898, F.O. 17/1340;
O'Conor to Salisbury, tel. 33, secret, of 22 Feb. 1898, F.O. 65/1559.

political problem, of meeting the Russian challenge in China, still remained.

The Search for a Positive Policy

By 1898 there was a growing concern in England about the country's international position. It was felt that a more positive policy was necessary if Great Britain were to maintain her rightful position overseas. To some, this could only be achieved if Great Britain accepted the need for allies, so as to allow her more effectively to oppose the Dual Alliance powers.

This opinion was strongly held by the Colonial Secretary, Joseph Chamberlain, who was possibly the strongest figure in Salisbury's administration. In the spring of 1898 an appreciable number in the Cabinet came to share the view. The result was a searching reappraisal of Great Britain's traditional outlook, as the need for, and the possibility of, an alliance was explored. The process began with an approach to the United States and ended with the signing of the Anglo-Japanese alliance, but Germany was generally regarded as the power most likely to help in opposing Russia and France.

Three overtures were made between 1898 and 1901 for an Anglo-German understanding, and the first and third of these stemmed directly from Great Britain's anxiety over her position in the east. It could be said that from the Port Arthur crisis sprang Chamberlain's ambition to be the architect of British foreign affairs, and it was through the Chinese situation that the value of a German alliance was examined at a practical level.[1]

[1] 'He talked of China and West Africa, and of France and Russia, with an amplitude of view and phrase that would have astonished Birmingham ten years ago. He has lately had a strong difference of opinion with Lord S(alisbury). He believes we are at the parting of the ways, and that we must stand fast for Imperial expansion now or never, whatever the result.' M. V. Brett (ed.), *Journals and Letters of Reginald, Viscount Esher*, 4 vols. (London, 1934–8), i. 210–11. The discussions between Chamberlain and Count Hatzfeldt, German Ambassador at London, for an Anglo-German alliance, referred to by Lord Balfour at the time as 'a curious episode of which no record will be found at the Foreign Office (and which) should not vanish without leaving a trace' (Balfour to Salisbury, 14 Apr. 1898, S.P. Chronological Series 1898, Foreign and Imperial, I, Germany), have since been extensively dealt with by various writers. See J. L. Garvin, *The Life of Joseph Chamberlain*, 3 vols., with vol. iv by J. Amery (London, 1932–51), iii. 254–95; B. E. C. Dugdale, *Arthur James Balfour, First Earl of Balfour*, 2 vols. (London, 1936), i. 256–61; J. M. Goudswaard, *Some Aspects of the End of Britain's 'Splendid Isolation', 1898–1904* (Rotterdam, 1952), 12–71; J. D. Bickford and E. N. Johnson, 'The

The division of opinion in the Cabinet on Great Britain's international position was inevitably reflected in the conduct of policy. This was all the more marked in that Salisbury, the staunchest opponent of a German alliance, was frequently abroad for reasons of health. These trips generally took place in the spring and autumn and, until Salisbury surrendered the Foreign Office in November 1900, it was during these absences that the forward moves in Great Britain's China policy occurred. At the time of the Port Arthur crisis, Lord Balfour, like Chamberlain an advocate of vigorous action, was left in charge of the Cabinet.

An additional factor which emerged during the winter of 1897–8 to complicate the Government's handling of the Chinese situation was the rise of public concern over the position in the Far East. Since 1895 there had been a certain amount of commercial agitation, but after the occupation of the northern ports public comment adopted a different tone. Criticism of the Government's inactivity, often scurrilously outspoken, was linked with repeated calls for a more spirited foreign policy.[1]

The campaign, which was prolonged over the spring and summer of 1898, had important consequences. The Cabinet, docile up to this moment, stirred under the weight of public agitation and began to interest themselves in the Chinese situation. Joseph Chamberlain, always sensitive to the mood of the electorate, was one of the first to move. 'I wish that you read all the papers just now', he wrote to Balfour on 3 February. 'If you did, you would, I think, agree with me that grave trouble is impending on the Government, if we do not adopt a more decided attitude in regard to China.'[2] The 'decided attitude' Chamberlain had in mind was a joint approach by the United States, Germany, and Great Britain to Russia to keep the recently occupied Chinese ports and all such future

Contemplated Anglo-German Alliance, 1890–1901', *PSQ*, 42 (1927), 1–57. J. A. S. Grenville, *Lord Salisbury and Foreign Policy* (London, 1964), 148–76.

[1] Garvin, *Chamberlain*, iii. 250–1; Elliot, *Goschen*, ii. 219–20. An example of the more violent form of attack is given in *Pall Mall Gazette*, 3 Sept. 1898: 'In these days of armed peace England longs for a leader as she has not longed since the news of Austerlitz killed Pitt. . . . Britain does not love the rule of valetudinarians . . .', etc. On 16 July a gross attack was made on Salisbury in the *Daily Mail* which Harmsworth hurriedly disowned.

[2] Chamberlain to Balfour, 3 Feb. 1898, Dugdale, *Balfour*, i. 252–3.

acquisitions open to international trade. If Russia should refuse, Chamberlain continued to Balfour, who was then in temporary charge of the Government because of Salisbury's illness, 'we should summon her fleet to leave Port Arthur and make her go if necessary'.[1]

The need for a positive decision became more pressing after 20 February, when the suggestion of a 'bargain' with Russia was rejected and it became clear that she would demand Port Arthur and Talienwan. On 23 February the Cabinet decided to approach the United States for its co-operation in maintaining the open door in China.[2] Salisbury, who was shortly to go abroad to recuperate, was against acting precipitately and the actual approach was delayed. However, the situation worsened during the next fortnight. On 25 February MacDonald reported that the Chinese Government was prepared to offer Great Britain the lease of Weihaiwei. Despite reports that Germany was likely to seize the port, Salisbury rejected the offer, which was likely to lead to the very situation he was trying to avoid.[3] Admiralty reports of the presence of seven French warships on the south China coast suggested urgency. Then, on 7 March, *The Times* reported that Russia was threatening to send troops to Manchuria, to claim the lease of Port Arthur and Talienwan.

Balfour, again in charge, acted decisively. MacDonald was instructed to demand first refusal of a lease of Weihaiwei.[4] On the same day (7 March) a telegram was sent to Sir Julian Pauncefote, British minister in Washington, instructing him to ask for the co-operation of the United States.[5]

Initially, the position appeared to be favourable. Pauncefote reported that he had transmitted the message to the President before a Cabinet meeting on the 8th. McKinley, who stated that he had expected the communication, promised an answer the next day. However, a week passed and on 15 March Pauncefote was told to press for an answer. An unofficial verbal reply explained rather lamely that the American legislature

---

[1] Ibid.　　　　　　　　　　　　　　[2] Grenville, *Salisbury*, 143.
[3] MacDonald to Salisbury, tel., separate and secret, of 25 Feb. 1898, Cab. 37/46/29. The message came through Sir Robert Hart.
[4] Salisbury to MacDonald, tel. 55, secret, of 7 Mar. 1898, Cab. 37/46/29.
[5] Salisbury to Sir J. Pauncefote, tel. 17, very confidential, of 7 Mar. 1898, Cab. 37/46/29; R. G. Neale, *Britain and American Imperialism, 1898–1900* (Brisbane, 1965), 97.

and not the executive determined ultimate policy and, while the President of the United States was in sympathy with a policy which maintained open trade in China, in his opinion none of the occupations which had taken place proposed to interfere with that trade. Pauncefote's report concluded soberly:

> On the contrary, the official communications which (he) has indicate there is no present purpose to close the China trade to the civilized world or to obtain exclusive commercial privileges therein. He does not see any present reason for the departure of the United States from its traditional policy respecting foreign alliances, and, as far as practicable, avoiding any interference in connection of European complications.[1]

It was small comfort that Assistant Secretary of State Day should observe, in delivering the reply, that it had been cautiously framed on account of the settled policy of the United States to avoid 'entangling alliances' and because of the impending trouble with Spain.[2]

From the middle of March, after the American rebuff, the Cabinet searched for a suitable policy to match Russia's provocative attitude in North China. Great Britain was not opposed to Russia acquiring an ice-free commercial harbour which would enable her to further her Siberian railway project. The extension of Russian influence in south Manchuria could also be tacitly accepted, but only if the area remained open to international trade. But if Russia intended to claim Port Arthur and Talienwan as closed ports, as all the reports suggested, it would openly challenge the concept of the open door. Initially, in seeking the leases, Russia had indicated that treaty rights in the ports would be respected. However, as neither port had been opened to treaty status it was recognized that this assurance was meaningless. Thus the only way of keeping the ports open would be to claim equal rights through the most-favoured-nation clause of the Treaty of Tientsin. This was the minimum that Great Britain could accept without openly abandoning the basic principles of her China policy.

On this basis Britain attempted to test Russia's intentions. On 11 March she asked for an assurance of equal rights under

---

[1] Pauncefote to Salisbury, tel. 18 of 16 Mar. 1898, Cab. 37/46/29.
[2] Pauncefote to Salisbury, tel. 19 of 16 Mar. 1898, Cab. 37/46/29.

the terms of the Tientsin treaty.[1] A week later she made a more specific approach by suggesting that Russia could lease Talienwan and have a rail extension to the port, if she agreed not to take Port Arthur, which was of no commercial use. In return, Great Britain undertook not to occupy a northern port in retaliation, nor to interfere in Manchurian affairs, so long as her treaty rights were respected.[2]

When Russia did not respond to this it became clear that she intended to occupy Port Arthur as a closed and fortified port. It was consequently a political move and Great Britain had to consider it in terms of its strategic and political significance.

The Occupation of Weihaiwei

The deliberations of the Cabinet were conditioned by the prevailing view that Russia would inevitably come to dominate China across her land frontier. It was in this belief that MacDonald urged, in his dispatches from Peking, that Great Britain should recognize Russia's commanding position and come to terms with her in order to preserve commercial access to Manchuria.[3] Balfour was ready to admit the strength of Russia's position and even that her occupation of Port Arthur could have no long-term prejudicial effect on the future of northern China 'since, with or without Port Arthur, this must inevitably fall to Russia'.[4] He was also ready to agree with MacDonald's view that the balance of power at Peking need not be upset by the Russian occupation. Nevertheless, he argued with some force that the occupation of a port whose whole importance derived solely from its military strength and strategic position would inevitably be considered in the Far East as a standing menace to Peking and the beginning of a partition of China.[5]

Consequently, some positive action by Great Britain was necessary, and British attention focused on the possibility of

[1] Salisbury to O'Conor, tel. 69 of 11 Mar. 1898, Cab. 37/46/29.
[2] Salisbury to O'Conor, tel., private, of 18 Mar.; Salisbury to MacDonald, tel. 99 of 22 Mar. 1898, Cab. 37/46/29.
[3] MacDonald to Salisbury, tel. 71 of 10 Mar. 1898; MacDonald to Balfour, tel. 90 of 21 Mar. 1898, Cab. 37/46/29.
[4] Balfour to MacDonald, tel. (A) of 19 Mar. 1898, Cab. 37/46/29.
[5] Salisbury (Balfour) to MacDonald, tel. 99 of 22 Mar. 1898, Cab. 37/46/29.

occupying Weihaiwei. In discussion with MacDonald, Balfour contemplated a choice between two policies:

the one allowing Russia to lease Port Arthur subject to engagements to preserve existing treaty rights, and possibly, though this is doubtful, to refrain from fortifying Port Arthur, we taking as a make-weight a lease of Wei-hai-wei.

The other requiring the Russians to abstain from leasing Port Arthur, we engaging to take no port in Gulf of Pechili and not to intervene in Manchuria.[1]

The first of these alternatives, as presented by Balfour, implied that Great Britain would try to force Russian compliance by threatening to occupy Weihaiwei. The second involved the possible use of force. In explaining this latter alternative, Balfour reasoned that, even at the risk of a general war, it offered the only possible way of checking Russia and preventing the imminent partition of the Chinese Empire. On the previous day he had asked O'Conor whether Russia would fight rather than give way, and the British minister had replied reassuringly that he thought she would not, although in his view relations would be very strained.[2] Despite this, during the crisis over Port Arthur Great Britain never seriously considered war as a possible solution.

Thus, the real issue which lay before the Cabinet was whether Great Britain should occupy Weihaiwei, and thereby indicate her opposition to the Russian move, or acquiesce in Russia's action and, by seeking compensation elsewhere, join in the partition of China.

The decision to occupy Weihaiwei was a difficult one, and it was argued through five Cabinet meetings. As late as 10 March MacDonald had reported that Weihaiwei was 'the only one remaining port, second to none from a naval point of view'.[3] However, the Cabinet was well aware of its limitations. Experts from the Admiralty, when called into consultation, offered a rather more reserved view of the port's suitability. It was actually not deep enough to meet modern naval purposes, so

---

[1] Balfour to MacDonald, tel. (A) of 19 Mar. 1898, Cab. 37/46/29.

[2] Balfour to O'Conor, tel., private, of 18 Mar. 1898; O'Conor to Balfour, tel., private, of 19 Mar. 1898, Cab. 37/46/29.

[3] MacDonald to Salisbury, tel. 71 of 10 Mar. 1898, Cab. 37/46/29.

that the cost of its maintenance could scarcely be justified.[1] Balfour indicated this clearly to MacDonald on 19 March:

> Weihaiwei, if obtained, would require too large a force for its defence, and, except for appearances, would be worth little to us if fortified, and still less if unfortified, and, therefore, would be no counterpoise to Port Arthur, which is so strong by nature, and still possesses forts of such strength that it can easily be made impregnable. . . .[2]

Another consideration which encouraged hesitation was that the port lay in an area where Germany was consolidating her interests. 'By occupying Weihaiwei', MacDonald warned the Cabinet, 'we should strike a death-blow at this aspiration, and incur her hostility.'[3] Nor did the combined counsels of MacDonald and O'Conor help to resolve the Cabinet's growing doubt. Throughout the period of decision the two ministers seemed united in a conspiracy to urge the Government to accept Russia's action and to follow a policy of spheres of influence, seeking compensation in the Yangtze region. 'It secures a share,' O'Conor urged, 'and a preponderant share, in the semi-disintegration of China which has already, unfortunately, commenced.'[4] It was a strong temptation: generally, the ministers who favoured a vigorous policy were also in favour of the consolidation of British influence in central China. However, the Cabinet realized that it could not afford a policy of spheres of influence. The issue which lay before them involved more than the support of British commercial interests in China. They were already painfully aware that the Russian occupation of Port Arthur would 'discredit England throughout the Far East'.[5] The compensatory policy urged by O'Conor could only worsen Great Britain's position. Lord Goschen noted bitterly of his dispatches that 'he did not realize the diplomatic defeat involved in the least'.[6]

[1] Marder, *British Naval Policy*, 302.

[2] Balfour to MacDonald, tel. (A) of 19 Mar. 1898, Cab. 37/46/29.

[3] MacDonald to Salisbury, tel. 71 of 10 Mar. 1898, Cab. 37/46/29.

[4] O'Conor to Salisbury, tel. 46, confidential, of 13 Mar. 1898, Cab. 37/46/29; O'Conor to Salisbury, tel. of 21 Mar. 1898; O'Conor to Salisbury, 24 Mar. 1898, circulated to the Cabinet, S.P. 129/37, 39; MacDonald to Salisbury, tels. 10, 12 of 13 Mar. 1898, Cab. 37/46/29.

[5] Balfour to MacDonald, tel. (A) of 19 Mar. 1898, Cab. 37/46/29.

[6] Minute on O'Conor to Salisbury, 24 Mar. 1898, circulated to the Cabinet, S.P. 129/39.

The Kaiser was later to describe the occupation of Weihaiwei as 'a departure from that practical common sense with which Englishmen were usually credited'.[1] In fact, Great Britain had no alternative but to occupy Weihaiwei, if she were to maintain her international reputation. In December 1897, when Lord Salisbury had first pondered the situation, he had concluded that this consideration could lead Great Britain to seek a port in the north.[2] By March 1898, after all that had occurred, Great Britain could not afford to pursue any alternative less positive measure. The only really adequate counterpoise to the preponderance of Russia and Germany in China was in the north.[3] This view was also strongly pressed by Lord Curzon, then parliamentary secretary and an acknowledged expert on Far Eastern affairs, when he was admitted to a special meeting of the Cabinet on 25 March to argue his case for the occupation of Weihaiwei.[4]

Great Britain was also aware that, if she abstained, Germany would occupy the port after it had been evacuated by Japan. Weihaiwei, as MacDonald had already pointed out, was the last remaining port of any significance in north China. After deliberating for three and a half hours on 25 March, the Cabinet decided to lease the port for as long as Russia occupied Port Arthur.[5]

On the day the decision to occupy it was taken, Balfour and Chamberlain began preliminary conversations for an Anglo-German understanding with Baron Hatzfeldt, the German Ambassador, and Baron Eckardstein, the first secretary of the

---

[1] Lascelles to Salisbury, No. 168, very confidential, of 26 May 1898, printed for the use of the Cabinet, Cab. 37/47/36.

[2] Memorandum by Sanderson of 23 Dec. 1897, Sanderson Papers, F.O. 800/2.

[3] Memorandum by Bertie of 14 Mar. 1898, *B.D.* i. 17–18.

[4] Curzon's own view of his influence was: 'Weihaiwei—which was in a particular sense my own child, since I first went and recommended its acquisition to Balfour and Chamberlain, then fought its case hard in a private Committee at the Admiralty with Goschen, Balfour, Devonshire, Lansdowne and the Admirals, and finally as you (Hamilton) may remember, reargued it in the Cabinet, to which I was admitted for the purpose. . . .' Curzon to Hamilton, 22 Aug. 1900, Hamilton Papers.

[5] F. Gosses, *The Management of British Foreign Policy before the First World War, especially during the period 1880–1914* (Leiden, 1948), 155 f.; Garvin, *Chamberlain*, iii. 248–9; Earl of Ronaldshay, *The Life of Lord Curzon*, 3 vols. (London, 1928), i. 276–81, 283–6. For the attitude of the Admiralty, Marder, *British Naval Policy*, 302 f. Generally, E-tu Zen Sun, 'The Lease of Wei-hai Wei', *PHR*, 19 (1950), 277–83.

German legation in London. This consideration undoubtedly influenced Chamberlain, for he was opposed to the taking of Weihaiwei.[1] To meet German objections, and possibly Chamberlain's, a clear assurance was given in Berlin that no railway development would be made from the port into the Shantung peninsula.[2]

The task of forcing the lease from China fell to MacDonald who, even after the decision had been taken, argued against the occupation. The diplomatic considerations which had preoccupied the Cabinet were not so clear in the east, where the consequences of the British action seemed only too apparent. The offer of the lease of Weihaiwei was one of the desperate measures which the harassed ministers of the Tsungli Yamen had devised to bolster up their crumbling diplomatic position in the negotiations with Russia over Port Arthur. Another, which provided the only note of light relief to the perplexed British Cabinet in its own deliberations, was a suggestion for an Anglo-Japanese-Chinese alliance against Russia.[3] At the end of March the Chinese ministers were understandably apprehensive that the grant of a lease of Weihaiwei to Great Britain would lead to counter-claims by the other foreign powers. Through several lengthy meetings MacDonald urged compliance and at one point the British minister contemplated the use of force. 'They will not, I think, give way except under great pressure, and an occupation of Chusan will probably be necessary as a (? first step).'[4] After further delay, during which China asked for the right to anchor her ships at the port, a convention for the lease was signed on 1 July 1898.

After Weihaiwei was obtained very little was done with it. Initially it was assumed that the port would be turned into a fortified naval base. However, because of the general unsuitability of the place, this would have involved the construction of a long breakwater and extensive dredging work in the

[1] Balfour to Salisbury, 14 Apr. 1898, S.P. Chronological Series, 1898, Foreign and Imperial, I, Germany.
[2] Sir Frank Lascelles, British Ambassador at Berlin, to Herr von Bülow, German Minister for Foreign Affairs, 20 Apr. 1898, B.D. i. 33–4.
[3] MacDonald to Salisbury, tel. 79, very confidential, of 15 Mar. 1898, Cab. 37/46/29.
[4] MacDonald to Salisbury, tel. 110 of 31 Mar.; tel. 107 of 28 Mar. 1898, F.O. 17/1358.

harbour at prohibitive cost. In any case, the establishment of permanent advanced bases did not conform with Admiralty policy at the time.[1] The Treasury also rejected a request by the Admiralty for a British cable between Woosung and Weihaiwei, which the Navy thought would be of immense advantage in the event of outbreak of war with Russia.[2] Although various schemes were put forward, no attempt was made to utilize the port as a strategic base and it was used chiefly as a naval rest centre.[3] A suggestion was made by Field-Marshal Wolseley, the Commander-in-Chief, that Chinese troops could be organized at Weihaiwei for use in other places, but the Chinese Government objected to recruits being enlisted in leased territories for general service.[4] Eventually a Chinese Regiment was formed for local defence. The venture was not successful. Between 1899 and 1901 over 800 men deserted.[5] Many of them moved straight into Chinese service after having passed through what came to be known as 'the Wei Hai Wei Military School'.[6] As the India Office pointed out, Great Britain was in effect furnishing 'a steady annual supply of trained soldiers' to China.[7]

The occupation of Weihaiwei was defended in Parliament on 5 April. While Balfour in the Commons emphasized the need to maintain Great Britain's commercial influence in the east, the Duke of Devonshire in the House of Lords was more outspoken. He presented the occupation of Weihaiwei as a necessary counterpoise to restore the naval equilibrium in northern Chinese waters, which had to be preserved in view of Russia's overwhelming preponderance on land in north China.[8]

From his holiday retreat at Beaulieu, Salisbury maintained an attitude of reserve. Not until Balfour sent the urgent message on 30 March that the Cabinet was 'unanimous in the opinion

---

[1] China, WHW. 1905, Cab. 17/65.

[2] Memorandum by Hicks Beach of 10 May 1899; Admiralty memorandum of 8 June 1899, S.P. Confidential Print.

[3] WHW., Schemes for utilization of place, Cab. 1/2/411.

[4] Memorandum by Wolseley of 1 Dec. 1898, Cab. 37/48/88. Memorandum by Colonial Defence Committee, 'Utilization of Native Troops in Colonial Garrisons', secret, No. 173 M, Apr. 1899, Cab. 8/2.

[5] Major-General Sir A. Dorward to Secretary of State, Colonial Office, secret, 12 Dec. 1901; WHW. 1901, C.O. 521/2; War Office to Foreign Office, 16 Dec. 1901, F.O. 17/1511.

[6] India Office to Foreign Office, 27 Nov. 1901, F.O. 17/1511.

[7] India Office to Foreign Office, 13 Nov. 1901, F.O. 17/1510.

[8] Parliamentary Debates, 4th Series, lvi, cols. 165–74, 224–39.

that at all costs Wei-hai-wei must be obtained and that any retrogression on our part in this matter would have the worst effect possible on this country' did he give his consent.[1] A month earlier he had refused a Chinese offer of the port and his change of front was clearly made to save the unity and confidence of his Cabinet.

He returned on 29 April to find that the Chinese situation had become the occasion of an intense and bitter political discussion. The publication a few days previously of a Blue Book on China made available information about the events of the previous winter. The earlier criticism of the Government's handling of the situation was revived. In particular, attention was focused on the withdrawal of the two British ships from Port Arthur, apparently after Russian representations. The *Globe*, violent in its criticism, labelled this 'the "hope-I-don't-intrude" incident'. The *Morning Post*, with more dignity but greater effectiveness, hoped that the dispatches, particularly those relating to the two ships, would be read and studied and their meaning pondered over in every constituency in the country. 'They embody in a few sentences', it remarked scathingly, 'the whole spirit or spiritlessness of the Government's policy.' Scorn was heaped on the Government's childlike faith in the assurances of the country's rivals. This, *The Times* remarked, was 'not the way to uphold the prestige of a great nation in the East'. The *Standard*, charitably, sought to defend Salisbury by stressing Russian duplicity.[2]

The situation was far from Salisbury's liking. China, in his opinion, was not a suitable platform on which a debate on Great Britain's isolated position in international affairs could profitably be conducted. On 4 May, speaking at the Albert Hall, he made an effort to remove China from the centre of controversy back to a peripheral position where differences could be settled pacifically as a regional issue.

The living nations will gradually encroach on the territory of the

[1] Balfour to Salisbury, 30 Mar. 1898; Salisbury to MacDonald, 31 Mar. 1898, S.P. Box 1, Drafts, Copies, Minutes, etc., 1897–1902. Salisbury's opinion on WHW. has been quoted as 'some territorial or cartographic consolation in China' to satisfy British opinion: 'It will not be useful and it will be expensive.' Garvin, *Chamberlain*, iii. 249. It seems that Salisbury was not aware of Chamberlain's dissent until Balfour's letter of 14 Apr.

[2] This, and the preceding newspaper references, all of 25 Apr. 1898.

dying, [he declared] and the seeds and causes of conflict among civilized nations will speedily appear. . . . We shall not allow England to be at a disadvantage in any rearrangement that may take place. On the other hand, we shall not be jealous if desolation and sterility are removed by the aggrandizement of a rival in regions to which our arms cannot extend.[1]

The plea was not responded to as he would have wished. On 13 May Chamberlain replied with his equally well-known speech which threw out the gibe against Russian duplicity:

. . . who sups with the devil must have a very long spoon. . . . If the policy of isolation which has hitherto been the policy of this country is to be maintained in the future then the fate of the Chinese Empire may be, and probably will be, hereafter decided without reference to our wishes and in defiance of our interests.[2]

The exchange revealed the differences of opinion which had emerged over the conduct of British policy in China because of the Port Arthur crisis. Salisbury's attempt to limit the field of application of British isolation in relation to the Dual Alliance by treating China as an area where differences could be adjusted pacifically was rejected by the militant members of his Cabinet.

However, their efforts resulted in a dangerous collision of Anglo-Russian interests which over the next few months appeared to weaken rather than to strengthen the British position in China.

[1] *The Times*, 5 May 1898.   [2] Ibid., 14 May 1898.

IV

THE SCRAMBLE FOR CONCESSIONS

THE occupation of the northern ports brought about a changed situation in China. Throughout 1898–9 a scramble for concessions developed between the powers as they worked to extend their interests in an apparently disintegrating Chinese Empire. The concessions which were obtained were ostensibly negotiated by private foreign interests and were generally for mineral and railway construction rights. In certain instances, attempts were made to obtain Chinese participation by arranging for the claims to be worked through Sino-Western companies or through Chinese companies in which foreign technical co-operation was allowed. However, the degree of foreign control which was written into the loan prospectuses was considerable and, for all practical purposes, the concessions were regarded as foreign enterprises and sought out on that basis through the exercise of diplomatic pressure at Peking.

The political aspect of this activity was emphasized by the fact that the concessions were generally sought for in specific areas on a national basis. This tendency had been introduced by France and Russia in 1895, when they claimed a special priority of rights in south-west China and Manchuria. The seizure of the northern ports in the winter of 1897–8 then accelerated the process in a way which threatened to disrupt the economic structure of the country as well as Chinese political control. The ports became convenient centres around which territorial claims could be made. Thus Russia was conveniently placed in south Manchuria, Germany on the Shantung promontory, and France in the area around Kwangchow Bay in the south. Later, Japan contemplated an area of special interest in the region of Amoy and Italy looked forward to the establishment of a sphere around San Mun Bay.

Spheres of interest had been tacitly recognized in China since 1895, but as these allowed the continued although possibly diminished participation of the other foreign powers they did not specifically violate the concept of the open door. Spheres of influence, on the other hand, implied a distinct economic and commercial exclusiveness, with a degree of political control over the area as well as an understood freedom to absorb the territory. This could not be admitted without altering the entire basis of the foreign treaty position in China.

The surge of foreign concession hunting was helped on by the attitude of the Chinese Government. During the eighteen-sixties, when the first tentative attempts had been made to introduce railways into China, the Manchu Court had maintained a hostile attitude to what was regarded as a foreign innovation. However, after the Sino-Japanese war of 1894–5 it began to regard the construction of railways as a possible means of national defence. Concessions were freely approved up to the end of 1898, when a growing concern over the consequences of foreign activity led to the promulgation of an imperial decree which indicated that no further concessions would be considered until those already granted had been taken up. This liberal attitude was not extended to mining enterprises, over which an attempt was made to enforce rigorous mining regulations so as to limit foreign control. However, as these mining enterprises were often linked to railway projects the distinction was often difficult to maintain and a significant amount of foreign control was established through the loan contracts.

The pattern which emerges from the scramble for railway concessions in the spring and summer of 1898 shows that China did all she could to prevent the formation of spheres of influence by granting concessions to the powers in areas in which they were likely to come into conflict with their European rivals. The fact that the concessions were regarded as private enterprises and that each had to be obtained separately from the Chinese Government gave China an element of continuing control which she used to advantage. As the concern of the Chinese Government grew over the expanding appetites of the powers it granted concessions in a way which interfered with the development of the exclusive control of an area by any single power. This display of initiative, delicately and tentatively applied, provided China with a moderately successful policy, in a period of otherwise general subjection. To an increasing extent, the powers found themselves encroaching on each other's spheres, with a consequent heightening of diplomatic tension. Whereas the anticipated spheres of influence could be easily defined at the beginning of 1898, they became increasingly blurred as the scramble continued. The multiplicity of concessions which were granted led to an indeterminate situation which in the end helped to frustrate the whole process.

Understandably, Great Britain was opposed to the emergence of spheres of influence in China. Although there had been a considerable disregard of the concept in the period after 1895, British policy was still based on the principle of the open door. However, Great Britain was also intent on avoiding any course of action which could align her against the other foreign powers and which would emphasize her diplomatic isolation in the east. The Port Arthur crisis had shown that she was not prepared to go to war over Chinese affairs, even if it could be assumed that an adequate defence of her position justified the step. Consequently, after 1895 British support of the open door tended to be interpreted in defensive terms as a determination to resist any containment of her existing interests. In practice this had become a policy of compensatory concessions against China. The pressure which she applied for an extension of the Burma railway into Yunnan; the demand for the non-alienation of the Yangtze region; her insistence on a British Inspector-General of the Maritime Customs and other claims which were made during the negotiation of the third indemnity loan did little to support the principle of the open door and much to undermine the very position which Great Britain wished to maintain.

Nevertheless, even if she were prepared to abandon the open door, Great Britain could not afford to accept a policy of spheres of influence in China. On a territorial assessment, she had an interest in central China, with a possible link with the interior. She had a stake in Hong Kong and an interest in a Burmese railway project, and consequently a special concern for south and south-west China. She had to retain her position in the north so that she could maintain her influence at Peking. She had even to display an interest in the remote provinces of the north-west, so as to prevent Russia from consolidating her hold on the area, with a possible effect on the balance of power in central Asia.

Yet it was clear that both Russia and Germany assumed that they had obtained spheres in Manchuria and Shantung. France too claimed a similar position in the south. From mid-February 1898 reports were current that she intended to claim a port either on Hainan Island, for which she had already secured a non-alienation agreement from China, or on the mainland in the vicinity of Hainan. A month later *The Times* reported that in reply to the British demand for the non-alienation of the Yangtze, China would extend a non-alienation agreement to France for the whole portion of China south of the Yangtze valley.[1] The alarm was immediately sounded by Sir John Ardagh, the D.G.M.I., who described this as a deliberate attempt to block the extension of British interests in Hong Kong and of the Burmese railway into Yunnan. Ardagh also objected to the use of the term *valley*, which had an ambiguous meaning and could limit the area of British control in the Yangtze to the lowland immediately adjacent to the course of the river. He urged that the correct expression should be 'the *basins* of the river Yangtze and all its affluents and tributaries'.[2]

Within a few weeks these British apprehensions were justified. On 9 April France acquired the lease of Kwangchow Bay and China's agreement to the non-alienation of the provinces of Kwangtung, Kwangsi, and Yunnan. A railway concession between Tongking and Yunnanfu and France's special rights on Hainan Island, both previously granted, were also publicly confirmed. In addition, it was agreed that a Frenchman would be given control of the Chinese Postal Service when the service was established.[3] Still more significantly, in mid-April the long-drawn-out negotiations over the construction of the vital Peking–Hankow–Canton railway took a turn which convinced the Foreign Office that a struggle for railway concessions was emerging along political lines.

The project of a trunk railway between Peking and Canton

[1] *The Times*, 'The French Demands', 19 Mar. 1898.
[2] Memorandum No. 35, Ardagh's Memoranda, vol. i, p. 340; P.R.O. 30/40/14, Pt. I.
[3] Joseph, *Foreign Diplomacy*, 307.

had been raised shortly after the Sino-Japanese war. China was eager to establish this link and an Imperial edict was issued on 20 October 1896 which sanctioned the Peking–Hankow section and authorized a Chinese company to contract a foreign loan for the construction of the line. Negotiations came under the control of Sheng Shuan-huai, Director-General of the Chinese Railway Bureau, who negotiated a preliminary agreement with an American firm, the American China Development Company.[1] When these negotiations fell through, the discussions were taken up by a Belgian syndicate, the Société d'Étude des Chemins de fer en Chine, which had a nominal capital of 45 million francs written down in Paris and Brussels. Two preliminary agreements for the construction of the line were signed with this company in May 1897.

Throughout 1897 there was some feeling in the Foreign Office that Great Britain should compete for the concession. In March 1898, at the height of the negotiations over the third indemnity loan, Salisbury thought that the concession could be demanded as part compensation for China's rejection of the British loan offer. The suggestion was put to O'Conor, who had been minister to China in 1896. O'Conor rejected the concession as 'trivial' and he urged strongly that Great Britain should concentrate her attention on the Burma–Yangtze railway project, which should not be 'bartered away' for the Peking–Hankow railway scheme.[2] O'Conor's preoccupation with the dream of a Chinese railway link with Burma and India was not only outdated but damaging to Great Britain's position on the Yangtze. By the spring of 1898 the Hankow–Canton section as well as the Peking–Hankow stretch were under consideration. The American China Development Company, whose interest had revived, negotiated a preliminary agreement for the southern section of the line on 14 April 1898. It then emerged that the Belgian syndicate holding the concession for the construction of the northern section was merely a cover for a French company, the Compagnie des Chemins de fer Chinois, which held 78,000 of the 133,000 shares which had been issued. It was also reported that Sheng, who harboured some doubts

---

[1] W. R. Braisted, 'The United States and the American China Development Company', *FEQ*, 11 (1952), 147–65.
[2] O'Conor to Salisbury, tel. of 12 Mar. 1898, S.P. 129/37.

as to whether the American company would take up their option on the southern section, had promised the Belgian syndicate preferential rights if the American contract fell through.

British apprehensions were immediately aroused by the political implications which surrounded the Peking–Hankow and Hankow–Canton railway concessions. By working through Belgium, France and Russia could control the vital trunk line which effectively cut through Great Britain's position on the Yangtze. Russia's part in this activity was emphasized in a leading article in *The Times* on 31 May, where it was pointed out that the northern section was in fact to be constructed with funds from the Russo-Chinese Bank.[1] The effectiveness of this type of state-controlled activity and the reluctance of the British Government to oppose it was the subject of a further article the following day. In caustic terms *The Times* pointed out that the article printed the previous day would possess but slight interest for British diplomatists and statesmen 'who cannot be expected, as we know by observation and on authority, to display an intelligent anticipation of events before they occur'. But *The Times* concluded that to 'plain men' it would have deep significance:

It shows quite clearly that a potent instrument for facilitating the creation of future claims of a political order within the Chinese Empire is already in existence, and that it is at this moment being used by our rivals with their accustomed pertinacity and foresight. ... The instrument in question is the grant of what are practically, if not nominally, state loans to China for purposes of railway construction.[2]

The possibility of obtaining positive financial support by the Government to oppose French and Russian activity was then taken up by the China Association. A request was made for a British Government guarantee of £125,000 a year to cover a loan of £5 million to China so as to oppose the Peking–Hankow railway concession. In pressing the suggestion the Association argued that the Russo-Chinese Bank was a state bank and that while private enterprises could compete against each other state finance had to be opposed by state finance. 'England is

1 'Railways in China', *The Times*, 31 May 1898.
2 Ibid., 1 June 1898.

interested in maintaining the Yangtze region intact,' it observed, 'and the control of its approaches is a matter of Imperial concern.'[1] After its experience in the third indemnity loan negotiations the Government could not respond to this suggestion for direct financial and political action. Nevertheless, it was clear that some sort of government backing was necessary. The indecisive policy of the Government over the winter of 1897–8 had led to a significant decline in British public confidence which compared unfavourably with the vigorous optimism shown by their foreign competitors. This was strikingly illustrated in the widely differing responses of British and German investors in subscribing to the third indemnity loan. When Germany's £8 million portion of the Chinese loan was issued at Berlin £38 million was applied for, yet when a similar amount was offered in London only £2 million was subscribed by the British public.[2]

Consequently, from the spring of 1898 certain British mercantile organizations were supported by the British Government. Foremost amongst these was the British and Chinese Corporation, which was formed by two leading British firms, the Hongkong and Shanghai Banking Corporation and Jardine Matheson and Company, when the Anglo-German, banking arrangement broke down in March. The arrangement was that the Bank would handle the financial aspect of British activity in China, while the Company would act as the contracting firm, building railways and supplying the engines and rolling stock.[3] The railway concessions which the Corporation obtained in the Yangtze valley, Manchuria, and between Canton and Kowloon constituted the major British gains during the scramble. Other British organizations which were given political support were the Peking Syndicate and the Yunnan Company.

A rather more cautious attitude was taken by the Government over the grant of subsidies to private trading companies. The issue was raised with the proliferation of such requests in 1898 and steps were taken to have it considered by a committee of the House of Commons. The report, which was delayed,

[1] Gundry to Foreign Office, 8 July 1898, F.O. 17/1440.
[2] Memorandum by Bertie, 24 Mar. 1898, F.O. 17/1357.
[3] M. Collis, *Wayfoong* (London, 1965), 118–20.

was not expected until 1902. Meanwhile British Government policy, laid down by the Treasury, was to consider Chinese ventures through the rulings laid down for Africa. In the rare instances when subsidies were granted in Africa they were strictly confined to lines of communication directly connecting British possessions and the Protectorates. An example of this was the £9,000 a year given to the British Indian Steam Navigation Company for a monthly service between Zanzibar and Aden.[1] This ruling, which was followed during 1899–1901, created considerable confusion both in the minds of the Foreign Office and the merchants applying for help. On the one hand, the Foreign Office wanted to extend British interests without actually committing the Government and it was reluctant to refuse any application for help. On the other, the various minor firms active in China were under a sincere misapprehension of the unvoiced reservations of the Foreign Office and solicited as their right the granting of government subsidies. However, few if any of the Chinese ventures conformed with the ruling which applied to Africa and subsidies were generally refused. The closest approach to direct financial aid was made by a minor British firm, the Yangtze Trading Company, which submitted a scheme to maintain a flotilla of river boats on the upper reaches of the Yangtze so as to open up British communication with Chungking. Even in this case the Foreign Office was only prepared to offer political rather than financial assistance. Lord Lansdowne, who had become Foreign Minister by 1901, observed when the Company made a final appeal before going into liquidation, 'we should certainly "support" such an enterprize in the sense of putting pressure upon the Chinese Government if they were to impede it'.[2]

This degree of political support was extended to all the smaller British speculators and concession hunters during the scramble. Concessionaires were encouraged to seek claims over as wide an area of China as possible. Although many of the schemes which were submitted were of an extremely dubious nature, there is little evidence of any official attempt to control or direct this activity. An extreme example is provided by the

[1] Treasury to Foreign Office, 18 Aug. 1898, in memorandum by Mallet, 17 Aug. 1901, F.O. 17/1508.
[2] Minute on Col. J. Denny to Lord Cranborne, 17 Aug. 1901, F.O. 17/1508.

activities of the Eastern Contract Company of Dublin which claimed a mining concession in Mongolia of 19 million acres, allegedly secured of a Prince T'san-pa-lo-no-esh-pu of Weng-nien-to for £360 a year.[1] By October 1898 Sir Claude Mac-Donald at Peking was driven to protest against the unrealistic demands of would-be investors who travelled out to China and claimed diplomatic support. The particular instance which aroused his exasperation was the arrival of two Members of Parliament with 'a modest little demand for exclusive mining rights in three provinces each about the size of Great Britain, a railway through the same with branch lines traversing China like a gridiron . . . really they ought not to have been let out without a keeper,' MacDonald reported, '. . . are many more M.P.'s afflicted this way?'[2] However, from the spring of 1898 the Foreign Office was faced with the extensive nature of France's gains in south China and by the increasingly disadvantageous position of Great Britain on the Yangtze because of the Peking–Canton railway concessions. It preferred to encourage as wide a range of British activity as possible so that Great Britain would not fall behind in the scramble which was emerging.

British Participation in the Scramble

The French acquisitions led to an immediate response by Great Britain. On 13 April MacDonald at Peking was instructed to demand five counter concessions from China; four of these were designed to offset the advantages which France had gained in the south. China was asked to grant all the land required for the military defence of Hong Kong; to give assurances that no exclusive privileges had been given to France in railway or mining matters, to fulfil a promise to make Nanning a treaty port, and to accept an Anglo-Chinese agreement for the non-alienation of the provinces of Kwangtung and Yunnan. The fifth demand, for a railway concession to Great Britain, aimed at consolidating the British position on the Yangtze.[3]

---

[1] The Eastern Contract Company to Secretary of State for Foreign Affairs, 17 Apr. 1901, F.O. 17/1503.

[2] MacDonald to McDonnell, 11 Oct. 1898, S.P. Chronological Series, Foreign and Imperial, II.

[3] Joseph, *Foreign Diplomacy*, 308–9.

Although difficulties were anticipated with France, the first diplomatic clash actually occurred with Germany over British rights in the Yangtze valley.

At the end of March 1898 the agreement of 1895 which the Hongkong and Shanghai Bank had with the Deutsch-Asiatische Bank was terminated when the latter refused to apply the principle of equal division in Shantung. A month later, the British and Chinese Corporation applied for the concession for a railway between Shanghai and Nanking as a political concession in return for the concessions which had been made to France. The claim was challenged by Germany, who took the attitude that while the Yangtze was still open to Germany, the agreement for the occupation of Kiaochow gave her a special position in Shantung, which was consequently not unreservedly open to British enterprise.[1] Thereafter, the two powers competed for the control of the Yangtze valley railway concessions and a loose accord was not re-established until September when the two banks agreed to divide the Tientsin–Chinkiang railway project at the frontier of Shantung.[2]

Despite Germany's attitude, British activity in the Yangtze valley was not seriously challenged by the other powers. In the early summer of 1898 the British and Chinese Corporation obtained all the railway concessions which were allowed by China in the area. On 13 May a preliminary agreement was signed with Sheng for the Shanghai–Nanking railway, and this was followed by a concession for the Soochow–Hangchow–Ningpo railway. At the time these were regarded as the beginning of an extensive Yangtze valley railway system which would eventually link up with Szechuan in the interior, and through it with the Burmese railway project to India. However, British policy during the scramble for concessions cannot be traced through British activity in central China but in the way in which Great Britain challenged the other powers in the spheres of influence which they were attempting to establish.

In this connection an early move was made to extend the territories of Hong Kong. For some time the inadequacies of the defences of Hong Kong had been considered by the Govern-

---

[1] Memorandum by Bertie of 3 May 1898, in memorandum by Mallet, 23 Apr. 1902, F.O. 17/1548.

[2] P. H. Kent, *Railway Enterprise in China* (London, 1907), 140–53.

ment. In 1895 a report of the Joint Naval and Military Committee on Defence advocated an extension and readjustment of the frontier on naval and military grounds. This was approved by the Secretary of State for War and the Lords Commissioners of the Admiralty. The strategical reasons which led to the recommendation of the Committee centred on the sufficiency or otherwise of the garrison which was considered far below what it ought to be for the adequate defence of British Kowloon, which involved the safety of the naval depot and the docks. It was felt that the adequate defence of Hong Kong required not only the absolute control of the waters between the island of Hong Kong and the mainland but also the command of the northern and southern shores flanking the Lyemun Pass. As the territory on the northern shore was under Chinese jurisdiction, its occupation in time of need could be taken as a *casus belli*. Thus its early acquisition was considered a matter of vital importance, although it was feared that any move could stir France into retaliation.[1]

After the French occupation of Kwangchow Bay only 210 miles to the south the matter took on an added urgency. Negotiations were pressed with the Chinese Government which indicated its willingness to lease the additional land as long as Chinese control over the native city in Kowloon was not interfered with. On 14 April 1898 the Foreign Office asked the Colonial Office for an opinion as to the exact boundary essential for the proper protection of Hong Kong. The Colonial Office referred the matter to the Colonial Defence Committee, which recommended an extension of the boundaries and, because of the French action, the establishment of a British sphere of influence round the Colony, within a line which followed suitable natural features from Lamkao Bay (Deep Bay) to Mirs Bay.[2] It was later stressed that the military object in view in acquiring the new territories was solely to improve the defence of the waters of Hong Kong and that it was not intended to make Mirs Bay a defended harbour for the British

[1] Report No. XVII of the Joint Naval and Military Committee on Defence of 13 May 1895; memorandum by Colonial Defence Committee, No. 74M of 12 Oct. 1896 in No. 85M, secret, of 12 Nov. 1896, Cab. 8/1. Memorandum by Bertie, 23 Dec. 1897, F.O. 17/1330.

[2] Memorandum by Colonial Defence Committee, No. 139M, secret, of 3 May 1898, Cab. 8/2.

fleet.[1] A convention for a ninety-nine-year lease of the New Territories was signed on 9 June 1898.[2] The actual occupation of the area, arranged for 1 July, was delayed for a short while because of the presence in Mirs Bay of units of the United States fleet under Admiral Dewey. To respect British neutrality rights, Dewey had moved there from Hong Kong during the Spanish-American war.[3]

A second measure pressed by Great Britain to offset French gains in the south was for a railway concession between Pakhoi and Nanning. Since 1895 Nanning had been an objective for both France and Great Britain in their competition to control the lines of communication in south China and to open up the trade of Yunnan. Nanning, which was the chief distributing centre for eastern Yunnan and western Kwangsi, was accessible by three routes. First, a 560-mile voyage up the West river from Hong Kong; secondly, a short land and boat journey from Pakhoi; and third, a longer land and boat journey from Haiphong via Phulang-thuong, Langson, and Lungchow. French policy, which was to attract the trade of south-west China to Tongking, was opposed to the opening of Nanning. This worked against the commercial interests of Hong Kong and British policy was to open up the area. From 1895 Great Britain pressed China to open up the West river to inland traffic and to declare Nanning a treaty port. However, the upper reaches of the West river were difficult and this route offered only limited access to the area. When the scramble for railway concessions developed in the summer of 1898 the British pressed for a railway concession between Pakhoi and Nanning, which had been described by the Lyons Commercial Mission of 1895–6 as 'la rivale la plus redoutable de la route française'. This was vigorously and successfully opposed by France. The issue was resolved in October 1899 when China sanctioned the construction of a French line between Nunkuan

[1] Memorandum by Colonial Defence Committee of 23 Jan. 1899, Cab. 8/2.

[2] 'Despatches and other Papers relating to the Extension of the Colony of Hong Kong', enclosed in Colonial Office to Foreign Office, 26 Jan. 1900, F.O. 17/1436. For correspondence on the definition of the boundary and over the control of the foreshores of Mirs Bay and Deep Bay see No. 31 of F.O. 228/1339; 18 Aug. 1900, F.O. 17/1444.

[3] R. G. Neale, *Britain and American Imperialism, 1898–1900* (Brisbane, 1965), 55–8.

(Lungchow) and Nanning, thus allowing a continuation of the Hanoi–Langson line.[1]

Meanwhile, Great Britain competed against France in south-west China. In July 1898 a Yunnan Company was formed with the specific objective of extending the Burmese railway into Yunnan. The project was readily supported by the Government and arrangements were made for two military officers to be lent to the Company to survey a route. When their reports were submitted it became clear that it was impossible to compete against the French from this route. Consequently Great Britain shifted her aims after 1898 and concentrated on improving the upper reaches of the Yangtze so as to provide a natural outlet down the river to Shanghai. The Yunnan Company, as well as a number of other British concession hunters, accepted this as a favourable alternative to the Burmese railway route, and further surveys were carried out until progress was interrupted by the Boxer rising.[2]

British concession hunting in the summer of 1898 ranged not only over south China and on to the upper reaches of the Yangtze but also into north China. There were two areas where Great Britain was significantly active in the north. The first area covered Shansi and Honan. Her activity there successfully refuted the view that British interests in a northwards direction could be contained within the narrow limits of the Yangtze valley. The second area was Manchuria, where she opposed Russia's claims.

The British concessions in Shansi and Honan were obtained through the Peking Syndicate, which was formed in 1897 to continue negotiations which had been begun by Italian business interests with the Chinese Government. In 1898 the organization secured sound financial backing from the financiers Carl Meyer and Lord Rothschild. During the scramble for concessions it obtained a sixty-year concession to develop the mineral resources of Shansi and Honan.[3] The Syndicate's

---

[1] Memorandum by Mallet of 17 May 1901, F.O. 17/1504; *Chinese Railways*, p. 73, 18 Dec. 1903, F.O. 17/1622; Joseph, *Foreign Diplomacy*, 229–31.

[2] W. J. Weightman, Note on the Reports of the Yunnan Expedition of 1898–9, 6 Jan. 1900, F.O. 17/1437; Capt. Wingate, Report on Railway Extension into China, F.O. 17/1438; Report by Capt. Peach, D.A.A.G., D.G.M.I., F.O. 17/1507.

[3] The concessions of the Peking Syndicate are to be found in B.P.P. China, No. 1 (1899), 154, 194.

record in this respect was a poor one. Because of opposition from local mining interests no actual mining was carried out in Shansi, and the interminable delays in commencing operations led Sir Ernest Satow, who became British minister at Peking in 1900, to conclude that it was a stock-jobbing affair.[1] However, the Syndicate was strongly supported by the Foreign Office because of the railway concessions which were incorporated in the mining agreement. By Article 17 of the agreement the Syndicate had the right to lay branch lines for the conveyance of minerals between the mines and any main lines or navigable waterways. The concession was taken up as a means of establishing a link with the Yangtze. The consent of China was obtained to establish a railway line from the mines to Siang-yang on the Han river, a tributary of the Yangtze. When the Han was surveyed in 1899 and found to be practically unnavigable a request was made for a line via Kaifeng to Pukow, opposite Nanking. Negotiations for this concession were then pressed against Chinese objections until interrupted by the Boxer rising. The motives of the Foreign Office were political. By establishing herself in this area Great Britain was in a position to oppose the consolidation of Franco-Russian control over the projected Peking–Hankow railway.

Political reasons also underlay Great Britain's interest in concession hunting in Manchuria. In 1898 British commercial activity in the area still outstripped that of the other powers.[2] A British engineer-in-chief, C. W. Kinder, controlled construction of the important Northern railway which ran from Tientsin through Taku to Shanhaikuan, and from there forty-odd miles beyond the Great Wall to Chunghouso. Despite this, Great Britain was prepared to accept the view that Russia had a special interest in Manchuria. When Russia began to build her own Chinese Eastern railway system and repeatedly attacked Kinder's position and pressed for his removal Great Britain did not take a strong stand. However, she refused to

---

[1] In 1908 the Syndicate surrendered its concession in Shansi for an indemnity of Taels 2,750,000. Copy of Agreement, Jordan to Grey, No. 7881 of 22 Jan. 1908, F.O. 371/413/637.

[2] By 1896 the growing trade of imports of English and American cotton goods to Niuchwang from Shanghai by coastal traffic aggregated 664,000 tons, of which 349,600 was carried under the British flag and only 3,628 under that of Russia. *The Times*, 28 Apr. 1898.

recognize a Russian sphere of influence in Manchuria. It has been seen that during the Port Arthur crisis Salisbury used the Chinese loan negotiations to combat this assumption. During the summer of 1898, for the same reason he encouraged the British and Chinese Corporation to compete for the concession to extend the Northern railway in Manchuria. China responded readily when approached. In June 1898 the Corporation arranged a sterling loan of £2,300,000 with Hu Yu-fen, Administrator-General of the Imperial Railways of north China, acting under the authority of the Chinese Government, for the extension of the Peking–Shanhaikuan, or Northern, railway to Newchwang, north of the Great Wall. Besides being unconditionally guaranteed by the Chinese Government, the loan was secured as a first charge on the existing railway lines between Peking and Shanhaikuan and on the earnings of the extramural sections of the line as they were constructed. In the event of default in the service of the loan it was agreed that the line and property of the Peking–Shanhaikuan railway should be taken over by the British and Chinese Corporation until the loan and the interest had been paid in full.[1] The concession gave Great Britain a hold on north China and also allowed her to probe into southern Manchuria, an area Russia had begun to look upon as her own.

The Diplomatic Compromise

By September the mid-summer madness of concession hunting had largely died away. The range and vigorous nature of Great Britain's activity and the feeling that the British Foreign Office was prepared to support this activity without regard for the spheres of influence which the other powers were trying to establish put them in a frame of mind to reach an understanding over their positions in China. Similarly, Great Britain realized that, despite the extensive gains which she had secured over the length and breadth of China, foreign control over the Peking–Canton railway concessions effectively loosened the British hold on the Yangtze. From the start Great Britain had joined the scramble for concessions not to oppose the other powers in their areas of special interest but to prevent those areas from

[1] See memorandum by Bertie, with enclosures, 21 Nov. 1900, F.O. 17/1450.

becoming spheres of influence. This point was clearly made by Balfour in the House of Commons at the end of April 1898. 'Spheres of influence we have never admitted,' he declared, 'spheres of interest we have never denied.'[1] Consequently, after the precarious activity of the summer the powers were inclined towards agreement in China.

An early move in this direction was the restoration of the Anglo-German banking arrangement which had broken down in March. On 2 September an agreement was signed between Herr von Hausemann, representing the German banks, and Mr. W. Keswick for the British and Chinese Corporation and Mr. (later Sir) Ewen Cameron and Mr. Julius Brussel representing the Hongkong and Shanghai Bank. By this arrangement the British sphere of interest for railway concessions was defined as the Yangtze valley, the provinces south of the Yangtze, and the province of Shansi. The German sphere was defined as the province of Shantung and the Hoang-ho valley. The Tientsin–Chinkiang railway concession was then divided on this basis. In 1902, after the Boxer rising had made it less possible for spheres of interest to develop in China, Great Britain denied that this understanding had any official backing. Lord Cranborne, who was asked to investigate the matter, reported that the 'understanding' could only be applied to the Tientsin–Chinkiang line, but that there was 'no signature to be found by any one qualified to represent either Great Britain or Germany which commits them even to this extent'.[2] Nevertheless, in the hectic days of 1898 when Great Britain was fighting for the recognition of her position on the Yangtze the arrangement was accepted without question by the Foreign Office.

A clear agreement was not reached by Great Britain with France over the delineation of their spheres of interest. Both powers, however, were aware that some working arrangement was necessary if they were to avoid a situation which Cambon, the French Ambassador in London, thought could lead to another Fashoda in the south of China.[3] During 1899 conciliatory moves were made at a private level which led to the establishment in October 1899 of a joint Anglo-French enter-

---

[1] 29 Apr. 1898, *Parliamentary Debate*, 4th Series, lvi, cols. 1582–3.
[2] Memorandum by Cranborne of 16 May 1902, F.O. 17/1549.
[3] Memorandum by Bertie of 21 Feb. 1900, F.O. 17/1437.

prise, the Syndicat du Yunnan. The object of the Syndicate was to acquire all rights and concessions in Yunnan in conformity with the Anglo-French agreement of 15 January 1896.[1]

These private efforts at co-operation were extended to the Hankow–Canton railway concession. By an agreement of 1 February 1899 the British and Chinese Corporation became entitled to a half share in any of the concessions of the American China Development Company. Because of the shaky finances of the American company the arrangement was not very successful.[2] But it did point to the future pattern of foreign financial activity in China. By 1905 the British and Chinese Corporation, the Peking Syndicate, and the French company joined to form the Chinese Central Railways Ltd. In 1908 Germany also joined in, followed by the United States.

The major settlement over the scramble for concessions was arranged between Great Britain and Russia. From the spring of 1898 British concession hunters had carried their activities into south Manchuria and Russian influence had spread in a southward direction in a way which aroused the apprehensions of both the powers. In this situation an attempt was made to revive the discussions begun the previous January.

Negotiations were opened in London in July 1898 by Lessar, the Russian chargé d'affaires, who suggested to Balfour that if Britain should undertake not to interest herself in railway and mining concessions in Manchuria, Russia would bind herself in a similar manner with regard to the Yangtze.[3]

After his conversations with Lessar, Balfour drew up a report for the Cabinet examining the various replies which could be made. While Balfour stressed that the existing mood of public opinion made it a simple matter to adopt a belligerent attitude towards Russia, he added, '*We* should be fighting because we want Manchuria and the Yangtze to be a common field for English and Russian concessionaires. *They* would be fighting because they preferred dividing the field into two portions, and giving the larger to England. A small matter to set the world on fire.' Mindful of Great Britain's unsatisfactory position in

[1] See enclosure, Nov. 1900, F.O. 228/1340. Art. 4 of the Salisbury–Councel Agreement laid it down that all concessions obtained in Yunnan should be for the joint benefit of England and France.

[2] Keswick to Sanderson, 4 Feb. 1901, F.O. 17/1506.

[3] Romanov, *Russia in Manchuria*, 128, 152–3, 166–7, 170–1.

relation to spheres, Balfour then concluded, 'We should then obtain from at least one Power a recognition, so far as she is concerned, of a sphere of interest much larger than we could easily demand in cold blood.'[1] At the end of August Balfour wrote to Salisbury, who was then on vacation, 'Chinese matters are muddling on . . . Russia is (I think deliberately) hanging back. . . . I want to drive them into making a distinct offer of spheres of interest (so far as concessions go)—i.e. Manchuria v basin of Yangtze:—they hint at this but do not distinctly propose it.[2]

After this, rapid moves were made towards an understanding. Salisbury returned to take up the negotiations, which were but a continuation of the overture he had regarded as necessary the previous January, now made more urgent by the anger aroused over Port Arthur. Russia, too, was in a conciliatory mood. The young Tsar Nicholas II, enthusiastic over the Hague Peace Conference, was pacifically inclined. Count Muraviev, the Russian Foreign Minister, faced with the financial burden of the Siberian railway and of capital ship construction, was also favourably disposed. Only Witte, who had just invested three million roubles in activities of the Russo-Chinese Bank south of any projected line of agreement, was initially reluctant.[3] However, he had urgent need to regain the confidence of the London money market and when assurances were given that the security taken for the Northern railway's loan did not give Britain control of the line north of the Great Wall, the way to agreement was open.

On 8 February 1899 Muraviev proposed that Russia and Great Britain should agree on a recognition of each other's sphere of interest in Manchuria and the Yangtze. Russian interests were to be confined north of the Great Wall, while Great Britain was to give the assurance that the Northern railway should remain under Chinese control. On 15 February Salisbury circularized the proposal to the Cabinet and argued for its acceptance. He observed that although Russia was unlikely to

[1] Memorandum by Balfour, confidential, of 13 July 1898, printed for the use of the Cabinet on 15 Aug. 1898, S.P. 89/33; Dugdale, *Balfour*, 265–6, gives a long extract.

[2] Balfour to Salisbury, 30 Aug. 1898, S.P., Correspondence from Balfour 1892–9.

[3] Romanov, *Russia in Manchuria*, 155–6, 162–3, 167–71.

make any serious attempt to encroach on the Yangtze, 'their acknowledgment of our preponderant interest there, and their engagement to respect it is of considerable value'.[1] On 21 February the Cabinet agreed to the convention. After further details had been arranged the agreement was signed on 28 April 1899.[2]

The Anglo-Russian Agreement became the basis of Salisbury's China policy. He recognized that the outbreak of concession hunting had made agreement along the lines of his January overture impossible and that if Great Britain and Russia were to exist amicably in the Far East it would have to be through a policy of spheres.[3] During the remainder of his stay at the Foreign Office (until November 1900) his determination to observe both the terms and the spirit of the Agreement is a noticeable aspect of his policy. He dissociated himself from any support of the British and Chinese Corporation's loan agreement for the extension of the Northern railway into Manchuria, for which Balfour had allowed the Government's approval to be written into the loan prospectus, to the extent that by the summer of 1899 the Corporation believed that the line could not be held, and would have to be sold on completion.[4] Throughout 1899 his aim was improved relations with Russia, and to that end he would not interfere in Manchurian affairs or encourage any step in the direction of an anti-Russian alignment.

An indication of this attitude is seen in his reaction to Lord Beresford's mission to the east at this time. By the summer of 1898 the amount of British capital invested in the Chinese

[1] (Draft) Cabinet memorandum by Salisbury of 15 Feb. 1899, S.P. 89/53. The background of negotiation may be followed through Sir C. Scott, British Ambassador at St. Petersburg, to Balfour, 25 Aug. 1898, Scott to Salisbury, 8 Sept., 3 Nov., 1 Dec. 1898, 9 and 23 Feb. 6 Mar. 1899, S.P. 129/47, 48, 49, 52, 55–7.
[2] MacMurray, *Treaties and Agreements*, i. 204–5.
[3] In taking up Muraviev's proposal Salisbury noted its 'scanty dimensions'. Salisbury to Scott, tel. 31 of 22 Feb. 1899, F.O. 65/1581.
[4] Even on the matter of the sale of the line Salisbury refused to interest himself and declared bluntly that as the Corporation had got into the mess they had to get themselves out of it. Cf. memorandum by Salisbury, 22 June 1899; memorandum by St. J. Brodrick, 8 June 1899, encl. memorandum by Bertie, 21 Nov. 1900, F.O. 17/1450. In July 1899 preliminary negotiations were begun by Russia to buy up the Hongkong and Shanghai Bank's £2,300,000 loan (Romanov, *Russia in Manchuria*, 170–1), but these were interrupted by the Boxer rising, when the Northern railway was to play a prominent part in Anglo-Russian relations, see below, pp. 298–300, 314–17, 407–18.

concessions had become a matter of interest to the Associated Chambers of Commerce, who felt that an observer should be sent out to report on the situation. Admiral Lord Charles Beresford was then appointed. His instructions were 'to obtain accurate information as to how security is to be insured to commercial men who may be disposed to embark their capital in trade enterprise in China'.[1] Salisbury was enthusiastic about the mission and although Beresford was to go out in an unofficial capacity, arrangements were made to meet his expenses with £750 from the Secret Service Fund.

Beresford travelled extensively in the east throughout the winter of 1898–9, lecturing both in China and Japan on the expansion of trade and the need for commercial alliances. On his return he wrote a book which created a stir in mercantile circles.[2] However, there was another side to Beresford's activity which displeased Salisbury even more than the Admiral's references to the need for commercial alliances. At the time of Beresford's visit the Chinese political situation was in a confused and explosive condition. In the spring of 1898 the Kuang Hsu Emperor had initiated a forced programme of reform of the Chinese administration. By September a conservative reaction had set in under the direction of the Empress Dowager Tzu-hsi. The fluid situation encouraged interference by the foreign powers, who looked upon the period of change as an opportunity for increasing their influence. Beresford engaged in this activity. He showed around some letters which had been given him by various members of the Cabinet in a way which intimated to the Chinese that he was on a secret mission. He then sought to prevail upon Yuan Shih-K'ai, the only capable military commander among the Chinese, then in north China, to use his cavalry against the Chinese capital. Yuan thought Beresford was speaking officially, and it was reported that he was ready to comply at a word from MacDonald, the British minister.[3] Beresford also engaged in political discussion with

[1] Sir Stafford Northcote (President of the Associated Chambers) to Beresford of 1 Aug. 1898, encl. Northcote to Salisbury, 3 Aug. 1898, S.P. Chronological Series, 1898, Foreign and Imperial, II.

[2] Lord Charles Beresford, *The Break-up of China. With an account of its present commerce, currency, waterways, armies, railways, politics, and future prospects* (New York and London, 1899). The book was published in May.

[3] MacDonald to Barrington, private, of 25 Dec. 1898, S.P. 106/18.

Prince Henry of Prussia, then on tour in the east. To the Prince he suggested that England, Germany, America, and Japan could put Russia out of Manchuria.[1]

Salisbury was so dissatisfied with this behaviour that Lord Northcote, President of the Associated Chambers, offered to cover the £750 promised Beresford for his expenses. Northcote's efforts to mollify Salisbury reveal the direction of the Prime Minister's anger. Northcote suggested that Beresford be told that 'the question of alliances is not one that is determined by English, American and German men of business, but by Cabinets'. Northcote added, 'The harm he has done . . . is in arousing Russian suspicions. . . .'[2]

The episode involved more than Beresford's personal irresponsibility. Since the spring of 1898 there had been talk, particularly by Chamberlain, of Anglo-Saxon and Teutonic alliances being applied to the Far Eastern situation. After the Beresford issue was brought before the Cabinet in January 1899, the possibility of these alliances became less a subject of ministerial utterance. From then, until the Boxer rising, control of Great Britain's China policy lay exclusively in Salisbury's hands, and a principle of that policy was to avoid any action which would foster an alignment of the powers and serve to commit British naval strength in the east. This consideration, already pertinent because of Great Britain's isolated international position, became a matter of dominant concern after October 1899, with the outbreak of the South African war.

To all intents the Anglo-Russian agreement of April reestablished the international equilibrium in the Far East. The powers who had secured a territorial foothold in China set about consolidating their newly gained positions, and showed a disinclination to support those powers who came forward with belated demands for concessions in China. Thus in March 1899 when the Chinese Government rejected an Italian demand for the lease of San Mun Bay and for the recognition of the coastal part of Chekiang province as an Italian sphere of influence, Italy was forced to withdraw the demand, largely because she

[1] Memorandum of an interview between Lord Charles Beresford and Prince Henry at Shanghai on 18 Nov. 1898, printed for the use of the Cabinet, 10 Jan. 1899, S.P. 89/50.
[2] Northcote to Salisbury, private, of 26 Feb. 1899, S.P. Chronological Series, 1899, Miscellaneous and Private, I.

was not in a position to press the claim through lack of inter-national support.[1] A similar coolness was displayed by the powers toward the diplomatic overtures of the United States who, reversing its cool attitude of the previous year, stepped forward to play a part in Far Eastern affairs.

The scramble for concessions which took place in China after the Sino-Japanese war convinced American business interests of the need for a fundamental change in American policy in the Far East. In 1895 the American China Develop-ment Company was formed, and a campaign to arouse govern-mental interest was carried out in the succeeding years. The seizure of the northern ports in the early part of 1898 then led interested business groups in the United States to form the American Asiatic Association.[2] This agitation, which was helped on by the general interest in Pacific and Far Eastern affairs aroused in the United States by the Spanish-American war of April–August 1898, led the McKinley administration to pay closer attention to the Chinese situation. A striking move in this direction, which would secure the approval of American business interests and reflect credit on the Government, was initiated by John Hay when he became Secretary of State. William Rockhill, Hay's adviser in Chinese affairs, was approached by Alfred Hippisley, an Englishman in the service of the Chinese Maritime Customs. Through this channel Hay obtained a closer acquaintance with the situation in China.[3] Hay then decided on a bold move which would help to safe-guard American commercial interests in the rapidly closing Chinese market. Between 6 September and 17 November 1899 he circularized notes to Great Britain, Russia, Germany, France, and Japan calling on the powers to recognize the continued existence of the treaty ports within their various spheres of interest, and to continue to apply the tariff, railroad charges, and port dues within those ports to the benefit of the Chinese Government. The powers, particularly Russia, were circum-

---

[1] Langer, *Diplomacy of Imperialism*, 683–4.
[2] C. S. Campbell, *Special Business Interests and the Open Door Policy* (Yale, 1951), ch. vi, *passim*; F. R. Dulles, *America's Rise to World Power, 1898–1954* (London, 1954), 63.
[3] A. W. Griswold, *The Far Eastern Policy of the United States* (New York, 1938), 62–86; P. A. Varg, *Open Door Diplomat: the Life of W. W. Rockhill* (New York, 1952), 30 f.; Campbell, *Special Business Interests*, ch. viii.

spect in their replies to this approach by the United States. Nevertheless, Hay overlooked this hesitation and declared the assent of the powers as final and definitive.[1]

When Russia's hesitation became known in London, the Government felt that Great Britain could hardly be bound by the notes while Russia remained free. St. John Brodrick, who was responsible for answering questions in the House of Commons, went to some lengths to stave off a debate on the subject, and felt that the matter should be reopened with the United States. Salisbury, however, thought it better not to raise the issue.[2]

As far as Salisbury was concerned the situation in the Far East had been settled on a practical basis, which was best left undisturbed.

---

[1] The text of the notes, and the replies, are given in United States Congress, Foreign Affairs Committee, *Papers relating to the Foreign Affairs of the United States, 1868–1912*, annual volumes (Washington, D.C.), 1899, pp. 128–43, hereafter cited as *Foreign Relations*.

[2] Memorandum by Brodrick to Salisbury of 7 May 1900, F.O. 17/1489. Hay's note is referred to as a 'Declaration as to foreign trade obtained by the United States from powers having leased territory in China'.

V

THE CHINESE RESPONSE

The Rise of Boxer Activity

LORD SALISBURY'S aim of isolating the Chinese situation was not to be realized. Although the 'midsummer madness' of concession hunting had died away by the end of 1898, it had led to a situation which careful diplomacy could not anticipate. Throughout 1899 and the early part of 1900 the mining and railway concessions became the centres of feverish activity. Entrepreneurs and construction engineers flooded into Manchuria, Shantung, and Shansi, while railway surveyors spread afield along the prospective routes. Whereas the actual claims had been a matter of negotiation between the Tsungli Yamen (Office of Foreign Affairs) and the legations, this activity brought the foreigners into direct contact with the people. In the process local authority and tradition were ruthlessly trampled under as the newcomers applied themselves to their work with an approach as unbending as the railway lines they proposed to lay.

The influx of foreigners came at an unfortunate moment. From 1897 the north China plain had suffered a series of devastating floods. In the spring of that year a heavy drought in the northern Kiangsu area contiguous to Shantung made the germination of the wheat and barley crop difficult, and a poor harvest followed. In the summer prolonged rain led to heavy floods, which recurred intermittently throughout the year. By the summer of 1898 the Huai-ho had overflowed repeatedly and an exodus of more than five million refugees was reported. By this time flooding had affected the Huang-ho, the central river system of the north China plain. In 1853-5 the river had burst its dykes at T'ung-wa-hsiang in Honan and changed its bed to flow to an outlet north of the Shantung peninsula. The Chinese Government, then preoccupied with the Taiping rebellion, left water conservancy measures to the villagers;

consequently the dykes were inefficiently maintained and the river flooded almost yearly. In August 1898 the banks were breached at four places in the Tung-a area and a flood, estimated to cover an area of over five thousand square miles, inundated most of the Shantung plain. By the winter starving villagers were on the move. In 1899 heavy drought and locust plagues followed the floods of the previous year.[1]

Inevitably, the resentment aroused by these catastrophes was directed at every tangible grievance. The railway projects became a natural focus. Since their inception, such innovations had been regarded with suspicion and the expansion of the railway into China was still a matter of superstitious fear for the populace.[2] Moreover, construction implied an alternative means of communication, likely to threaten the livelihood of the thousands of carriers and porters, and of the bargemen of the river system and the Grand Canal. Within living memory the consequences of an alternative means of transport had been impressed upon the industrious river folk. In 1853 the northern swerve of the Yellow river had severed communication with the Grand Canal. For twelve years the grain tribute was transported by sea and the Canal never fully recovered its earlier traffic.[3] These were the years when the Canal area was devastated by the violent Nien Rebellion (1853–65).[4] In 1900 indigent canal bargemen were to figure prominently in the unrest directed against the railroads.[5]

A second focus was provided by the work of the missionaries. Throughout the nineteenth century there was a long-standing

[1] A. H. Smith, *China in Convulsion* (Edinburgh and New York, 1901), i. 162; C. T. Hu, 'The Yellow River Administration in the Ch'ing Dynasty', *FEQ*, 14 (Aug. 1955), 505 f.; Yuji Muramatsu, 'The Boxers in 1898–9, the Origin of the I-ho-ch'uan Uprising', *Annals of the Hitotsuhashi Academy*, 3 (Apr. 1953), 257–8; China, Imperial Maritime Customs, *Decennial Reports* (Shanghai, 1892–1901), i. 60–1.

[2] For example, in May 1900 reports of an impending government raid to secure children for immolation in the foundations of the Kowloon–Canton railway led the parents of the little fishing village of Aberdeen outside Hong Kong to oppose the police with antiquated iron guns. Cf. Blake to Chamberlain, 25 Sept. 1900, encl. 1 in Colonial Office to Foreign Office, 8 Nov. 1900, F.O. 17/1449.

[3] H. C. Hinton, *The Grain Tribute System of China* (Harvard, 1956), 16 f.

[4] Chiang Siang-tseh, *The Nien Rebellion* (Seattle, 1954).

[5] See 'Yu-kuan I-ho-t'uan Jen-wu chien-piao' (A brief table concerning the figures of the I Ho T'uan) in Chien Po-tsan, ed., *I-ho-t'uan (tzu-liao ts'ung-k'an)* (Source Materials on the Boxer War), 4 vols., 3rd ed. (Shanghai, 1953), iv. 503 f. Hereafter cited as *I.H.T.*

history of opposition to missionary endeavour in China. This was partly due to the superstitious resistance of the populace, partly to the xenophobia of the gentry, who regarded the missionary, with his privileged extra-territorial position, as a subversive influence which undermined official control.[1] This antagonism took on a clearer form after 1860, when the right of missionaries to reside and travel in the interior of China was written into the treaties.[2] Between 1860 and 1895, as missionaries of various denominations penetrated into the interior to carry out their work of conversion, there was a steady growth in anti-foreign feeling which manifested itself in sporadic outbursts of violence on the part of the populace.[3]

The issue took a serious turn at the end of the nineteenth century when missionary work became associated in the minds of the Chinese with the political activity of the foreign powers. Since the eighteen-forties France had arrogated to herself the role of official protector of the Catholic missionaries in China. This claim was recognized in Article 13 of the French Treaty of Tientsin of 1858 and it became the practice for Catholic missionaries to go to China on French passports. During the eighteen-eighties, after Father Anzer had been sent out from Germany by the Steyl mission to found a mission in southern Shantung, Germany began to question France's control. The issue was decided in 1890, when Father Anzer decided to place himself under German protection.[4]

The murders of Fathers Nies and Henle, both of Anzer's mission, in November 1897 led to the German occupation of Kiaochow and introduced an unfortunate element into missionary endeavour. The feeling became general among the

---

[1] J. K. Fairbank, 'Patterns behind the Tientsin Massacre', *Harvard Journal of Asiatic Studies*, 20 (1957), 494. Hereafter cited as *HJAS*.

[2] K. S. Latourette, *A History of Christian Missions in China* (London, 1929), 274–5; S. T. Wang, *The Margary Affair and the Chefoo Agreement* (London, 1940), 18.

[3] Latourette, *Christian Missions in China*, 303–485; Morse, *International Relations*, ii. 220–38; P. A. Cohen, 'The Hunan-Kiangsi Anti-Missionary Incidents of 1862', Harvard University: *Papers on China*, xii (1958), 1–27; J. K. Fairbank, 'Patterns behind the Tientsin Massacre', *HJAS*, 20 (1957), 480–511; North China Herald, *The Anti-foreign Riots of 1891* (Shanghai, 1892); A. Cunningham, *History of the Szechuan Riots, May–June 1895* (Shanghai, 1895).

[4] R. A. Norem, 'German Catholic Missions in Shantung', *Chinese Social and Political Science Review*, 19 (Apr. 1935), 45–64; Latourette, *Christian Missions in China*, 306–7, 311–13.

Chinese that the work of conversion was to be upheld by force. At the same time, with the struggle for influence which developed between the powers in China, the proselytizing fervour of the missionaries took on a new character. Competition developed between the various denominations to secure converts and to increase their area control. To encourage conversion they displayed a readiness to protect their converts against interference by the local authorities. In December 1899 the British consul at Ningpo observed the 'daily increasing tendency on the part of missionaries to take up the secular disputes or difficulties of the converts and to try to enlist Consular support for them'.[1] This form of activity was widespread, and the result was disastrous. Dissident elements in the community took advantage of the protection thus offered and declared themselves converts either to escape retribution or to secure backing in their inter-village disputes. All too frequently local native pastors used their positions to press their private interests. Thus at Hsien-yang (near Hankow) an inter-village dispute of twenty years' standing over the control of the local lake resulted in a lawsuit. The losers then joined the Roman Catholic mission and the case was stirred up again by the native priest. Not to be outdone, the others then joined the London Mission, to considerable official embarrassment.[2] Such neophytes were accepted and aided without question. 'If we refuse to help them with the officials,' a Church Missionary Society member noted, 'we shall lose them—they will join the Catholics or some other mission where they can get help.'[1] In the Foochow area a dispute arose between converts and villagers over the control of communal trees. In the resultant fight the converts were beaten and had their chapel wrecked. They then complained to the local Archdeacon, who brought pressure to bear on the *taotai* (Intendant of circuit) who imprisoned the villagers without question.[3] In the event of non-compliance immediate application was made for consular or even diplomatic support. In places questionable assistance was given by the local consular officials. The widespread risings in Yunnan in 1900 were provoked when the French representative insisted on shipping in

[1] Ningpo Intelligence Report, ending 31 Dec. 1899, F.O. 228/1363.
[2] Hankow Intelligence Report, ending 31 Mar. 1900, F.O. 228/1361.
[3] Foochow Intelligence Report, June quarter 1900, F.O. 228/1357.

forty cases of arms for the use of missionaries in spite of Chinese protestations.[1] In other places, French fathers fought against investigation even by their own consuls.[2]

The result was seriously to undermine local Chinese authority. In certain areas an entire breakdown of the administration was threatened. In Swatow the Hakka community joined the Roman Catholic mission in a body and then virtually warred against local officialdom. Defensively, the other inhabitants revived a moribund Buddhist sect originally dedicated to the worship of bridges and roads and turned it into an anti-Christian association 'for the purpose of counteracting the immense power wielded by the Roman Catholic hierarchy'.[3]

When the unrest centred on Shantung and Chihli (Hopei) in the north, the dissatisfied populace drew on a similar fund of sectarian belief to express their discontent. Under the impulse of flood, famine, and foreign interference, the secret societies endemic to the north China plain revived. Chief among these were the sect of the Eight Trigrams (Pa kua chiao), the Big Swords (Ta tao hui), and the Fists of Righteous Harmony or, as they became known, the Boxers (I ho ch'uan). These were subsects with an alleged lineal connection with the White Lotus (Pai lien chiao), the major society which had operated at an earlier time over the north China plain. This connection was tenuous, but the claim arose from the general tendency, after any rising, for the fugitive sectaries to transfer their allegiance to any subsect holding out a promise of a more potent mystique. Thus, after the suppression of the widespread White Lotus uprising of 1795–1804, the subsect of the Eight Trigrams, with its cosmogonic ritual elaborated from the divinistic Book of Changes, rapidly assumed the mantle of the White Lotus. Increasing social discontent in the first half of the nine-

[1] Report of Acting-Consul Carey (Yunnan) of 3 Nov. 1900 in Satow to Lansdowne, No. 90 of 4 Mar. 1901, F.O. 17/1471; J. G. Scott, Memorandum on the Situation in China . . ., India Office to Bertie, 7 Oct. 1900, F.O. 17/1448; C. Clementi, Report of a tour of S-W. China, pp. 14–15, Colonial Office to Foreign Office, 2 Sept. 1902, F.O. 17/1552. The French reply to the Chinese complaint was to appoint M. François, the representative concerned, to the Legion of Honour.

[2] Ningpo Intelligence Report, ending 30 Apr. 1900, F.O. 228/1363.

[3] 'Memorandum on Persecution of Converts at Swatow', encl. in Hurst to MacDonald, No. 9 of 29 Aug. 1900, F.O. 228/1363; Swatow Intelligence Reports, Dec. 1899, June 1900, F.O. 228/1363; Smith, China in Convulsion, i. 55. The sect was the T'ai-hong hui.

teenth century led to sporadic outbreaks under the aegis of this society. One such was the T'ien li chiao rising of 1812; another, ruinous in its effect, was the Nien rebellion of 1853–68. After the Nien had been subdued, sectarian activity was quiescent for a generation in northern China until it was revived at the end of the century. Again the various subsects stressed the common basis of esoteric doctrine which established the lineal connection with the earlier societies. This provided the cohesive element which gave the sectarian movement its force. Similarly, after an emergent period, dissident elements gravitated into the sect offering the mystique with the greatest promise of success. Thus, after 1895, when the populace was acutely conscious of the superiority of foreign military strength, the Boxers assumed prominence, for this sect promised a mystical invulnerability against weapons through the practice of a form of pugilistic gymnastics.[1]

The expansion of the sect was aided by the attitude of the Court. After the Sino-Japanese war the Chinese entered into a period of intense political and military self-appraisal. On the one hand, there was a movement toward governmental reform, which was connected with the activity of K'ang Yu-wei, Liang Ch'i-ch'ao, and other Chinese reformers who turned to administrative change as a means of bringing about a Chinese revival. This culminated in a hectic and unsuccessful attempt at reform by the Kuang-hsu Emperor in the summer of 1898.[2] On the other hand, there was a determined effort on the part of the Government in the direction of military reorganization. Jung-lu, a prominent Manchu bannerman and trusted confidant of the Empress Dowager Tz'u-hsi, was made President of the

---

[1] This section is based on Lao Nai-hsüan, 'I-ho-ch'üan chiao-men yuan-liu k'ao' (A study of the origin of the I-ho-ch'uan), reprinted in *I.H.T.* iv. 431–9; Li Shih-yu, *Religions secrètes contemporaines dans le Nord de la Chine* (French title, Chinese text), Studia Seria monographs, Series B, No. 4 (Chengtu, 1948); J. J. M. de Groot, *Sectarianism and Religious Persecution in China* (Amsterdam, 1903–4); B. Favre, *Les Sociétés secrètes en Chine* (Paris, 1933); Chiang Siang-tseh, *The Nien Rebellion* (Seattle, 1954); D. H. Porter, 'Secret Sects in Shantung', *Chinese Recorder*, 17 (1886), 1–10, 64 f.; Edkins, 'Religious Sects in North China', ibid. 245 f.; Ch'en chieh, *I-ho-t'uan yun-tung shih* (A history of the Boxer Movement) (Shanghai, 1931); Chih Pi-hu, 'Hsu I-ho-ch'uan yuan-liu k'ao' (A continuation of the study of the origin of the I-ho-ch'uan), reprinted in *I.H.T.* iv. 441–5.

[2] M. E. Cameron, *The Reform Movement in China, 1898–1912* (Stanford, 1931), 23–55; Ho Ping-ti, 'Weng T'ung-ho and the One Hundred Days of Reform', *FEQ*, 10 (Feb. 1951), 125–35.

Board of War. Under him various army units were concentrated in the Peking area. With the seizure of the northern ports, and after the failure of the reform movement of 1898 when the Emperor was removed from power by the conservative Empress Dowager, these measures were consolidated. The military forces in north China were integrated into an army corps organized in five groups. The first was under Jung-lu himself and was based in the Imperial Hunting Park in Peking; the other four were placed strategically to guard the approaches to the capital.[1] At the same time attempts were made to reduce the Government's military expenditure by dismissing effete units in the traditional army forces and by a rigorous investigation into the widespread peculation which was rife among army commanders, who claimed supplies for fictitious troops.[2] To balance this the village militia was reorganized and expanded as a means of local defence.

The consequences of these measures were serious. First, groups of unemployed and wandering ex-soldiers appeared as a factor of social unrest. Secondly, because the Government wished to encourage a spirit of local defence, it failed to appreciate the essentially dissident and heretical nature of the groups emerging among the populace as an expression of anti-convert feeling. When reports of these self-protective community groups were received in May 1898, the Court ordered an investigation of the 'group of people who call themselves without official sanction the righteous people (i-min hiu) on the borders of Shantung and Chihli . . .'.[3] Chang Ju-mei, the governor concerned, replied that the 'righteous people' were Boxers and that when the village militia units were reorganized he would incorporate the Boxers in them so as to place the latter under control.[3] This attitude was subsequently adopted by the Court, which received with approbation reports that the Boxers'

practice of pugilism was only for the protection of themselves and

[1] A. W. Hummel, *Eminent Chinese of the Ch'ing Period*, 2 vols. (Washington, 1943–4), 406–7; R. L. Powell, *The Rise of Chinese Military Power, 1895–1912* (Princeton, 1955), 51 f.

[2] Muramatsu, 'The Boxers in 1898–9', *Annals of the Hitotsubashi Academy*, 3 (1953), 243–8.

[3] *Ta-ch'ing li-ch'ao shih-lu* (Veritable records of the Ch'ing Dynasty) (Tokyo, 1937–8), 418 2b. Hereafter cited *T.T.S.L.*

their families. They possess all sorts of expert skills, none of which are not marvellous (so that they) never need to rely upon force to create a disturbance. By disposition (they believe in) personal loyalty and mutual help, their minds must be straightforward. . . .[1]

This original impulse was not sustained. Through the following year, groups of ex-soldiers, disgruntled officials, candidates who had failed in the Imperial examinations, unemployed bargemen, and others permeated the ranks of the self-protective groups, whose nature they changed. To an increasing extent these units became the means by which local opposition was raised against the privileged position of the Christian converts, who were vilified for relying on foreign support. Moreover, in its desire to utilize every possible means of resistance, the Court failed to make up its mind whether the groups were 'righteous people' or heretical elements, and this indecision encouraged adhesion and led the majority of the minor officials to hesitate over repressive measures; other officials, particularly Yu Hsien, who succeeded Chang Ju-mei as governor of Shantung, gave them active support. By the winter of 1899–1900 a confused situation had developed, where government troops were sent out against the Boxers and then their officers were cashiered for carrying out repressive measures.[2] The combination of government indecision, Boxer bellicosity, and missionary pressure put the officials in an impossible position. 'The officials could not hold a balance between passion and law . . .', Lao Nai-hsuan, a magistrate of the time, noted:

When the Boxers were weak they repressed them in order to flatter the converts . . . and that faction was aware that the officials despised the weak and feared the strong, thus still more they banded themselves together so that they could act recklessly . . . (and) when

[1] Quoted Lao Nai-hsuan, 'Ch'uan-an ts'a-ts'un' (Addenda to the Boxer Cases), *I.H.T.* iv. 453.

[2] Particularly the P'ing-yuan incident; see the magistrate Chiang K'ai's account, 'P'ing-yuan ch'uan-fei chi-shih' (Record of the affair of the Boxer rebels at P'ing-yuan), *I.H.T.* i. 351–62. It was in the P'ing-yuan area that the Nien rebels were finally encircled and annihilated in 1868. Jan-p'ing, the reputed birthplace of Chu Hung-teng, the only Boxer leader to achieve any prominence before the movement was taken up by the Manchu conservatives at the Court, lies in the final circle of Nien resistance, bounded by the T'u-hsieh river, the Yellow river, and the Grand Canal.

officials summoned Boxers (to trial) several hundred of their faction would gather in the hall (of justice) and there were officials who would keep silence and not dare to question (them); others imposed monetary fines, or found for both Boxers and converts. (For the Boxers) crowded together in great numbers, their weapons stood like a forest, they incited and burned and killed. The officials were accustomed to this and none dared to make enquiries, regulations and laws were destroyed, how could they hope there would be no rebellion.[1]

Throughout the winter of 1899–1900 the situation deteriorated rapidly. Boxer depredations, which up to the outbreak at P'ing-yuan (October–November 1899) had been directed against the converts, were carried out against other sections of the populace. Sectaries openly sported the insignia of the Eight Trigrams, strutted about the provincial towns and villages, declared they had the support of the governor Yu Hsien, and prophesied the imminent approach of a cataclysm, the Kalpa.[2]

The Diplomatic Reply

In November 1899 notice of this unrest was taken by the diplomatic body in Peking. The lead was taken by Edwin H. Conger, the American minister, acting on a report of the American Board Mission in Shantung. The cumulative revelation of Chinese weakness since 1895 had fostered a disdain of Chinese administrative ability and representations were made, in a spirit of ministerial dictation, on the need for anticipatory measures. Conger demanded the dismissal of the governor Yu

[1] Lao Nai-hsuan, 'Ch'uan-an ts'a-ts'un,' *I.H.T.* iv. 451. Lao Nai-hsuan was one of the earliest of the contemporary writers on the Boxers, and perhaps the first to stress the heretical and secret society origin of the sect. Despite the attempt of G. N. Steiger to refute this view (*China and the Occident*, New Haven, 1927) by stressing the connection which the sectaries had with the militia, Chinese scholars give due weight to Lao's researches. Lao's three principal works were put forward in pamphlet form in 1899–1900 in an attempt to stir the Government to action, and were then issued in a block-printed edition in 1902, *Ch'uan-an san-chung.* Lao himself survived the rising and enjoyed a successful career as a civil servant and educationalist, and died at the age of 79. For his memoir see *Ch'ing-shih kao,* Draft history of the Ch'ing dynasty (Movable type ed., 1927), L.C. 259, pp. 6a–b.

[2] The central tenet of sectarian belief was the ideal of the readvent of Maitreya, the Coming Buddha, who would appear at the Kalpa, the millennium, to alleviate the suffering of the people. See Li Shih-yu, *Religions secrètes contemporaines,* 5–7, 23–4, 46–7.

Hsien on the ground that his support of the Boxers could lead to an outbreak against foreigners.[1]

This was the development the Court had sought to avoid. In March 1899 an attempt had been made to resolve the missionary problem by conferring an official status upon the Catholic hierarchy. Thus, bishops were correlated with viceroys and governors, and lesser church officials with their equivalents in the Chinese administrative structure. The Court's purpose was twofold: by assimilating the missionaries they would give them official responsibility and thus less freedom to intervene in legal cases; secondly, the issue would be decentralized and diplomatic pressure removed from the Court.[2] In November 1899 the Court, or rather, the Empress Dowager, was still undecided whether the Boxers would turn into an anti-dynastic rising or whether, as Yu Hsien insisted, they could be used to strengthen resistance to the foreign powers.[3]

Any tendency to restraint was not helped by the attitude of the ministers in Peking. After further pressure from Conger, Yu Hsien was recalled to the capital in December. His presence influenced decisively the attitude of the Court. The embittered ex-governor's advocacy of the Boxer cause, and the displays of sectarian invulnerability which he staged for the Empress Dowager's benefit, served to sway Court opinion to his views. On 11 January 1900 an edict was issued at the insistence of the foreign ministers. However, while calling for the cessation of Boxer activity, the edict observed that although people were demanding the suppression and punishment of the Boxers

. . . it occurs to Us that a distinction should be made within the group (between) the reckless followers who have joined the faction and pledged themselves to its support and relied on numbers to

[1] Conger's action is discussed in G. N. Steiger, *China and the Occident* (New Haven, 1927), 173 f.

[2] Latourette, *Christian Missions in China*, 499–501; Wu Chao-kwang, *The International Aspect of the Missionary Movement in China* (Baltimore and London, 1930), 201–7.

[3] Both the Court's anxiety over the Boxers and its determination to resist foreign encroachment are revealed by the decrees of this time. 'If this lawlessness is not subdued at an early stage it will put forth tendrils which will create difficulties . . . (but) many Italian warships have arrived . . . and their purpose is really unfathomable. It is particularly necessary that preparations be made in time for the frontier defence . . .' (edict of K25/10/19 (21 Nov. 1899), *T.T.S.L.* 453/6a); also cf. edicts of 21, 28 Nov. 1899, *T.T.S.L.* 453/5a–6a, 14b.

raise trouble and have thus placed themselves amongst those whom the law cannot pardon, and the peace-loving people who have practiced (this Boxer) skill in order to protect themselves and their families and have joined village groups in order mutually to protect their villages which is the righteous (way) of mutual aid and protection. . . .[1]

The decree, which exhorted local officials to take care to observe the distinction which had been drawn, was considered so inflammatory by the diplomatic body that a protest was determined on by the British, French, German, and United States ministers at a meeting held at the British legation on 25 January 1900. The protest was made in the form of an Identical Note which drew the Court's attention to the presence of the two societies, the Boxers and the Big Swords, to the unfortunate ambiguity of the Imperial decree of 11 January, and to the need for a further decree which would definitely prohibit membership of the two societies. It was handed to the Chinese on 27 January.[2]

In this step Sir Claude MacDonald, the British minister, took the lead because, a few days before the decree of 11 January was published in the *Peking Gazette*, a report had been received of the murder of a British missionary, the first European casualty.

The Revd. S. M. Brooks, a young clergyman of the Society for the Propagation of the Gospel, was attacked and killed in the Fei-ch'eng district of Shantung by a group of ruffians on 30 December 1899.[3] The Court ordered an immediate inquiry.[4] Yuan Shih-k'ai, who had succeeded Yu Hsien as governor of Shantung and who was in the process of stamping out Boxer activity within his jurisdiction, acted promptly. Within a few days three of the five men responsible for the outrage had been arrested.[5] Extensive investigations were then carried out, culminating in the trial and punishment of the guilty men by the end of March 1900. Two of the men were sentenced to death,

[1] Given in Pao Shih-ch'ieh, 'Ch'uan-shih shang-yu' (Imperial edicts of the Boxer period), *I.H.T.* iv. 124.
[2] British minister to Tsungli Yamen, No. 4 of 1900, F.O. 228/1350.
[3] MacDonald to Salisbury, tel. 2 of 4 Jan. 1900, F.O. 17/1418; Morse, *International Relations*, iii. 178 f.; P. H. Clements, *The Boxer Rebellion* (New York, 1915), 81–2.
[4] Decree of K25/12/4 (4 Jan. 1900), *T.T.S.L.* 456/5a.
[5] MacDonald to Salisbury, tel. 8 of 13 Jan. 1900, F.O. 17/1418.

one was imprisoned for life, one for ten years, and one banished for two years. 7,500 taels (£1,125) were paid over for a memorial chapel, 1,500 taels for a memorial at Canterbury, and 500 taels for a tablet at the scene of the crime. The magistrate of Fei-ch'eng was dismissed from office.[1]

While these findings were being made MacDonald had continued his representations against the Imperial decree of 11 January. On 21 February he asked for a reply to the Identical Note of 27 January and when the Tsungli Yamen replied evasively on the 25th he demanded, on 27 February, that a decree of prohibition against subversive sects be published in the *Peking Gazette*.[2]

The pressure was unwise. On 19 February the Tsungli Yamen had prevailed upon the Court to issue an edict calling for the posting of proclamations forbidding adhesion to the Boxer sect. This had been sent out and the proclamations had been posted by Yu Lu, viceroy of Chihli, by 21 February.[3] However, the Chinese found it difficult to respond to the attitude adopted by MacDonald and these measures were not revealed to him.

Moreover, throughout January and February the Court had become increasingly resentful at the interference by the diplomatic body in matters which it considered to be of private concern. In December 1899 and again in February 1900 the Court had issued decrees offering a reward for the capture or assassination of K'ang Yu-wei, who had fled to the British colony of Hong Kong after the failure of the reform attempt of 1898.[4] The Colonial Office questioned whether Great Britain should acquiesce in this situation, which was tantamount to sanctioning

---

[1] Correspondence on Brooks given Misc. 1900, F.O. 228/1343; Campbell's Chinanfu series, F.O. 228/1348. The magistrate had sent an officer to try to dissuade Brooks from making the journey; it was also reported that Brooks first approached the men at the village inn in an attempt to convert them. Further correspondence on Brooks is to be found in the archives of the Society for the Propagation of the Gospel. See *S.P.G. Original Letters Received*, Asia, vol. 2, 1900.

[2] British minister to Tsungli Yamen, Nos. 7 and 9 of 25, 27 Feb. 1900, F.O. 228/1350.

[3] The edict is given *T.T.S.L.* 458/12b–13a; the proclamation is noticed in Lao Nai-hsuan, 'Keng-tzu feng-chin I-ho-ch'uan hui-lu' (A collection of records on receiving the prohibition against the I-ho-ch'uan in 1900), *I.H.T.* iv. 477–8.

[4] Decree given *T.T.S.L.* 432/10; transmitted by MacDonald, No. 348 of 22 Dec. 1899, F.O. 228/1332; MacDonald to (?), private letter of 15 Feb. 1900, F.O. 17/1718.

the assassination of K'ang on British soil, and Salisbury instructed MacDonald to protest against the reward notices.[1] Although MacDonald, who thought that China was justified in issuing the decrees and that Great Britain had no basis for an official complaint, confined his protests to informal representations at Peking, a noticeable degree of Chinese resentment was apparent.[2] A second issue which aroused Chinese hostility was related to British protests against the imprisonment, after the conservatives assumed power at the Court in the autumn of 1898, of the officials who had been responsible for the granting of foreign concessions earlier in the year.[3] A third issue was more intimately connected with Court politics. During the winter of 1899–1900 there had been a movement among the conservative faction at the Court towards the strengthening of their position by the removal of the Kuang-hsu Emperor, who had been kept incommunicado since the Empress Dowager's *coup d'état* of September 1898. The New Year celebrations of 1900 were cancelled because of his 'illness' and reports were rife of his impending deposition. On 14 January Li Hung-chang, an influential Chinese statesman, told Baron von Ketteler, the German minister, that the Emperor was mentally and physically incapable and that his successor had been decided on. This was followed, on 24 January, by the appointment of an heir apparent. The diplomatic body then intimated that if the Emperor were removed (i.e. murdered) an unfavourable impression would be created among the foreign powers which would have unfortunate results.[4]

The irritation felt by the Court at this foreign interference was undoubtedly a factor which helped on the rising. By the end of February Boxer groups, driven out of Shantung by Yuan Shih-k'ai, had become active in the metropolitan province of Chihli. A growing faction at the Court, led by Prince Tuan, the father of the new heir apparent, spoke in their support, with

---

[1] Colonial Office to Foreign Office, 26 Dec. 1899, F.O. 17/1718; idem, 7 Feb. 1900, F.O. 17/1437; Salisbury to MacDonald, tel. 16 of 5 Feb. 1900, F.O. 228/1332.

[2] MacDonald to Salisbury, No. 36, confidential, of 16 Feb. 1900, F.O. 17/1718.

[3] British representations centred on the arrest of Wu Shih-chao, President of the Yu-feng Company which had drawn up the Honan agreement with the Peking Syndicate. Syndicate to MacDonald, 26 Feb. 1900, F.O. 228/1343; MacDonald to Salisbury, No. 37 of 18 Mar. 1900, F.O. 17/1718.

[4] MacDonald to Salisbury, tels. 11, 17, 19, 23 of 14, 24, 25 Jan., 5 Feb. 1900, F.O. 17/1418; Hummel, *Eminent Chinese*, 391–2, 732.

the implication that if the Empress Dowager did not tolerate the movement others would.

On 10 March MacDonald, exasperated by the continued evasiveness of the Tsungli Yamen, told the Chinese that if no satisfaction were offered in the matter of the decree of 11 January the governments concerned in the Identical Note of 27 January would adopt other measures for the protection of the life and property of their nationals in China.[1] To the Foreign Office MacDonald suggested that a combined naval demonstration should be made in north China waters.[2]

This was the development Salisbury had sought to avoid. In each of the issues which had come up during the winter of 1899–1900 he had urged restraint on MacDonald. When the British minister had stated in mid-February that 'nothing short of a concentration of the Fleet followed by actively hostile measures' would secure the withdrawal of the reward notice for K'ang Yu-wei, Salisbury had immediately instructed him to withdraw all pressure.[3] Similar restraint was shown on a much more important issue. In February a clash occurred between British and Chinese troops over the demarcation of the Burma border in the region of the valley of the N'Mai Kha in the Myitkyina district of the Kachin Hill tract. The disturbance was brought sharply into attention when two British officers were murdered by Wa natives at Mengkan on 9 February. The incident was comparable with Margery's murder in 1875 and MacDonald felt that a strong line should be taken. He suggested that if the bodyguard of the Chinese commissioner were responsible, as it was believed, Britain should abstain from attending the annual new year audiences then about to be held. To this Salisbury returned that even if the bodyguard were responsible the fact was to be ignored until after the ceremonies.[4]

On the missionary issue Salisbury was even less inclined to

[1] British minister to Tsungli Yamen, No. 11 of 10 Mar. 1900, F.O. 228/1350.
[2] MacDonald to Salisbury, tel. 33 of 10 Mar. 1900, F.O. 17/1418.
[3] MacDonald to Salisbury, tel. 27 of 15 Feb. 1900, F.O. 17/1718; Salisbury to MacDonald, tel. 24 of 22 Feb. 1900, F.O. 228/1332.
[4] MacDonald to Salisbury, tel. 26 of 15 Feb. 1900, F.O. 17/1418; Salisbury to MacDonald, tel. 20 of 16 Feb. 1900, F.O. 17/1417. The background of the incident is given in the Confidential Report on the North Eastern Frontier, 1899–1900, pp. 2, 9–10, 19–20, F.O. 17/1499. All reference to the affair was excised from the published report.

vigorous action. The practice of coercion which had developed over these matters was deplored by many in the Government. Over the earlier murder of the British missionary Fleming, in 1898, the Cabinet had decided not to resort to a naval demonstration, 'merely for the sake of dismissing a Governor, who has failed to arrest a Headman, who is supposed, but by no means proved, to have been an accomplice in the murder for which two men have already been executed'.[1] Similarly, when MacDonald reported the findings of the Brooks murder and then expressed his dissatisfaction that the two magistrates of the surrounding districts had not also been dismissed, Salisbury remarked laconically, 'They never tell me how they are so confident of the complicity of the persons they name . . .' and had the matter dropped.[2]

But the British attitude to the missionary issue is shown most clearly over the edict conferring official status on the Catholic hierarchy. The prevalent feeling of the time was that any concession granted should as a matter of policy be claimed by all. However, various Protestant groups in China submitted resolutions opposing the claim and, as some doubt was also felt at the Foreign Office about the ethical nature of the privilege, the matter was referred to the Archbishop of Canterbury. The Archbishop was opposed to the claim and replied:

> I find that many of the Chinese are fully alive to the mischief done by the incessant interference of the Roman Catholic Missionaries of all ranks in the civil administration of their country and especially in the administration of justice. And this interference is in its nature so mischievous a thing that although it may help the missionaries to obtain Converts, it must of necessity lower the aspect of Christianity in the view of the people at large.[3]

The detached attitude which this opinion invited led the Foreign Office to view with calm the reports of rising antimissionary unrest among the Chinese. Brooks's murder was regarded as a natural hazard of that type of work, and classed with the numerous other outrages of that nature which had

---

[1] Confidential print of 13 Sept. 1899, S.P. 89/52; Latourette, *Christian Missions in China*, 501.

[2] Minute on MacDonald to Salisbury, tel. 40 of 29 Mar. 1900, F.O. 17/1418.

[3] Archbishop of Canterbury to Salisbury, 16 Feb. 1900, F.O. 228/1339; Wu, *The International Aspect of the Missionary Movement in China*, 207.

occurred over the years. Consequently, it was with a feeling of shock that the Foreign Office received the news that MacDonald had taken the initiative over the missionary problem and that he had raised the matter of a naval demonstration with his colleagues. 'It was stupid of him to do this without asking me', Salisbury observed. 'One of the demonstrating powers will take the opportunity of appropriating something nice and we with our engagements in South Africa will have to grin and look pleasant.'[1] The next day MacDonald was instructed that it was in Britain's interest 'to be very quiet just at present. The matter may be a little delayed before we come to any naval action.'[2]

The instruction put MacDonald in a difficult position. On 15 March the Court appointed Yu Hsien to the governorship of Shansi. Although it was not a decisive step in that direction, the appointment indicated that the Court was moving towards a toleration of the Boxers. To the diplomatic body it was a definite sign that the Court was hedging on the matter of repression and, more galling, that it was ignoring their authoritative advice. MacDonald regarded Yu Hsien's reinstatement as 'a counter move to our demand for an Imperial Decree'.[3] As the threat to use force had been made, for reasons of prestige the naval ships had to be called up, and MacDonald asked for a naval force at Taku, the port of entry to Peking. Two ships were then sent, but with specific instructions to confine their activity to the protection of British life and not to join with the ships of foreign powers in the use of force.[4]

Thereafter, in April and May, events moved rapidly. The situation was aggravated by mutual apprehension. The Court, conscious of the presence of foreign naval ships off Taku, hesitated over the Boxers; the sectaries, thriving on this indecision, became completely out of hand; and the diplomatic body, because of the growing unrest, called for increased legation

---

[1] Minute on MacDonald to Salisbury, tel. 33 of 10 Mar. 1900, F.O. 17/1418.

[2] Salisbury to MacDonald, tel. 29 of 11 Mar. 1900, F.O. 17/1417.

[3] This observation was made in a draft telegram to Salisbury (tel. 36 of 15 Mar. 1900, F.O. 228/1334) but erased from the report actually sent (ibid., F.O. 17/1418). By comparing the drafts in the Embassy files with the telegrams in the Foreign Office files it is to be noticed that from this time in his reports MacDonald deliberately tried to suppress all indications of bellicosity or references to the use of force.

[4] Foreign Office to Admiralty, secret and immediate, of 24 Mar. 1900, draft, F.O. 17/1438; Salisbury to MacDonald, tel. 37 of 25 Mar. 1900, F.O. 17/1417.

guards and a greater show of naval force. Investigators sent out by the Empress Dowager to report on the nature of Boxer activity returned favourable reports designed according to their interpretation of what would please her, or to further the interests of the Manchu faction, which was now openly flaunting its support of the Boxers. By the latter part of May Boxer activity was noticeable along the Paotingfu railway, while red-turbanned bands forayed in the thick Peking dust up to the city walls. On 16 May a local paper reported a great secret scheme by the conservative faction to crush all foreigners except the Russians, using the Peking Field Force, the Banner Corps, the Glorified Tigers, and the Imperial Guards. This impressive list of all the regular forces available was the 'Army of Avengers' to which the Boxers would serve as auxiliaries.[1]

The foreign diplomats had acted in the belief that a naval demonstration would rapidly bring the Chinese to a more pliable frame of mind; instead it had inflamed rather than intimidated the populace and led to a noticeable hardening of resistance on the part of the Court. The diplomatic body met repeatedly to deliberate on the various measures which could be taken. One suggestion was that the combined naval demonstration should be extended from Taku to Shanhaikuan or Chinwangtao in the north, but in general the discussions were inconclusive; the naval demonstration at Taku had been the strongest threat they intended and little hope was entertained that an extension of the threat would prove more successful. It was difficult to accept a defensive role and admit the need for additional legation guards in Peking. The dominant feeling was of exasperation that the Chinese should persist in an obstinate but futile stand against the combined disapproval of the powers.

Baron von Ketteler, the German minister, openly believed that the naval demonstration should be followed by drastic measures of intervention by the powers. He put these views so forcibly at a meeting of 20 May that the other ministers became apprehensive over this possible consequence of the policy of bluff.[2] The next day Giers, the Russian minister, suggested to

[1] *The North China Herald and S(upreme) C(ourt) and C(onsular) Gazette* (Shanghai, 1860–1912), 16 May 1900, p. 868.

[2] MacDonald to Salisbury, tel. 75 of 21 May 1900, F.O. 17/1418. The report of Giers, the Russian minister, is given in Steiger, *China and the Occident*, 197–8.

MacDonald that as Britain and Russia were the only powers seriously interested in China it would be wise if they could agree to deprecate further naval demonstrations or landing of guards.[1]

In London, Salisbury received the reports of the developing situation in China with disquiet. He had consistently fought against involvement in China. He viewed with alarm the prospect of combined naval operations in north China waters and, more particularly, the German suggestion of joint intervention by the powers against Peking. Immediately on receiving MacDonald's report of Ketteler's suggestion, Salisbury replied that 'H(er) M(ajesty's) Gov(ernmen)t would view with uneasiness a "concert of Europe" in China'.[2] Three days later this feeling was given expression in a more deliberate instruction. 'Keep in the background as much as possible,' MacDonald was informed, 'and let any suggestions for further action come from others.'[3] At the beginning of June Salisbury was disturbed by yet a further indication that international complications could develop out of Chinese affairs. A rumour became current that the Empress Dowager was about to flee to Hsi-an (Sian) to escape the Boxers. When Giers, the Russian minister, let it be known that he had been authorized to offer Russian support for the maintenance of the dynasty, Salisbury immediately instructed MacDonald to take the same stand.[4]

However, by that time none of the ministers was thinking in terms of political rivalry. Chinese intractability had bound them together with a common outlook. On 28 May they agreed on the need for additional legation guards at Peking. The issue then was whether they should call up further reinforcements against the wishes of the Chinese. To do so might bring about a crisis which had to be avoided if possible; their duty was to assess the intentions of the Court before taking a decisive step. The differences of opinion which led the ministers to hesitate until 9 June before sending for additional guards were centred on this issue, not on the possibility of opportunistic action by any one power. It was assumed that the reinforcements from Taku would be international.

[1] MacDonald to Salisbury, tel. 74 of 21 May 1900, F.O. 17/1418.
[2] Salisbury to MacDonald, tel. 58 of 22 May 1900, F.O. 17/1417.
[3] Salisbury to MacDonald, tel. 59 of 25 May 1900, F.O. 17/1417.
[4] MacDonald to Salisbury, tel. 93 of 2 June 1900, F.O. 17/1418; Salisbury to MacDonald, tel. 62 of 3 June 1900, F.O. 17/1417.

In the end a growing sense of isolation drove MacDonald to action. Throughout the first week of June there were signs of increasing violence in the surrounding countryside and, at the same time, it became correspondingly difficult to approach a suitable authority in Peking with whom representations could be lodged. At the beginning of June, Robinson and Norman, two missionaries of the Church of England mission at Yung-ching, were murdered.[1] When MacDonald made representations on 5 June the Tsungli Yamen showed itself indifferent. This was so contrary to the usual abject response that MacDonald immediately explained to Salisbury the impossibility of effacing himself any longer, as he was next in seniority to the doyen of the diplomatic body, who had neither guards nor force at his disposal. At the same time, he asked Admiral Seymour at Taku for a further legation guard of seventy-five men, and came to the conclusion that the only remaining resort was to make representations directly to the Emperor and Empress Dowager.[2] These reports led the Foreign Office to abandon the policy of restraint and on 6 June control was placed in the hands of the British authorities on the spot.[3]

Meanwhile, the diplomatic body in Peking made a further attempt to overcome the indifference of the Tsungli Yamen. On 6 June, the day on which MacDonald had telegraphed Salisbury that this was the only possible resort, Giers attempted unsuccessfully to secure an audience with the Empress Dowager to persuade her to bring about the suppression of the Boxers.[4] The failure of this move led the diplomatic body to despair of obtaining any form of reassurance through official channels. Two days later, on 8 June, the withdrawal of General Nieh Shih-cheng's troops from the Tientsin area was reported.[5]

---

[1] MacDonald to Salisbury, tels. 94, 96, 97 of 4 and 5 June 1900, F.O. 17/1418.

[2] MacDonald to Salisbury, tel. 100 of 6 June 1900, F.O. 17/1418. The doyen was Cologan, the Spanish minister.

[3] Admiralty to C.-in-C., China Station, tel. 79 of 6 June 1900, Adm. 116/117.

[4] Giers's approach, made through Prince Ching, the head of the Tsungli Yamen, was a matter of common knowledge to the foreign community, although MacDonald does not appear to have informed Salisbury of the move. Cf. Malozemoff, *Russian Far Eastern Policy*, 126; the approach appears to have failed because the Tsungli Yamen did not dare to submit Giers's request for an audience. See Li Hsi-sheng, 'Keng-tzu kuo-pien chi', entry of 10th day of the 5th month (6 June), *I.H.T.* i. 12.

[5] MacDonald to Salisbury, tel. 104 of 8 June 1900, F.O. 17/1418.

Nieh was one of the few capable officers in the Chinese army at that time. He was known to have been in action against the Boxers and his troops were regarded by the foreign community as a bulwark which would prevent any larger scale encroachment of the Boxer bands into Peking.[1] The withdrawal made the diplomatic body fear that both rail and telegraphic communication would be cut. In the next two days foreigners were menaced in the streets of Peking; then, on 10 June, two developments led MacDonald to hesitate no longer. First, the *Peking Gazette* announced the appointment of Prince Tuan and other reactionaries to the control of the Tsungli Yamen, and, secondly, the summer quarters of the British legations outside Peking were reported destroyed. MacDonald sent to Seymour for reinforcements.[2]

The Seymour Expedition

By the beginning of June 1900, Vice-Admiral Seymour, Commander-in-Chief, China Station, was at Taku with eight British ships which formed a nucleus around which the vessels of the other powers were grouped. Seymour was the senior officer present.

Taku lay at the mouth of the Pei-ho, thirty miles east of Tientsin, ninety miles south-east of Peking. It was defended by three forts at the mouth of the river, two on the north bank, one on the south. Four new Chinese destroyers lay in the mouth of the river. The lower reaches of the Pei-ho were navigable to tugs and cargo-lighters; larger ships were forced to anchor outside the Taku bar, four miles from the mouth of the river.

---

[1] MacDonald to Salisbury, tel. 99 of 5 June 1900, F.O. 17/1418.

[2] MacDonald to Salisbury, tel. 108 of 11 June 1900 (via Kiachta), F.O. 17/1418. Steiger raises the speculation that MacDonald's call for reinforcements may have been made to anticipate a Russian move (*China and the Occident*, 216, n. 7). No evidence has been traced in the Foreign Office Correspondence, the Embassy archives, or the Admiralty files to support such a view. It may be assumed that if this factor determined MacDonald's action he would have made Salisbury aware of it, since he knew that the latter deplored the appeal to force and was apprehensive of Russian action. Of the telegrams sent out by MacDonald at this time, other than those already referred to, only two have a bearing on the Russian issue, which was to loom so large later in the crisis. The first was on 30 May (tel. 85 of 30 May. F.O. 17/1418) when he passed on the information that five Russian ships were outside the Taku bar; the other was on 14 June (tel. 110 of 14 June, via Kiachta? F.O. 17/1418) where he stated that Russia had embarked 2,000 troops at Port Arthur for Taku, that Japan was expected to send a force, and that to maintain her political position Britain should send at least an equal force.

The only practical route to Peking lay along the Northern railway line. The rail terminus for Taku was Tangku, which lay five miles up the Pei-ho, defended by a fourth fort at the bend of the river. From Tangku there was a single track of twenty-seven miles to Tientsin; from Tientsin there was a double track of eighty-four miles to Peking.[1]

Seymour had no reliable knowledge of the situation in Peking, nor of the state of the country between Tientsin and Peking. After his arrival he based his actions on the reports of Carles, the British consul in Tientsin.

Carles was in a state of nervous excitement. On 4 June he called on Yu Lu, viceroy of Chihli, about the murder of Robinson and Norman. There was no traffic on the roads and the shops were deserted; unruly crowds gathered outside the viceroy's Yamen. Carles rushed back to the consular quarters, gathered the British residents together, formed a home guard and sent to Taku for reinforcements.[2]

On 6 June, when control was placed in his hands by the Admiralty, Seymour called a meeting of the senior naval officers of France, Germany, Italy, Russia, Austria, the United States, and Japan aboard his flagship, H.M.S. *Centurion*, to arrange details of concerted action. A guard of seventy-five had already been sent to Peking and 104 to Tientsin. At the meeting of 6 June Seymour suggested the joint command of the Tientsin forces under Colonel Wogack, the Russian senior military commander at Tientsin.[3] This move was not approved in London. The next day Seymour received an instruction from the Admiralty, which Salisbury sent concurrently to MacDonald, warning him that the most serious danger he had to guard against was in taking any step which would lead Russia to occupy Peking, and that if she did so Seymour was to attempt to occupy a part of the city simultaneously.[4]

On 10 June Seymour received this message from MacDonald: 'Situation extremely grave. Unless arrangements are made for immediate advance to Peking it will be too late.'[5] The Admiral

---

[1] See map.

[2] Carles to MacDonald, encl. 1 in Carles to Salisbury, No. 3 of 5 June 1900, F.O. 17/1428.

[3] C.-in-C. to Admiralty, tel. 84 of 6 June 1900, Adm. 116/117.

[4] Admiralty to C.-in-C., tel. 80 of 7 June 1900, Adm. 116/117.

[5] C.-in-C. to Admiralty, tel. 88 of 10 June 1900, Adm. 116/117.

did not hesitate. He informed the other naval commanders that he was leading a contingent to Peking, invited them to join him, collected all available men and set out at 3 a.m. on the morning of 11 June, leaving supply and communication lines to be settled in his wake. By the evening of that day he was at Lofa, thirty miles along the route. On 12 June he left Tientsin with an international force of about 2,300 men. At Langfang, about twelve miles outside Tientsin, he clashed with a force of Boxers, killed about fifty of them and moved on to Yangts'un, where the allied force met 4,000 Chinese regulars under the command of General Nieh Shih-ch'eng. The two forces 'exchanged friendly greeting, crossed the river, and went on . . .'.[1]

Next day, 13 June, the Court acted. A decree was issued stating that there were already more than a thousand legation guards in Peking which were ample for protection, that if further foreign detachments were allowed to 'come one after another the consequences would be unthinkable'. Yu Lu was to order Nieh Shih-ch'eng, commander of the regular forces in the Tientsin area, and Lo Jung-kuang, the commandant of the Taku forts, to resist the advance of any further detachments.[2] Nieh then turned back and engaged Seymour's force.

By 17 June the Admiral had been forced back to Langfang, where he was marooned. On the 19th he decided to abandon the troop trains and return to Tientsin along the left bank of the Pei-ho, the railway having been destroyed by Boxer activity. By 21 June the force had lost its artillery, and only two maxim guns remained. The next day they stumbled on a Chinese arsenal at Hsi-ku. Incapacitated by 230 wounded, they stayed at the arsenal until relieved by a force from Tientsin on 26 June. Seymour's report stated: 'Success was only possible on the assumption that the Imperial troops . . . would at least be neutral. . . .'[3]

Seymour's attempt was gallant, but questionable. Mac-Donald had been thinking in terms of legation guards,

[1] Sir E. H. Seymour, *My Naval Career* (London, 1911), 344–5.
[2] Grand Council to Yu Lu K26/5/17 (13 June), quoted C. C. Tan, *The Boxer Catastrophe* (New York, 1955), 71.
[3] C.-in-C. to Admiralty, 'Events leading up to Combined Naval Expedition to attempt relief of Legations at Peking', 27 June 1900, Adm. 116/114. Total casualties were 65 killed, 230 wounded. British casualties 30 killed (1 officer), 97 wounded (8 naval officers), W.O. 32/137/7842/1003.

permission for which was being negotiated with the Chinese. Seymour's action was a resort to military force. The news of the expedition and its repulse swept around the countryside. In Peking the massacre of the native Christians began on 13 June, and skirmishing against the legations started. In Tientsin the Boxers had taken over the native city by the 15th.

A second consequence affected British policy more directly. Seymour's vulnerable position made extensive relief operations obligatory. Russian troops at Port Arthur were the only ones immediately available and the urgency of the situation placed Russia in a position of military preponderance. Further, owing to Seymour's decision to lead the contingents in person, the allied naval forces came under the command of the Russian Vice-Admiral Hildebrandt, the next in seniority. Seymour had been aware of this problem before he started and had attempted to deal with it by placating the Russians; thus he suggested Wogack for the chief command in Tientsin and that a Russian colonel should act as his chief-of-staff on the expedition.[1] The reason he gave later for leading the expedition in person was that he did not wish British troops to come under a foreign command.[2]

By 13 June the naval forces at Taku were out of touch with Seymour. Next day it was reported that all rolling-stock had been ordered up the line to bring a Chinese army from Tientsin to Tangku. Vice-Admiral Hildebrandt immediately called a Council of Admirals and Senior Naval Officers aboard his flagship, the *Rossia*, and proposed that in view of this report (which by this time had been elaborated into the immediate descent of 2,000 Chinese regular troops to cut communication between Taku and Tientsin) the eight naval units in the Pei-ho, with the Russian Captain Dobrovolsky of the *Bobre* in command, should seize the railway station, prevent the removal of the rolling-stock, and hold the terminus at Tangku. If the Chinese offered resistance the naval units were authorized to employ force at the railway station and to attack the forts. Next day, 15 June, it was reported that the Chinese were mining the mouth of the Pei-ho. This led to a second Conference of Admirals on the afternoon of 16 June, when it was decided that notice

---

[1] Seymour to Admiralty, tel. 86 of 8 June 1900, F.O. 17/1439.
[2] Seymour, *Career*, 343.

be given to the Viceroy of Chihli and the Commandant of the Taku Forts that the forts would be occupied at 2 a.m. on 17 June.[1]

The decision was made by a group of officers in closed session off Taku, on the basis of the reports which had been received. No attempt was made to assess the political significance of the action, nor to investigate the true situation in the surrounding territory. The only mines in the Pei-ho were those which already lay in the vicinity of the forts. The last report on General Nieh's movements had come from Carles; this stated that Nieh had taken 1,500 to 2,000 troops to Lofa to subdue about 4,000 Boxers, but that he had been instructed secretly by Jung Lu not to use force.[2] The only sign of hostility among the populace apparent to the naval commanders was the excitement which was shown by the local Chinese at Tangku; Chinese porters helped the disembarkation of supplies. The reason for the decision to take the forts was given later by Rear-Admiral Bruce, second-in-command of the China Station:

> If we lost the forts we lost the entrance to the river and all communication with our forces at Tientsin and the front, and our only other available base of operations was Pei-ta-ho about 120 miles to the north, with a destroyed railway, two large Chinese Military camps in front of us and 120 miles march to Tientsin through a country totally devoid of any supplies. . . .[3]

At one a.m. on the morning of 17 June the Taku forts opened fire on the naval units which were moving up to seize the four Chinese destroyers which lay beyond the bend of the river. By 6.30 a.m. the forts had been reduced and the destroyers taken. The naval side of the offensive was undertaken by the smaller naval units capable of crossing the Taku bar; one Russian and all the British ships made a creditable showing. The military side of the manœuvre was dominated by the Japanese who

---

[1] Rear-Admiral Bruce to Admiralty, No. 4 of 17 June 1900, Adm. 116/114. The American commander, Admiral Kempff, did not join in the ultimatum on the ground that no act of war had been committed by the Chinese; but later he joined the other forces in the attack on the forts after the Chinese had fired on the American ship. Cf. Steiger, *China and the Occident*, 225 f., who treats these events in greater detail. Bruce did not mention the American abstention.

[2] Carles to Seymour, encl. in Carles to Salisbury, 7 June 1900, F.O. 17/1428.

[3] Bruce to Goschen, 25 June 1900, Adm. 116/114.

landed marine contingents and attacked the forts from their land approaches with considerable bravery, suffering heavy casualties. Throughout the subsequent campaign the Japanese forces fought much more efficiently than the other foreign contingents. In the taking of the Taku forts they produced steam lighters, shallow draught vessels adapted for the Taku bar, sampans, coolies, and land searchlights, all 'as if an invasion of the Pei-ho were a normal task'.[1]

After the taking of the forts, the naval forces turned to the consolidation of the territory between Taku and Tientsin. On 20 June the Council of Admirals issued a proclamation stating that the powers were only fighting against Boxers and against those Chinese who threatened foreign life and property.[2] Admiral Alexieff, commander of the Russian squadron in the Pacific, arrived from Port Arthur to take over the presidency of the Council of Admirals. The disembarkation of troops and supplies continued and, by 30 June, 520 officers and 13,500 men had been landed, while further Russian and Japanese reinforcements were expected to give a total of 20,000 men. The admirals considered that this force was sufficient to hold Taku, Tientsin, and perhaps Peitaho, but that it would be impossible to advance beyond Tientsin.[3] On 2 July Seymour, who returned to Taku after being relieved, reported that he considered the 'first violent outbreak of hostility now over'.[4]

On the day of the attack on the Taku forts, Sunday 17 June, the foreign quarter in Tientsin was attacked by the Chinese. Thereafter, until 13 July, the city was considered to be under siege. In reality, the Chinese who held the native quarter of the city were the more hard-pressed. One thousand seven hundred Russian troops, who had moved up to join Seymour's force and had been delayed in Tientsin by a broken railway line, gave the city a garrison strength of 2,700. Communication was freely maintained with Taku; expeditions were sent into the countryside. By 25 June sufficient reinforcements had been brought up to relieve Seymour. The foreign residents of

[1] (W. H. Coish) *Tientsin Besieged and After the Siege* (Shanghai, 1900), 29.

[2] Bruce to Admiralty, encl. 4, No. 24 of 27 June 1900, Adm. 116/115. It was promulgated in French and English and sent to the German consul at Chefoo, the doyen of the consular body there.

[3] Bruce to Admiralty, tels. 12 and 13 of 30 June 1900, Adm. 116/117.

[4] C.-in-C. to Admiralty, tel. 95 of 2 July 1900, Adm. 116/117.

Tientsin believed themselves in a perilous position, but the close proximity of the allied fleet did not give this belief substance. 'As regards Boxers we have no fear, and Imperial troops not much', the correspondent of the *North China Daily News* admitted. 'Indeed, we aspire to have the honour of pricking this monstrous Boxer bubble. . . .'[1]

The Siege of the Peking Legations

In Peking the situation was more critical. From 13 June numerous bands of Boxers roamed the city. The massacre of native converts which began on the night of 12 June continued without respite. The houses of the 'secondary hairy ones', as the converts were known, were marked out with crosses for the attention of the Boxers; in the slaughter of these innocents lay the tragedy of the rising. Within a few days the depredations were out of hand. Between 13 and 16 June, Imperial decrees were promulgated repeatedly ordering the suppression of the Boxers,[2] but the Imperial troops lay passive as the Court tried to make up its mind. Only the unruly Kansu forces of the anti-foreign commander Tung Fu-hsiang were prominent and these added to rather than controlled the unrest. On the morning of 16 June the entire residential quarter in the Cheng-yang men area went up in flames and the homes of more than 4,000 rich Chinese merchants were devastated. The fire burnt for three days and was attended by widespread looting.

Against this background the Empress Dowager tried to come to a decision. A powerful and vociferous group led by Prince Tuan pressed for the extermination of the foreigners. Jung Lu, the one man with enough influence to sway the Empress Dowager, and who had command of all the Metropolitan forces, followed a devious waiting policy. Only a few courageous officials risked, and later lost, their heads in urging a policy of moderation. Between 16 and 19 June three Imperial Councils were summoned by the Empress Dowager to advise her on a course of action; they were attended by all the Manchu princes

---

[1] (W. H. Coish) *Tientsin Besieged*, 2. A description of the fighting at Tientsin and the official report of the capture of the Taku forts is given in China Letter No. 24 of 27 June 1900, F.O. 17/1446.

[2] Li Hsi-sheng, 'Keng-tzu kuo-pien chi', *I.H.T.* i. 12.

and officials of any consequence at Court.[1] The meetings were stormy; the moderate ministers were shouted down by their bellicose colleagues. At the meeting of 17 June the Empress Dowager produced a note which purported to put forward four demands by the foreign powers. Three of these she passed on to her courtiers. The foreign powers, she informed them, demanded that the Emperor be rehoused in a suitable residence, that they be given the management of the provincial revenues and the control of Chinese military power. The fourth demand, which she apparently forbore to mention, was that the Emperor should be restored to administrative control. These demands were reputedly made through a minor official named Lo Chia-chieh who forwarded them to Jung Lu. The spurious document has been regarded as a move by Prince Tuan to goad the Empress Dowager into declaring war. It clearly aroused her anger; when she showed Lo's letter to the assembled officials, an observer noted, 'they all turned their heads away and shrank back; none dared be the first to rise'.[2]

Despite this, the decision to oppose the powers was delayed for three days. After the first meeting two of the moderate ministers were sent to Yangts'un to persuade Seymour's force not to advance, but they were met on the road, robbed, and turned back. After the next meeting three more ministers were sent to the legations to secure the reversal of the order for re-inforcements. The failure of these missions destroyed the arguments of the moderate party. On 19 June the Court received Yu Lu's report of the admirals' ultimatum at Taku. It was then decided to break off diplomatic relations with the powers and the diplomatic body was ordered to leave Peking within twenty-four hours. On 21 June a further memorial was received from Yu Lu reporting the outbreak of hostilities at Taku and Tientsin; an Imperial edict was issued on the same day declaring war on the powers.[3]

---

[1] Yun Yu-ting, 'Ch'ung Ling ch'uan hsin lu' (The true story of the Kuang-hsu Emperor), *I.H.T.* i. 47-8; Li Hsi-sheng, 'Keng-tzu kuo-pien chi', *I.H.T.* i. 12-13. Yun places the meetings on 16, 17, and 19 June; Li places the third on 18 June. Both accounts were written by minor officials some time after the events. Yun published his work in 1911, Li died in 1905. Yun is the usual source given for these audiences, but Li's less deliberate account gives greater actuality.

[2] Li Hsi-sheng, 'Keng-tzu kuo-pien chi', *I.H.T.* i. 12. Li states that Lo's letter was made known to the officials on 16 June.

[3] Tan, *The Boxer Catastrophe*, 75. Teng Ssu-yu notes (in Li Chien-nung, *The*

The impression received from reading reports of these palace audiences, reports written by minor officials after the events and thus not altogether satisfactory, is of a natural desire in the Empress Dowager to expel the foreigners, restrained by her conviction of the impossibility of the task. This conviction had to combat the obstreperous attitude of the reactionary party, the refusal of the diplomatic body to co-operate on anything but the most humiliating terms, and the need to give the uncontrollable Boxer bands a target other than the Imperial throne. Understandably, her resistance became increasingly weaker. The many officials, whose personal safety depended on the imperial favour, observed the signs and tempered their attitude accordingly, so that no one 'did not grasp the wrist of his neighbour and start up and speak of exterminating the foreigner'.[1] The final trace of indecision was then removed by the news of the attack on Taku. But, though from this time the Court professed its belief in Boxer invulnerability, and the officials vied with each other in Boxer practices and talked of dragons rising from the sea to sink the foreign ships and of the efficacy of old and defunct sects, these avowals bore the stamp of desperation. By 13 July, an edict of 29 June, forwarded by the Board of War to the provincial treasurer of Chihli for transmission to the various ministers abroad through the *taotai* of Shanghai, had been handed in at the British Foreign Office by Sir Chihchen Lofenglu, the Chinese minister in London. 'It was the duty of Lo Yung-kwang to hold the Forts,' the message stated, 'so he had no alternative but to refuse the demand. . . . No false estimate of her power led her (China) to measure her forces with those of the combined fleets. She fought because she could not do otherwise than resist.'[2]

While the Court was deciding on a course of action, defensive preparations were being made in the legation quarter in Peking. At first only desultory efforts were made, for the foreign community moved slowly towards the idea of a siege. For the first week in June attention was on the question of additional legation guards. The civilian community, made anxious by the

Political History of China (trans. Teng and Ingalls), p. 510, n. 12) a declaration of war of 20 June.
    [1] Li Hsi-sheng, 'Keng-tzu kuo-pien chi', *I.H.T.* i. 14.
    [2] Communicated by the Chinese minister (Sir Chihchen Lofenglu), 13 July 1900, F.O. 17/1435.

badly equipped contingent which had arrived from Tientsin on 31 May, pressed for greater security; while the various ministers, except for Baron von Ketteler, the German minister, hesitated over a step which would so clearly antagonize the Chinese.[1]

On 11 June, just before telegraphic communication with Tientsin was cut, it was reported in Peking that Admiral Seymour's force was at Langfang. Thereafter the foreign community lived in the hourly expectation of the arrival of reinforcements. In small groups, even singly, they went repeatedly to the railway station to meet the incoming troop trains, and were consequently menaced by the increasingly hostile populace. In this way Sugiyama, a secretary of the Japanese legation, was killed on 11 June. On 13 June, in view of the growing Boxer activity in the city, and because of the non-arrival of Seymour's force, efforts were made to put the legations in a condition of defence. These efforts were haphazard; no one believed that the Chinese would dare to oppose the allied contingents; the delay in their arrival was attributed to the breakdown in rail communication. Between 13 and 19 June this expectation of immediate relief encouraged an attitude in the foreign community which seriously inflamed the rising. Bands of foreigners went out into the city to rescue Chinese converts, to collect supplies, and, more frequently, to hunt down the Boxers.

On 19 June the foreign representatives were thrown into confusion when identical notes were received from the Tsungli Yamen stating that as an attack had been made on Taku by the allied fleet, the protection of the foreign ministers and their families could no longer be assured and that they were to leave for the coast under escort within twenty-four hours. A meeting was held immediately by the diplomatic body. The general feeling was that the order should be complied with; but a note was sent to the Tsungli Yamen asking for assurances of safety and also for an extended period of time, as it was considered

---

[1] The contingent arrived with an antiquated five-barrelled Nordenfeldt of an 1887 pattern, which jammed at every fourth round; the Russian party brought 80 rounds for a 12-pounder, but left the gun on the platform at Tientsin. The events leading up to the siege of the legations are only referred to briefly, for they have been treated exhaustively in contemporary and later accounts, notably Steiger, *China and the Occident*, 201 f. Peter Fleming, *The Siege at Peking* (London, 1959), 15–22, 60–73, 91–112.

impossible to make adequate transport arrangements in one day. Also, an interview was requested of the Yamen for the next day. That night practically the whole of the foreign community except the British legation started to pack; MacDonald had little faith in any protective measures the Chinese were likely to provide. When he heard of the admirals' ultimatum at Taku he observed that the action had tipped the scales and swamped the moderate party at the Court, and he wrote Carles that 'they had sounded the death knell of the foreigners in Peking'.[1]

By the next morning no answer had been received from the Tsungli Yamen. Despite the efforts of his colleagues to dissuade him, Baron von Ketteler insisted on setting out for the Yamen with his secretary and two out-riders. Shortly afterwards he was shot and killed on the road by a Chinese soldier; his secretary was seriously wounded. The murder was not officially admitted by the Chinese until 18 July, but a few hours later a further note was received from the Yamen which allowed an extension of the twenty-four-hour time limit, as it was admitted to be unsafe for the diplomatic body to leave Peking just then.[2]

Nevertheless, promptly on expiration of the original time limit, at 4 p.m. on 20 June, Chinese troops opened fire on the legations, which were then under siege until they were relieved on 14 August. Fire was continual from 20 to 25 June, and a sniping siege was maintained until 18 July. From 18 to 25 July there was a truce, during which sellers of fruit and ice were allowed into the legations. Hostilities were then resumed until 14 August, when the legations were relieved.

It was not an impressive siege. At no time were the Chinese attacks pressed home and after the first few days the beleaguered were aware of this restraint in the enemy. On 18 July MacDonald could suggest to Jung Lu that ammunition should be denied the attackers.[3] The period of greatest pressure was at

---

[1] Sir Ernest Satow's Journal (hereafter cited S.J.) from the Satow Papers, P.R.O. 30/33/16/3; entry of 22 Oct. 1900.

[2] The general feeling in Peking after the legations had been relieved was that Ketteler had been killed by his own obstinacy and that he had been deliberately marked out for punishment because of his harsh treatment of the Boxers in the period before the siege. Cf. S.J., 21 Oct. 1900; Satow to Lansdowne, 8 Feb. 1901, Lansdowne Papers.

[3] MacDonald to Yamen, No. 116 of 18 July 1900, F.O. 228/1351.

the end of July, after the anti-foreign official, Li Ping-heng, arrived in Peking to infuse new vigour into the Boxer movement. The greatest trial of the defenders was the heat.[1]

[1] British casualties in the defence of the legations were: military—3 killed (1 officer), 22 wounded (2 officers); W.O. 32/137/7842/1003. Civilian—2 killed, several wounded.

VI

THE NEGOTIATIONS FOR THE RELIEF OF THE LEGATIONS

THE decision of 6 June which placed control in the hands of the British authorities on the spot was followed by a period of waiting in London. It had become, as Sir Ernest Satow, the British minister at Tokyo, noted, 'an affair of admirals'.[1] This period, which lasted until the repulse of Seymour indicated the necessity for extraordinary measures, was given to anxious speculation, much handicapped by the lack of reliable information.

Initially, a large-scale native uprising against foreigners was not foreseen. The unrest was attributed to inter-factional activity among the Chinese, instigated possibly by the reformists with the aim of dynastic change. Reports indicating this possibility had been current since spring. On 22 March Satow had written of repeated rumours that China was ripe for rebellion;[2] from as far afield as Malaya, Sir Frank Swettenham reported on 29 March a prediction by the Chinese Reform Party at Penang that a rising would take place in China in three months time.[3] In June, in view of the developments in China, these isolated reports acquired added force. Attention was focused on this interpretation of the unrest by the publication on the front page of the *Daily Express* of 12 June of a long article which was reputedly an appeal by the Kuang Hsu Emperor that the foreign powers should rescue him from Peking, take him to Nanking or Hankow, declare the Empress Dowager and her party usurpers, and establish a protectorate over the government of China through the Kuang Hsu Emperor, who had the support of the people.[4]

[1] S.J., 25 June 1900.
[2] Satow to Salisbury, letter of 22 Mar. 1900, P.R.O. 30/33/14/11.
[3] Salisbury to MacDonald, tel. 38 of 29 Mar. 1900, F.O. 228/1341.
[4] *Daily Express*, 12 June 1900. The article was by Henry O'Shea, editor of the *China Gazette*.

On this basis the Boxers were regarded as an element in a dynastic upheaval, involving the possible collapse of Manchu authority. Attempts were made by the popular press to identify them with the Hung, or Triad, Society and thus to credit them with the driving force which had led to the Taiping rebellion.[1] But by responsible opinion they were regarded as a mob. Satow, who had by this time arrived home on leave, felt that they would never manage to force the gates of Peking.[2]

Nevertheless, recognition of the inherent weakness of the Boxers was offset by the possible consequences of their activity, which gave much concern. From MacDonald's reports it was by no means certain that the Court would not attempt to save itself by condoning mob rule, which would endanger the foreign community and, in Francis Bertie's opinion, cause the powers to use 'such strong measures against the Empress Dowager as will bring China to the ground and hasten partition'.[2] Apart from such joint action by the powers, it was feared that Russia would take advantage of the unrest to intervene in China either to prop or to replace the tottering dynasty. By 1900 there was much speculation on the possible consequences of the Siberian railway project, the construction of which had begun in Manchuria in 1898. Reports of rising Russo-Japanese hostility over Masampo and Korea gave credibility to the possibility of a preventive war by Japan, a view which was strongly held by Morrison, the persuasive correspondent of The Times.[3] Again, rumours were current in mid-May that Russia had obtained a concession for a railroad overland from Kiachta to Peking.[4] The disturbed situation in north China was recognized as a factor likely to encourage Russia to further her ambitions, since the appeal for military support by the legations had given her a reason for the dispatch of troops. On 8 June, writing to Northcote, Governor of Bombay, Salisbury stated of Russia that 'when her Siberian railway is ready, she will want

[1] Daily Chronicle, 18 June 1900.
[2] S.J., 31 May 1900.
[3] See Morrison's article in The Times, 7 June 1900. Satow, with his eye on the incomplete state of Japan's military preparations, thought such a war unlikely until after 1903 as the Japanese 'do not change their plans easily, for their intellect is not supple enough'. Satow to Salisbury, letter of 22 Mar. 1900, P.R.O. 30/33/14/11.
[4] Salisbury to MacDonald, tel. 51 of 11 May 1900, F.O. 228/1341.

to be mistress of the greater part of China'.[1] Two days previously, when he had placed control in the hands of MacDonald and Seymour, he had written explicitly:

There are many possible dangers, the most serious is that Russia should be moved to occupy the whole or part of Peking. It would be very difficult to move her out. We should therefore, if possible, avoid making her wish to occupy Peking, but if she shows signs of intending to do so we should occupy some important part simultaneously so far as our resources enable us to do so. Arrangements of course will be made with the other Powers, but they are less important.[2]

With this in mind, Salisbury was led to resist the desire of Queen Victoria that MacDonald should be withdrawn, a step which he felt would leave the Dual Alliance powers supreme. 'Russia not China', he maintained, 'seems to me the gravest danger of the moment.'[3]

Despite these feelings, Salisbury was reluctant to take any step which could encourage Russia. He felt that Great Britain should wait on Russian action before taking active measures. The alternative view, expressed most coherently by Francis Bertie, now in charge of the China Department at the Foreign Office, was that Great Britain should act on the assumption that north China was lost to Russia and that if in the circumstances Great Britain were not to offer armed opposition she 'ought to take some security for the control of the Yangtze such as the seizure of the Chusan Islands and the Forts at Nanking'.[4]

This was the division of opinion over the conduct of policy in China which had been revealed during the Port Arthur crisis of the spring of 1898, and which had been pushed into the background by Salisbury's Anglo-Russian Agreement of April 1899. Now, with the apparent breakdown of that arrangement, and with the prospect of a general collapse, the first thought was again for the consolidation of the Yangtze. This argument

---

[1] Salisbury to Northcote, letter of 8 June 1900, S.P., quoted in J. A. S. Grenville, 'British Foreign Policy, 1899–1902', unpublished Ph.D. thesis (London University, 1954), 167.
[2] Salisbury to MacDonald, tel. 64, secret, of 7 June 1900, F.O. 17/1417; Admiralty to C.-in-C. China Station, tel. 80 of 7 June 1900, Adm. 116/117.
[3] Salisbury to the Queen, 10 June 1900, copy S.P. 84/112.
[4] Memorandum by Bertie, with Salisbury's minutes, of 7 June 1900, F.O. 17/1439.

was put forward by Bertie to all who came to him for the latest reports on China; and the attractive nature of his solution, for he spoke loftily of establishing a scion of the Mings in the south, compared favourably with Salisbury's policy of inaction.[1]

I believe that the cardinal blunder of our policy throughout the East . . . [Hamilton wrote to Curzon on 6 June in a strain which reflected the feeling of many of the Government] is the belief that by asserting and maintaining the so-called independence of these Governments we are promoting and protecting our own interests. . . . I cannot see that we can hope to improve our position so long as we fatuously adhere to what seems to me to be an obsolete policy. . . .[2]

Eventually, the attention Bertie had focused on the Yangtze was decisive. Although Salisbury repeated his argument that Great Britain should reserve her action until Russia had shown her hand, and that the naval units which were being concentrated should go to Taku, 'the point of danger',[3] he was persuaded to a change of front when St. John Brodrick, then parliamentary secretary, pressed the incontrovertible argument that while Great Britain was waiting on Russian action, France and Germany might take a stronger line and occupy the area. Consequently, on 13 June, the Admiralty was instructed to take steps to forestall any foreign occupation of Chusan and the Nanking forts in the event of a general collapse.[4]

This was a precautionary measure which at that particular moment seemed unlikely to be called into operation. From 10 June, when Admiral Seymour landed with his contingents, successive telegraphic reports traced the smooth passage of over 2,000 troops under British control along the road to Peking. On the 13th Seymour expressed confidence in his ability to enter the capital and the concern shown over Russian ambitions seemed unjustified. Salisbury regained his optimism and cheerfully maintained that the Boxers would not come to much.[5]

This mood was rapidly shattered. From 14 June reports took

[1] S.J., 25 June 1900.

[2] Hamilton to Curzon, 6 June 1900, Hamilton Papers.

[3] Memoranda by Campbell, Barrington, and Brodrick of 16 June 1900, with minutes, F.O. 17/1440.

[4] Foreign Office to Admiralty, secret, of 13 June 1900, F.O. 17/1440; Brodrick to Salisbury, memorandum of 9 June 1900 enclosed. For the situation on the Yangtze, see Chapter VII below.

[5] S.J., 12 June 1900.

an alarming turn. Seymour had disappeared into the Chinese countryside, leaving his exact whereabouts a matter of intense speculation both at Taku and in London. At the same time, Pelham Warren, the British acting consul-general at Shanghai, reported a worsening situation on the Yangtze. From Tientsin Carles, the British consul, sent the incredible news that the Empress Dowager had resolved to destroy the legations and that the Viceroy of the metropolitan provinces, Yu Lu, was about to ask for sanctuary on a British ship.[1] Both in the Commons and the Lords the Government confessed to an inability to understand the situation.[2] Communication with Tientsin and Taku was cut and the Admiralty was driven to seek information from the Senior Naval Officer at Liukuntao, the naval station off Weihaiwei. Commander Gaunt responded with the news of the intention to bombard the Taku forts, which was followed the next day (18 June) by reports from Washington and Berlin of the actual attack.[3] Rear-Admiral Bruce's report of the ultimatum, sent off at 12.24 p.m. on 17 June via Port Arthur, did not arrive in London until 8.15 p.m. on 25 June, while news of the capture of the forts and the admirals' proclamation of 20 June, reported via Chefoo, was known on the 21st.[4]

The admirals' proclamation of 20 June was the only indication to the Government of the attitude being adopted by the commanders in north China, and since it offered a means of limiting the conflict, Salisbury made it the basis of his policy. It was applied in the Yangtze region, where negotiations were being carried out for an occupation of the Nanking forts, and in London, when Sir Chihchen Lofenglu, the Chinese Ambassador, made anxious inquiry on 22 June, on Li Hung-chang's behalf, whether the powers considered themselves at war with

---

[1] Carles to Salisbury, tel. 11 of 14 June, tel. of 15 June 1900, F.O. 17/1429. Sanctuary was offered to the Viceroy, see Salisbury to Carles, tel. 3 of 16 June 1900, F.O. 17/1429, Foreign Office to Admiralty, 15 June 1900, draft, F.O. 17/1440.

[2] *Parliamentary Debates*, lxxxiv. 12–14, 259.

[3] Senior Naval Officer, Liukuntao, to Admiralty, tel. of 17 June 1900, Adm. 116/117. Commander Gaunt's information came from a letter written by Rear-Admiral Bruce, second in command on the China Station; Admiralty to Rear-Admiral at Taku, tel. 7 of 18 June 1900, Adm. 116/117; *The Times*, 18 June 1900.

[4] Rear-Admiral to Admiralty, tel. of 17 June, tel. 1 of 20 June 1900, Adm. 116/117.

China.[1] However, the diplomatic basis of foreign intervention was not the immediate concern. The urgent problem was to find reinforcements, Admiral Seymour's failure having revealed the inadequacy of the naval contingents at Taku.

Salisbury's Proposal for the Use of Japanese Troops

As soon as the critical position of the legations was known Salisbury cast aside his earlier restraint and applied himself to the provision of an adequate relief force which could be sent to north China with the least possible delay. The Hong Kong Regiment had already been ordered to the north, and five regiments of infantry and one regiment of cavalry were on their way from India.[2] But these British forces could not be expected to arrive for some time. Nor did Australia, though reassuringly willing to help, seem likely to be able to send reinforcements in the immediate future.[3] It was clear that if the legations were to be saved, troops would have to be sent by either Russia or Japan, the only powers with adequate military forces in the vicinity.

As early as 9 June Viscount Aoki, the Japanese Foreign Minister, had indicated Japan's readiness to dispatch a land force at short notice; but in making the offer he had stipulated the need for prior consultation with Great Britain and had stressed the desirability of obtaining German and American support, 'so as to be in a majority of the powers concerned'.[4] Brodrick, Balfour, and Chamberlain had been in favour of the move and had suggested that Russia and Japan should each be called upon to send 4,000 troops, while Great Britain would send 2,000.[5] This had been opposed by Salisbury, for he believed that while Russia should not be encouraged to send troops in on her own, the conditions Japan had stipulated for the sending of Japanese troops would patently involve Great Britain in an

---

[1] Salisbury to British consul, Canton, tel. 2 of 22 June 1900, copy, Adm. 116/117.

[2] Goschen to Salisbury, private, of 18 June 1900, S.P. 93/59; India Office to Foreign Office, 20 June 1900, F.O. 17/1440. Particulars regarding the dispatch of the Expeditionary Force to China are conveniently given in 'Military notes' for Aug. 1900, *JRUSI*, 44 (1900), 943–6, 1079.

[3] See R. H. Wilde, 'The Boxer Affair and Australian Responsibility for Imperial Defence', *PHR*, 26 (Feb. 1957), 51–65.

[4] Whitehead to Salisbury, tel. 8 of June 1900, F.O. 46/531.

[5] S.J., 13 June 1900.

anti-Russian combination in the Far East. Nevertheless, when Rear-Admiral Bruce at Taku appealed on 21 June for reinforcements desperately needed to save Tientsin,[1] Salisbury pushed his doubts aside and immediately approached Japan.[2]

By this time Japan had also received a call for reinforcements from the Japanese Admiral at Taku, upon which Aoki convened a meeting in Tokyo on 23 June to ascertain the views of the representatives of the powers concerned. After the meeting J. B. Whitehead, the British chargé d'affaires, privately communicated Salisbury's request, which Aoki promised would receive the immediate consideration of the Japanese Cabinet. From Aoki's observations at the time, however, Whitehead concluded that Japan would 'not take energetic action unless guaranteed support by at least Great Britain and Germany, so as to provide against complications with Russia and France'.[3] This was the condition Japan had stipulated in her offer of 9 June, and from this position, through all the tortuous negotiations which followed, she refused to retreat.

Great pains were taken by the Japanese to make themselves understood. On the evening of 24 June Aoki went to see Whitehead and stressed that the Japanese Government was aware, on information received from Chinese sources, that after the *coup d'état* of 1898 the conservative faction which had come to power, including Prince Tuan and possibly the Empress Dowager herself, had been inveigled into Russian pay, and that there was an active group in the Manchu Court which contemplated making the Hwangho the frontier of the Chinese Empire, ceding the northern part to Russia. Aoki then concluded that Russia intended using the Boxer disturbances to obtain this end, and that if Japan sent troops collision was likely. Consequently, Aoki urged the 'imperative necessity for (an) understanding between Great Britain, Germany and Japan to counteract Russian designs', and that if the powers were in a state of war with China a 'collective declaration of war should be made to give a basis of co-operation and to prevent independent action by any one power'.[4] At the same time the

---

[1] Rear-Admiral, Taku, to Admiralty, 21 June 1900, F.O. 17/1440.
[2] Salisbury to Whitehead, tel. 29 of 22 June 1900, F.O. 46/530.
[3] Whitehead to Salisbury, tels. 20 and 21 of 23 June 1900, copies, Adm. 116/117.
[4] Whitehead to Salisbury, private and confidential, tel. of 25 June 1900, circulated to Queen and Cabinet, F.O. 46/531.

Japanese chargé d'affaires in London approached Salisbury on the urgent need for an assurance that any effective assistance provided by Japan would not lead to collision with Russia. Japan also let it be known that a division (about 13,000 men) was mobilized and ready for use; the Japanese military attaché in London called on Sir John Ardagh, the Director of Military Intelligence, to discuss the military side of the intervention.[1]

However, Salisbury refused to contemplate the Japanese proposal on these terms. Instead, he acted on the assumption that the relief of the legations was an international matter, and that the assurance sought by Japan could be met by obtaining Russia's consent. He instructed Sir Charles Scott, the British Ambassador at St. Petersburg, to secure Russian approval of a Japanese expedition of 20,000 to 30,000 men.[2] At the same time he sought to tip the scales by approaching Germany for assistance in obtaining this assurance.[3]

The move was unsuccessful. The immediate reaction at St. Petersburg to the rising had been one of apprehension of the very development that Salisbury now proposed. At the time of Seymour's landing Count Muraviev, the Russian Foreign Minister, had suggested to the Tsar that 4,000 Russian troops should be sent to Tientsin 'to avert the danger of Japanese or other foreign troops being summoned to the defence'.[4] Four thousand troops were accordingly embarked at Port Arthur for north China, where they arrived in time to take part in the military activities around Tientsin.[5] At the same time, Russia tried to adopt a political attitude which would allow her to maintain the special position of friendship which had been built up with China since 1896. On 17 June Muraviev submitted a further memorandum to the Tsar which stressed that, while participating in any joint expeditionary force to relieve the legations, Russia should not assume a prominent role which would attract the hostility of the Chinese. This received the Tsar's approval and became the basis of Russian policy in the crisis.[6]

---

[1] Whitehead to Salisbury, tel. 22 of 26 June 1900, copy, Adm. 116/117; Memorandum by Sir Thomas Sanderson of 26 June 1900, F.O. 17/1440.

[2] Salisbury to Scott, tel. 74 of 25 June 1900, F.O. 65/1603.

[3] Salisbury to Gough, tel. 65 of 26 June 1900, F.O. 64/1496.

[4] Quoted Romanov, *Russia in Manchuria*, 178.

[5] Malozemoff, *Russian Far Eastern Policy*, 127.

[6] Ibid., 127–8.

Then, with the spread of the rising after the taking of the Taku forts, Russia became concerned for her position in Manchuria. Consequently, when Li Hung-chang submitted a request for advice to St. Petersburg on 26 June, Witte seized the opportunity and replied immediately to the Chinese states-man that Russia would not declare war on China and that Prince Ukhtomsky (a confidant of the Tsar frequently employed on missions of this nature) would travel to China to discuss a Manchurian settlement with Li. At the same time, Witte hurriedly placed a sum of money with the chief engineer of the Chinese Eastern railway to be used to bribe the officials of the three Manchurian provinces.[1]

This policy was thwarted by Russia's own activity. On the one hand, the Russian militarists, encouraged by General Kuropatkin, the Minister of War, displayed an aggressive attitude in north China. Admiral Alexieff, Commander of the Russian squadron in the Pacific, arrived at Taku and took over control of the Council of Admirals. He then worked to consoli-date Russia's hold on the territory between Taku and Tientsin; and in the process he appropriated the British-owned section of the Northern railway which lay in this area.[2] On the other hand, Witte was led, out of concern for the safety of his railway, to support the sending of troops into Manchuria. This overt military move incited the populace to violence and the regular Chinese troops to active resistance, and Russia forfeited any chance of coming to an agreement for neutrality over Man-churia, on a basis similar to that which Great Britain was then negotiating with the viceroys of the Yangtze.

Nevertheless, Salisbury's inquiry coincided with the depar-ture of Ukhtomsky's mission to negotiate with Li Hung-chang. Until agreement had been reached with China it was in Russia's interest to maintain the fiction of separate action, to stress the disparate nature of Russian policy upon the Chinese, and to delay a military offensive on Peking. Thus, in the initial stage of the Boxer rising, while Russian military activity

[1] Romanov, *Russia in Manchuria*, 179–80.

[2] This aspect is treated in greater detail in Chapter XI below. Malozemoff states (*Russian Far Eastern Policy*, 127) that Alexieff telegraphed Yu Lu, viceroy of Chihli, advising him to block the movement of foreign troops from Tientsin to Peking. No corroborative evidence has been uncovered to support this extreme view.

displayed an aggressiveness and rapacity second to none, Russian diplomacy remained consistently on the defensive both in relation to China and to the other powers. Salisbury's proposal for the use of Japanese troops had therefore to be deflected without giving offence, and the Russian reply received in London was skilfully phrased:

We can only highly appreciate the sentiments expressed by Japan under (the) present circumstances as also her view of Chinese affairs. We have no desire to seek to hinder her liberty of action, particularly after her expression of a firm intention to conform her action to that of the other Powers. . . .[1]

Germany's response to Salisbury's suggestion was even more unsatisfactory. Instead of using her good offices with Russia she deliberately sought to create Anglo-Russian friction by assuming that Salisbury's proposal was in effect a British attempt to secure a separate mandate of action for Japan. While Russia had veiled her refusal, Germany's was openly expressed, with a deliberate misinterpretation which offended Salisbury deeply:

They are not informed as to the particulars of the proposed Japanese intervention [the reply ran] and cannot judge whether it would leave the interests of third Powers untouched, nor whether Germany can undertake responsibility of supporting it. Only by preserving the accord hitherto maintained among the Powers can order be restored in China, and the existence of that Empire and of the peace in the world be continued. Thus Germany would only take part in the steps proposed by Her Majesty's Government if she, from the outset, entertained the certainty that they could not endanger the above-mentioned indispensable accord.[2]

The reply was withheld until Russia had made her views known; and in this timing, of which Salisbury was aware, was a deliberate attempt to win favour at St. Petersburg. On 19 June a premature report of the murder of Baron von Ketteler, the German minister at Peking, had arrived in Europe.[3] The Kaiser had then expressed himself strongly in favour of immediate reprisals, and had called for the mobilization of the marine infantry to raze Peking to the ground. Count von Bulow, the

[1] Scott to Salisbury, tel. 58 of 28 June 1900, F.O. 65/1604.
[2] Gough to Salisbury, tel. 10 of 1 July 1900, copy, Adm. 116/117.
[3] The curious premature report of von Ketteler's death is discussed in Morse, *International Relations*, iii. 224.

German Minister for Foreign Affairs, had then exerted himself to persuade Wilhelm II to adopt a more cautious approach and to wait until Anglo-Japanese and Franco-Russian antagonism had emerged sufficiently to ensure that the chief command in any joint punitive expedition should pass to neutral Germany.[1] This advice was in accordance with the political philosophy, at the time, of both von Bulow and Count von Holstein, the *eminence grise* of the German Foreign Office: that if Germany maintained a position independent of both Russia and Great Britain, the growing tension between these two great powers would cause them to neutralize one another, leaving a decisive control of affairs in the hands of Germany.[2] While this was the goal of German statesmen, the exigencies of Germany's European situation fostered a sensitive awareness of Russian displeasure. The result was that, from a British perspective, their policy was all too frequently moulded to that of their eastern neighbour; in tow, *à la remorque* as Sir Frank Lascelles, British Ambassador at Berlin, gibingly put it when he returned to Berlin after the German attitude over the use of Japanese troops had become known.[3]

It was soon apparent that Germany expected Russia to respond warmly to this evidence of harmony. Immediately after Salisbury's suggestion for the use of Japanese troops had been rejected, the authentic news of von Ketteler's death was received (2 July). Once again the Kaiser broke into an extravagant diatribe.[4] His call for immediate action was made in the expectation of a whole-hearted Russian response. In this he was disappointed. Instead, Wilhelm II's hysterical outburst was received with alarm by Russia. By the end of June the Boxer rising had spread to Manchuria and with this development the Russians were painfully aware that they had insufficient troops to safeguard their own interests, much less encourage the

[1] *Grosse Politik*, xvi. 14, 18–19; F. D. Djang, *The Diplomatic Relations between China and Germany since 1898* (Shanghai, 1936), 108–9.

[2] J. M. Goudswaard, *Some Aspects of the End of Britain's 'Splendid Isolation', 1898–1904* (Rotterdam, 1952), 31.

[3] Lascelles to Salisbury, 1 Aug. 1900, *B.D.* ii. 5–6.

[4] *Grosse Politik*, xvi. 27–8 note. The German Emperor's public speeches in relation to the Chinese crisis (2 July, when the first battalion of Marines left for China; 27 July, when further troops sailed from Bremerhaven; and 18 Aug., at Cassel, before Waldersee left) are given in L. Elkind, *The German Emperor's Speeches* (London, 1904), 313–17.

interests of others. General Kuropatkin, the Minister for War, bluntly retorted that Russia was not interested in snatching other people's chestnuts from the fire.[1] Although the remark was softened diplomatically a few days later, it was nevertheless clear to Germany that Russia's attitude was dictated by the situation in Manchuria, and that just as she was ready to discard Great Britain, Russia was ready to discard her.

The extreme stand taken by the Kaiser led to a modification of Russia's attitude over the use of Japanese troops. The Emperor's resounding speeches presaged the impending disintegration of China. In the face of this danger Russia began to modify her policy of non-participation with the other powers in favour of agreed joint action which would serve to keep the German Emperor under a certain measure of control. Consequently, at the beginning of July, Count Lamsdorff carefully intimated to Scott, the British minister at St. Petersburg, that Japanese reinforcements were welcome 'to co-operate in the common aim which all the Powers, sinking every other consideration, must exclusively set before them' and that he regarded the German Emperor's speech as 'a little too impulsive'.[2]

At this point Japan again took up the negotiations. The optimism which had led her to expect the formation of a natural anti-Russian combination had been largely dissipated under the coolness of Salisbury's response. By the beginning of July it seemed as though a policy of individual aggression were about to start in view of Germany's belligerent statements and the large number of troops Russia was rushing into Manchuria. Japan feared a possible Russian invasion of Korea.[3] She could not afford to act alone, nor could she stand aside. Consequently, unaware that Russia was also filled with anxiety, and that Lamsdorff was at that moment (4 July) advocating a similar course of action, Japan circulated a memorandum to the effect that as

the troubles in (the) North of China (were) much more deep-rooted and of far wider bearing than might appear . . . it was highly advisable that (the) Powers concerned should now exchange views as to the joint measures to be taken to meet all eventualities.[4]

[1] Romanov, *Russia in Manchuria*, 181; *Grosse Politik*, xvi. 40–2.
[2] Scott to Salisbury, tel. 61 of 4 July 1900, F.O. 65/1604.
[3] Whitehead to Salisbury, tel. 24 of 4 July 1900, F.O. 46/531.
[4] Whitehead to Salisbury, tel. 25 of 5 July 1900, copy, Adm. 116/117.

Aoki did not define the joint measures he had in mind, and this reticence led Whitehead to fail to grasp the change of front contained in the Japanese memorandum. He assumed that Aoki meant agreement for the use of Japanese troops and for a financial arrangement on the cost of the expedition.[1] In turn, this assumption misled Salisbury. If the Japanese were prepared to overcome their earlier scruples he was more than ready to meet them. By the end of June, 520 officers and 13,500 men had been landed at Taku.[2] The assembled naval authorities considered that this force was sufficient only to hold the territory between Taku and Tientsin, but that any advance beyond this would need a force of 30,000 to 40,000 men. The attack on the native city of Tientsin, planned for 3 July, was postponed for ten days on the report of 10,000 Chinese troops in the neighbourhood. Despite repeated promises of further reinforcements the contingents could not be exhorted to greater efforts, for the Seymour fiasco had led to a marked reluctance to advance beyond Tientsin. By 13 July Admiral Seymour was calmly reporting that an advance by land was not feasible 'until after the rains say early September'.[3]

The decision to delay the advance on Peking aroused deep pessimism in London. Satow felt strongly that Great Britain had followed the wrong policy over the past forty years and that 'the old gunboat policy was the best'; Sir Thomas Sanderson, Permanent Under-Secretary of State for Foreign Affairs, usually calm and fair-minded, felt that the Imperial city should be razed to the ground if any massacre had taken place.[4] But the dominant mood was a brooding sense of helplessness which encouraged the conviction that the legations were lost.[5] 'I feel quite ill at the thought of the poor MacDonalds and ladies and children', the Queen wrote Salisbury. 'It haunts me day and night.'[6] Three weeks previously the Prime Minister had refused the Queen's request for MacDonald's withdrawal and he could find no adequate words to console her. Every alternative measure

---

[1] Ibid.   [2] C.-in-C. to Admiralty, tel. 95 of 2 July 1900, Adm. 116/117.
[3] C.-in-C. to Admiralty, tel. 108 of 13 July 1900, Adm. 116/117.
[4] S.J., 3 July 1900.
[5] Hamilton to Curzon, 6 July 1900, Hamilton Papers; Chamberlain to Mrs. Chamberlain, 5 July 1900, quoted Garvin, *Chamberlain*, iii. 585; W. S. Blunt, *My Diaries*, single vol. ed. (London, 1932), 369.
[6] The Queen to Salisbury, 5 July 1900, S.P. 83/165.

by which the legations could be saved had already been explored, apparently without success.

One proposal was to threaten the destruction of the Imperial Mausolea, the dynastic tombs of the Emperors, much revered by the Chinese. This step, which recalls the drastic action taken by Elgin in 1860, was first proposed by Carles, the British consul at Tientsin, on 26 June.[1] When it was taken up in the chancelleries of Europe it was pressed avidly by Germany in the face of persistent British reluctance. Although Eckardstein in London attempted to preserve German decorum by emphasizing Germany's reluctance and by stressing that she would only try it as a 'last extremity'.[2] Baron Richthofen, German Under-Secretary of State for Foreign Affairs, was more outspoken in Berlin and bluntly asked Viscount Gough, the British chargé d'affaires, whether Great Britain had a better measure to propose which would have an immediate effect 'and whether it would not be assuming a great responsibility to refuse (a) proposal made unanimously by (the) best informed persons on the spot'.[3]

Lord Salisbury's declared reasons for opposing the measure were threefold: (1) that the opinion of the army and naval commanders was unknown, (2) that the Mausolea were situated in Manchuria, thus an expedition of considerable strength would be needed to accomplish the task, and (3) that he was unable to sanction a measure so offensive to European opinion unless it were recommended on much stronger authority than that of the consular corps at Tientsin. 'The threat', he concluded, 'appears very unlikely to have any effect upon a riotous mob or upon a mutinous soldiery, and these are the factors which make the situation of the legations so perilous.'[4]

Of the three reasons, two were not valid. When reporting the proposal Carles had stressed that he had Admiral Seymour's approval, while the tombs suggested were not the western Mausolea near Mukden but the eastern tombs near Peking. Salisbury was guided by a natural repugnance to the measure, in which the sharp criticism which arose when Kitchener

---

[1] Carles to Salisbury, tel. 22 of 26 June 1900, F.O. 17/1429. On Elgin's action see Costin, *Great Britain and China*, 332–7.

[2] Memorandum by Sanderson of 2 July 1900, F.O. 17/1441.

[3] Gough to Salisbury, tel. 11 of 2 July 1900, copy, Adm. 116/117.

[4] Salisbury to Gough, tel. 77 of 2 July 1900, F.O. 64/1496.

destroyed the Mahdi's tomb after taking Khartoum may not have been without effect. Another possible deterrent was the prospect of complications with Russia and France, for Baron Whettnall, the Belgian minister, had promptly presented himself at the Foreign Office, as a 'stalking horse' for Russia and France (for so he appeared to Sir Thomas Sanderson who saw him), to sound out Great Britain's reaction to the proposal.[1] But undoubtedly the strongest reason for Lord Salisbury's reluctance lay in his distrust of German aggressiveness.

To distract attention from this unsavoury measure Salisbury then advanced the counter-suggestion of 'a collective declaration by all the Powers that all authorities at Peking of whatever rank will be held responsible in person and property for any act of violence against the Legations'.[2] This was acceptable to France, for the idea had occurred simultaneously to M. Delcasse, the French Minister for Foreign Affairs, and to Germany, who could be relied upon to support any retaliatory measures; but it could not find support from Russia, Lamsdorff making the devious reply that it would be impossible to find any authority now in Peking 'to whom it could be delivered with good effect'.[3]

By the time the Russian view had become known the declaration had been handed to Lofenglu, the Chinese minister in London, who promised to forward it to the Court through the provincial viceroys. To a limited extent the 'declaration of guilt' served its purpose. After deliberation the provincial viceroys forwarded it to the Tsungli Yamen, where it helped to swing the Court to a more sober frame of mind, leading to the mid-July truce in the attacks on the legations.

However, these measures could not disguise the fact that the lives of the diplomatic body at Peking depended on the prompt sending of reinforcements. Consequently, when Whitehead's dispatch appeared to indicate Japan's readiness to send troops, Salisbury responded at once. Japan was the only power which could act with any hope of success in saving the legations, he replied, 'and heavy responsibility must rest with them if they

[1] Memorandum by Sanderson of 2 July 1900, F.O. 17/1441.
[2] Salisbury to Gough, tel. 78 of 2 July 1900, F.O. 64/1496.
[3] Scott to Salisbury, tel. 62 of 7 July 1900; Gough to Salisbury, tel. 14 of 5 July 1900, copies, Adm. 116/117; memorandum by Sanderson of 4 July 1900, F.O. 17/1441.

delay'. At the same time he sought to facilitate the expedition and remove international discord by emphasizing a sharp distinction between 'immediate operations which may yet save the legations and any ulterior operations. All questions as to the latter may be left to the future.' He also stressed that Great Britain would provide any financial assistance which was necessary.[1] The prospect of reaching international agreement on the basis of this distinction grew in Salisbury's mind after the sending of this telegram and later in the day (6 July) again he telegraphed Whitehead to repeat that Great Britain would undertake the financial responsibility 'because international negotiations on the point would involve a fatal expenditure of time'.[2] Further, to secure European consent, he circularized this latest British suggestion to the powers.[3]

The overture was as brusquely treated as the first. The other powers were still concerned with possible political groupings and with their positions in relation to a possible territorial partition of China. M. Paul Cambon, the French Ambassador in London, was reported through St. Petersburg as saying that Great Britain had declared she would only operate with Japanese troops; and although this was immediately denied, the sting of the allegation remained.[4] Further, on the assumption that Great Britain may have said one thing while meaning another, Japan made discreet inquiries of the form the British offer of financial assistance would take.[5] When Salisbury abruptly replied that one million pounds sterling would be provided to cover the cost of providing 20,000 additional troops for the sole purpose of relieving the legations and not for any other operations, equally abruptly Aoki returned that it was not opportune to send further troops 'as no combined plan of campaign has been agreed upon'.[6]

---

[1] Salisbury to Whitehead, tel. 58 of 6 July 1900, F.O. 46/530.

[2] Salisbury to Whitehead, tel. 60 of 6 July 1900, F.O. 46/530. The telegram was actually sent off by Balfour, Salisbury having gone to a levee.

[3] Salisbury to Monson, tel. 101 of 6 July 1900; Salisbury to Scott, tel. 98 of 6 July 1900, copies, Adm. 116/117. There is no evidence of a similar communication to Germany, but the telegram may have been misplaced, as were those to France and Russia, which were located in the Admiralty files.

[4] Scott to Salisbury, tel. 63 of 8 July; Salisbury to Scott, tel. 102 of 9 July; Scott to Salisbury, tel. 66 of 10 July 1900, Adm. 116/117.

[5] Whitehead to Salisbury, tel. 31, confidential, of 11 July 1900, Adm. 116/117.

[6] Salisbury to Whitehead, tel. 68 of 12 July 1900, copy, Adm. 116/117; tel. 70

This exchange led to a rawness in Anglo-Japanese relations which took some time to heal. Later it was revealed that the Japanese had been much hurt by the purely financial offer of assistance Great Britain had proposed.

International Recognition of Chinese Territorial Integrity

By the first week of July, the negotiations on Lord Salisbury's proposal for the use of Japanese troops had made it clear that an international understanding would have to be reached before troops sufficient in number to satisfy the military commanders at Taku could be allowed in. Such an agreement, short of arranging the partition of China, could only be in the nature of a declaration by each power of its attitude toward China. In this the lead was given from a wholly unexpected quarter. On 3 July the United States sent out a circular note proclaiming that she did not consider herself at war with China and that the territorial integrity of China should be preserved.[1]

The circular has become noted as the second and more important of the Open Door notes and has subsequently been held up as a triumph of American diplomacy. But its importance must not be overstressed. At the time Lord Salisbury was concerned with practical measures which would facilitate the relief of the legations, not with declarations of principle on the territorial integrity of China. Much of Hay's message went disregarded. In his report to the Queen, Salisbury said that the United States 'still decline to regard the situation as that of war with China' and that Joseph Choate, the United States Ambassador at London, 'regards the condition of Pekin as one of anarchy whereby power and responsibility practically devolved on the local provincial authorities. It seems to me', Salisbury concluded, 'that we should maintain a similar attitude.'[2]

The question of the territorial integrity of China was taken up at this time by the British Cabinet, but not on the American note. On the evening of the next day (6 July) Lofenglu communicated a proposal from Li Hung-chang to the effect that the powers should agree to a guarantee of Chinese territorial

of 13 July 1900, F.O. 46/530; Whitehead to Salisbury, tel. 33 of 14 July 1900, copy, Adm. 116/117.

[1] *Foreign Relations*, 1901, App., p. 12.
[2] Salisbury to the Queen, 5 July 1900, S.P. 84/116.

integrity, or a 'self-denying ordinance'. Li had thoughtfully added the vital information that Russia had already expressed her consent. Salisbury immediately stated that the 'policy apparently pursued by Russia was entirely in harmony with the principles and objects of this country' and promised to lay the matter before his colleagues. The proposal, which was circulated to the whole Cabinet, was slow in making the rounds and by 10 July had not been seen by the majority. The only outstanding observation was appended by Lord Lansdowne, the Minister of War, who presumed that 'any assurance would depend on the conduct of the Chinese Government (if there is such a thing) during the present crisis'. Most of the Cabinet supported this suggestion. The Duke of Devonshire, Lord President of the Council, confused the origin of the communication, and thereby explained the general interest with which the overture had been received, when he wrote that a more substantive source than the Chinese minister should be obtained for the Russian proposal.[1]

Li Hung-chang's proposal may well have had its origin in St. Petersburg, though there is no evidence to support this view. By this time Russia was anxious to come to a basis of agreement in China. It was not to Lamsdorff's liking that while Russia was occupied in Manchuria, Japan should be encouraged by Great Britain on the one hand, while Germany engaged in extensive preparations for a military expedition on the other. Russia was unaware of the purely pecuniary nature of the British offer of assistance toward the use of Japanese troops. A separate mandate of action for Japan might allow her exclusive claims in a future indemnity and, at this stage, it had not been established that the indemnity claims were not to be of a territorial nature. Li's self-denying ordinance might well have been seized on by Russia had it not coincided with Hay's circular note. This was a much more satisfactory opening for Lamsdorff's purpose, as it would allow Russia to clarify her position in the form of a reply. Consequently, on 13 July a Russian note was presented at the Foreign Office defining Russian objectives in China as the preservation of the lives and property of Europeans, the relief of the legations and the maintenance of the integrity of China.[2]

---

[1] See the minutes appended to Salisbury's circular, S.P. 89/68.
[2] Salisbury to Scott, tel. 107 of 15 July 1900, F.O. 65/1603.

It was clear that Russia's action hinged on her fear of Salisbury's plan to use Japanese troops. On 16 July Choate stated that Count Cassini, the Russian minister at Washington, had specifically asked Hay whether the United States had joined in giving any directions to Japan. On 19 July it was revealed through the French chargé d'affaires in London that the Russian note to France of 14 July had displayed a similar anxiety over possible exclusive Japanese claims for the use of her troops. Sanderson observed, 'it rather intimated that we had suggested some special arrangement for Japan—which was a misconception for we had not done so'.[1] Rather than have Japan placed in such an advantageous position, Russia was prepared to call for the integrity of China. Later, when her own hold on Manchuria seemed assured, this declaration was to be used with effect against her. From this point of view Lord Salisbury's otherwise abortive overture for the use of Japanese troops bore valuable fruit.

The Appointment of the Chief Command

Recognition of the territorial integrity of China marked the end of the first phase of diplomatic activity between the powers in relation to the Boxer rising. It resulted from jealousy and the fear of international complications, the factors which had brought Salisbury's efforts to a grinding halt. Nevertheless, only lip-service was paid to the declarations so gravely handed round the chancelleries of Europe. While denying what Salisbury had called for openly, the powers rushed to northern China all their available troops. At the same time, a genuine concern for the safety of the beleagued foreigners in Peking stirred European opinion. It was reported that the Pope was ready to encourage a crusade.[2] The burgomasters of Brussels, Ghent, Liege, and Antwerp called for donations to finance a corps of volunteers.[3] The result of this activity was that during July a sizeable body of international troops was gathered at Taku. On 14 July the native city of Tientsin was taken. This

---

[1] Memoranda by Sanderson of 16 and 20 July 1900, French text and reply enclosed, F.O. 17/1442.

[2] Sir H. Drummond Wolff (Madrid), tel. 42, very confidential, of 18 July 1900, copy, Adm. 116/117.

[3] Memorandum by Sanderson of 26 July 1900, F.O. 17/1443.

success then encouraged the allied commanders to draw up tentative plans for an advance on Peking on or about 1 August.[1] This mounting offensive brought the delicate question of the chief command of this international force to the forefront of the diplomatic scene.

The question of the chief command had been a matter of anxiety in London since the beginning of the crisis. It has been noticed that Vice-Admiral Seymour's decision to lead the naval contingents to Peking in person gave Russia seniority of command at Taku, at first under Vice-Admiral Hildebrandt and then under Vice-Admiral Alexieff.[2] In the excitement of the initial stages, the other naval commanders had readily acquiesced in this situation. Rear-Admiral Bruce, in command of the British squadron after Seymour's departure, even suggested to the Admiralty that as the Council of Admirals which had been formed at Taku was under a Russian president, the officer commanding land forces should also belong to the same nation 'in order to avoid opportunities of friction'.[3]

Bruce's enthusiasm was not shared in London. Questions had been asked in the House which Brodrick and Balfour had difficulty in answering.[4] After Seymour's return to Taku, Alexieff had remained in command although he was two years junior in rank to Seymour. On 2 July the Admiralty tentatively inquired of Seymour whether the Russian held local rank and whether the question of the chief command had been raised at Taku.[5]

After making inquiries Seymour discovered that he had been misinformed. Alexieff did hold local rank, but of a military and civil standing, while in naval matters Seymour was still superior. The issue was too delicate to be raised locally and Seymour referred it back for Cabinet decision.[6]

By this time the question of the chief command had been raised by the other powers in connection with Salisbury's

[1] Dairy of the Tientsin–Peking operations, P.R.O. 30/33/7/11. Brigadier-General Dorward's reports of the advance from Taku and the capture of Tientsin are given 11 and 19 July 1900, C.O. 521/1, War.
[2] See above, pp. 120–2.
[3] Rear-Admiral Bruce to Admiralty, tel. 5 of 23 June 1900, Adm. 116/117.
[4] *Parliamentary Debates*, lxxxiv. 205, 628–9; lxxxv. 1305.
[5] Admiralty to C.-in-C. tel. 88 of 2 July 1900, Adm. 116/117.
[6] Seymour to Admiralty, tel. (unnumbered) and tel. 108 of 13 July 1900 Adm. 116/117.

suggestion of the use of Japanese troops. In rejecting the request Aoki had questioned the expediency of Alexieff, a naval officer, having supreme command of the allied forces and had expressed the hope to Whitehead that an English or German general of senior standing would be sent to China.[1] Discussion was then helped on by the coincidence of Russian anxiety over a separate mandate of action for the Japanese. On 11 July Lamsdorff informally suggested to Scott at St. Petersburg the need for 'some sort of agreement which would secure united action and direction in any large combined effort'.[2] Two days later, in the communication relating to Chinese territorial integrity, Russia stressed that she considered it a matter of urgency that an immediate positive understanding concerning the ulterior military measures necessary in China should be arranged. This should also cover the question of the unity of action of all the international detachments on Chinese territory. In this respect Russia suggested 'the concentration in one single hand' of the general command and direction of all the detachments.[3]

The Russian communication coincided with the final breakdown of the negotiations for the use of Japanese troops. It also coincided with the taking of Tientsin by the allied contingents already in north China. It will be seen that this military advance aroused the apprehension of the foreign community in Shanghai, who feared retaliatory measures by the Chinese in the Yangtze area to divert foreign pressure from Peking.[4] Within a few days the hysterical mood prevalent at Shanghai led to a report from that city that the entire diplomatic body in Peking had been massacred. This was believed in London and on 17 July the obituaries of MacDonald, Hart, and Morrison were published in *The Times*. Thereafter Salisbury withdrew; throughout the remainder of the month his conduct of policy was listless and aloof. It was during this period that Salisbury's political reputation suffered, as his persistent inaction aroused the exasperation of his colleagues. At the root of this mood lay his disillusion with the political machinations which had so

---

[1] Whitehead to Salisbury, tel. 28 of 8 July 1900, copy, Adm. 116/117.
[2] Scott to Salisbury, tel. 67 of 11 July 1900, F.O. 65/1604.
[3] Salisbury to Scott, tel. 107 of 15 July 1900, F.O. 65/1603.
[4] See below, p. 169.

obviously sealed the fate of the foreign community in Peking. Only at the end of the month, when it became clear that the legations were still holding out, did he spring again into life. Lord George Hamilton, a vigorous critic of Salisbury's indecision, wrote on 3 August that the Cabinet meetings were then becoming more satisfactory. 'I think I am now able to fathom the Prime Minister's mind', he confided to Curzon. 'He believed the legations to have been massacred and did not want to use British troops to extend Russian and German influence; but (he) acted as soon as he heard the legations were safe.'[1]

Thus it was in this mood, in the belief that the legations were already lost, that Salisbury had to turn during the latter part of July to the question of the appointment of the chief command. Any arrangement would only further the political ambitions of the powers, and Salisbury could show no enthusiasm for placing British troops under foreign control to carry out measures of political reprisal. Moreover, if the establishment of the chief command were not to be by seniority of rank or on a numerical basis, it would be by invitation from the powers. There was little likelihood of Great Britain securing the appointment. Instead, by a process of elimination it seemed likely that Germany would secure the nomination. Prince Henry, who had travelled in the east, was the most promising candidate. Hamilton, who did not share Salisbury's distrust of Germany, suggested him as 'a good fellow and very friendly to us'.[2] The Prime Minister was not impressed. On 18 July Eckardstein went to Eric Barrington, Salisbury's private secretary, and 'talked mysteriously' about intrigues against Great Britain in the Far East, of 'how Russia was trying to frighten Europe about the awful possibilities of an Anglo-Japanese "terror"' and of a possible revival of the triple *entente*. Having prepared the ground Eckardstein revealed the reason for his visit: France, he said, was about to propose a German commander but the Kaiser would be 'gratified beyond anything' if England would forestall the other powers with the proposal.[3] Although Eckardstein gave this as his own opinion, he had clearly been prompted by the Kaiser.

[1] Hamilton to Curzon, 3 Aug. 1900, Hamilton Papers.
[2] Hamilton to Salisbury, 16 July 1900, S.P. unclassified.
[3] Memorandum, Barrington to Salisbury, 18 July 1900, S.P. 122/87.

Against this background of growing intrigue and thrusting opportunism the Cabinet met on 19 July to consider the Russian communication. It was to be expected that Salisbury should consider the Russian suggestion with critical reserve. Lamsdorff's use of the phrases 'ulterior military measures' and 'single hand' were questioned. Salisbury personally drafted a telegram to Scott to find out the Russian view of how a single commander was to be chosen and of the nature, scope, and object of the military operations contemplated. This cool response put Lamsdorff on the defensive and in reply he stated that Russia's only object had been to clear herself of the charges made in the Press that she had hesitated to accept the assistance of Japan.[1] Thereafter negotiations were dropped.

Salisbury's coldness placed the Germans at a loss. The Kaiser was desperately anxious to secure the chief command. Prestige was an obvious motive; a second consideration was the desire to secure European approval of the German expeditionary force then being assembled. At the end of July events moved in the Kaiser's favour. Shortly before the expedition sailed it became known that the legations were still standing. Wilhelm II was given a pretext for prompt action which was difficult to refute. To secure his aim he tried a personal approach, for the Kaiser was a firm believer in the continued control of affairs by royalty. On 31 July he wrote to the Prince of Wales to express his elation at the successful send-off given to the German troops. As Eckardstein's earlier tactic had obviously produced the wrong effect, the Kaiser carefully stressed the absence of a Russo-German alliance and expressed his regret that the Prince thought Great Britain and Germany could not pull together.[2]

With Russia the Kaiser had more success. While discussing the matter of a single commander-in-chief, General Kuropatkin made the chance remark that if Prince Henry of Prussia had still been in China, or if General Liegnitz, who had been popular with the Russians during the Russo-Turkish war, had been on the spot, he would have recommended that Russian

[1] Salisbury to Scott, tel. 109 of 20 July 1900, F.O. 65/1603; Scott to Salisbury, tel. 73 of 22 July 1900, F.O. 65/1604.
[2] Kaiser to Prince of Wales, 31 July 1900, S.P. 86/26. Hatzfeldt had reported that Salisbury had indicated Britain could act without a unified command, *Grosse Politik*, xvi. 75–6.

troops be placed under their command. This was reported to the Kaiser, who seized on the opening and on 5 August made a direct approach to Nicholas II suggesting the appointment of Field-Marshal Waldersee. The move was successful for the Tsar impulsively gave his consent.[1]

Waldersee's appointment was announced by the Kaiser as soon as the Tsar's reply was received. It now became necessary for the German Foreign Office to smooth over the Kaiser's action diplomatically to secure the concurrence of Great Britain and France. On 7 August Herr von Derenthall, German acting Under-Secretary of State for Foreign Affairs, handed a *note verbale* to Lascelles which intimated that Russia had invited the nomination of the German Field-Marshal; at the same time he expressed his conviction that France must have agreed previously to this Russian move. However, the Austrian chargé d'affaires, Count Thuin, had caught a glimpse of Nicholas II's telegram while it was in the Kaiser's hand and the origin of the overture was obvious.[2]

Several of the Cabinet met to consider the situation on 9 August. There was a strong feeling that Great Britain was being hustled into acquiescence. But Bertie had observed that if Britain did not accept the situation the Kaiser would make it a pretext to renew the triple *entente* against Great Britain in China. He also argued that by the time Waldersee got to Tientsin the Peking campaign should be over, which would make the appointment of less critical importance.[3]

These considerations, and the obvious need for continuing the advance on Peking, decided the Cabinet, which agreed after much discussion to accept a German commander-in-chief 'if the Powers who have forces in Pechili determine to put those forces under the supreme direction (the phrase general command was rejected) of Count Waldersee'. Salisbury reported to the Queen, 'It is a case in which there are serious objections both to accepting and refusing.'[4]

---

[1] Scott to Salisbury, No. 262 of 13 Aug. 1900 (received 27 Aug.), copy, Adm. 116/118, Section XVI; *Grosse Politik*, xvi. 82 n.–83.

[2] Lascelles to Salisbury, tel. 20 of 7 Aug., tel. 21, secret, of 8 Aug. 1900, F.O. 64/1496; Lascelles to Salisbury, private, of 10 Aug. 1900, S.P. 121/60.

[3] Bertie to Salisbury, encl. in Lascelles to Salisbury, tel. 20 of 7 Aug. 1900, F.O. 64/1496.

[4] Salisbury to the Queen, 9 Aug. 1900, S.P. 84/117–18; Salisbury to Lascelles tel. 117 of 9 Aug. 1900, F.O. 64/1496.

The doubt felt in London was shared in St. Petersburg. Lamsdorff reasoned with Scott that it would take a month for Waldersee to get to China and that when he did his command could be confined to the single province of Chihli. Lamsdorff was following a line of reasoning that had occurred to Bertie, but he was completely misunderstood by the British Ambassador, who had persistently failed to notice the change in Russian policy after the Kaiser's belligerent speeches. Consequently Scott interpreted Lamsdorff's remarks as indicating Kuropatkin's desire to hold the chief command himself and that the appointment of Waldersee 'looks like an attempt to renew the Triple Alliance of the Treaty of Shimonoseki'.[1]

In reality Lamsdorff was busy unravelling the consequences of Nicholas II's impulsive response. Russian strength in the Far East owed much to the Dual Alliance. By direct loans to Russia, and indirectly by the Russo-Chinese Bank, Russia had been bolstered by French finance, but France was getting little return for this outlay. Russia had shown reserve over Egypt; in China there was a similar lack of co-operation. Nicholas II's response to the Kaiser added further grit to the smooth-running of Franco-Russian relations. Derenthall's assumption that Russia had only responded after prior French approval was a justifiable surmise, but unfounded. When Sir Edward Monson, the British Ambassador at Paris, approached Delcasse on 9 August the latter replied tartly that he knew only what had been reported in the Press.[2]

When the French realized the full implications of the slight, they showed considerable irritation. In fact, they had hoped for the chief command for themselves and in mid-July when the issue was quite fluid they had openly revealed their ambition in unofficial quarters. Initially, they hoped that Seymour would be recalled through illness and that the French Admiral Pottier would then succeed to the command.[3] When the question of the chief command moved from seniority in the Council of Admirals to a direct military appointment, the candidature of General Dodds was rumoured. Dodds had a high military

[1] Scott to Salisbury, 9 Aug. 1900, S.P. 129/84.
[2] Monson to Salisbury, tel. 60 of 9 Aug. 1900, F.O. 27/3499.
[3] This was Pottier's personal ambition, revealed to Admiral Caneraro. Cf. C.-in-C., Mediterranean, to Admiralty, tel. 386 of 18 July 1900, Adm. 116/118, Case 266, vol. 5.

reputation and it was believed by observers that he had not been appointed to the command of the French contingent which had been sent to China so that he could be reserved for the supreme command.[1]

When the French showed their peevishness over the appointment of Waldersee, Lamsdorff tried to get out of the difficulty in which he had been placed by stressing that the original proposal had merely offered Waldersee for the general direction and command of international operations in Chihli. He argued that if this interpretation were emphasized it would facilitate acceptance by the French. In a further attempt to hide France's wounded pride behind a constitutional shield, he admitted the difficulty the French would have in obtaining sanction of the Chambers for placing French troops under a foreign command.[2]

The French answer to Waldersee's appointment was given understandably late. No unwillingness to conform to the example set by the other powers was indicated, but the French implied that their consent was based exclusively upon acknowledged considerations of military etiquette. After Waldersee had arrived in China, the French reply ran:

> . . . and shall have taken in the Councils of the Commanders of the International Corps d'Armée the eminent position due to his superior rank, General Voyron, the Commander of the French Expeditionary Corps will not fail to place his relations with the Marshal upon a proper footing (ne manquera pas d'assurer ses relations avec le Marechal).[3]

The reserve shown by France could not dampen the Kaiser's elation. A special request was made to the Prince of Wales for a staff officer to serve under Waldersee; but this mark of gratitude was dwarfed by the gesture made to Russia; the commander of the German contingent in China was ordered to place himself under the orders of the senior Russian general until Waldersee's arrival.[4]

---

[1] Memorandum Cartwright, 16 July 1900, F.O. 17/1442.
[2] Scott to Salisbury, tel. 88 of 14 Aug. 1900, F.O. 65/1604.
[3] Monson to Salisbury, No. 425 of 17 Aug. 1900, copy, Adm. 116/118, Section XVI.
[4] Salisbury to Lascelles, tel. 122 of 11 Aug. 1900; Lascelles to Salisbury, tel. 27 of 13 Aug. 1900, F.O. 64/1496.

This enthusiasm was not shared. The other powers felt strongly that they had been tricked into the appointment. It will be seen that the combined command failed to achieve any degree of coherence. From the beginning, Waldersee's authority was hedged with reservations. The most significant of these was that his control was confined to the province of Chihli. By the time the Field-Marshal reached China the bulk of the Chinese forces had been withdrawn beyond the boundaries of that province and the restricted position in which he found himself rapidly dissipated Waldersee's enthusiasm. Even before he sailed it was anticipated that his headquarters staff would be riddled with intrigue. The British officer seconded to this duty should have been drawn normally from the forces in India, but it was recognized that any such officer would have been able to join Waldersee only at Singapore, by which time 'the officers on his staff would have formed themselves into cliques' so an appointment was made from England. Moreover, Salisbury deliberately warned against the choice of a 'philo-German' which would have facilitated the formation of a European combination against Great Britain in the east.[1] Aboard ship, while on the way to China, Engalitscheff, the Russian staff officer, declared openly that Waldersee had only been appointed for the combined movement on Peking and as by that time the city had been taken he was no longer commander-in-chief of the Russian forces. To emphasize his point, Engalitscheff consistently refused to wear his uniform.[2] After his arrival Waldersee exercised little real control. The French and Russians ignored him, the Japanese barely tolerated him, the Americans thought him amusing. General Gaselee, in command of the British contingent, was given careful instructions on his attitude to Waldersee. Command of British troops was to rest always with Gaselee, although their special sphere of action or their part in a particular operation could be decided by the Field-Marshal. All orders to British troops were to be given only through their own officers. The British were to maintain their own control of supplies. Orders might suitably be prefaced 'at the request of Count Waldersee . . .' but not 'by order

[1] Hamilton to Salisbury, 12 Aug. 1900, S.P. 91/44.
[2] Grierson (the British staff officer) to Sir William Everett, 10 Sept. 1900, encl. Intelligence Division to Foreign Office, 15 Oct. 1900, F.O. 17/1448.

of . . .'. Gaselee's own military views were always to be stated frankly.[1]

Waldersee was to realize the effect of these precautions after his arrival, but even before he left Europe he was to experience a great disappointment. It has been noticed that after the taking of Tientsin on 14 July the allied commanders decided to move on Peking at the beginning of August. Chinese resistance was concentrated in two desperate stands in the battles of Yangts'un (6 August) and Hosiwu (9 August). The resultant defeat and deaths of Yu Lu, the Viceroy of Chihli province, and of Li Ping-heng, the last of the Boxer adherents with any military ability, left Peking open to attack. Led by the Japanese contingent, the allied forces moved along the road to Peking, until by 12 August the walled city of Tungchow, fifteen miles from Peking, had been occupied. Here a brief halt was called while the rear contingents of the allied column came up, for by this time some of the units were practically a day's march behind the Japanese force. A concerted attack on Peking was planned for 15 August.[2]

Meanwhile, frantic efforts for a truce were initiated by the Chinese Government through Li Hung-chang. The Chinese minister in London was instructed to communicate an Imperial Edict for the safe conduct of the legations to Tientsin. To this Li added the further plea that Salisbury should take the lead in mediating an early settlement. The elaborate preparations being made in Europe had not been lost on the Chinese. Salisbury could make his own conditions Lofenglu told Bertie, such as the removal of the anti-foreign faction 'not excepting even the Empress Dowager'. The Chinese minister then concluded with delightful Chinese logic which nevertheless betrayed the real apprehension of the Chinese, 'Lord Salisbury's superiority in age to the German Emperor entitled him to treat His Majesty as a boy who required restraint and if Lord Salisbury took the lead the other powers would follow'.[3]

---

[1] The correspondence on the appointment of Gaselee is given in Adm. 116/118, Section XVI, Case 266, vol. 5; Draft Instructions, 2 Aug. 1900, F.O. 17/1443; India Office to Sir A. Gaselee, tel. 18 of 5 Oct. 1900, F.O. 17/1448.

[2] Diary of the Tientsin–Peking operations, P.R.O. 30/33/7/11. Various accounts written by participants are given in the Bibliography.

[3] Memorandum to Bertie on a conversation with Lofenglu, 8 Aug. 1900, F.O. 17/1435.

Li Hung-chang's request for British mediation was flattering but unpractical; the suggestion of a truce, however, was explored. Responsible military opinion had stressed the adverse effect to be expected if an advance on Peking were made with insufficient force, and it was felt that a protracted siege would mean the massacre of all the foreigners within the city.[1] But when MacDonald was approached through Chinese channels he declared flatly that a Chinese escort was not to be trusted to conduct the diplomatic body out of Peking, and while a solution was being sought to this objection, a competitive rush led by the Russians was made on the Chinese capital by the assembled contingents at Tungchow. On 14 August the legations were relieved.[2]

Five days later Waldersee left to take up the chief command. By that time attention in Europe had swerved to the Yangtze, and a diplomatic crisis had developed over the British occupation of Shanghai.

[1] 'D.M.I. Assessment of the situation in China', Ardagh's Memorandum 66 of 15 Aug. 1900, P.R.O. 30/40/14, Pt. 2.
[2] Diary of the Tientsin–Peking operations, P.R.O. 30/33/7/11.

VII

GREAT BRITAIN AND THE YANGTZE

ALTHOUGH by 1900 Boxer activity was concentrated in the Metropolitan province of Chihli, it had been noted that the anti-foreign unrest which had led to the movement was also present in other parts of the country which foreign influence had permeated. In June, when the Court began to support the Boxers, it became possible that the various provincial officials would obey the flow of edicts urging them to anti-foreign activity, and encourage the nascent unrest within their jurisdictions, leading to a general outbreak all over the country. The Council of Admirals at Taku had tried to prevent this by stressing in their proclamation of 20 June that their measures were directed specifically against the Boxers, not the Chinese people. In general, however, the attitude of the provincial authorities depended on the extent of their personal antipathy to the foreigner, on the proximity of their provinces to the capital, and on the behaviour of the foreign powers active within their jurisdictions.

Thus the violent xenophobe Yu Hsien participated zealously in the movement and massacred the missionaries of Shansi. Yüan Shih-k'ai, on the other hand, displayed the political acumen which was to raise him to the presidency in the early Republican period, and maintained a rigid neutrality in Shantung. In Manchuria, the Russian authorities carried out a military occupation of the country as a precautionary measure, which aroused the populace. However, the extent of the rising in north China really depended on the attitude of officials of the central and southern provinces.

The major officials concerned were Liu K'un-i, Viceroy at Nanking, Chang Chih-tung, Viceroy at Hankow, and Li Hungchang, Viceroy at Canton. These men, with Yüan Shih-k'ai, exercised sufficient authority to ensure that their decision would be obeyed by all the lesser provincial officials whose reason had not been swamped by the xenophobia raised by the Boxers.

Li Hung-chang was the most senior of these officials; but in the early stages of the rising Li adopted a policy of cautious reserve and procrastinated at Canton despite the repeated injunctions of the Chinese Government for his attendance at Court. The decision thus devolved on Chang Chih-tung and Liu K'un-i at Hankow and Nanking. As the Yangtze was a British sphere of interest the attitude of the viceroys was a matter of direct concern to Great Britain. Consequently, Pelham Warren, the British acting consul-general at Shanghai, assumed control of the negotiations with the Chinese authorities. Valdez, the senior ranking Portuguese consul-general, was swept into the background by the urgency of the situation.

The Neutralization of the Yangtze

The possibility of securing the neutrality of the Yangtze occurred to Warren as soon as the landing of Seymour's force was known. 'I am convinced that we ought to arrive at an early understanding with the Viceroys at Nanking and Hankow', he telegraphed to Salisbury on 14 June. 'If they are assured of the effective support of H.M. Government, I feel certain they will do their utmost to keep peace in their districts.' Warren suggested that Great Britain should offer naval aid to the Yangtze viceroys.[1]

It will be remembered that the position on the Yangtze was already a matter of concern in London and that on 13 June the Admiralty had been instructed to anticipate any foreign interference in the area. Consequently Warren's suggestion was welcomed in London, for it arrived at the same time as a report that a Russian transport with a small number of troops had gone up to Hankow.[2] H.M.S. *Hermione*, a second-class cruiser, was directed to Nanking and the gunboat *Linnett* to Hankow to assure the viceroys of British support.[3] The cruiser H.M.S. *Undaunted* was ordered up from Hong Kong to Woosung, just outside Shanghai, where the bulk of the Chinese fleet was stationed. In addition, although Rear-Admiral Bruce had ordered from Taku that ships concentrated from Manila

[1] Warren to Salisbury, tel. of 14 June 1900, F.O. 17/1427.
[2] Salisbury to Warren, tels. 3 and 4 of 15 June 1900, F.O. 17/1426.
[3] Memorandum Foreign Office to Admiralty of 15 June, Adm. 116/116; Admiralty to Senior Naval Officer, Shanghai, 16 June 1900, Adm. 116/117.

M

and elsewhere should be sent to the north, contrary to these orders, units being assembled were deliberately held back in case of a flare-up over the whole of China and in order to be available for the immediate support of the Yangtze viceroys.[1]

On 16 June Sundius, the British consul at Nanking, called on Viceroy Liu K'un-i to secure his approval of these measures. Liu had recently returned from a visit to Peking and Sundius found the aged viceroy despondent and unnerved by the spread of reactionary influence in court circles. To Sundius Liu expressed the hope that after Great Britain had settled the South African war, she would turn to China and help to bring about a better state of affairs. Liu confided further that he regarded the government of the Empress Dowager as finished, and doubted his ability to keep order. Consequently he welcomed the offer of British naval protection and asked that the ships should be sent without delay. The only condition expressed by Liu was that the Kiangyin forts, which commanded Nanking, should not be taken as a *sine qua non* as that would expose his weakness and lead to disorder.[2]

Liu made this decision after an unsuccessful appeal to Li Hung-chang for leadership.[3] Telegraphic messages to the Court had remained unanswered, and it was clear that he would have to make the decision on his own responsibility. In a last attempt to secure a common basis of action with his colleagues, he telegraphed a verbatim report of his conversation with Sundius to Chang Chih-tung at Hankow. In his reply on 18 June, Chang displayed a more militant independence. He maintained that the two viceroys could keep order without foreign help and that the foreign men-of-war should be asked to leave. In conversation with Fraser, British consul at Hankow, Chang emphasized his desire for friendly relations with Great Britain, but expressed his determination to maintain peace and afford the protection due under treaty to foreign nationals through his own exertions.[4]

[1] Admiralty to Commodore, Hong Kong, 20 June 1900, Adm. 116/117.
[2] Sundius, Report to Warren of 30 Aug. 1900 in Warren to Salisbury, No. 174, of 26 Sept. 1900, F.O. 17/1425.
[3] C. C. Tan, *The Boxer Catastrophe*, 76.
[4] Fraser to Warren of 29 Aug. 1900, encl. 13 in Warren to Salisbury, No. 161 of 25 Sept. 1900, F.O. 17/1425. Chang maintained that both viceroys were of one mind as to the advisability of acting with Britain; the phrase used was 'binding themselves to England'. Fraser to Warren, No. 145 of 18 June 1900, F.O. 17/1422.

On this, Liu changed his stance and asked that ships should be reduced to a minimum. The extent to which this change of front was directed by his stronger-minded colleague was revealed in a telegram from Chang to Liu which the latter showed to Captain Cumming of H.M.S. *Hermione,* suggesting the undesirability of any foreign ships remaining in the Yangtze. Liu himself thought that two ships could be kept in the river at Nanking and Hankow. Both viceroys feared the presence of ships of other nations.[1] By this time Lofenglu, the Chinese minister in London, had also forwarded a communication deprecating any demonstration on the part of a British naval force. In view of this, the British ships at Nanking and Hankow were ordered to exercise restraint.[2]

These preliminary moves were then followed up by Warren, who wanted to establish Great Britain's control over the Yangtze region on a more substantial basis. On 19 June rumours circulated in Shanghai of an imminent move by the continental powers on the Woosung forts. To counteract this possible intrusion into the British sphere, Warren suggested to Liu that a joint Anglo-Chinese occupation of the forts should be arranged. Liu replied by asking whether, in the event of his acquiescence, Great Britain would 'be prepared to stop any ships passing, by force if necessary?'[3] Before a satisfactory answer could be found, the Yangtze was involved in the conflux of events at Peking. By 21 June alarming rumours, which alleged that Prince Tuan had killed the Emperor and driven the Empress Dowager into flight, led Liu to modify his stand. In a secret message through Sundius he stated that if Great Britain would dissuade the other foreign powers from engaging in military operations on the Yangtze, and that if the British would work with him in maintaining order, he would consent to a joint Anglo-Chinese occupation of the Yangtze forts. The details of this co-operation could be arranged between Warren and the *taotai* at Shanghai, who would be given secret instructions.[4]

[1] C.O. H.M.S. *Hermione* to Admiralty, 19 June 1900, Adm. 116/117.
[2] Foreign Office to Admiralty, draft of 20 June 1900, encl. memorandum by Chinese minister of 19 June, F.O. 17/1440. Admiralty to Senior Naval Officer, Woosung, 22 June 1900, Adm. 116/117. Lo was carrying out the wishes of the provincial viceroys, not the Court.
[3] Warren to Salisbury, No. 26 of 23 June 1900, F.O. 17/1424.
[4] Warren to Salisbury, tel. 11 of 22 June 1900, F.O. 17/1427.

This suggestion was not carried out as originally intended. Before any move could be made, news of the repulse of Seymour and the bombardment of the Taku forts filtered through to the Yangtze and caused uproar. Li Ping-heng, in command at the Kiangyin forts, let it be known that he would sink any foreign ships that came into sight. Several thousand modern-armed Chinese troops were reported at Woosung; five thousand more at Soochow to the south. The Chinese populace fled Shanghai in their thousands.[1] The consuls were driven to the posting of proclamations stating that the foreign warships on the Yangtze were only for defence.[2] Warren realized that the opportunity for a peaceful occupation of the Yangtze forts by Great Britain had been missed. On 24 June he reported that 'the time had even now gone by for carrying out joint occupation suggested by the Viceroy at Nanking unless a very strong force was present here at Woosung as otherwise the Chinese soldiers would in all probability at once attack Shanghai as in the case of Tientsin after the taking of the Taku forts'.[3]

The news from the north also had an effect on the attitude of the Chinese authorities. Apart from being impressed by the gravity of the situation they were also made aware of the Imperial proclamation of war of 20 June against the foreign powers. A feverish exchange of views then followed between the provincial viceroys to decide on a suitable course of action. Eventually, through the constructive advice of Sheng Hsüan-huai, the Chinese Director of Railways and Telegraphs, then in Shanghai, it was decided to treat the proclamation of war as a forged document issued by a usurping faction at Court. The viceroys then decided on a policy of neutrality toward the events in the north, while stressing their loyalty to the Manchu Court.[4]

Consequently, they adopted a more determined attitude toward the foreign powers. To convince the consuls at Shanghai that they had the power to negotiate, they made known to them a decree of 20 June which antedated the declaration of

[1] Warren to Salisbury, No. 27 of 28 June 1900, F.O. 17/1424.
[2] Warren to Salisbury, No. 27 of 28 June 1900, F.O. 17/1424. The proclamation is given in *Foreign Relations* (1900), 250.
[3] Warren to Salisbury, tel. 13 of 24 June 1900, F.O. 17/1427.
[4] See 'Yu-kuan tung-nan hu-pao tzu liao' (Material concerning (the policy of) mutual defence in the east and south), *I.H.T.* iii. 323–62, and the appended record given on pp. 517–39.

war and which exhorted the viceroys and governors to protect
their provinces as well as to render assistance to the capital.
The decree was genuine;[1] but in bringing it to the notice of the
foreign consuls through Drummond, legal adviser to Liu, they
implied that they regarded it 'as the testamentary command of
a dying government' which placed absolute powers in the hands
of the viceroys.[2] While preparing the ground in this way, the
viceroys turned with greater confidence to the discussions
which had been arranged between the *taotai* and the consuls at
Shanghai for 26 June.

At this meeting the Chinese presented nine articles on which
they were prepared to guarantee peace in the Yangtze. These
maintained that the consular representatives should act 'con-
jointly' with them in protecting native and foreign life and
property. Shanghai was to be protected by the powers, while
the Yangtze valley and the region to the south was to be the
responsibility of the Chinese administrators. They also stipulated that no foreign naval ships should cruise in the river or
approach the Chinese forts or arsenals. The ships of war
already at the treaty ports could remain but as a precautionary
measure, to avoid exciting the populace, they should not disembark their crews; and during the outbreak foreigners should
refrain from travelling in the interior where their protection
would be difficult.[3]

This loss of initiative was not to Warren's liking. Instead
of securing possession of the forts and thereby strengthening
Great Britain's hold on the Yangtze, he found himself expected
to agree to a limitation of foreign influence. With the support
of the other consuls he deflected the Chinese demand by
referring to the allied admirals' proclamation of 20 June. As
this stated that the powers were only fighting against Boxers, it
implied that if there were no breach of the peace by the Chinese
there would be no foreign attack.[4]

Lord Salisbury approved this action as soon as it was reported
to him.[5] Thus when the nine articles were submitted to him by

[1] Given *T.T.S.L.* 464/12a.
[2] Warren to Salisbury, tel. 19 of 29 June 1900, F.O. 17/1427.
[3] The text is in Lofenglu's communication to Salisbury of 28 June 1900, F.O.
17/1435.
[4] Warren to Salisbury, tel. 16 of 27 June 1900, F.O. 17/1427.
[5] Salisbury to Warren, tel. of 27 June 1900, F.O. 17/1426.

the Chinese minister on the following day (28 June), while applauding the excellent spirit in which the proposal had been framed, Salisbury declared the terms 'quite inadmissible' in their restriction of existing treaty rights,[1] and added further on 12 July 'that they imposed on H.M. Government duties which properly belonged to the Chinese Government, and . . . that so far as it appeared to H.M. Government expedient to execute their provisions they would gladly do so but that each case must be judged on its merits and that we could not accept them as a contract we were bound to execute'.[2] This was the extent to which formal negotiations were taken by the British Government for the neutralization of the Yangtze.

These reservations placed the viceroys in a difficult position. The Imperial declaration of war was incompatible with the admirals' proclamation. If the Manchu dynasty were still in power after the rising, their sole defence against a charge of treason would be the claim that by their action they had preserved the territorial integrity of their provinces. Without an assurance of non-intervention from the powers this stand was precarious. Consequently, throughout July the object of their diplomacy in London and in ǀShanghai was to elicit this assurance. At the same time, the urgency of the situation demanded immediate measures, and so they adopted the only sensible course and acted on the assumption that agreement had been reached.

By mid-July the consuls at the various treaty ports were reporting a reputed arrangement for the preservation of peace. A proclamation issued jointly by the Viceroy of Hankow and Governor Yu of Hupeh was posted in places as far south as Hong Kong and it may be taken as a prototype of those issued:

Arrangements have been made by us with the consuls of the various powers that the lives and property of foreigners shall be protected by local officials as long as ships of war do not come to the Yangtze. Pekin has been notified by telegram of this Agreement.[3]

Instructions issued by Liu modified this arrangement slightly to cover the tacit agreement with Captain Cumming of H.M.S.

[1] Minute on Lofenglu to Salisbury of 28 June 1900, F.O. 17/1435.
[2] Salisbury to Warren, tel. 21 of 12 July 1900, F.O. 17/1426.
[3] Governor Blake (Hong Kong) to Colonial Office, tel. of 10 July 1900 in Colonial Office to Foreign Office, 11 July 1900, F.O. 17/1441.

Hermione allowing one British ship at each treaty port, with one or two additional ships cruising on the river. But Chinese determination not to concede more than this was evident. When the *Linnet* and the *Woodcock* arrived simultaneously at Kiukiang on 7 July, the *chentai* lodged an immediate complaint, stating that he was acting on orders from Nanking.

The officials appear imbued with the idea [Acting-Consul Clennell noted], that an Agreement exists under which our Government undertakes not to enter the Yangtze in force or to occupy Wusung [*sic*], and have expressed themselves several times in conversation, and at least once in a Proclamation, as if their obligation to protect us were contingent on our adhering to this understanding.[1]

Further, although news-sheets of Boxer victories had been circulated at the port, Clennell noted that the behaviour of the troops was 'scrupulously correct'. When the *Hermione* arrived at Chinkiang the *taotai* expressed his satisfaction, but when the ship was replaced by the *Esk*, *Rosario*, and *Pigmy* he voiced his disquiet at the presence of three vessels.[2]

In Chekiang, where the violence of the mob led to the murder of several Europeans, the responsible officials were immediately dismissed, frequent references being made to the understanding 'between Her Majesty's Government and the Yangtze Viceroys'.[3] In Soochow, Governor Lu Ch'uan-lin spoke bitterly against missionaries, but he reassured the consul that he would do his duty in keeping order.[4] From Chungking came evidence of the influence of the Yangtze viceroys in the interior. The Viceroy of Szechuan and the Generalissimo in charge of troops issued a proclamation on an agreement between the foreign powers and the Yangtze viceroys and, Consul Fraser noted, the 'wording is such as to make this appear as a condition for China protecting foreigners inland'.[5] From Foochow, Consul Playfair

[1] Report by Clennell of 6 Aug. 1900, encl. in Warren to Salisbury, No. 98 of 11 Aug. 1900, F.O. 17/1424; Clennell to Warren, 28 Aug. 1900, encl. in Warren to Salisbury of 25 Sept. 1900, F.O. 17/1425.

[2] Acting-consul Willis to Warren of 17, 18 Aug. 1900, encl. in Warren to Salisbury, 25 Sept. 1900, F.O. 17/1425.

[3] Acting-consul King to Warren, encl. in Warren to Salisbury, No. 160 of 25 Sept. 1900, F.O. 17/1425.

[4] E. G. Carvill to Warren of 5 July 1900, encl. 2 in Warren to Salisbury, No. 160 of 25 Sept. 1900, F.O. 17/1425.

[5] Fraser to Salisbury, No. 3 of 23 July 1900, F.O. 17/1430.

telegraphed direct to London for permission to sign a 'convention' embodying this agreement.[1] The nature of the stringent measures taken by the Chinese to maintain order can be adduced from Liu's own efforts at Nanking. Nightly patrols of reliable soldiers were sent out and guards were placed on all mission buildings; teashops and other gathering places were closed at 9 p.m. and a curfew was operated until dawn.[2]

Further evidence of the deliberate limitation of the conflict is shown in the movement of Chinese ships. The Chinese admiral at Chefoo informed Rear-Admiral Bruce that Yüan Shih-k'ai had ordered him south to try to maintain friendly relations with the foreign powers.[3] In the Yangtze area, because of the uneasiness of the foreigners at Shanghai, Liu ordered five of the larger cruisers from the bulk of the Chinese fleet lying between Shanghai and Woosung up to Nanking 'to give every assistance to British ships in preserving order if it is necessary'.[4]

There is little doubt that the Yangtze viceroys prevented a general uprising by this stratagem. The authority in which they were held influenced the majority; only in places where the populace was encouraged by violently anti-foreign officials did massacres take place. The assumption that the central and southern provinces of China remained in ignorance of the situation in the north cannot be maintained: at an early stage of the crisis Boxer placards imitating those posted in Peking had appeared throughout the countryside. The Imperial decree of 25 June giving the Chinese version of the events at Taku had been published in the Canton newspapers by the 29th.[5]

When the reputed agreement was brought to Lord Salisbury's notice by roundabout channels—through Hong Kong or the unusual telegram from Playfair asking permission to sign the 'convention'—with the scrupulous honesty with which he conducted foreign affairs, Salisbury instructed Warren to

---

[1] Playfair to Salisbury, tel. of 14 July 1900, F.O. 17/1430. The text of the proposed convention is given in Playfair to Salisbury, No. 120 of 23 July 1900, F.O. 17/1430.

[2] Sundius to Warren of 30 Aug. 1900, in Warren to Salisbury, No. 174 of 26 Sept. 1900, F.O. 17/1425.

[3] Rear-Admiral to Admiralty, tel. 6 of 24 June 1900, Adm. 116/117.

[4] C.O. H.M.S. *Undaunted*, Woosung, to Admiralty, tel. of 24 June 1900, Adm. 116/117.

[5] Consul Scott to Salisbury, No. 28 of 5 July 1900, F.O. 17/1422.

repeat to the viceroys the reservations he had made to the Chinese minister.[1] It is not clear that Warren did so. His telegrams remained discreetly silent on this point; the full consular reports describing the situation, which are referred to above, were only sent to London by sea after the crisis.

The Occupation of Shanghai

Warren's reticence is understandable. Throughout the entire crisis the position of the foreigner in Shanghai was particularly unhappy: for the besieged in Peking doubts were resolved in the straightforward issue of courage; for the missionary of the interior either disaster struck suddenly or the trouble was heard only as a distant thunder, muted by the protection of the Chinese administrators; but for the inhabitants of Shanghai, fed by rumour, believing daily in the imminent spread of the outbreak, life must have been intolerable. The accumulated wealth of the treaty port meant that it would be the principal objective in any rising on the Yangtze. During the latter part of June and throughout July they felt as if they were sitting on a powder magazine, to which the nearby Woosung forts were the fuse.

News which was 'absolutely reliable', though it was impossible to trace the source, stated that Jung-lu had implored the foreign powers to rescue their nationals before it was too late, that the Boxers had been victorious in the north and that the provincial viceroys were to make immediate preparations for a campaign, that 100,000 Boxers were attacking the two remaining legations in Peking, and that Prince Tuan had ordered Yüan Shih-k'ai to march on Nanking with 18,000 troops. With apparent inevitability, the progress of a punitive force was traced down the Grand Canal and out along the Yangtze: encirclement was complete, for the Boxers were reported drilling in Wenchow to the south.[2]

In general, these rumours were stirred up by the conviction of the foreign residents of Shanghai that the Chinese would carry out diversionary measures on the Yangtze to relieve

[1] Salisbury to Warren, tel. 21 of 12 July 1900, F.O. 17/1426; minute by Salisbury on Blake to C.O., tel. of 10 July 1900, F.O. 17/1441.

[2] Warren to Salisbury, tels. 19, 20, 22, 24 of 29 June, 1, 3, 4 July 1900, F.O. 17/1427.

foreign military pressure on the north. Thus, apprehension was intensified at Shanghai at the beginning of July when it became known that a foreign attack was planned on Tientsin, and it rose to hysterical heights after the taking of that city on 14 July when it was assumed that an advance would be made on Peking.

These rumours aroused a feeling of increasing insecurity on the Yangtze which influenced the formulation of policy in London. With the South African war on their hands and increasing international complications in the north of China, the Government did not want involvement in the Yangtze. But two considerations were of overriding importance: the safety of British nationals in the area and the possibility of intrusive action by one of the other powers. Warren's reports pointed to a critical position at Shanghai, and these formed the material on which decisions had to be based. Moreover, they were corroborated by a 'Yangtze' lobby which was active in London at the time.

This group had stirred itself early in the crisis. On 28 June Walton, Colquhoun, Dudgeon, Jamieson, Yerburgh, and others of the China Association had formed the China League with the avowed intention of seeking

by means of popular addresses, pamphlets, etc., to build up in the country at large a sound body of public opinion on the Far Eastern question; and, secondly, through a strong Parliamentary party it would endeavour to assist and support Her Majesty's Government in the task of formulating and maintaining a clear and consistent line of policy.[1]

The group had been baffled in its aim by the high-level diplomacy which had developed between the powers and had been consistently turned away in questions in the House. But over the Yangtze they came into their own. In Byron Brenan, the British consul-general at Shanghai, then on leave in London, and in Warren, sympathetically mellowed in the camaraderie of Shanghai's clubland, they found authoritative spokesmen who could command the ear of the Government. Warren became their idol; they pressed for his appointment as attaché to direct

---

[1] See *The Extra-Parliamentary Hansard* (1899–1900), 788. The China League Manifesto is given op. cit. (1900–1), 497–8.

Chinese affairs, and it will be seen that the consul exerted himself on their behalf.

Thus at the beginning of July various memoranda were submitted to the Foreign Office advising the Government on a suitable course of action. One of these was put forward by H. B. Morse, the historian who was later to make his name by his work on Chinese foreign affairs. Morse argued that the Yangtze valley was the British sphere of influence and that it could best be pacified by throwing a screen of British and German troops between the valley and the rebellion. The Yangtze viceroys should be informed in advance and their troops impressed, but only as roadmakers, for 'at the front they will be useless and even a danger'. Morse then discouraged British commitment in the north of China where the situation could be left to the other powers, with Great Britain only showing her co-operation by attaching a single company of English, but not Indian, troops to each of the allied forces. The natural line of British action, Morse concluded, was from the south 'and the military disadvantage of eccentric action will be more than counterbalanced by the political gain'.[1] Similar advice was offered by Brenan on 4 July. Brenan argued that by the time the allied armies entered the capital the Court would have fled and there would be no responsible person to treat with. A palace revolution, which was then in progress, would continue and take two months to work itself out. During this upheaval the provincial authorities would watch the situation warily to estimate the relative strength of the foreigners and Prince Tuan, the leader of the reactionaries, who was attempting to usurp the throne. It was up to Great Britain to encourage the allegiance of Chang Chih-tung and Liu K'un-i, the Yangtze viceroys, who would in turn influence Li Hung-chang; she must be prepared for anarchy as the provinces might not accept the rule of Prince Tuan. It would be useful to have an alternative candidate to the throne ready. Brenan suggested Duke Kung, lineal descendant of Confucius, who would be helped to the throne by Yüan Shih-k'ai because of his connections with the province of Shantung.[2]

[1] H. B. Morse, Notes on the Situation in China, 4 July 1900, encl. in J. D. Campbell to Bertie, 6 July 1900, F.O. 17/1441.

[2] Brenan's memorandum may be found enclosed in Warren to Salisbury, No. 32 of 30 June 1900, F.O. 17/1424.

These and other similar views had an indirect influence on the conduct of affairs; they were accepted by a busy Foreign Office staff and repeated in minutes and inter-departmental memoranda, even to the phraseology used. The Government was convinced when these reports were supported by reports from Warren, arguing the same case. They were accepted by Francis Bertie, who controlled the China Department at the Foreign Office, and later used by him to persuade Salisbury to a waiting policy during the urgent strategical scramble which developed between the powers in north China after the legations had been relieved. They were also used by Major-General Ardagh, the Director of Military Intelligence, when he drafted two memoranda on 5 and 7 July which became the basis of British action on the Yangtze.[1]

On the afternoon of Sunday, 8 July, a meeting was arranged at St. John Brodrick's house. Those who took part were Ardagh, Brodrick, Lansdowne, Goschen, Hamilton, Browne, the Intelligence Officer for China, Brenan, and Norton of Naval Intelligence.[2] All shared a common approach to the conduct of British policy in China. The presence of Lansdowne, Goschen, and Hamilton, the three ministers whose interest in the Chinese question was most sustained, ensured sufficient coherence to sway Cabinet support; they could rely on all in the Government who were in favour of a vigorous policy.

At the meeting discussion centred on the considerations raised in Ardagh's two memoranda of 5 and 7 July. These argued from the premiss that as the provincial viceroys were either no longer able or were unwilling to maintain their neutral attitude, precautionary measures should be considered for the protection of foreigners in the Yangtze area and the south. Ardagh suggested that all out-lying groups of foreigners should be concentrated in the localities suitable for defence and in touch with the Navy. 'Of the interior,' he declared categorically, 'it may at once be admitted that the writ of the Powers does not now run where a gunboat cannot reach; and that military operations are out of the question.' Foreigners were to be grouped at the treaty ports and, supported by ships of war,

---

[1] Memorandum 58, Measures of Precaution for Safety of Foreigners, P.R.O. 30/40/14, Pt. 2, pp. 207–17; memorandum of 5 July 1900, F.O. 17/1441.
[2] Ardagh Diary, 1900, P.R.O. 30/40/6.

formed into local corps under the control of military officers.¹ Arms and ammunition (20,000 rifles) would be sent from India. If Prince Tuan's orders for the capture of Nanking were obeyed the Shanghai forts would have to be taken; the guns in these could be rendered innocuous by the removal of a few irreplaceable parts. If the viceroys co-operated, a definite promise of naval and if necessary, military, force should be made. In the event of a general outbreak of fanaticism an ultimate withdrawal to Shanghai would be necessary. If the situation became acute the force then on its way from India to northern China should be directed to Shanghai. The powers should mandate the defence of the Yangtze to Great Britain, the power most interested, but clear international understanding should precede any action. This assessment of the situation was approved at the meeting. In fact, the position on the Yangtze seemed so precarious that preliminary measures had already been authorized.

The strategic problem centred on the control of the mouth of the Grand Canal to prevent a southward drive by the Chinese while the foreigners were being withdrawn. Chinkiang, fifty miles above the Kiangyin forts, was the point from which a watch could be kept on all three outlets of the Canal, which was the only route by which the rebellion could gain the Yangtze during the rainy season. Consequently, on 5 July H.M.S. *Hermione* was instructed to report on the position at Nanking and to take steps to resist a troop attack from the north; this step was to be taken without communicating with the Chinese.²

Meanwhile Warren had been active in Shanghai. Wenchow, where Boxer activity had been reported, was completely evacuated by 10 July. The isolated position of Chungking made the position there more precarious. As no gunboat could ascend the river until late October a private vessel was retained, at a cost of £100 a day to the Treasury. Fraser, the consul there, had a miserable time. At the first sign of an exodus the Chinese population turned hostile and Fraser was forced to abandon

¹ In 1900 there were approximately 15,000 foreigners in China; of these 7,000 were in Shanghai, 1,568 in the Yangtze hinterland, 400 at Hankow, 740 at Kiukiang.
² Admiralty to Senior Naval Officer, Woosung, 5 July 1900, Adm. 116/117; Browne to St. John Brodrick, 7 July 1900, Precautions in the Event of the Boxer Rising Spreading, F.O. 17/1441; Admiralty to Senior Naval Officer, Woosung, 6 July 1900, Adm. 116/117.

both stragglers and diplomatic cyphers in his haste. For this he was censured, but his panic was understandable; he had been led to believe that the whole of the lower Yangtze was up in arms.[1]

This preliminary activity was insignificant compared with the crisis which developed a few days later when news was received in Shanghai of the proposed advance on Tientsin. In a spate of telegrams Warren reported that the situation had become urgent and might 'well develop into a Chinese national uprising against foreigners throughout the Empire'.[2] Again: 'The governors of Kuangsi, Shansi, Shensi, Honan and Hupeh had all declared in favour of the rising; the Viceroy of Hankow was still firm but may be swept away.'[3] It was at this time that the report emanated from Shanghai that everyone in Peking had been massacred.

The alarming situation was complicated further when Warren reported that private American interests were intriguing with Viceroy Liu to weaken British influence; that the American Asiatic Association at Shanghai, alarmed by the situation, proposed to ask the United States Government for a force to occupy Shanghai 'either alone or jointly with Britain'; that with the report of the massacre at Peking intrigues had developed over the succession to the Inspectorate of the Maritime Customs, as Sir Robert Hart was presumed lost.[4]

In London it was assumed that the critical situation envisaged in Ardagh's memorandum of 7 July had developed. An urgent message was sent to the officer in command of the troops which were on the way from India to Tientsin.

Ominous reports as to the spread of revolt and consequent danger to Shanghai [the message ran]. 'Stop there on your way North, and, if in your judgment the position is critical, divert such troops as seem absolutely necessary for its defence. Whilst we are alive to the necessity of rapidly augmenting the international forces at Tientsin, European interests at Shanghai are too important to be imperilled.[5]

[1] Warren to Salisbury, tel. 45 of 14 July 1900, F.O. 17/1427; Fraser to Salisbury, No. 3 of 23 July 1900, F.O. 17/1430.
[2] Warren to Salisbury, tel. 45 of 14 July 1900, F.O. 17/1427.
[3] Warren to Salisbury, tel. 51 of 17 July 1900, F.O. 17/1427.
[4] Warren to Salisbury, tels. 36A and 49 of 11, 16 July 1900, F.O. 17/1427.
[5] Secretary of State for War to G.O.C., Hong Kong, 18 July 1900, misplaced following 7 Jan. 1901 in F.O. 17/1499.

The officer sent by General Gaselee was rapidly overwhelmed by the business interests at Shanghai. The Shanghai Municipal Council emphasized the defenceless state of the city and demanded 10,000 troops. The officer thought a force of 3,000 adequate, and this recommendation was accordingly sent off.[1] The basis of this decision must be noted. Fear of retaliation for the taking of Tientsin had driven Shanghai business interests into an illogical fear for their own safety. When the officer sent by Gaselee made his report, he based it on the purely military consideration of the number of troops necessary for an adequate defence of the city.

By this time Warren had the bit firmly between his teeth; he was convinced that if he did not act the other consuls would do so without him. When Sheng Hsüan-huai attempted to correct the report on the destruction of the legations, Warren refused to believe him, and thought it a subterfuge by the Chinese to gain time. He refused to hold his hand when the Chinese told him that Li Hung-chang was on his way north to negotiate a settlement. Instead, he sent an urgent message to London that no negotiations should be entered into with the southern viceroy, with such effect that Salisbury was led to reverse his earlier opinion favouring a mediatory effort by the Chinese statesman. Scott, the British consul at Canton, was instructed to suggest to Li that it would be better for him to stay where he was.[2] Moreover, without waiting for permission, Warren approached Liu K'un-i to persuade the reluctant viceroy to agree to the landing of British troops. Warren's hand was strengthened by the Shansi and Shensi massacres which were being reported in the local press at this time, and by the Ch'u-chou massacre of 21 and 22 July.[3] Similarly, these atrocities weakened Liu's resistance. On 27 July Warren dispatched the jubilant telegram: 'Secret. *Send for the troops.* Viceroy leaves the number to your discretion.'[4]

[1] Gaselee to India Office, tel. of 22 July 1900, F.O. 17/1442.
[2] Warren to Salisbury, tel. 43 of 14 July 1900; Salisbury to Scott, tel. 5 of 14 July 1900, Adm. 116/117.
[3] The notorious Shansi atrocities were connected with the anti-foreign activity of Yu Hsien. The Ch'u-chou massacre was an isolated incident in Chekiang. Governor Liu Shu-tang issued a proclamation ordering a general massacre, withdrew it two days later and issued another ordering peace, but by then it was too late.
[4] Warren to Salisbury, tel. 65 of 27 July 1900, F.O. 17/1427.

Some intimation of the narrow reasoning which had prompted this decisive step was felt by Lord Salisbury, who determined to hold his hand until Admiral Seymour, who had been instructed to make a personal investigation, could make his report. Seymour was asked to assess the real situation in regard to Warren's reports, to verify whether Liu had agreed to the landing of troops and to judge whether such a move might not precipitate an anti-foreign rising. 'The dangers from precipitate action have to be weighed against the risk of being too late. . . .' His instructions concluded soberly, 'Policy of Her Majesty's Government must largely depend on your report as to your views and what you consider practicable. They rely much on your cool judgment.'[1]

When Seymour arrived in Shanghai at the end of July he found the situation chaotic. The old fear of retaliation was again dominant. It had surged up at the end of June when the move on Tientsin was first projected; it had risen again in mid-July when the town was actually taken. Now, at the end of July, indications of an advance on Peking brought anxiety back a hundredfold, reinforced with fresh argument, of which the following message from the Shanghai branch of the China Association is an example: 'Considered certain that the Chinese will attempt to create a diversion here and elsewhere to prevent an advance on Peking.'[2] The British community urged Seymour that a further force, a minimum of 5,000 but preferably 10,000, was immediately necessary; these should be American and British and should arrive before any advance on Peking. Moreover, Seymour found that because of the 'foolish timidity of the residents' the Chinese ships which had been co-operating successfully with the allied fleet at Woosung had now been moved away to a stronger position just above the Kiangyin forts. Their commanders were friendly, he noted, but would act on Liu's orders. Undoubtedly preparations were being made by the Chinese, but a general outbreak depended on Liu's inclination. Seymour concluded that the best approach was to keep in with the Yangtze viceroys and 'to take the line that we are not at war with the Supreme Government'. Active British

---

[1] Admiralty to C.-in-C., tel. 122 of 27 July 1900, Adm. 116/117.
[2] C.A., Shanghai, to Hongkong and Shanghai Bank, London, 28 July 1900, encl. in Cameron to Bertie, 29 July 1900, F.O. 17/1443, circulated to Cabinet.

interference, he stressed, 'would at once precipitate general war here'.[1]

Nevertheless, Seymour felt himself obliged to make arrangements to cover any probable outbreak on the Yangtze. He went up to Nanking to persuade Liu K'un-i to agree to the landing of troops if necessary. Liu was 'indisposed by heat' and the interview did not take place until 2 August. Then Liu repeated his conviction that there was no need for troops at Shanghai, but if they had to come he agreed to a limit of 3,000, preferably British.[2]

By this time both in London and in Shanghai the situation was getting out of hand. A description of the confusion existing in the Government has been preserved in a letter by Hamilton to Curzon of 20 July. The War Office, Foreign Office, and the Admiralty each received daily reports of conditions and remedies to be taken, Hamilton noted:

And so we go on from day to day with urgent appeals for help counteracted by the more experienced advice of the Naval men, whilst here, so far from there being any one strong single man to take command of the policy, we have so far been absolutely unable to agree on any course of procedure except to wait upon events.[3]

In Shanghai the confusion was even more widespread. Warren sent a circular telegram to the various inland stations inquiring about the possible consequences of an occupation of Shanghai. This caused a panic which communicated itself to the Chinese. 'The effect', the consul at Chungking urgently replied, 'would be the extermination of all foreigners at Chungking and inland.'[4] Despite this, measures for an occupation went on. Seymour had advocated a policy of co-operation with the Yangtze viceroys, yet, as has been noted, he drew an assurance from Liu for the landing of 3,000 troops. Again, he ordered the withdrawal of isolated ships from the riverine ports, leaving only Hankow, Nanking, Kiukiang, and Chinkiang protected.[5]

---

[1] C.-in-C. to Admiralty, tels. 122, 130, 135 of 27 and 29 July 1900, Adm. 116/117; Admiralty to Foreign Office of 30 July 1900, F.O. 17/1443.

[2] C.-in-C. to Admiralty, tel. 142 of 2 Aug. 1900, Adm. 116/117.

[3] Hamilton to Curzon, 20 July 1900, Hamilton Papers. Hamilton might have added his own department, the India Office, to the list, for he had the direction of the Indian Expeditionary Force, but was equally at a loss.

[4] Warren to Salisbury, tel. 68 of 31 July 1900, F.O. 17/1427.

[5] C.-in-C. to Admiralty, tel. 137 of 30 July 1900, Adm. 116/117.

The reason for Liu's reticence with Seymour was soon known. The Chinese reaction to the preparations for an allied offensive on the capital was not a general retaliatory rising throughout the provinces, but an outburst of intense fervour at Peking. On 26 July Li Ping-heng, who had shown himself so obstructive while in charge of the Kiangyin forts, arrived in the capital to infuse the Boxer movement with fresh vigour. The trend toward a settlement, general since the mid-July report of Li's mission of pacification, was brought to an abrupt halt by the execution of the two moderate ministers Hsu Ching-cheng and Yuan Ch'ang. The executions caused considerable unrest along the Yangtze. An edict ordering the degradation and execution of the provincial authorities was expected daily. Rumours led to suicide; once again refugees were everywhere.[1] Sheng applied for British protection; it was anticipated that Li Hung-chang would make a similar request. This sharp reminder of the continued authority of the Court, coupled with their gradual loss of faith in the assurances by the British Government that forces would not be landed in the Yangtze area, exerted a powerful influence on Liu K'un-i and Chang Chih-tung. On 1 August they declared themselves unconditionally loyal to the Empress Dowager, and stated that unless it was distinctly guaranteed that her person would be respected it would be impossible to carry out the agreement of neutrality.[2]

This step by the viceroys was a logical consequence of a month of unsuccessful effort to stabilize their position by a definite assurance which would preserve the integrity of their jurisdictions. British activity at the end of July made it obvious that even tacit neutrality in this respect was not to be observed. Since Salisbury's 'declaration of guilt' of 5 July on the personal responsibility of the government of Peking for the safety of foreigners, the provincial viceroys had pressed for assurances that the Empress Dowager should be exempt from this indictment. At the time Warren had observed that 'Any threat to hold her responsible might affect their present attitude.'[3] Their stand was not one of fawning servility, for the old queen was

---

[1] Tower to Eric Barrington, letter of 9 Aug. 1900, S.P. 106/31.
[2] Warren to Salisbury, tels. 71, 72, 73, 74 of 1, 2, 3, 4 Aug. 1900, F.O. 17/1427.
[3] Warren to Salisbury, tel. 27 of 6 July 1900, F.O. 17/1427. On the 'declaration of guilt' see above, p. 145.

held in genuine affection by her equally aged servants. More pertinently, if they acquiesced in her responsibility it would make a mockery of the convenient belief on which they based their neutrality; for if she were responsible she would be still in control and the assumption that Prince Tuan had usurped the throne, widely circulated since 21 June, could no longer be maintained. But Salisbury was adamant in his refusal to except her from responsibility. This, with the impending British occupation, increased the deterioration of trust on the Yangtze.

By this time measures for the landing of troops had been begun. The general plan had been laid down in Ardagh's memorandum of 7 July, but each department acted on its own initiative, adding to the confusion. The India Office had diverted part of General Gaselee's Indian force to Shanghai, where they were to remain for a fortnight uncomfortably crowded into troop transports off Woosung. The Admiralty had counselled restraint on the basis of Seymour's report, yet it approved his measures for the withdrawal of naval ships, a step likely to agitate the Chinese. The Foreign Office approved Seymour's report, yet Chungking was ordered to be evacuated as 'Naval and military authorities at Shanghai would be much hampered in any operations until all Europeans are withdrawn from riverine ports'.[1]

Moreover, in his summary Ardagh had stressed the importance of maintaining all possible co-operation with the viceroys and, secondly, of preceding any British move by a clear international understanding. The Government's handling of both these crucial issues was inadequate. On 2 August a statement was made in the House of Commons that British policy rested on the preservation of the integrity of China. 'As regards the Yangtze district and the adjacent regions,' the statement went on to declare, 'assurances have been given to the Viceroys that the ships and forces of Great Britain will co-operate as far as possible with them in quieting unrest and securing order, and provision is being made for the due fulfilment of this assurance.'[2]

This confidence was not felt by the Government in private.

---

[1] Salisbury to Warren, tel. 41 of 1 Aug. 1900, F.O. 17/1426.
[2] *Parliamentary Debates*, 4th Series, lxxxvii. 490. The draft of this announcement is given F.O. 17/1444.

They were by no means sure of the Yangtze viceroys. Despite Warren's repeated assurances, Seymour was asked on 3 August 'to make sure that Liu had agreed to accept the 3,000 at Shanghai . . .'.[1] Yet when his consent was confirmed the decisive order for occupation was still withheld. With Chang Chih-tung at Hankow the position was even more precarious. On the very day Warren had sent the jubilant 'send for the troops' telegram (27 July) the wily viceroy had submitted a request for a loan of 500,000 taels (£75,000). His ostensible reason was the urgent need to pay his troops who would otherwise rise in revolt. However, the meagre security of his cotton mills, which was all he was prepared to offer for a British Government guarantee of the loan, made it clear that the money was to be a bribe for his complaisance. It was a test, Bertie observed, to see 'if we are to keep in friendly concert with the Yangtze viceroys'. To which Lord Salisbury retorted, '. . . a test which, if it is successful, will be so satisfactory that it cannot be renewed too often'.[2]

The negotiation of the loan provides a revealing sidelight on Chang's attitude to British dominance in the Yangtze valley. In a normal situation the principle of a government guaranteed loan would have been rejected out of hand by Great Britain. Even if it were considered, a delay of several months would have been involved. Yet within a few days of making his demand Chang had let it be known that he was entertaining Belgian offers through the Russo-Chinese Bank, and German offers through M. Arnhold Karberg & Company.[3] In addition, he intimated discreetly to Warren that without the loan he would lose his authority 'and have to go over to the other side'.[4] Chang played his advantage with a masterly hand and, short of jeopardizing the projected occupation, the British Government had no choice. There was bitter feeling in the Cabinet that Great Britain should have to pay his troops when there was evidence he was sending them north. It was also realized the loan would serve no purpose unless the promise were given that the person of the Empress Dowager would be respected. Sir Michael Hicks Beach, the Chancellor of the Exchequer,

---

[1] Admiralty to C.-in-C., tel. 144 of 3 Aug. 1900, C.-in-C. to Admiralty, tel. 145 of 5 Aug. 1900, Adm. 116/117.

[2] Memorandum by Bertie of 28 July 1900, F.O. 17/1443.

[3] Warren to Salisbury, tels. 75, 76 of 5 Aug. 1900, F.O. 17/1427.

[4] Warren to Salisbury, tel. 70 of 1 Aug. 1900, F.O. 17/1427.

had a momentary impulse to call Chang's bluff and let the Russo-Chinese Bank take over, but Salisbury firmly believed that, although the loan was being demanded on 'as bad a security as I can imagine', it was essentially a political matter and would have to be made.[1] By 10 August the loan issue had loomed so large that Salisbury considered any delay dangerous and pressed the Treasury for an immediate decision.[2] Promise of the loan was made the same day; and the agreement was signed on 28 August on the unsatisfactory security of a second mortgage on the Ichang Salt Likin which was already charged with the service of the Chinese Imperial Government $4\frac{1}{2}$ per cent loan of 1898.[3]

Heartened by his success, even as the loan was being signed, Chang intimated his need for a further loan in three months time. Then, before the second application could be considered, notice was given on the possible need of a third. 'I see no end to these applications', Salisbury remarked dismally and stiffened in his determination that the loan extorted at the height of the crisis should not be established as a precedent.[4] Nevertheless, Chang's importunate demands for financial assistance throughout the peace negotiations of the winter of 1900–1, conveyed in each instance with the implied threat of the transference of his allegiance, did much to disillusion British statesmen on the strength of the bond with the Yangtze viceroys. Chang was an ambitious man, deeply jealous of Li Hung-chang's pre-eminence. In the Yangtze, where Liu K'un-i approached Great Britain with consistent friendliness, Chang did so with cold calculation. Later he lamented openly that the British should be reluctant to give him the kind of support afforded by Russia to Li Hung-chang.[5]

Their preoccupation with the loan issue in the first week of

[1] Minutes on Warren's telegrams 64, 70 of 27 July, 1 Aug. 1900, F.O. 17/1427; memorandum by Hicks Beach of 6 Aug. 1900, F.O. 17/1443.

[2] Salisbury to Treasury, 10 Aug. 1900, F.O. 17/1444.

[3] Salisbury to Warren, tel. 64 of 10 Aug. 1900, F.O. 17/1426; Warren to Salisbury, tel. 107 of 29 Aug. 1900, F.O. 17/1427; memorandum by Bertie of 9 Nov. 1900; memorandum by Campbell, encl. F.O. 17/1449; text given with drafts in Warren to Salisbury, No. 120, encl. 1 of 21 Aug. 1900, F.O. 17/1424, and Warren to Salisbury, No. 126, encl. 2 of 1 Sept. 1900, F.O. 17/1425.

[4] Memorandum by Guy Hillier of 5 Sept. 1900, encl. 1 in Warren to Salisbury, No. 129 of 5 Sept. 1900, F.O. 17/1425.

[5] At an interview with Chirol of *The Times* on 27 Jan. 1901. Intelligence Report, Hankow, Sept. 1900–Jan. 1901, F.O. 17/1442.

August led the Government to neglect a more serious consequence of the projected occupation. In his memorandum
Ardagh had stressed the need for Great Britain to obtain a clear
mandate from the powers before any action was taken. Apart
from the inadequate statement in the House of Commons of
2 August no steps were taken in this direction. From the outbreak of the rising the other powers had shown an interest in
the possible fate of the Yangtze. The close nature of the negotiations between Great Britain and the viceroys had discouraged
interference, though it was attempted when openings occurred.
One such loophole was the viceroys' neutralization proclamation at the end of June. After this had become known the Belgian
minister in London duly presented himself at the Foreign Office
to inquire whether an *entente* had been arranged among the
powers in regard to the Yangtze and the south, on the lines that
had been agreed on in the north. To this indirect approach
Bertie had returned an even more indirect reply, and after
saying vaguely that the viceroys had announced their ability to
maintain order he began ostentatiously to talk about the
weather.[1] This method of discouraging interest could not be
sustained. The intrigues of the various foreign interests in
Shanghai during the middle of July have been noted; at the
beginning of August, when it became clear from the movement
of British naval and military units that an occupation was to
take place, a violent eruption of feeling occurred. The Comte
de Bezaure, the French consul-general at Shanghai, linked his
protest with the immediate recommendation to his Government
to send a French detachment from Tongking. Goodnow, the
American consul-general and quondam adviser to the *taotai*
at Shanghai, gave him warm support.[2] To avoid the appearance
of openly criticizing British action on the Yangtze, Aoki, the
Japanese Foreign Minister, expressed his anxiety indirectly
through Whitehead to Seymour.[3]

Moreover, in his enthusiasm to bring about the British landing, Warren had failed to emphasize sufficiently Liu's reservations
on his attitude in the event of similar action by the other powers.

---

[1] Memorandum by Bertie of 10 July 1900, F.O. 17/1441.

[2] Warren to Salisbury, tel. 81 of 8 Aug. 1900, F.O. 17/1427; Warren to Salisbury,
No. 95 of 8 Aug. 1900, F.O. 17/1424.

[3] Whitehead to Salisbury, tel. 45, confidential, of 9 Aug. 1900, Adm. 116/117.

Liu was an octagenarian addicted to his opium pipe and inclined to be swayed against his better judgement by Warren's vigorous argument. The prospect of French and American action gave him a chance again to retract the consent he had given to Warren, retracted, and then given again to Seymour. On 9 August, through Minister Lofenglu in London, he pointed out that Seymour had misunderstood his agreement on the landing of troops at Shanghai and that his intention had been to allow a small force; but as Great Britain's determination to land 2,000 troops would lead to inevitable panic among the populace and retaliatory action by France and the United States, she should desist. This appeal was repeated the next day, with the support of Li Hung-chang, Chang Chih-tung, and Sheng Hsüan-huai.[1]

It was clear to Salisbury that Great Britain was not going to be allowed to slip into Shanghai without objection from the other powers, and that the strongest opposition would come from France. Accordingly on 9 August he instructed Monson, British Ambassador at Paris, to make a tentative approach to the French Foreign Minister, Delcasse, to explain that Great Britain had neither territorial nor exclusive designs on Shanghai, but that British interests were so preponderant she could not allow them to remain without protection. It was clear, also, that Salisbury recognized the futility of the step, for Monson was told to offer these assurances 'only . . . if you think they are likely to have a salutary effect. They seem to me to run the risk of raising his suspicions.'[2]

Salisbury's doubt was understandable. France had just swallowed the bitter pill of having a German commander-in-chief for the China Expedition, she could not be expected to take kindly to the further one Salisbury proposed to offer. Monson at Paris was having a miserable time. He confided to Salisbury that Delcasse 'has latterly shown me so little confidence that I am bound to deal very carefully with him. He has not only been uncommunicative, but I fear untruthful.'[3] At first he tried to

[1] Communications by Lo of 9, 10 Aug. 1900, F.O. 17/1435; Salisbury to Warren, tel. 65 of 10 Aug. 1900, F.O. 17/1426. Even in his disclaimer Liu could not get himself to admit to the correct figure of 3,000.

[2] Salisbury to Monson, tel. (?) of 9 Aug. 1900, copy, Adm. 116/117.

[3] Monson to Salisbury, tel. 61, confidential, of 10 Aug. 1900, copy, Adm. 116/117.

avoid making the approach on the ground that the Press had reported that French troops were already in Shanghai, but Salisbury pinned him to the task and he saw Delcasse on 11 August. The result was as expected. Delcasse declared 'with great animation' that if Great Britain landed troops at Shanghai France would at once follow suit.[1]

This seemed to settle the matter. Liu K'un-i at Nanking, with the support of the other provincial officials, had expressed himself against a landing; France had declared she would follow Great Britain in. Lord Salisbury and Goschen met to discuss the situation and decided to abandon all thoughts of carrying out the occupation. On the evening of 12 August Warren was instructed that except in the case of an evident emergency no actual landing should be made without further orders. Next day, arrangements were made for the transports outside Woosung to be diverted to strengthen Gaselee's force at Weihaiwei.[2]

This decision was not accepted by the British authorities in Shanghai. While Salisbury and Goschen were pondering on the situation in London, Admiral Seymour had approached Liu to persuade him to yet another change of front. Under his pressure the pliant Liu withdrew his objections to the landing of a British brigade, though he maintained his reluctance in respect of the other powers. When this was reported, however, the Government refused to be committed on these terms.[3] To Goschen, who knew nothing of the pressure which was being applied to Liu, the change of front seemed suspicious; he thought the viceroys were probably trying to create international friction.[4]

By this time control of the situation was out of the hands of both the Cabinet in London and Liu in Nanking. The British authorities in Shanghai were plainly determined on occupation. In spite of the Foreign Office and Admiralty telegrams of 13 August, renewed efforts were made to secure Liu's com-

[1] Monson to Salisbury, tel. 63 of 11 Aug. 1900, copy, Adm. 116/117.

[2] Salisbury to Warren, tel. 68 of 12 Aug. 1900, F.O. 17/1426; Foreign Office to Admiralty, immediate and confidential, of 13 Aug. 1900, Adm. 116/118, Section XVIII; Admiralty to C.-in-C., tel. 167 of 13 Aug. 1900, Adm. 116/117.

[3] C.-in-C. to Admiralty, tel. 156 of 13 Aug. 1900; Admiralty to C.-in-C., tel. 169 of 14 Aug. 1900, Adm. 116/117.

[4] Minute of 13 Aug. 1900, Adm. 116/118, Section XVIII.

pliance. Admiral Seymour kept the transports at Woosung. Further, on 14 August, with Warren and General Creagh, officer in command of British troops in Shanghai, he met a representative of Liu in Shanghai and persuaded him to waive all objections. On the same day an arrangement was agreed on among all the consuls in Shanghai that telegrams should be sent to their respective governments stating that withdrawal would jeopardize the safety of Shanghai and proposing a joint landing by international agreement.[1]

This was the situation that Salisbury had sought to avoid, and that had led him to abandon the idea of occupation when Delcasse had made the French stand clear. Yet now it was being proposed by the British authorities in Shanghai. On 10 August, in conversation with Sanderson at Hatfield, he had decided to send Sir Ernest Satow, who had been nominated to replace MacDonald at Peking, out east at once, as it was clearly necessary to have the presence of 'some one with more coolness than our present acting Consul General at Shanghai'.[2]

However, on 15 August Salisbury left for a much-needed holiday at Schlucht. A Cabinet committee of three, composed of Hamilton, Goschen, and Lansdowne, was left in charge of the Chinese situation in his absence.[3] From his discussions with Salisbury on 12 August it is possible to infer that Goschen was alive to the danger of giving France an excuse for sending troops to the Yangtze. Indeed, on 14 August he voiced his suspicions of the French and also of the Chinese viceroys explicitly to Seymour.[4] But this reserve was only momentary, nor was he helped by his two colleagues. Throughout the summer Hamilton had fretted at the lack of a vigorous policy, now he had the power to act. Similarly, Lansdowne could be expected to favour any decisive move which would help to remove the unfortunate effect of his handling of the South African war. All three men were temperamentally unsuited to the waiting game; they lacked Lord Salisbury's massive

[1] Warren to Salisbury, tels. 89, 91, 92 of 13, 14, 15 Aug. 1900, F.O. 17/1427.
[2] Sanderson to Satow, 11 Aug. 1900, P.R.O. 30/33/7/1.
[3] Some light is thrown on this interesting administrative point in a letter by Hamilton to Salisbury of 2 Aug. (S.P. unclassified) where he suggests that the Cabinet going into recess should give Salisbury 'small committee power' on direction of events in China.
[4] Admiralty to C.-in-C., tel. 169 of 14 Aug. 1900, Adm. 116/117.

capacity for inaction. Finally, all three ministers had spoken on previous occasions in favour of the consolidation of Great Britain's position on the Yangtze. It has been seen that at the time of the Port Arthur crisis of 1898, during Salisbury's absence, they had favoured the occupation of Weihaiwei. In August 1900, again in Salisbury's absence, they decided on the occupation of Shanghai.

On 15 August the Chinese minister communicated a telegram from Liu K'un-i stating that arrangements had been made with Seymour and Warren for the landing of several hundred troops at Shanghai.[1] This tipped the scales for the Committee. They overlooked that this was merely a delayed report on Seymour's efforts of 13 August. Liu's reference to 'several hundred troops' similarly escaped notice. Ardagh made a last effort to keep the attention of the Committee on the international consequences of occupation. Because of the appointment of Waldersee, the Fashoda crisis, and the Dreyfus scandal, he pointed out, 'France is in a highly irritable and explosive mood'. He suggested, 'It is not too late to propose the policy of mandates for exclusive local action, or for collective action under the Power whose interests were locally paramount.'[2] But the prospect of embarking on tedious and extended negotiations with France deterred the Committee, and when Goschen, Lansdowne, and Hamilton met on 15 August they decided to occupy Shanghai. Their reasons, as cabled to Salisbury, were that as the consular body felt troops were desirable, arrangements would be made 'for landing troops with consent of Chinese authorities but without any guarantee as to action of any other Power, and that we should inform the Powers that this has been done purely as a temporary measure of protection in view of the immense amount of British property involved'.[3]

Salisbury clearly deplored the move, and he sought to salvage what he could. A formal circular or defence in the capitals of Europe, he replied, would lead to claims and reserves from the foreign powers 'to which afterwards they will feel bound to

---

[1] Bertie to Salisbury, tel. of 15 Aug. 1900, S.P. Schlucht. Telegrams to and from Salisbury while he was abroad (15 Aug.–12 Sept. 1900) are grouped S.P. Chronological Series, 1900, Foreign and Imperial, I. For ease of reference these are cited with the cypher S.P. Schlucht.

[2] Memorandum 66 of 15 Aug. 1900, P.R.O. 30/40/14, Pt. 2.

[3] Sanderson to Salisbury, tel. of 15 Aug. 1900, S.P. Schlucht.

adhere'. With the exception of France, where the delicate negotiation would have to be put into Monson's hands, he suggested it would be better to work informally through Warren. In his reply, Salisbury's realization of the overriding need for Cabinet unity in his absence was revealed. He stated explicitly that if the Committee of Three were agreed he would give way.[1] By this time the order to disembark the troops had been given,[2] and Salisbury's suggestion was lost in the frenzied rush which developed as the other foreign powers followed the British example and moved to an occupation of Shanghai. Within a week of the Committee's decision Hamilton was to observe soberly: 'We allowed the hysterical element in Shanghai to so far dominate us as to force us to send troops to Shanghai giving the powers the chance to occupy where our interests predominate.'[3]

It should be noted that by the time the order was given for British troops to disembark at Shanghai, Peking had been taken; and the fears of the Shanghai residents on the inevitability of retaliatory action by the Chinese proved unfounded. Chinese resistance after 6 August was negligible; from that date an armistice was under negotiation. Liu's final concurrence had been extracted in the shadow of an utter and catastrophic Chinese collapse. Yet the occupation of Shanghai was frenziedly pressed by Warren, in the ultimate stages directly in contravention of the declared intention of the Government. The reason was simple and, in its illogicality, unanswerable. Withdrawal, after the stated intention of occupying, would have been a severe blow to British prestige in the eyes of the Chinese.[4] Rather than submit to this, Warren was prepared to accept the participation of the other powers.

The first move in this direction was made by Germany. On 22 August, in conversation with the Prince of Wales, the Kaiser, while intimating his lack of surprise at French objections to the British landing at Shanghai, stated that Great Britain would find Germany by her side if she would make

[1] Salisbury to Prodrome, London (code address?), of 17 Aug. 1900, SP. Schlucht.
[2] Admiralty to C.-in-C., tel. 173 of 16 Aug. 1900, Adm. 116/117; Salisbury to Warren, tel. 85 of 16 Aug. 1900, F.O. 17/1426.
[3] Hamilton to Curzon, letter of 22 Aug. 1900, Hamilton Papers.
[4] Warren to Salisbury, tel. 92 of 15 Aug. 1900, F.O. 17/1427; China Association to Foreign Office, 14 and 15 Aug. 1900, F.O. 17/1444.

some formal declaration on the open door.[1] When this was reported in London, Goschen and Lansdowne, who were dismayed by the consequences of the occupation of Shanghai, immediately decided that the assurances should be given.[2] Salisbury saw it as a German design to secure a foothold on the Yangtze and showed more reserve. He agreed to consider the matter carefully, but added, 'at the first blush I am averse to giving special assurances to the German Emperor. I do not see what he has got to do with it, and his observations look very much like an attempt to make a quarrel between France and us.'[3]

During the next week the British position on the Yangtze deteriorated rapidly. By the end of the month the French had landed 600 marines, a mountain battery, and a company of Annamites. When Chang Chih-tung suggested that the powers should ask France to limit her troops to the proportion of her share of vested interests to be defended at Shanghai, Salisbury replied dryly that the French were really sending their troops to prevent the British occupation from becoming permanent. 'We can hardly expect the French', he observed wryly, 'to take our advice as to the amount of force which is necessary for this purpose.'[4] Japan and Germany began measures for the quartering of troops. From their activity it seemed that they had a permanent occupation in mind. Germany in particular showed her deliberate intention by beginning the construction of barracks for 2,000 troops, strategically situated on the Pootung side of the narrow Whangpoo river, directly opposite Shanghai's great commercial bund.[5]

However, the chief anxiety of the Government was not over the intrusion of foreign troops into Shanghai, where the international nature of the city's commercial activity had already placed Great Britain in the role of *primus inter pares*, but over the obvious intention of the powers to press their activity into the whole Yangtze area, thus challenging the British in their own sphere.

In this respect France, who had been most vociferous, showed

[1] Lascelles to Salisbury, tel. 29 of 22 Aug. 1900, F.O. 64/1496.
[2] Bertie to Salisbury, 23 Aug. 1900, S.P. Schlucht.
[3] Salisbury to Bertie, 24 Aug. 1900, S.P. Schlucht.
[4] Salisbury to Bertie, 21 Aug. 1900, S.P. Schlucht.
[5] Warren to Salisbury, tel. 117 of 1 Sept. 1900, F.O. 17/1427.

the least initiative. Her attention was confined to Shanghai, where, following the lead shown by the other powers, she declared her intention of building barracks on a semi-permanent basis. On the whole, French behaviour was remarkable for its restraint; Delcasse's belligerent outburst was merely an attempt to regain the prestige lost over the appointment of Waldersee.

Japan, however, showed an unexpected burst of activity when on 24 August she landed troops at Amoy. The attention of the British Government was then on Germany and they were inclined to belittle this Japanese move. But of all the schemes entertained by the foreign powers to secure a footing in south China at the time, this had been most carefully worked out.

Throughout the summer a rising body of opinion in Japan had begun to demand a firm and independent policy in China to counteract Russia's moves in Manchuria. When Aoki failed to swing Salisbury into an anti-Russian combination, the Japanese Cabinet, realizing that they could not oppose Russia alone, began to think in terms of compensation. On this account, the activity of Kodama Gentaro, Governor-General of Formosa, becomes a matter of interest. Kodama was a man of driving ambition, with the ability to create, rather than to wait for, openings. In this he displayed a leaning toward subversive and violent activity. Later he was to become known for his connection with the notorious Amur River Society (Black Dragon Society or Kokuryukai). In 1900, while governor of Formosa, he satisfied this interest by intriguing with Sun Yat-sen and the Chinese reformers to use Formosa as a base for a descent on the Chinese coast.

Sun's original intention had been to work from Hong Kong, where his activity came to the attention of the Governor, Sir Henry Blake, who was sympathetically inclined. Sir Henry suggested that Great Britain should offer to 'press any fair and reasonable reforms that the people may demand' in the forthcoming peace settlement on condition that Sun and his party, with whom Sir Henry linked K'ang Yu-wei, should abstain from their activity. However, Salisbury, on Bertie's advice, had the reformers deported from Hong Kong.[1] By this time Sun had turned to Kodama, with whom connection had been established through Chinese revolutionary circles in Japan.

[1] Bertie to Salisbury, minutes, 19 Aug. 1900, S.P. Schlucht.

The plan was to capture Waichow, a hundred miles east of Canton, with the help of Chinese secret societies along the Kwangtung coast, and then to move toward the central provinces, gathering support on the way. The scheme was put into operation, but broke down for lack of careful planning and because of Sun's failure to secure supplies and ammunition.

Meanwhile, Kodama had acted and had prevailed upon the Japanese Cabinet to agree to the occupation of Amoy. The Yamagata administration were confirmed expansionists, in particular Yamamoto Gombei, the navy minister, who, like later naval opinion, looked to expansion in the south. Opposition came from Ito Hirobumi, head of the Privy Council who advised caution in case of adverse European reaction to the move. But Yamagata pointed to Russia's activity in Manchuria, and by 10 August Kodama in Formosa had been told to be ready to carry out an occupation on 29 August.

At this point two factors disrupted this careful plan. In the early hours of the morning of 24 August a Japanese temple in Amoy was burnt to the ground. By all accounts it was clearly instigated; the temple, which was really a shack hired a few weeks previously, was cleared of its contents by its two Buddhist caretakers before the fire began. It is not clear whether the premature move was an accidental confusion of dates by the Buddhist provocateurs, or whether Kodama decided to advance his operation because of the British landing at Shanghai. In any case, Uyeno, the Japanese consul at Amoy, lost his head and ordered the immediate landing of a Japanese naval contingent. This proved to be large enough to excite, but not to control, the populace, and panic ensued; 50,000 Chinese fled into the interior, and large numbers were drowned.[1] It was still possible for Kodama to carry out the original Japanese intention, but on 28 August he was instructed by Tokyo that the cabinet had decided to postpone the invasion. The reason for this disastrous volte-face, ordered after the occupation had begun, was that two days previously news had been received of Russia's intention to propose a general withdrawal of the foreign powers from north China.[2] This demolished Yamagata's only valid

---

[1] Amoy Intelligence Report, Sept. quarter, 1900, F.O. 228/1357; Mansfield to Salisbury, tel. of 26 Aug. 1900, F.O. 17/1430.

[2] See below, pp. 198–9.

argument and enabled Ito to carry out a postponement of the Amoy plan.[1] In Amoy the unrest was rapidly quelled after the arrival of H.M.S. *Isis* on 29 August, and by 5 September both powers had withdrawn.

The Japanese explanation of the incident, made by their minister in London on 29 August, was that Amoy formed a base for dangerous attempts on Formosa and that after rioting had broken out at the port a small Japanese force had been landed to protect the foreign community. This was accepted by Salisbury, who approved Bertie's comment that the affair 'will probably settle itself if no notice be taken of our Consul's appeals to worry the Japanese'.[2]

For Salisbury, the problem of foreign activity on the Yangtze centred on the behaviour of Germany. At the end of August it was widely felt that the German expeditionary force which had left Bremerhaven at the end of July would attempt some belligerent action as it passed the Yangtze. Li Hung-chang, who had not proved amenable to Salisbury's advice and who was at this time in the Yangtze on his way north, urged Chang Chih-tung to withdraw the Chinese fleet from the area to avoid capture 'should Germany pick a quarrel'.[3] General Creagh, in command of British troops at Shanghai, was equally apprehensive and asked Gaselee for reinforcements. These fears seemed justified when Mumm, the German minister who was sent out to succeed von Ketteler, arrived in Shanghai on 27 August and stated Germany's intention to send a man-of-war up to Hankow. Warren asked the Foreign Office for an indication of British policy in view of the assembling of the German fleet.[4] At the same time Admiral Seymour asked for definite instructions on what he was to do if the Germans engaged in hostile action against the Chinese forts.[5]

[1] Japan's action over Amoy is discussed in M. B. Jensen, 'Opportunists in South China during the Boxer Rebellion', *PHR* 20 (Aug. 1951), 241 f.

[2] Minute by Bertie on Whitehead to Salisbury, tel. 57 of 4 Sept. 1900, F.O. 46/531; Salisbury to Whitehead, tel. 86 of 29 Aug. 1900, copy, Adm. 116/117. The only reference to the expansionist impulse of the Yamagata Administration in relation to this incident traced in the contemporary material is in J. T. Pratt, 'Japanese activity in Southern China September–December 1900', encl. Intelligence Report, Dec. quarter, encl. in Satow to Lansdowne, No. 70 of 18 Feb. 1901, F.O. 17/1470.

[3] Warren to Salisbury, tel. 126A of 10 Sept. 1900, F.O. 17/1427.

[4] Warren to Salisbury, tels. 109, 111 of 29, 30 Aug. 1900, F.O. 17/1427.

[5] C.-in-C. to Admiralty, tel. 174 of 30 Aug. 1900, Adm. 116/117.

The Government's reply revealed the full extent to which Great Britain's position on the Yangtze had been weakened by the occupation of Shanghai. Seymour was instructed:

All influence should be used to prevent such a disaster. If collision (between the Germans and the Chinese) should be probable you should avoid, if possible, being present; but if H.M. ships are present and the necessity is very serious you should assist Germans.[1]

[1] Foreign Office to Admiralty, 30 Aug. 1900, F.O. 17/1445; Admiralty to C.-in-C., tel. 190 of 31 Aug. 1900, Adm. 116/117.

VIII

THE ANGLO-GERMAN AGREEMENT

AFTER the fall of Peking on 14 August the Manchu Court fled to Sian in Shensi, the Chinese armies were dispersed beyond the boundaries of the Metropolitan province and no effective Chinese authority was left in the capital. North China was in a chaotic condition.

Control lay in the hands of the foreign military forces. The Council of Admirals directed affairs at Taku, while Tientsin was controlled by a provisional military government whose three members were explicitly responsible not to the powers but to the allied generals.[1] Peking was divided into sectors, ostensibly for policing purposes, in reality as a solution to international rivalry.[2] Each contingent of the allied force maintained a rigid individuality of action. In conference, the influence of the various commanders depended on the strength of their contingents. This had been realized even before the taking of Peking, while the fiction of concerted action was being scrupulously maintained. General Gaselee, who had arrived by that time to command the British force, called for more troops to give Great Britain a greater weight in Council.[3]

The whole of the allied force engaged in widespread looting; discipline was lax. Troops ignored the orders of foreign officers and treated their own with derisive respect. Scavengers formed themselves into self-protective bands, against which their commanders were helpless, and forayed into the countryside avowedly in search of 'booty and blood'.[4]

[1] Dorward to War Office, 2 Aug. 1900, F.O. 17/1443. The regulations of the Council are given in Satow to Lansdowne, No. 92, and encl. of 5 Mar. 1901, F.O. 17/1471.
[2] The British sector was the Chinese city lying east of the mainstreet from Ch'ien men and the Tartar city west of Shun Chih men and south of Ping tze men street. The Russians demanded passports in their area and insulted the foreign residents in an attempt to drive them out; cf. Sir Edmund Backhouse's complaint of 4 Sept. 1900, Misc. 105, F.O. 228/1343.
[3] Gaselee to India Office of 13 Aug. 1900, F.O. 17/1444.
[4] Report of C. H. Powell, encl. in Intelligence Division to Foreign Office, 12 Nov. 1900, F.O. 17/1449.

At first General Gaselee tried to keep the British contingent from participating in this looting. But he found this impossible without causing the gravest discontent among his troops, who saw the activities of the other contingents in this respect openly tolerated. Accordingly on 16 August he cancelled his previous orders against looting and did his best to regulate the practice by limiting the confiscation of property to unoccupied houses and by instituting the practice of prize money.[1] 'All nationalities loot quite impartially and indiscriminately wherever they choose', he reported to MacDonald. 'It is quite impossible to maintain order.'[2] 'From Taku to Peking', an observer noted, 'there is a continuous belt of devastated country. Not a town or village along the line of march has escaped pillage, accompanied, in many instances by atrocities. . . .'[3] Two months later, when Sir Earnest Satow entered Peking, he noted: 'It was like entering a huge city of the dead where the tombs had been thrown down and enveloped in dust.'[4] In November he wrote to Salisbury:

> Whatever any one finds unguarded he feels it his duty to appropriate lest some one else should take it after he has passed by. . . . It reminds one of the Papal Bulls that gave all the property of the heathen nations to the Kings of Spain and Portugal. No Chinese is recognized as being capable of ownership of moveables.[5]

More significantly, the province of Chihli was faced with famine. Boxer activity the previous May had left the spring crop unharvested; by September rice was being sold at an exorbitant price. In Peking the Japanese attempted some relief by distributing the stock in the thirteen Imperial granaries; but the lack of food was critical and rapidly making the province militarily untenable. Gaselee was inclined to move his winter headquarters to Shanghai.[6]

[1] Correspondence given W.O. 32/137/7842/1224.
[2] Gaselee to MacDonald, No. 94 of 16 Aug. 1900, F.O. 228/1343.
[3] W. C. Hillier to Eric Barrington, 31 Aug. 1900, S.P. 106/32.
[4] S.J., 20 Oct. 1900. This was echoed by a Chinese observer: 'The wards and markets of the city were desolate and bleak, foxes appeared in the daytime, where in former days people thronged shoulder to shoulder with hub striking on hub now one found himself walking as though amongst the old tombs.' Li Hsi-sheng, 'Keng-tzu kuo pien-chi', I.H.T. i. 24.
[5] Satow to Salisbury, 8 Nov. 1900, S.P. Chronological Series, Imperial and Foreign, III.
[6] Gaselee to Hamilton (India Office), No. 229 of 29 Aug. 1900, F.O. 17/1446.

In this chaotic situation there was ample evidence of growing friction between the allied contingents. Recriminations were levelled against the Russians for breaking the agreement for a concerted attack on Peking, and their motives were deeply suspect to the other military authorities as the various contingents set about occupying strategic points.

In this respect, as far as the British were concerned, the Russians displayed an adeptness which indicated a deliberate plan. Immediately after the allied attack on the Taku forts in June, a Russian detachment had occupied the head office of the Northern railway administration in Tientsin and then systematically destroyed the title deeds to the sale of land connected with the railway project.[1] On 8 July, during the allied advance on the native city of Tientsin, the Russians seized the Tangku–Tientsin section of the line, and turned out the British manager, Kinder, and his staff on the ground of military necessity. On 16 July the Council of Admirals decided that the section should be managed by the Russian army until the settlement; this proposal was made by Admiral Alexieff, the Russian chairman of the Council, and carried by majority against British, Japanese, and American objections.[2] At the time, the Russian action was brought to the attention of the Foreign Office by the British and Chinese Corporation.[3] Major-General Ardagh had then observed that if Russian administration of this vital stretch of line were allowed it would be difficult later to dispossess her, and that '. . . the episode savours of something more than a mere military detail, and looks like fishing in troubled waters for a reversal of the understanding between Great Britain and Russia as to the railway of which this is a section'. He suggested releasing British rights over the line to Russia in exchange for a free hand at Shanghai.[4] However, Salisbury rejected the idea of a bargain and confined his action to a mild note to Russia stating that Great Britain had no objection to the transfer on

Also, see S. D. Gamble, 'Prices, Wages and the Standard of Living in Peking', *CSPSR* 10 (1926), July Supplement, pp. 11–12, 25.

[1] C. W. Kinder and A. N. Bruce, Report on total destruction of Imperial Chinese Railway, Head Office, Tientsin, encl. 4 in Admiralty to Foreign Office, 5 Oct. 1900, F.O. 17/1448.

[2] Minutes of Meeting of Senior Naval Officers on H.B.M.S. *Centurion* on 16 July 1900, encl. 2 in China Letter 530/3874 of 24 Aug. 1900, Adm. 116/115.

[3] B. & C. Corporation to Foreign Office, 14 July 1900, F.O. 17/1442.

[4] Memorandum by Ardagh of 16 July 1900, F.O. 17/1442.

condition the line reverted to British ownership on termination of hostilities.[1]

After he had been overruled in Council on 16 July, Admiral Seymour advised General Doward, then in command of British military forces in north China, to make every effort to keep the next section of the line, which lay between Tientsin and Peking, in British hands by commencing repairs on it as soon as possible.[2] This aim was forestalled by the Russians when they began work on the line north of Tientsin on 9 August; Dorward, who arrived belatedly to offer British assistance, was ignored.[3]

After the relief of the legations the matter was taken up by Sir Claude MacDonald, who saw that it was but a matter of time before the Russians would occupy the remaining sections of the line which had been missed in the final rush on Peking. In a series of telegrams he asked for instructions, culminating on 28 August in the message:

> More troops urgently needed to offset Russian occupation of lines of communication and points of vantage. They already have Summer Palace and Peking terminus of Railway; unless forestalled will occupy Shanhaikuan, Chinwangtao and Tongshan Railway, giving them whole of Shanhaikuan–Peking line; they already have Taku–Tientsin line. Japanese show no enterprise—reluctance perhaps due to our weakness and doubts on our intentions.[4]

On the same day MacDonald suggested to General Gaselee, who had by this time arrived to take over from General Dorward, that British forces should occupy a point on the Peking–Tientsin section of the line north of the stretch on which the Russians were already working. Gaselee acted promptly and the little station of Feng-t'ai was occupied on 30 August. The Russians immediately posted a detachment in front of the station. General Linevich, in command of the Russian military forces, protested formally to Gaselee on 18 September that the whole line from Taku to Peking had been handed over to Russia by the agreement of the Council of Admirals of 16 July. The British rejected this contention and, with the help of the Japanese, began repairs on the line between Feng-t'ai and

[1] Salisbury to Scott, tel. 113 of 25 July 1900, F.O. 65/1603.
[2] C.-in-C. to Admiralty, tel. 163 of 19 Aug. 1900, copy, F.O. 17/1444.
[3] Carles to Salisbury, tel. 47 of 9 Aug. 1900, F.O. 17/1429.
[4] MacDonald to Salisbury, tel. 115 of 28 Aug. 1900, F.O. 17/1418.

Yangts'un. A deadlock then followed, and the flags of the two powers were hoisted over the different sections of the line to mark possession.[1]

In London, after the relief of the legations, there was at first a misconception of the probable course of events in China. The Government were then preoccupied with the occupation of Shanghai. Francis Bertie believed that a civil war was inevitable in China before any peaceful settlement could be obtained, and that in the forthcoming débâcle the Yangtze viceroys should be assured of British protection and support.[2] On 20 August, in a memorandum to Salisbury, who was still on holiday at Schlucht, Bertie argued that as the Empress Dowager and Prince Tuan were reputedly reactionary:

. . . they will go for the Viceroys of the Yangtze who have hitherto taken the other line, and will subdue them or get knocked out themselves. I believe that there must be a considerable amount of fighting amongst the various factions in China before we can see which of them will be boss and until such time the Powers would do wisely not to interfere except to protect Treaty ports and European lives and property near enough to the coasts or rivers to be easily defended. We certainly cannot impose a Government on a nation of 400,000,000. Let them fight it out if they are inclined to do so.[3]

To Salisbury, always critical of impulsive action, this advice was sound. 'The steps to be taken next will be a matter of great difficulty,' he cabled the Queen, 'but no decision ought to be taken till we have received the written reports describing the recent crisis and its causes.'[4]

However, because of the disruption in communications, it was difficult to obtain reliable information during the latter part of August. MacDonald was forced to send his reports along devious routes, by telegraph from Tientsin, or by steamer to Shanghai or Nagasaki before transmission, which delayed them considerably. His telegram of 28 August concerning the Northern railway did not reach the Foreign Office until

[1] MacDonald to Gaselee, Misc. 96 of 28 Aug.; Gaselee to Secretary of State for India, No. 21 of 20 Sept. (Misc. 104A); Linevich to Gaselee, No. 564 of 6/18 Sept.; Gaselee's reply, No. 1474 of 20 Sept. 1900, F.O. 228/1343.
[2] S.J., 20 Aug. 1900.
[3] Bertie to Salisbury, 20 Aug. 1900, F.O. 17/1444.
[4] Salisbury to the Queen, tel. of 20 Aug. 1900. S.P. Schlucht.

8 September.[1] A message which did come through on 24 August tended to confuse rather than to enlighten the Government. In it, MacDonald stressed the need for crushing completely Chinese military power in the vicinity before beginning negotiations.[2] The report seemed to confirm a fear which Salisbury had entertained since the beginning of the crisis, that after the collapse of Chinese resistance the powers would extend the field of operations to suit their own aims. '. . . I should, if we had no allies, reply that the wisest course is to allow the Chinese situation to develop further before taking any action,' he told MacDonald, '(but we have) impatient allies (so matters are left) to your discretion (with the) single reservation . . . that in the attempt to carry out punishment you must not engage in any dangerous or costly expedition.'[3] Two days later Salisbury's uneasiness was revealed in a second instruction to MacDonald: he stressed that it would be impossible to crush Chinese resistance with any hope of success, and that, with the limited number of troops at her disposal, it was impossible for Great Britain to attempt to maintain order in north China 'even if we stood alone. But as it would certainly produce a collision between ourselves and our allies it would only end disastrously.'[4]

On 25 August Russia circulated a proposal to the powers suggesting that as the relief of the legations had been completed and as no responsible government remained in Peking, the legations and troops of the allied powers should be withdrawn to Tientsin, and that all attempts at a settlement with China should be postponed until the Chinese Court had returned to Peking and had re-established normal diplomatic relations with

[1] At the time, telegraphic communication from Peking and Tientsin was by (1) the Shanghai–Tientsin overland line, (2) the Kiachta–Peking line, (3) the Helampo–Kirin–Manchurian line, and (4) via Japan and Korea. Except for the laborious sea route everything was in the hands of the Russians. It is difficult to say whether there was deliberate suppression, but when the delayed telegrams were received on 8 September their cyphers were corrupt and had obviously been tampered with. Eventually the Foreign Office realized their disadvantage and everything was duplicated to Warren at Shanghai, and when this proved equally unsatisfactory, triplicated through Whitehead at Tokyo.

[2] MacDonald to Salisbury, tel. 112 of 19 Aug. 1900, F.O. 228/1334. This telegram is missing from the Foreign Office Correspondence, but from the nature of Salisbury's reply it was obviously received, so it has been quoted from the Consular Archives.

[3] Salisbury to MacDonald, tel. 82 of 24 Aug. 1900, F.O. 17/1417.

[4] Salisbury to MacDonald, tel. 83 of 26 Aug. 1900, F.O. 17/1417.

THE ANGLO-GERMAN AGREEMENT 199

the powers.[1] The suggestion was received with consternation in Germany. Field-Marshal Waldersee, who had been sent off with such pomp, would cut a ridiculous figure if he arrived to find everyone gone. Baron Eckardstein hurriedly presented himself at the Foreign Office and declared that Germany would pledge herself to remain if two other great powers did likewise; and that Japan was to count as a great power.[2] Four days later, on 4 September, Eckardstein enlarged on this offer: Great Britain would get support over the Tientsin–Peking railway, Bertie reported, 'provided we make up our minds to keep hold of Peking in company with Japan and Germany. If we determine not to hold on, Waldersee will probably be stopped and Germany will sit in Kiaochow and leave things in Manchuria to slide.'[3]

The Russian and German counter-proposals were received with great excitement in London. The Committee had become increasingly depressed at the turn of events in Shanghai. The Kaiser's overture of 22 August, which promised to stabilize the situation on the Yangtze at least in respect of one power, had been coldly received by Salisbury. There was a rising sense of irritation at the Prime Minister's obstinacy. Nor did the Committee show confidence in themselves. On 29 August Hamilton confessed to Curzon that they would have to meet to consider the Russian proposal 'to try and either come to some conclusions ourselves, or to get the Prime Minister to state more definitely what he intends to do'.[4] Three days previously Lansdowne, Minister for War, had placed his resignation in Salisbury's hands because of the criticism of his conduct of the South African war. Lansdowne seemed particularly dispirited. He was in favour of withdrawing from Peking on the grounds that continued occupation would lead to unpleasant complications, and that it would be difficult to maintain forces there over the winter.[5] Hamilton thought the War Office pressed withdrawal because of jealousy that the China expedition was in the hands of the India Office.[6]

[1] Scott to Salisbury, tel. 93 of 29 Aug. 1900, F.O. 65/1604.
[2] Bertie to Salisbury, 31 Aug. 1900, S.P. Schlucht.
[3] Bertie to Salisbury, 4 Sept. 1900, S.P. Schlucht; Eckardstein claimed later that these conditions had been put forward on his own initiative; cf. Baron Eckardstein, *Ten Years at the Court of St. James* (London, 1921), 175.
[4] Hamilton to Curzon, 29 Aug. 1900, Hamilton Papers.
[5] Lansdowne to Salisbury, tel. of 31 Aug. 1900, S.P. 89/69.
[6] Hamilton to Curzon, 5 Sept. 1900, Hamilton Papers.

Consequently, the change in Germany's attitude brought an invigorating sense of optimism, tempered only by the fear that Salisbury would remain obdurate. From the start they misread Germany's intentions and moved from an attitude of defensive concessions on the Yangtze to the concept of an Anglo-German understanding covering the whole field of policy. After Eckardstein's first visit, Goschen, who took the lead, wrote to Chamberlain, to whom the matter was of obvious interest:

> . . . The latest Russian move as to retreating from Peking which is distasteful to Germany, furnishes a good opportunity for opening of conversations and exchange of ideas with the Emperor, but we hang back, are open with nobody, and shall practically stand alone, or come in at the tail of other Powers on every occasion.
>
> If I see any opening that may be utilized I would ask you and Balfour to come to London to meet Lansdowne and G. Hamilton, who, like myself, are in despair of our present attitude. . . .[1]

Eckardstein's second visit of 4 September and the specific conditions which he outlined provided the necessary opening.

Chamberlain's attention was then on the forthcoming election. On 31 August he had written to Salisbury that, on the whole, China seemed 'in a less critical condition' and that in this quarter there was little public interest.[2] This may have been merely a manœuvre to persuade Salisbury to an early dissolution, the Prime Minister having declared an election inadvisable until the situation had cleared. But the chance of opening Anglo-German negotiations could not be missed and, when the Committee of Three met on 4 September to discuss the Chinese situation, Chamberlain was present.

The joint telegraphic summary of the discussion which was sent to Salisbury after the meeting put the case well. The ministers drew Salisbury's attention to the adverse public opinion which could be aroused by a premature withdrawal from Peking without previous arrangement of terms with the Chinese. Having thus raised the ghost of the 1898 agitation over Port Arthur, they then introduced their weightier arguments. Withdrawal would 'be considered as leaving the game in the hands of Russia, whose interest is clearly to draw the Allies

---

[1] Goschen to Chamberlain, 1 Sept. 1900, quoted Amery, *Chamberlain*, iv. 138.
[2] Garvin, *Chamberlain*, iii. 591.

away from Pekin while still occupying Newchang and parts of Manchuria'; it would also be interpreted as evidence of fear, leading to further outrages. It was important to use the recent Russian action to bind the German Emperor closer to Great Britain, and if he were helped to avoid humiliation after his brave words he would support Great Britain over the Northern railway and give assurances with regard to the British position on the Yangtze. For this purpose an interchange of views should be arranged with Germany. Lansdowne, the report concluded triumphantly, was concerned with the military position, but he would concur. Balfour's concurrence was also indicated.[1]

The ministers were clearly elated by Great Britain's apparently improved position. Since 1898 a section of the Cabinet, under Chamberlain's guidance, had skirmished unsuccessfully for a German alliance. Each of the two previous attempts had failed against two objections to which no satisfactory reply could be given. The first was Salisbury's insistence on the fact that an alliance with Germany would be of little avail to Great Britain where she needed it; the second was the irritating German indication that short of committing herself to the Triple Alliance in Europe Great Britain could be of little use to Germany. Now in the pattern of Chinese affairs these points had found their connection. 'We have an opportunity', Hamilton wrote jubilantly to Curzon, 'such as we have never had before of separating Germany from Russia.'[2]

Salisbury replied from Schlucht with a coolness which exasperated his colleagues. Where, in their enthusiasm, Chamberlain and the other ministers saw the making of an Anglo-German bridge, Salisbury saw only the pitfalls. He agreed against withdrawal from Peking, but objected to developing this resolution into a general acceptance of German policy, which in his view was more dangerous and required careful reflection. 'What does Germany want from us?' he asked Goschen with a bluntness which anticipated his famous memorandum of May 1901, 'What can she give us in return?'[3]

[1] Goschen to Salisbury, tel. of 4 Sept. 1900, S.P. 69/70. The rejected draft (S.P. 89/71) also argued the opportunity of joining Japan in taking advantage of Germany's position to detach her from Russia and France.

[2] Hamilton to Curzon, 5 Sept. 1900, Hamilton Papers.

[3] Salisbury to Goschen, tel. of 5 Sept. 1900, S.P. Schlucht. The disillusionment

This difference in opinion between Salisbury and the influential section of his Cabinet, chiefly Chamberlain, Goschen, Hamilton, and, to a lesser extent, Lansdowne, can be briefly analysed. These ministers believed that if Russia were to be stopped successfully a vigorous policy was necessary. The obvious way to this was by close combination with Germany, with the possible co-operation of Japan and the United States. In reality their perspective was conditioned by a long-standing Russophobia, and they looked through the China problem without actually seeing it, to the concept of an Anglo-German alliance which seemed to lie beyond.

Salisbury, on the other hand, although apprehensive of Russia's recent conduct in China, refused to condemn her out of hand. His aim was to maintain the Anglo-Russian Agreement of April 1899. Until this agreement was deliberately transgressed he refused to act. He would not embark on a policy of anticipation; British interests depended on concert not combination in China. Further, Salisbury's deep-rooted suspicions of Germany were given fresh application when focused on the Far East. Before sending Satow out to replace MacDonald he impressed on Satow that he suspected Wilhelm II of big designs in China.[1] This fear seemed only too tangible when it was reported by Bertie on 1 September that the Kaiser had ordered two companies of the German East Asiatic Corps to land at Shanghai, and by Warren on 3 September that there was considerable native unrest over a rumoured German intention of seizing the Kiangyin forts.[2] It will be remembered that a few days previously Admiral Seymour had been instructed not to oppose German action on the Yangtze. Throughout the Boxer crisis, as far as Germany was concerned, Salisbury's aim was not to search for German co-operation, but to keep that power under control.

On 11 September Bertie reported that Count Hatzfeldt, the German Ambassador at London, wished to take up the discussions which had been begun by the Kaiser on 22 August. Bertie added that Hatzfeldt had suggested that discussion should

occasioned by this reply is indicated in Amery, *Chamberlain*, iv. 139. Amery's date of 4 Sept. raises the possibility of a previous telegram. However, 5 Sept. is confirmed in S.P. 89/73.   [1] S.J., 20, 24 Aug. 1900.

[2] Bertie to Salisbury, 1 Sept. 1900; Warren to Salisbury (through Bertie), 3 Sept. 1900, S.P. Schlucht.

be on the basis of a general self-denying declaration by Great Britain and Germany that neither power would seek territorial compensation in China because of the existing complications. The suggestion aroused Salisbury's interest, and he agreed to see the German minister on 14 September, two days after he returned.[1]

When Salisbury returned to London he found the Cabinet greatly excited. MacDonald's telegram of 28 August reporting Russian seizures on the Northern railway had arrived on 8 September; on 10 September the Russian proposal for a general withdrawal had been rejected.[2] On the same day Chamberlain had taken the lead and in a lengthy Cabinet memorandum had presented in greater detail the arguments Goschen had sent Salisbury a week previously.

If Great Britain stood by the Kaiser, Chamberlain reasoned, the German Emperor's position would become tenable and he would be saved from humiliation. For this 'signal service' satisfactory assurances could be obtained in return. Great Britain was not strong enough alone to maintain the integrity of China or to enforce the Open Door, and it would be some time before harmony of action could be achieved with the United States to this end; meanwhile, to resist the immediate threat of Russian expansion, Great Britain should work closely with Germany and Japan, supporting the special claims of these two powers in Shantung and Korea. In return, Great Britain should obtain written assurances recognizing her claim to predominant interest and influence in the Yangtze valley. Chamberlain concluded:

. . . Both in China and elsewhere it is our interest that Germany should throw herself across the path of Russia. An alliance between Germany and Russia, entailing, as it would, the co-operation of France, is the one thing we have to dread, and the clash of German and Russian interests, whether in China or Asia Minor, would be the guarantee for our safety. I think, then, our policy clearly is to encourage good relations between ourselves and Germany, as well as between ourselves and Japan and the United States, and we should endeavour to emphasize the breach between Russia and Germany, and Russia and Japan. . . .[3]

[1] Bertie to Salisbury, 11 Sept. 1900, S.P. Schlucht.
[2] Salisbury to Scott, tel. 166 of 10 Sept. 1900, F.O. 65/1603.
[3] The memorandum is summarized in Amery, *Chamberlain*, iv. 140; the quotation given ibid. 159.

On 13 September, the day before Salisbury was due to meet Hatzfeldt, Bertie wrote a memorandum on Anglo-German relations in China. Any tendency Salisbury may have had to act upon Chamberlain's analysis was halted by Bertie's pessimistic appraisal. 'We may be able to arrange a "modus vivendi" with Germany to tide over the present crisis', Bertie stated bluntly, 'but mere "open door" or "open port" and tariff declarations are not likely to satisfy her.' Germany's pretensions were large; she claimed a special position in Shantung which cut Great Britain out, but she also made a claim in the Yangtze. 'What Germany will claim as her special field', Bertie continued, 'will probably be Shantung and the valley of the Yellow R(iver). We shall have to undertake not to support any British application in that region.' Germany would also want to share everything between the Yellow river and the Yangtze. Great Britain would be pushed south where she would come into collision with France. Nor could Germany be regarded as a buffer against Russia's southward move, for if that power secured enough territory and if the capital remained at Peking after the settlement, Russia and Germany would control China between them.[1]

Salisbury and Hatzfeldt met in two preliminary meetings on 14 and 18 September. On the 24th Hatzfeldt presented a German draft agreement, to which Salisbury responded with a British counter-draft the following day. With this exchange in writing the real negotiations began. Both drafts contained three articles.

Article one dealt with the freedom of trade. The German draft confined the declaration on the open door specifically to the Yangtze. The British counter-draft maintained that 'the ports on the rivers and littoral of China should remain free and open to trade and to every other legitimate form of economic activity...'. Article two covered the assurance that neither power would take advantage of the situation in China. On this, Germany merely proposed agreement on a self-denying ordinance, while Great Britain added the vital provision that the

[1] Memorandum by Bertie of 13 Sept. 1900, F.O. 17/1446. The memorandum was put into print. Bertie expressed his surprise at the importance attached to it but 'had no feeling one way or another as to it being recorded'. On reflection it was taken out of print and prevented from going abroad in the China Series. The confidential print was found by the editors of the British Documents, cf. *B.D.* ii. 11.

two powers would 'oppose, in such manner as may be agreed upon between the two Powers, any attempt on the part of any other Powers to obtain territorial advantages in a similar manner'. Article three was identical in both drafts. This stated that if any other power should endeavour to obtain territorial acquisitions and if the two powers should 'consequently consider it necessary themselves to proceed to territorial acquisitions' then they would come to a previous understanding on the subject.[1]

The differences revealed were striking; Germany was intent on a strictly limited agreement which would allow her to share in the lucrative Yangtze trade, Great Britain on an undertaking which could possibly commit Germany to oppose Russian acquisitions in north China and Manchuria. Salisbury's intention was to distract German attention from the Yangtze. The tactic was excellent, but he was put at a disadvantage in the subsequent negotiations because his geography was poor.

At the beginning of October Hatzfeldt pointed out to Salisbury, in respect of article one, that the German Government could hardly be expected to uphold the principle of the freedom of trade in China on the terms suggested by Salisbury, for that would commit Germany to press it on Russia in areas of Manchuria where international commercial rights were not secured by any treaty.[2] Salisbury then agreed to a suggestion, which was apparently put forward by Hatzfeldt, that the two powers should uphold the open door in China by renouncing 'all special commercial restrictions for all the rivers and for the littoral of China south of parallel 38 of north latitude' which 'would include all the territories over which the two Governments had influence, without implying any consent on their part to provisions of a different character under the influence of other Powers'.[3] In effect, Salisbury was ready to stand by the

[1] B.D. ii. 12–13.

[2] Salisbury to Lascelles, No. 224 of 15 Oct. 1900, F.O. 64/1491; B.D. ii. 15. Sections of this dispatch, which surveyed the whole course of negotiation, were deleted before being sent.

[3] Salisbury to Lascelles, No. 224 of 15 Oct. 1900, F.O. 64/1491. On 5 Oct. Bülow told Lascelles in Berlin that Salisbury had proposed that the arrangement under negotiation should not be confined to the Yangtze. When Lascelles asked whether it were to include Manchuria, Bülow replied that Salisbury 'had drawn a line across the map of China to the south of Manchuria' (Lascelles to Salisbury, 5 Oct. 1900, S.P. 121/61). In 1902, after the terms of the agreement had become a matter

Anglo-Russian Agreement of 1899 and tacitly to accept the absorption of Manchuria by Russia. His aim in negotiating was to meet Germany's efforts to intrude into the Yangtze area by claiming a reciprocal right by Great Britain to enter Germany's sphere in Shantung.

However, the 38th parallel did not lie along the Great Wall but along a line running just north of the Shantung peninsula and the mouth of the Yellow river, a full 200 miles south of Peking. Salisbury had agreed to exclude not only Manchuria but also most of north China. When Sir Thomas Sanderson brought the discrepancy to the Prime Minister's attention he was forced to retrieve the position as best he could.[1]

After considerable discussion, the declaration on the freedom of trade was defined as applying to the ports and littoral of China, the two powers agreeing 'to uphold the same for all Chinese territory as far as they can exercise influence'.[2] In addition, Salisbury suggested the addition of a clause by which the powers undertook to maintain their interests in China and their rights under existing treaties. Hatzfeldt agreed to this on the understanding that this referred only to treaties which were published and known. Finally, article two was rephrased less precisely. Instead of Salisbury's suggestion that Great Britain and Germany should 'oppose, in such manner as may be agreed upon between the two Powers, any attempt on the part of any other Powers to obtain territorial advantages', Bülow proposed the reading that the powers 'will direct their policy towards maintaining undiminished the territorial condition of the Chinese Empire'. Salisbury accepted this, apparently with reluctance.[3] The agreement was then signed on 16 October 1900.

---

of dispute between Great Britain and Germany, Mallet of the Foreign Office told Lascelles that the 38th parallel had been proposed by Hatzfeldt on 4 Oct. (memorandum by Mallet to Lascelles, private, of 5 Mar. encl. 12 Mar. 1902, F.O. 17/1547).

[1] Memorandum by Sanderson of 4 Oct. 1900, F.O. 64/1507. The mistake may have been helped on in that Bertie, who usually kept a watchful eye on details of this sort, was on leave from the beginning of Oct.

[2] Salisbury to Lascelles, No. 224 of 15 Oct. 1900, F.O. 64/1491; memorandum by Mallet, 12 Mar. 1902, F.O. 17/1547.

[3] Hatzfeldt to Salisbury, 4 Oct. 1900, F.O. 64/1506. Drafts of the Agreement of 6, 9, 13 Oct. 1900 are given in F.O. 17/1448. The Agreement is reprinted in B.D. ii. 15–16.

As an Anglo-German understanding for the preservation of the territorial integrity of China the wording of the final agreement was thus dangerously obscure; the phrase 'as far as they can exercise influence' was susceptible of various interpretations. Within six months of negotiation it was to be disputed in relation to the Manchurian crisis of the spring of 1901. Lansdowne, who had then replaced Salisbury at the Foreign Office, acted in the belief that the Anglo-German Agreement applied to Manchuria, while Germany maintained that Manchuria had been excluded. This difference of opinion will be examined in a later chapter, but Salisbury's purpose in negotiating the Agreement should be noted here.

Salisbury's aim was not an alignment against Russia but an arrangement to bring Germany under a certain measure of control. The Prime Minister's easy acquiescence in Bülow's counter-suggestions and in the vague wording of the Agreement is explicable only if this intention is grasped. When it became clear at the end of August that Germany would possibly take advantage of the opening provided by the international occupation of Shanghai to engage in an aggressive policy against the Chinese on the Yangtze, an understanding became essential.

It must be remembered that Salisbury negotiated the Agreement against the background of a deteriorating situation in China. Throughout September and the early part of October, alarming reports came in from Warren at Shanghai. The substance of these was that vindictive officials at the fugitive Manchu Court were determined on reprisals against the Yangtze viceroys. At the end of September Warren suggested that a British punitive expedition should make a two-pronged attack on the exiled Court, from the north and up the Yangtze, to punish the reactionary officials who were threatening Chang and Liu.[1] When Salisbury rejected this suggestion Warren pressed that Great Britain should guarantee that the viceroys would not be removed from their posts, adding on 13 October, 'I trust H.M. Government will allow me to assure them of *material* support in case of need.'[2]

In north China the position was equally precarious. After the Russian proposal for a general withdrawal from Peking had

[1] Warren to Salisbury, tel. 150 of 24 Sept. 1900, F.O. 17/1427.
[2] Warren to Salisbury, tel. 170 of 13 Oct. 1900, F.O. 17/1427.

been rejected by the powers, Russia then suggested on 15 September that the powers should accept Li Hung-chang and Prince Ching as Chinese plenipotentiaries and agree to an immediate start to peace negotiations.[1] Li Hung-chang was then generally regarded as being favourably inclined toward Russia and, since July, there was a feeling among British commercial interests that the Chinese statesman should be forcibly prevented from travelling north. By September this view had been accepted by the military authorities in north China, and a movement was made to detain Li on an allied ship. Although Salisbury was aware of Li Hung-chang's pro-Russian leanings he was anxious to see an early start to the peace negotiations, for a continued state of chaotic military activity in north China was to Great Britain's disadvantage. When asked for a decision he stated categorically that he saw 'no reason for refusing L.H.C. or any other Chinaman as negotiator, if he is properly accredited'.[2]

However, Germany had no desire to see an early settlement with the Chinese. The German reply to the Russian proposal was a counter-circular on 18 September, maintaining that before there could be any talk of peace it would be necessary to punish the guilty Chinese officials.[3] Her aim was that north China should continue in the state of unrest which would be most suited to the extension of Waldersee's military authority.

When Waldersee arrived in north China on 26 September he attempted to establish a system of German military control. Colonel Grierson, the British representative, arrived at Waldersee's headquarters to find a complete staff of thirty German officers already established. The allied liaison officers were deliberately excluded. 'All that was wanted of us,' Grierson noted, 'was that we should act as a "means of communication", i.e. as translating and post offices between the Headquarters Staff and those of the contingents.'[4] They were barred from executive work and not consulted on operations. The German flag was always carried behind Waldersee; the Headquarters'

[1] Salisbury to MacDonald, tel. 109 of 2 Oct. 1900, F.O. 17/1417.

[2] Minute on Whitehead to Salisbury, tel. 62, confidential, of 13 Sept. 1900, F.O. 46/531.

[3] Salisbury to MacDonald, tel. 96 of 24 Sept. 1900, F.O. 17/1417.

[4] Grierson to War Office, Final Report . . . 24 July 1901, Intelligence Division to Foreign Office, 12 Aug. 1901, F.O. 17/1508.

guard was always German. German flags were even hoisted over latrines and henhouses. It was clear to everyone at the time that the German intention was 'to exploit their position as a huge advertisement for German prestige—military and political—in China'.[1]

Moreover, Waldersee's military control was conducted in a manner clearly detrimental to British interests. It will be remembered that at the end of August MacDonald decided to anticipate the Russians over the control of the Northern railway. An opportunity for this occurred in the first week of September, when the Chinese general in charge of the forts at Pehtang (near Taku) and at Shanhaikuan let it be known privately that he wished to surrender through the British.[2] When Salisbury was informed he repudiated MacDonald's policy of anticipation and stated bluntly that as Great Britain would protest if the action were undertaken by Russia as being contrary 'to the spirit of the arrangement of April 1899' she would not embark on such a course herself.[3] When Waldersee arrived in north China he declared that the forts at Shanhai-kuan would be placed under combined allied control. Arrangements were made for France and Russia each to occupy a fort, Germany, Italy, and Austria were to hold a third, while Great Britain and Japan were to control the fourth. This arrangement was only entered into under protest by the Russians; Admiral Alexieff stated formally that he considered Shanhai-kuan 'the left wing of Russian operations in Manchuria and their sphere' but that he would hoist his flag with the others.[4] The port controlled the Northern railway at its juncture with the Great Wall, and Russia's determination to control it was revealed during the process of occupation.

To meet the Chinese commandant's wishes Sir Walter Hillier of the Hongkong and Shanghai Bank was detailed to precede the international detachments to arrange a peaceful trans-ference through British hands. This allowed a small escort which Hillier had taken with him for the purpose, ostensibly for protection, to occupy the all-important railway station

[1] See note 4 on page 208.
[2] Chinese correspondence given in No. 124 of 13 Sept. 1900, F.O. 228/1334.
[3] Salisbury to MacDonald, tel. 87 of 7 Sept. 1900, F.O. 17/1417.
[4] C.-in-C. to Admiralty, tels. 206 and 210 of 27 Sept. and 1 Oct. 1900, Adm. 116/117.

which Waldersee had forgotten to allocate. When the forces of the other powers arrived on 1 October the Russians ignored their fort but rushed to the railway station and were chagrined to find the British in possession. By 3 October 7,000 Russian troops had been transferred from Tongshan and Port Arthur. When these had to be withdrawn for service in Manchuria a major-general of three years' standing was left in command of two weak battalions, thus ensuring Russia administrative control of the port. It was 'a really intolerable state of things in North China', Hamilton observed when seeking Salisbury's approval for the occupation of the port (two weeks after the occupation had in fact been carried out), but Great Britain had to take part, otherwise 'it might result in our being put altogether on one side'.[1] To regain control Reid, the British general next in seniority, was given his promotion, thus placing him in charge. Twenty-four hours later the Russian announced his promotion. In the face of such dauntless determination the matter was allowed to drop.[2]

Similarly, Russian activity in respect of the Northern railway was condoned, if not encouraged, by Waldersee. The line had been built and run by the British; it was the 'last remaining wedge of British influence'[3] in the north, without which she could surrender any pretensions to an influential position at the Court. Russia already controlled the Taku–Tientsin stretch; she was also working on the line from Tientsin to Peking and had only been stopped from advancing further by MacDonald's anticipatory action in occupying Feng-t'ai outside Yangts'un. The last stretch lay along the eastern arm, from Taku up to Shanhaikuan. During the extensive troop movements which followed the occupation of Shanhaikuan, a Russian column under General Tzerpidsky quietly moved in and took possession of the stretch by the simple strategem of picketing 3,000 troops along the line. This was in open defiance of Waldersee's order that no occupation should be made except by his direction. The Russians, however, refused to move and claimed the line by right of conquest. Later, after the signing of the Anglo-

[1] Hamilton to Salisbury, 13 Oct. 1900, S.P. 91/45.
[2] Gaselee to India Office, tel. 42 of 9 Oct. 1900, F.O. 17/1448; Powell to India Office of 6 Nov. 1900 in India Office to Foreign Office, 31 Dec. 1900, F.O. 17/1451.
[3] Memorandum by Hillier, The British Position in China, encl. 22 Mar. 1900, F.O. 17/1438.

German Agreement, when Great Britain and Germany showed a greater tendency to confide in each other, Waldersee maintained to MacDonald that 'short of fighting' he was forced to acquiesce.[1] But at the time there was a different complexion to Waldersee's complaisance. Gaselee returned from Tientsin on 4 October to report that Waldersee had decided that the Russians should have control and construction rights on the railway from Taku to Yangts'un, while the remaining Yangts'un–Peking stretch should be worked by the Germans assisted by the other powers. Waldersee also intimated that the Russians should be allowed to keep the Taku–Shanhaikuan stretch.[2] Although Salisbury immediately ordered a protest to be made in Berlin and although, on American initiative, the American, Japanese, and British generals protested to Waldersee, the Field-Marshal persisted in his intention. On 8 October an Army Order was issued confirming these appropriations.[3] 'I assert', Grierson stated categorically, 'that the attitude of the Headquarters Staff towards the Russians here is dictated by considerations of purely German policy and by fear of them. . . .'[4]

Thus within a fortnight of Waldersee taking over, which coincided with the time immediately preceding the conclusion of the Anglo-German Agreement, Great Britain had been deprived of every strategic position, losing even the points which MacDonald had previously secured. She was given the administration of certain coastal harbour works, but it was expressly stipulated that these should be equally available to all nations. No such condition was made in respect of the Russians. The railway, which had become the symbol of control in north China, had passed out of her hands; within a few days the Russians were painting the rolling stock with the colours of the Siberian Railway.[5]

[1] MacDonald to Salisbury, tel. 174 of 23 Oct. 1900, F.O. 17/1418.
[2] MacDonald to Salisbury, tel. 143 of 4 Oct. 1900, F.O. 228/1334. References to Taku in the text are made to emphasize the strategic location; strictly the line passed through Tangku, the railhead of the port.
[3] Salisbury to Lascelles, tel. 188 of 7 Oct. 1900, F.O. 64/1496; MacDonald to Salisbury, tel. 149 of 11 Oct. 1900, F.O. 17/1418; the Army Order (Army H.Q., Tientsin, 1A, No. 599 of 8 Oct. 1900) is given in Misc. 118A/1900, F.O. 228/1343.
[4] Grierson to Under-Secretary of State for War, secret, No. 1 of 2 Oct. 1900 in War Office to Foreign Office, 11 Dec. 1900, F.O. 17/1451.
[5] MacDonald to Salisbury, tel. 149 of 11 Oct. 1900, F.O. 17/1418.

On 12 October Sir Thomas Sanderson wrote to Satow:

We do not know
  What the Chinese Court is at
  What Waldersee is after
  What the Russians mean to do
  The only thing established beyond doubt or contradiction is
    that everybody is grabbing our railway.[1]

Negotiations for an Anglo-German Agreement were carried out against this background. While aggressive action could be expected of the Russian military, when supported by Germany it became significant. No peace moves toward the Chinese had been made. The prospect was of indefinite military control in north China under German leadership and based on a policy of reprisal. On 4 October this activity was initiated by a joint military expedition to Paotingfu. Waldersee also showed a desire to extend these punitive expeditions beyond the boundaries of Chihli. When this was resisted Germany pressed for the interdiction of all supplies to the fugitive Court, so that it would be forced back to Peking.[2]

Salisbury refused to contemplate any measures designed to starve the Court out of its retreat. He declared that although Germany was very anxious to 'do something' he was 'averse to piratical proceedings'.[3] If the Court were starved out and forced to return, he noted, 'a rivalry for influence will be set up of which we shall get the worst'.[4]

Salisbury's aim was to limit the disturbed area, to confine Waldersee's military control to the Metropolitan province, and to discourage punitive expeditions into the interior. He wished to preserve the Anglo-Russian Agreement of 1899. Thus, he was tolerant of the provocative behaviour of the Russian military in north China and he refused to sanction retaliatory measures by the British. He wanted an early start to the peace negotiations.

All this was impossible if Germany were to support Russia in an expansionist policy, or if Great Britain should negotiate an anti-Russian alignment. The only solution was to curb

[1] Sanderson to Satow, 12 Oct. 1900, P.R.O. 30/33/7/1.
[2] Memorandum by Sanderson of 11 Oct. 1900, F.O. 17/1448.
[3] Minute on memorandum by Sanderson of 14 Oct. 1900, F.O. 17/1448.
[4] Minute by Salisbury on Bertie's memorandum of 18 Oct. 1900, F.O. 17/1448.

Germany by getting her to agree not to take advantage of the existing situation in China. Such an arrangement should not violate the agreement already reached with Russia; Anglo-Russian relations could then return to normal without embarking on tedious and precarious negotiations. In agreeing to confine the German agreement to an area south of the 38th parallel Salisbury had conceded more than this, but the mistake was soon rectified. In the final reading all reference to the 38th parallel was dropped; instead a defence of existing British treaty rights was written into the agreement. An examination of the Anglo-German Agreement of 16 October 1900 shows that Salisbury succeeded in his objective; Germany's promising offensive in the Yangtze area was neatly deflected and her tendency to arbitrary and opportunist activity in the north was halted. At the same time, Great Britain's right to the Northern railway was reaffirmed and the Anglo-Russian Agreement of 1899 was not transgressed.

The Agreement was received with disappointment by the Cabinet. In Hamilton's opinion it only repeated 'some archaic self-denying ordinances'.[1] At the same time Hamilton observed that it was important in that it brought Great Britain and Germany together. This consideration came to dominate the approach of the Germanophile ministers. Unlike Salisbury, they regarded it as a favourable beginning to an alignment against Russia in the Far East. In the spring of 1901 they attempted to apply it against Russia in Manchuria. The disappointment occasioned then by Germany's repudiation of this interpretation did much to turn them away from the idea of an Anglo-German alliance. Nevertheless, over the winter of 1900–1 the belief that Great Britain and Germany had reached a community of aim served a useful purpose. In November Lansdowne succeeded Salisbury at the Foreign Office and the Anglo-German Agreement enabled him to face the China problem in the confidence that he had behind him the one necessary alignment.

[1] Hamilton to Curzon, 24 Oct. 1900, Hamilton Papers.

IX

THE JOINT NOTE

O N 4 October Delcasse, the French Foreign Minister, circularized a note to the powers presenting six points on which a settlement could be arranged with the Chinese. The move came at an opportune moment. In the two months which had elapsed since the relief of the legations, the effect of the Russian proposal for a withdrawal together with the German demand for the preliminary punishment of offenders had created a situation in which an early start to formal peace negotiations had become increasingly remote. Delcasse proposed that the following six points should be accepted as a common basis of approach for a settlement:

1. Punishment of the principal culprits, who would be designated by the representatives of the Powers at Peking.
2. Maintenance of the regulations between the Powers for the prohibition of the importation of arms.
3. Equitable indemnities for states, societies, and individuals.
4. The establishment by each Power of a permanent guard for its legation at Peking.
5. The dismantlement of the forts at Taku.
6. The military occupation of certain points to be determined by an agreement between the Powers which would keep the road always open for the legations wishing to reach the sea, or for forces from the sea wishing to proceed to the capital.[1]

The list was modest. To the demand for punishment, which had hitherto filled the diplomatic horizon, the French had added five other points covering indemnities and adequate measures for the safety of foreigners in China. No mention was made of the future status of the Chinese Empire. After two and a half months of arduous negotiation by the powers, carried out through their representatives at Peking, the six points became

[1] Communicated by Salisbury to MacDonald, tel. 115 of 6 Oct. 1900, F.O. 17/1417. Published China, No. 5 (1901), p. 5 with slight verbal changes.

the basis of a Joint Note which was presented to the Chinese for their acceptance on 24 December. The negotiations were then continued at Peking until a settlement was reached with China in September 1901.

These negotiations formed but a part of the Boxer settlement. In fact, they were overshadowed by larger political issues concerning the powers, which could not be brought to the conference table at Peking. Thus, while an international crisis raged over Manchuria and while the military forces of the powers in north China stood in dangerous opposition over the control of the Northern railway and other strategic points, the assembled foreign plenipotentiaries, with an apparent show of unanimity, arranged a settlement with the Chinese.

Upon receiving the French proposals Salisbury immediately sent them to MacDonald for his opinion. MacDonald's reply of 12 October proposed a number of additional points which were brought up for consideration at Peking at the end of the month.

On 9 October Cambon, the French Ambassador in London, approached Salisbury for his reaction. Salisbury agreed to all but the last of the proposals. Instead of the occupation by an international force of a string of forts between Peking–Tientsin–Taku, which was the French conception of how point six was to be implemented, Salisbury held that each power that wished could hold a fort of its own as near as practicable to the sea.[1] In a further conversation a few days later, 16 October, Salisbury reaffirmed this, and also expressed some anxiety whether the permanent guard for the legations, provided in point four, was to be a collective body or was to be maintained as a separate unit by each power. He also preferred an identic rather than a collective note.[2]

Salisbury's stand on point six was a hardening of his reaction to a French suggestion made in August, soon after the relief. In conversation with Bertie on 24 August, Cambon had suggested that it would be necessary for the powers to hold the Taku forts permanently; Salisbury had then agreed on

---

[1] Salisbury to MacDonald, tel. 125 of 11 Oct. 1900, F.O. 228/1341.

[2] Cambon to Salisbury, résumé of conversations on Delcasse's bases for negotiations; discussion of points 6 and 4 with Salisbury's answer; Cambon's answer S.P. 119/83, 84, 87.

condition that each power should have a separate fort.[1] Salisbury's reserve was caused by, first, a reluctance to commit Great Britain to joint action or to expose British troops to foreign command; and, secondly, his determination to avoid any sense of obligation, especially in relation to the garrisoning of a legation guard.

France proposed, on 17 October, that as Delcasse's bases had been accepted by all the powers, the Chinese representatives should be approached. Salisbury assumed that his reservations had been incorporated and consequently instructed MacDonald to join in an identical note.[2] However, when the new wording of the note was submitted to the Foreign Office two days later it was seen that Delcasse's proposal of an open road (*la route ouverte*), which signified a chain of posts between the capital and the sea, had been preserved. Sanderson, who received the note, agreed that, as the French proposals had gone out, Salisbury would accept the wording as it stood and that further modifications could be made in discussion at Peking.[3] When informed, Salisbury bluntly stated that Cambon had misinterpreted their conversation and that he could not assent.[4] However, on reflection, he was persuaded to Sanderson's point of view. Word had come from Hardinge, British chargé d'affaires at St. Petersburg, that, since circumstances had been changed by the French proposals, Russia reserved the right of communication with the Chinese plenipotentiaries. This was, in effect, the abandonment of her policy of withdrawal. Again, Eckardstein had come forward to say that although France had promised not to oppose Salisbury's reservations, Germany felt it would be a mistake to begin negotiations until the powers were thoroughly agreed on the bases. Anything was preferable to the state of chaos so suitable to Germany's military ambitions, and Salisbury replied through Bertie that it was immaterial whether reservations were inserted before or at Peking so long as they formed part of the identic note and that MacDonald had been

---

[1] Memorandum by Bertie on conversation with Cambon, 24 Aug. 1900, F.O. 17/1445.

[2] Salisbury to MacDonald, tel. 130 of 17 Oct. 1900, F.O. 17/1417.

[3] Memorandum by Sanderson of 19 Oct. 1900, F.O. 17/1448.

[4] Salisbury to Sanderson, 19 Oct. 1900, F.O. 17/1448. It is difficult to say whether Delcasse committed a real or a deliberate mistake. The extent of Russian pre-knowledge of the French proposals is also a matter of much interest.

instructed accordingly.[1] In fact, MacDonald had not been instructed; but Salisbury would not risk a show of indecision to Germany. Not until three days later was MacDonald authorized to enter into negotiation, and then on condition of an amendment to point six which allowed for Salisbury's reservation. This read: '(The) Right of each Power to occupy and fortify a point accessible from the sea where the Legations may in case of need take refuge.'[2]

When negotiations opened at Peking at the end of the month the representatives made a bad start. M. N. de Giers, the Russian minister, let it be known that he intended to propose an armistice at the initial meeting on 26 October. When the representatives met, however, Mumm von Schwarzenstein, the new German minister, seized the lead and spoke out strongly against any cessation of hostilities. Mumm was so successful that the meeting was entirely taken up with the question of punishment. Discussion centred on an Imperial decree of 25 September, which the Court had issued, detailing the punishment of officials responsible for the rising. The ministers considered both the list and the degree of punishment indicated by the Chinese as inadequate. They had already expressed their dissatisfaction in this respect on 8 October, particularly in connection with the absence of the names of Yu Hsien and Tung Fu-hsiang from the list of guilty officials. On the 26th the matter was taken up again.

Sir Ernest Satow took a prominent part in the discussion. He had taken over from MacDonald on the previous day and was anxious to establish his standing with the other diplomats. He was also new to Peking and somewhat overwhelmed by the accounts of the siege and by his recent reading in the consular reports of the 'fiendish cruelty' of the Boxers towards the missionaries in the provinces.[3] Consequently, when the subject of punishment came up he proposed that the death penalty (la peine de mort) should be demanded for the guilty Chinese officials.[4] Delighted, Mumm gave him warm support and the two ministers, with the help of Salvago Raggi, the Italian

[1] Memorandum by Bertie of 23 Oct. 1900, F.O. 17/1448.
[2] Salisbury to MacDonald, tel. 141 of 26 Oct. 1900, F.O. 17/1427.
[3] Satow to Lansdowne, letter of 6 Dec. 1900, Lansdowne Papers.
[4] S.J., 26 Oct. 1900.

minister, carried this demand against the bitter opposition of Giers, who proposed the phrase 'severest punishment' (*la punition la plus sévère*). Finally, a resolution was adopted *ad referendum*, which read: 'The Diplomatic body agrees in demanding in form of an ultimatum death penalty against the guilty persons named in Imperial Decree (i.e. of 25 September) besides Tung Fu-hsiang and Yu Hsien.'[1]

On 28 October Giers put forward his proposal for an armistice. The United States and Japan declared themselves in favour of the motion. Satow, who wished to mollify Giers, also gave his support. However, when Li Hung-chang approached Satow the next day on the question of a cease-fire, Satow cleared the room and then told Li that Great Britain was in favour of an armistice, but for the whole of China not just Chihli.[2] This meant Manchuria, the only other place where military operations were officially in progress, and Giers immediately abandoned his proposal.[3]

On 5 November Germany proposed that supplies should be denied the fugitive Manchu Court in order to force it to return to Peking. The motion was rejected. From his report, it is clear that Satow assumed that Great Britain was in favour of the return of the Court, but that for reasons of prestige she preferred that the proposal should be made from the Chinese side.[4]

Satow's attitude requires closer examination. On 20 August, five days before he left for the Far East, Satow had a long conversation with Bertie at the Foreign Office for a final briefing on the Chinese situation. Bertie was then still working on the assumption of a civil war in China. A critical situation was envisaged on the Yangtze. This was the reason why Salisbury decided at Hatfield on 10 August to send out Satow immediately. And, with the appointment of Waldersee, prolonged operations were anticipated in north China. In respect of Russian activity in

[1] Satow to Salisbury, tel. 177 of 26 Oct. 1900, F.O. 17/1418.
[2] S.J., 29 Oct. 1900.
[3] Satow to Salisbury, tel. 189 of 30 Oct. 1900, F.O. 17/1418. In this and the following chapters, concerned with the negotiations at Peking, Satow's telegraphic reports are supplemented by the accounts given in the Procès-verbaux of the sittings of the Council of Ministers. These are located in the Diplomatic Dispatches for 1900 and 1901, F.O. 17/1414–16, 1469–81.
[4] Satow to Salisbury, tel. 194 of 6 Nov. 1900, F.O. 17/1418.

this fluid situation, Satow observed: 'Russia would have enough to do to absorb Manchuria.'[1] On 8 October, from Shanghai, Satow wrote privately to Salisbury to confirm his conception of his mission. He understood British policy to be 'to act in concert with the rest of the Plenipotentiaries and to save as much of an independent China as is possible under the circumstances'.[2] In conference, he had then spoken for the death penalty for the guilty Chinese officials and had supported the Russian proposal for an armistice. In private, he had implied that this should extend to Manchuria. No evidence has been uncovered to show that Salisbury was determined to wrest Manchuria from Russia at this time. In fact, when Giers made his proposal the Anglo-German Agreement, which excluded Manchuria, had just been concluded, although publication of this had been deferred for ten days. Satow's declared reasons for his action, which he arrived at in consultation with the British military authorities in north China, were that he would support an armistice if Manchuria were included because:

(a) no military operations were possible in winter, and

(b) it would facilitate the return of the Court.[3] It has been seen that he assumed that Salisbury was in favour of the Court's return.

Up to this time the Cabinet had made no clear decision on the matter of an armistice. Russia's call for a general withdrawal at the end of August had been rejected. However, when Satow reported that he had supported Russia's call for an armistice no reply was sent. Perhaps it was realized more clearly in London that the condition he had stipulated removed any chance of Russian acceptance. Germany's endeavour in the middle of October to secure British co-operation to starve the Court out of its retreat had been repudiated. But when Mumm brought it up again at Peking and it was seen that Great Britain was in favour of the return of the Court it was necessary to clear the position. Salisbury replied immediately and, 'keeping in mind the geographical relations of Russia and China', questioned Satow's wish to secure the return of the Court.[4]

[1] S.J., 20 Aug. 1900.
[2] Satow to Salisbury, 8 Oct. 1900, P.R.O. 30/33/14/11.
[3] Satow to Salisbury, tel. 179, secret, of 27 Oct. 1900, F.O. 17/1418.
[4] Salisbury to Satow, tel. 156, secret, of 6 Nov. 1900, F.O. 17/1417.

This consideration had been much in the minds of the Government since the beginning of the crisis. Throughout the summer, as Russia appeared to consolidate her hold on northern China, the 'inevitable historical episode' which O'Conor had stressed at the time of the Port Arthur crisis, seemed on the point of being realized. A possible solution was to work for a change of the Chinese capital to a position where it would be under greater British control. This long-standing issue had been raised at the beginning of the crisis in a letter by Mitford to *The Times*. Out of a sense of outrage at Boxer activity Mitford had argued that the capital should be moved to Nanking so that 'the retrograde cliques would be broken up, just as the rookeries in London's slums are destroyed by new building schemes'.[1] After the flight of the Court this became politically possible and at the beginning of September Bertie argued:

> If we can make a return to Peking repugnant to the Chinese Gov't and so lead them to establish themselves elsewhere permanently it will be better for us—even if the new capital is in the interior— than that it should be at Peking saved by and under the paw of Russia.[2]

A similar view was put forward by Satow after he had been made aware of the Government's feeling about the return of the Court.

> . . . Seeing that with Port Arthur in her possession and the Manchurian Railway completed [he stated], Russia would be in a position to seize the north of China in any case (and I do not see how we could prevent a *coup-de-main*), I am of opinion that our policy should be to ensure that the queen bee is not at home when the hive is taken.[3]

However, two considerations prevented the Cabinet from pressing this policy actively. The first was indicated by Lansdowne in his reply to Satow's policy of the beehive. The theory was attractive, he wrote, 'but will the swarm be allowed to settle elsewhere than at Peking'.[4] The second was that a move-

---

[1] A. B. Freeman Mitford, *The Times*, 22 June 1900. Mitford was a friend of Lansdowne's and close to government circles.

[2] Memorandum by Bertie of 6 Sept. 1900 in Warren to Salisbury, tel. 120 of 3 Sept. 1900, F.O. 17/1427.

[3] Satow to Salisbury, tel. 202, secret, of 12 Nov. 1900, F.O. 17/1418.

[4] Lansdowne to Satow, letter of 14 Nov. 1900, Lansdowne Papers. From 11 Nov.

ment of the capital to the south would effectively abandon the
north to Russia and drive Great Britain into a policy of spheres.
This extreme step had to be avoided if possible, although at
times it seemed almost necessary during the autumn of 1900. The
Cabinet were not to know that Russia was then equally anxious
and was trying to work through Li Hung-chang for a transfer
of the Court to Mukden, 'the cradle of the Manchu dynasty'.[1]

Consequently, an indeterminate attitude was adopted by
Great Britain; no move was made to encourage the return of the
Court to Peking, either by supporting Germany on the 'supplies' issue or Russia in the cease fire, since there it could fall
under Russian domination. On the other hand, she pressed for
the early opening of formal negotiations with the Chinese, for
with the limited forces which she had available, the conference
room was the only place where she could counter the predatory
ambitions of Russia and Germany with any success.

Meanwhile, while the Russian and German proposals were
being considered and the demand for the death penalty referred
back to the home governments, rapid progress was made by the
representatives on the less controversial issues of the proposed
Joint Note.

After receiving Delcasse's six points MacDonald had proposed, on 11 October, the addition of several articles designed
to widen the content of the Note. To Delcasse's punishment
clause MacDonald proposed the addition of all those officials
who had connived at massacres in provincial areas and the
abolition of official examinations where persecutions had taken
place. The specific reference to the provinces was resisted by
the other powers, who felt the phrase 'and for those whom the
Representatives of the Powers shall subsequently designate' in
Delcasse's text sufficient to cover this provision. This did not
prove to be the case. One of Satow's most tiresome tasks during
1901 was concerned with provincial punishments. Also, on
MacDonald's suggestion, the suspension of official examinations
was limited to five years (Art. 2b).[2] An additional article by

Foreign Office correspondence was dealt with by Lansdowne, but the latter
frequently sought Salisbury's advice.

[1] The approach was made through Ukhtomsky, then in Peking to negotiate a
separate Manchurian settlement. Romanov, *Russia in Manchuria*, 195.

[2] The final placing of British proposals or amendments in the Joint Note is
indicated in parentheses. The text of the Note is given Appendix II, below.

MacDonald for the posting of an Imperial edict (*a*) prohibiting Boxer membership and (*b*) stating the punishments inflicted, was passed unanimously (Art. 10a). His suggestion for the abolition of the Tsungli Yamen, the appointment of a Chinese Minister for Foreign Affairs, and the establishment of relations with the Court on a sensible basis was accepted, with reservations, against the opposition of Russia, France, and Japan (Art. 12).

When Satow took up the negotiations Delcasse's clauses were defined more precisely and widened still further. On the defensive clauses, Salisbury's reservation on the separate nature of the legations' guards was accepted (Art. 7 with modifications); but a compromise was reached between Delcasse's proposal of a chain of posts between Taku and Peking and Salisbury's reservation of the right of a single post. The compromise was fortunate; in his anxiety to avoid committing British troops to land-locked duties by calling for the 'right of each Power to occupy and fortify a point accessible from the sea', Salisbury had provided an opening for further territorial claims on the Port Arthur model. On the other hand, the compromise amendment prevented this; by stipulating the occupation of certain points 'to be determined by agreement among the Powers', such separate claims were effectively barred. The question of the prohibition of the importation of arms was a more delicate issue. It was included because of the stress laid on it during the siege. Eventually it was incorporated in the Joint Note, with the duration of the prohibition left for further discussion.

An important addition in respect of commercial revision was put forward by Satow on 5 November and carried against the opposition of Russia and France. On 15 October, while the powers were busy assessing Delcasse's bases, an isolated attempt was made by the Chinese to provide a basis of settlement. The proposal was embodied in five articles: 1, 2, and 5 confirmed the appointment of Li Hung-chang and Prince Ching as Chinese plenipotentiaries, admitted Chinese guilt and her liability to indemnity, and called for a preliminary suspension of hostilities. Articles 3 and 4 were of more significance. These read:

(3) Powers must decide on procedure (in respect of) future trade

and intercourse; whether existing treaties are to be maintained and to some extent extended, or whether entirely new treaties are to be drawn up according to special requirements (of each power? text obscure).

(4) A Convention as a general basis of negotiation between China and the Powers; in addition each power will negotiate separate conventions for the settlement—these will be arranged in order (of powers? territorial areas? text obscure).

The Addendum stated that the separate conventions of Article 4 and the commercial treaties of Article 3 had no connection with each other.[1]

Article 3 was plainly directed at the powers in favour of the open door and of tariff and likin revision, and in particular at Great Britain; Article 4 at the powers who were more inclined to spheres of influence. In fact, this article pointed directly to Russia's separate convention over Manchuria which, unknown to the powers, was then in its initial stages of negotiation.

Mercantile circles in London and Shanghai had been violently opposed to Satow's appointment at Peking because it was felt he was not sufficiently a man of action capable of protecting their interests. When the change with MacDonald became known, the China Association announced their determination to publish their objections (made to the Foreign Office) in order 'to formulate the strongest possible public and private protest . . . that the occasion calls for a very different man'.[2] This virulent attack may have hardened Satow's determination. As soon as he reached Peking he seized on Article 3 of the Chinese proposals of 15 October as 'a useful handle'[3] to enable Great Britain to insert an article in the Joint Note providing for a subsequent commercial convention. Satow nursed this aim through the negotiations (Art. 11), guarded it jealously against interference by the other powers throughout 1901, and, with satisfaction, saw it develop into the Mackay Treaty of 1902, negotiated at Shanghai under British control. In refutation of his mercantile critics, the ground which Satow laid so carefully

[1] Ching and Li to H.M. representative, 15 Oct. 1900 (Kuang Hsu 26–8A–22), No. 51, enclosure, F.O. 228/1350.
[2] Gundry to Campbell, 21 Sept. 1900, F.O. 17/1447; cf. Pelcovits, *Old China Hands*, 271–5.
[3] S.J., 23 Oct. 1900; Satow to Salisbury, tel. 177 of 26 Oct. 1900, F.O. 17/1418.

for Mackay was unquestionably one of the most important British gains of the peace settlement.

On the sticky question of indemnities discussion was deliberately kept general until information could be received. However, early in October MacDonald had added the humane proposal that the Chinese servants of foreigners who had been viciously persecuted should also be compensated (incorporated Art. 6). He had also suggested that preliminary agreement should be reached by the powers in respect of the extent and method of guarantee of the indemnity 'to prevent deferred claims being used as a lever to extract concessions'.[1] MacDonald thus anticipated the direction of the later indemnity negotiations; but in his suggestions on the method to be adopted he veered towards an acceptance of the international control of Chinese resources, which meant the international control of the Chinese Customs, a jealously guarded British preserve. It was obviously too early to speak out on this point, but the balance of the Joint Note was preserved by a compromise Italian proposal which was inserted as an addendum to Delcasse's third point. Initially this read: 'China will take financial measures on lines which the Powers will indicate, in order to guarantee payment of the indemnities and guarantees of the loans.' Russia, with some Japanese support, maintained her opposition to this clause until the end of November and was only persuaded to a change of front when 'financial measures acceptable to the Powers' was substituted for 'on the lines which the Powers will indicate'.[2]

Additional proposals accepted without objection by the representatives provided for the sending of a Chinese mission to Europe to pay penance for the murder of Ketteler. This was given pride of place in the Joint Note. The Japanese thereupon asked for a similar though more moderate recognition of the murder of Sugiyama, incorporated as Article 3. Further concessions were made to foreign prestige by the demand for the erection of expiatory monuments to mark the desecrated graves in foreign cemeteries.

By the end of November the main outline of a Joint Note had been worked out on (1) the French bases and (2) the

[1] MacDonald to Salisbury, tel. 151 of 11 Oct. 1900, F.O. 17/1418.
[2] Satow to Lansdowne, tels. 214, 215 of 23, 24 Nov. 1900, F.O. 17/1418.

amendments adopted, and agreement was thus reached on everything but the matter of punishment.

The proposal adopted *ad referendum* at the initial meeting of 26 October had stipulated that the death penalty would be demanded, in the form of an ultimatum, for the guilty officials named in the Imperial decree of 25 September as well as for Tung Fu-hsiang and Yu Hsien. It was also assumed that Delcasse's first base, which provided for the inclusion of the offenders to be pointed out by the representatives, would be incorporated. This was an uncompromising approach which placed the question of punishment entirely in the hands of the foreign powers. The history of the Joint Note from the end of November until its presentation a month later was a general retreat from this vigorous stand.

The process was begun by Great Britain. When the proposal of 26 October was received in London Sir Thomas Sanderson immediately observed that the wording was rather sweeping and indefinite and could be taken to include the Empress Dowager. Sanderson was concerned with Great Britain's relations with the Yangtze viceroys, an assurance on the Empress Dowager's safety having recently been given after Warren had successfully argued that they would revolt unless her person were respected. Sanderson thought that if an ultimatum were to be made it should be confined to 'officials or private individuals'.[1] Salisbury went further and expressed his dislike of the whole idea of an ultimatum. 'The Government may be mad enough to refuse,' he remarked, 'what are we to do then?'[2] Consequently Satow was reminded that if the purpose of the representatives was to indicate that no counter-proposal would be considered then 'we run the risk of coming to a deadlock at the commencement of the negotiations', especially if the demand for the death penalty could be made at will by the representatives, for the Chinese would feel that 'no one from the Empress Dowager downwards would be safe'.[3]

---

[1] Memorandum by Sanderson on Satow, tel. 177 of 26 Oct., F.O. 17/1448.

[2] Minute on memorandum by Sanderson above.

[3] Salisbury to Satow, tel. 147 of 29 Oct. 1900, F.O. 17/1417 (not to be sent to Shanghai or elsewhere by telegram). This reservation, bracketed, indicated the Government's efforts to restrain Warren's inflammatory behaviour by denying him explosive information; the practice then being to repeat all Peking messages to Shanghai and Tokyo.

In reply, Satow admitted that the term 'ultimatum' had been used rather loosely by the representatives, that it would be avoided in future, and that no one was asking for the punishment of the Empress Dowager. On 13 November 'ultimatum' in the punishment clause was formally dropped.[1]

By this time the representatives were having second thoughts on their vigorous stand. With ultimatum out of the way discussion pivoted on the death penalty. Of the guilty Chinese the two most powerful officials were Prince Tuan and Tung Fu-hsiang. All reference to Prince Tuan had been carefully avoided by even the most belligerent of the ministers, but the proposal of 26 October had specifically referred to Tung Fu-hsiang by name. Tung had a considerable body of devoted troops at his command and it was felt that he would 'take the bit between his teeth if this demand for his head is pressed'.[2] By the end of the month this sobering thought had blunted the determination of the representatives. Satow, who had proposed the death penalty in the first place, concluded that it was futile to ask the unattainable.[3]

This mood communicated itself to the various governments. By 23 November the Cabinet was aware that the United States, Russia, France, and Japan deprecated any insistence on the demand for capital punishment of high officials whom the Chinese Government might not be able to produce, thus jeopardizing the peace negotiations. This view was also aired in Berlin and there were signs that Germany would not stand fast.[4] 'It is becoming clear', Lansdowne wrote to Salisbury, 'that something like a stampede in the matter of the death penalty is commencing.'[5] Cambon, the French Ambassador, then came forward to say that after *pourparlers* between France and Russia because of American and Japanese circulars objecting to an insistence on capital punishment, France was ready to substitute 'severest punishment' for 'the death

---

[1] Satow to Salisbury, tels. 192, 204 of 3, 13 Nov. 1900, F.O. 17/1418.

[2] Satow to Lansdowne, letter of 15 Nov. 1900, Lansdowne Papers.

[3] Satow to Lansdowne, letter of 6 Dec. 1900, Lansdowne Papers. Conger wrote to Hay of Tung: 'I have urged my colleagues to leave his name out of the first demand, so that he might carry out the Imperial order for the execution of the others.' *Foreign Relations* (1900), 229.

[4] Memorandum by Bertie of 22 Nov. 1900, F.O. 17/1450; Lansdowne to Satow, tel. 171 of 23 Nov. 1900, F.O. 17/1450.

[5] Lansdowne to Salisbury, memorandum of 27 Nov. 1900, F.O. 17/1450.

penalty'.[1] After a month of arduous discussion Giers's rejected rendering had been restored.

It was now for the powers who had spoken most strongly in favour of the death penalty to accept the situation as best they could. Lascelles after a conversation with Hatzfeldt gathered that Germany desired 'to make use of H.M. Gov't as the ladder by which they may climb down. . . . They want to be the last to give way.'[2]

This seemed to be Germany's intention; Mumm, in Peking, was instructed not to sign until Satow had declared himself. It was a matter of prestige which Lansdowne thought could be resolved by private agreement; Salisbury, always more uncompromising with regard to Germany, bluntly declared that Great Britain should not satisfy Germany by taking the lead.[3]

In these circumstances, the Cabinet became increasingly aware of the difficulty of working from Satow's brief and cryptic telegraphic reports. Lansdowne asked for a full text. When this arrived on 2 December it was seen that all reference to an ultimatum and to the death penalty had been dropped. It was also noticed that a preamble had been included which outlined the general charge of Chinese guilt and then concluded with a reference to 'the irrevocable conditions' (i.e. the articles of the Joint Note) which would have to be satisfied before peaceful relations could be restored.[4] At the same time, Satow reported a feeling among the representatives against the word 'irrevocable' which, it was thought, admitted of no compromise. It was also felt at Peking that the term 'absolutely indispensable' should be substituted instead; and further, that all names in the punishment clause should be removed.

The draft was discussed in the Cabinet on 9 December, when it was decided that the substitution of the weaker formula was unfortunate and that a reference to the death penalty should be retained in the punishment clause. Satow was instructed: 'You should place on record that in the opinion of Her Majesty's Government the new formula implies the death penalty for the worst criminals and that you are instructed to press for it in

[1] Memorandum by Bertie of 30 Nov. 1900, F.O. 17/1450.
[2] Memorandum by Bertie of 1 Dec. 1900, F.O. 17/1450.
[3] Sanderson memorandum of 6 Dec. 1900, F.O. 17/1450; Salisbury minute on Lansdowne to Salisbury, 27 Nov. 1900, F.O. 17/1450.
[4] Satow to Lansdowne, tel. 217 of 30 Nov. 1900, F.O. 17/1418.

the negotiations with the Chinese plenipotentiaries. . . .'[1] The Cabinet also objected to the word 'irrevocable' or its substitute 'absolutely indispensable' on the grounds that in the event of non-compliance by the Chinese, Great Britain would be committed to punitive joint action, the scope of which was not defined. Accordingly, the Cabinet suggested the omission of these expressions from the preamble and the substitution of the phrase: 'the conditions enumerated below which would provide the fitting expiation for the crimes committed and the best means of preventing their recurrence.'[2] The Cabinet had committed themselves without fully understanding the situation. As with all negotiations of this nature, to avoid the need for a public retreat in conference, any attitude had to be assessed carefully in relation to the possible responses of the other powers. As it was believed that the other powers were also in favour of removing the word 'irrevocable', the Cabinet were encouraged to an open stand.

However, after the instruction had been sent to Satow, events took a serious turn. Satow reported that a vote had been taken by the representatives. Six of the powers had voted for the original text, retaining the word 'irrevocable', only four for the British amendment—these were the United States, Japan, Russia, and Great Britain. Conger, the United States minister, had then informed his Government that the majority favoured 'irrevocable' and he had been told to change his vote; whereupon Russia and Japan, who were largely indifferent to the reading, also went over.[3] Great Britain was thus left in a minority of one.

It was strongly felt in London that Satow had not kept them sufficiently informed on the attitudes of the other powers.[4] Lansdowne was particularly bitter, because he did not believe that the term 'absolutely indispensable' committed Great Britain to possible ulterior measures, but he had been overruled by the Cabinet. Now, within a month of his assumption of the Foreign Office, Great Britain had been placed in a position of diplomatic isolation at one of the most widely representative

[1] Lansdowne to Satow, tel. 179 of 9 Dec. 1900, F.O. 17/1417.
[2] Ibid.; Lansdowne to Satow, No. 180 of 26 Dec. 1900, F.O. 228/1340.
[3] Satow to Lansdowne, tel. 122 of 12 Dec. 1900, F.O. 17/1418.
[4] Bertie to Satow, tel., private, of 12 Dec. 1900, F.O. 17/1417.

conferences since the Congress of Berlin. The position grieved Lansdowne, especially as it had not been of his making. He thought that Great Britain had to adhere to her expressed opinion, but he was not sure, and so he wrote to Salisbury asking whether Satow were to stand by the British amendment. At the same time, he tried to explain his view:

To my mind there is a difference between laying down 'irrevocable conditions' and saying that you specify conditions which you '*deem* to be absolutely indispensable to expiate the crimes committed, and to prevent their recurrence'. But the Cabinet thought otherwise and without authority from you I am not prepared to reopen that question.[1]

Salisbury repudiated the argument, and agreed with the Cabinet decision already arrived at. He replied:

I am unable to conceive of a decision by which this country would purpose to declare a certain course indispensable and at the same time count on dispensing with it in case of need.[2]

The Prime Minister anticipated difficulties in the Commons and called a Cabinet meeting for the next day (14 December). The whole situation was distasteful to him and his feeling burst forth in sharp censure, rare in a man so tolerant and so loyal to his permanent officials: 'I think Satow has behaved very badly. I am ashamed of having nominated him.'[3]

It is not known what passed in the Cabinet on the 14th, but after the meeting an instruction was sent to Satow which revealed the conclusions reached. It emphasized their anxiety not to stand in the way of an early commencement of negotiations, but pointed out that the words accepted by the other powers 'seem to us open to objection as committing us to possible ulterior operations, the scope of which is not defined'. Therefore it was suggested that the following limiting clause should be added at the end of the Note:

Until the Chinese Gov(ernment) have complied with the above conditions to the satisfaction of the Powers the undersigned can hold out no expectation that the occupation of Peking and the

---

[1] Lansdowne to Salisbury, 13 Dec. 1900, Lansdowne Papers.
[2] Salisbury to Lansdowne, 13 Dec. 1900, Lansdowne Papers.
[3] Ibid.

province of Pechili by the Allied Forces can be brought to a conclusion.[1]

In Peking, Satow also was distressed at the turn of events. He, too, was new to his post and anxious to prove himself. Mumm agreed to support the British addition, and with him Italy and Austria-Hungary, Germany's European allies; Giers promised to telegraph St. Petersburg; but Japan was doubtful and Satow was out of humour with the United States minister. He admitted to Cologan that he had given all his 'support to Conger in getting rid of irrevocable, and now Conger went back on me'.[2] Conger had worked himself into an impossible position. He had changed his stand so often the other powers had begun to disregard him. Washington obviously did not want the word 'irrevocable' yet Conger was pressing it. His action may have been dictated by the fact that, with Czikann, the Austrian minister, and d'Anthouard, First Secretary of the French Legation, he had been responsible for the drafting of the preamble to the Note. Or his confusion may have arisen from his lack of French. He was forced to sit uncomprehending through the diplomatic meetings, dependent on the translations offered by the other ministers. On 15 December he tried again to change his stand and approached Satow for support to remove 'irrevocable'. Satow refused flatly.[3] By this time Lansdowne had agreed to the inclusion of the word 'irrevocable' in the preamble,[4] relying on acceptance of the British limiting clause to safeguard Great Britain's determination not to commit herself to unspecified ulterior measures in the event of non-compliance by the Chinese.[5]

On 19 December Satow announced the British stand on the

[1] Lansdowne to Satow, tel. 184 of 14 Dec. 1900, F.O.17/1417.
[2] S.J., 14 Dec. 1900; Satow to Lansdowne, tel. 229 of 15 Dec. 1900, F.O. 17/1418.
[3] S.J., 15 Dec. 1900.
[4] This instruction has not been traced in either the Diplomatic or the Consular files, but it is noted S.J., 15 Dec. 1900.
[5] On the British limiting clause the powers expressed their opinion, not openly but indirectly, through the discussion which arose when it was translated into French. Differences were revealed over the possible rendering of 'complied with', and the translations which were offered faithfully reflected the attitudes of the powers. Russia and Japan wanted 'accepté'; Germany, the stronger term 'rempli'. Lansdowne stated that 'accepté' was wrong and that it would have to be 'rempli'. The deadlock seemed insoluble, but the French, who were ready to agree to either reading, suggested 'se conformer à' which everyone accepted with relief.

death penalty, on which the Cabinet had instructed him on 9 December, but which had been pushed into the background by the flurry over the preamble. It was supported by Germany, France, and Italy; the United States also gave her support, but with the reservation that if it could not be implemented she would settle for something less; Russia thought Prince Tuan guilty but that it would be impossible to secure his punishment. But no one was prepared to reopen the discussion, and as Satow had merely been asked to place the British opinion on record, he pushed it willingly into the procès-verbal.

Everything had now been settled and arrangements were made to sign the Note on 20 December. However, Conger's troubles were not ended. On the 19th Washington stated that they were 'strenuously opposed' to any note which would commit them to a prolonged occupation or further military operations. Conger informed the representatives that he would concur with them over the Joint Note, on his own responsibility.[1] This show of initiative displeased the State Department. The next day, as the representatives were gathering to sign the Note, Conger received a telegram *en clair* 'Insist on omission of irrevocable'. The peremptory and public command caused consternation among the diplomats, to whom the humiliation of their colleague was excruciating. Satow was of the opinion that if Conger had asked for a rewriting it would have been done; only Mumm said he would have to refer home.[2] But Conger did not force his position and the other ten representatives signed; Conger added his signature on the 22nd.

The final reading of the disputed passage in the preamble ran:

. . . China, having recognized her responsibility, expressed her regrets, and manifested her desire to see an end put to the situation created by the disturbances referred to, the Powers have decided to accede to her request on the irrevocable conditions enumerated

---

[1] Satow to Lansdowne, tel. 236 of 19 Dec. 1900, F.O. 17/1418.

[2] S.J., 20 Dec. 1900; Satow to Lansdowne, tel. 238 of 20 Dec. 1900, F.O. 17/1418. The explanation published by the United States was that a telegraphic misreading occurred. While the State Department wrote on 5 Dec. that Conger should sign the Note as *transmitted*, i.e. without 'irrevocable', Conger had read *majorities*. See *Foreign Relations* (1900), 240–1, 243. However, the material available from the British side indicates that Conger played an active rather than a passive role.

below, which they deem indispensable to expiate the crimes committed and prevent their recurrence.

The terms which the powers had agreed on then followed.

The Joint Note was collective; Salisbury, who would have preferred it to be identic, gave way on this point. It was signed in alphabetical order (French reading) and presented to Prince Ching on 24 December. Li Hung-chang stated that he had a cold and did not attend. At the meeting Cologan, doyen of the diplomatic body, foolishly asked Ching for his credentials. The Chinese produced full powers and then created confusion by asking the representatives to show their credentials in return. None could be produced and the meeting was abandoned hurriedly. The incident was a fitting climax to the confusion which had attended the negotiations.

The Missionary Issue

Brief mention must be made of the British attitude to the missionary question. It will have been noticed that throughout the period of the siege, the post-relief period, and during the negotiation of the Joint Note, little mention has been made of an issue which could be expected to figure prominently both when the Boxers were active and later when the charges of guilt were being levelled at the Chinese Government. Throughout the summer of 1900, accounts of the outrages suffered by the missionaries and stirring reports of their escapes from the interior were published in the national press, although not as extensively as they were reported in the foreign language newspapers published in China, such as the *North China Daily News*. No attempt was made to stir up public sympathy through these accounts, although the Government were sorely in need of public approval of the extra expenditure entailed by the Chinese entanglement, which loomed large in the public mind because of the heavy financial burden brought on by the South African war.[1]

[1] The Budget of 1900 was introduced on 5 Mar. In July a supplementary estimate had to be made of £11½ million of which £3 million was for China. In Dec. there was a further call for a vote of £16 million of which £½ million was for China. By the end of the year the additional war expenditure over and above the budget estimate of 5 Mar. 1900 of £38 million had amounted to £30½ million. During the second reading of the Supplementary War Loan Bill in the Commons on 1 Aug.

Lord Salisbury's opinion on this aspect of the rising was given on 19 June 1900, when the first reports of the rising were becoming known and when public concern over the fate of the foreigners in China was at its strongest. Speaking at a public meeting at the Exeter Hall in connection with the celebration of the bicentenary of the Society for the Propagation of the Gospel in Foreign Parts, he declared:

> If an evangelist or an apostle, a Boniface or a Columba, preached in the middle ages, he faced the difficulties, he underwent the martyrdom, he braved the torments to which he was exposed, and the whole of the great moral and spiritual influence of his self-devotion acted without hindrance on the people whom he addressed. But now, if a Boniface or a Columba is exposed to this martyrdom the result is an appeal to the Consul and the mission of a gunboat. . . . They have a proverb in the East—first the missionary, then the Consul, then the General. . . . Just look at this Chinese matter. You observe that all the people who are slaughtered are Christians. Do you imagine that they are slaughtered simply because the Chinese dislike their religion? There is no nation in the world so indifferent on the subject of religion as the Chinese. It is because they and other nations have got the idea that missionary work is a mere instrument of the secular government in order to achieve the objects it has in view.[1]

Throughout the rising, attention was centred on the diplomatic issue of the relief of the legations and on the safety of foreigners in general. Evidence of Chinese hostility towards missionaries and converts was deliberately hushed up by Salisbury, largely because of his distrust of Germany's ulterior intentions.[2] Informed people condemned missionary activity in the protection of converts as the origin of the anti-foreign unrest.[3]

After the rising, Great Britain might have been expected to take up the missionary cause, as the majority of the casualties were British nationals. This Satow was reluctant to do. Before

1900 Sir William Harcourt, while criticizing the Government's expenditure stressed that the £3 million for China would be as adequate to uphold Britain's position in the east as the £10 million which had originally been assessed as the cost of the South African war. *Parliamentary Debates*, 4th Series, lxxxvii. 336–8.

[1] *The Extra-Parliamentary Hansard*, Section VIII (1899–1900), 757–8.

[2] Hamilton to Curzon, 13 Sept. 1900, Hamilton Papers.

[3] Notably T. L. Bullock, Professor of Chinese at the University of Oxford; cf. S.J., 1 Aug. 1900.

going out as plenipotentiary he suggested a policy of protection of the persons and property of missionaries, but thought that arrangements regarding their work should be left under the control of the native authorities.[1] When he arrived in Peking Satow pressed the view that missionaries should be protected only as British subjects, while converts had to look to their own protection, unless they received a wage (which would accord them the same privilege as servants of foreigners). He wrote to Bertie:

I hope I may be left to pursue my own line in respect of missionaries, and to say to my colleagues: as I did yesterday that tho' I have no prejudices against the missionaries, I regard the insertion in the Tientsin treaty of clauses about mission work as the most impolitic thing ever done in China.[2]

This feeling, held also by other foreigners, brought about a change in public opinion, late in the autumn of 1900, on the nature of Chinese excesses. The process was helped by the publication of several articles by Sir Robert Hart in the *Fortnightly Review* from November onwards. Although these articles were described by Reuter as the 'phantasms of a too sensitive imagination' they successfully pleaded the Chinese case and were later incorporated into a book.[3]

Over the winter of 1900–1, when various accounts of the rising began to appear, Lord Cranborne anticipated a possible interest in Parliament in the massacre and the heroism of the missionaries. He observed to Lansdowne:

But ought we not to take the opportunity of placing upon record the disapproval of H.M. Government of some of the missionary methods and their attitude towards the native authorities on behalf of their converts. It seems to have been pre-eminently this attitude combined with the aggression of Europe which produced the crisis.[4]

Lansdowne thought that the Roman Catholic missionaries were the greatest culprits.[5] This was not a view which could be

---

[1] S.J., 20 Aug. 1900.

[2] Satow to Bertie, 1 Nov. 1900, P.R.O. 30/33/14/11.

[3] Sir Robert Hart, 'These from the Land of Sinim', *Essays on the Chinese Question* (London, 1901).

[4] Cranborne to Lansdowne, memorandum of 27 Jan. 1901, F.O. 17/1500.

[5] Minute on above.

openly expressed. When Satow wrote to him in February 1901 to explain that all references to the missionaries had been deliberately left out of the Joint Note he approved the action. He also agreed with Satow's argument that the policy of allowing missionaries redress at Peking was a mistake.[1] Lansdowne replied: 'A good deal of harm has I fancy been done by the indiscriminate support which has been given to these persons. Chinese administration is so much decentralized that in this and other matters we must to some extent decentralize our diplomacy.'[2]

Missionary status was too delicate an issue to take up before the assembled representatives in Peking, much less with the Chinese plenipotentiaries. Consequently, when the Chinese, who persistently regarded the rising as a conflict between 'converts and people', submitted for approval draft decrees for the prohibition of anti-foreign societies under Article 10 of the Joint Note, Satow acquiesced in the unanimous opinion of the foreign representatives that they should be edited. Explicit references to religion were struck out; 'missions' were changed to 'les établissements étrangers', 'des sociétés anti-religieuses' became '. . . anti-étrangères', etc.[3] The peace settlement was then conducted along strictly political lines.

[1] Satow to Lansdowne, 8 Feb. 1901, Lansdowne Papers.
[2] Lansdowne to Satow, 9 Apr. 1901, P.R.O. 30/33/7/1.
[3] Cf. Satow to Lansdowne, No. 58 of 9 Feb. 1901, F.O. 17/1470.

X

THE IMPLEMENTATION OF THE
JOINT NOTE

The Concert of the Powers, with a great amount of self-
restraint on the part of some of them and mental reservations
on the part of all or nearly all of them, has lasted just sufficiently long to get a note settled, signed and presented. . . .
The Concert may now be expected to break up into Sections.[1]

THE presentation of the Joint Note marked the high point
of co-operation among the powers. Only the urgent need
to present a common front towards the Chinese had made
agreement possible. It was clear that in future meetings little
progress would be made towards a peace settlement if each step
must meet with the unanimous approval of the assembled
powers. It was also clear that the majority principle would work
to the disadvantage of the powers in the minority.

Great Britain's position in this respect was viewed with some
uneasiness by the Government. Eleven powers were involved in
the peace settlement. It was assumed that these would fall into
two major groups. The nucleus of one group would be Great
Britain and Germany, working together under the Anglo-
German Agreement. With them would be linked Austria-
Hungary and Italy, Germany's European allies. This seemed
the depressing limit to their voting security. France and Russia
formed a solid bloc. Japan had taken an independent stand in
favour of moderation. Similarly, during the negotiation of the
Joint Note, the United States had revealed a strong tendency
to press for withdrawal. Lord Pauncefote, British Ambassador
at Washington, felt that this was because President McKinley
had half an eye on the Presidential election of that year and
wished to please the anti-expansionists.[2] This factor may have
influenced American behaviour; in any case, the feeling in

[1] Memorandum by Bertie of 27 Dec. 1900, F.O. 17/1451.
[2] Pauncefote to Salisbury, private, of 14 Sept. 1900, S.P. 140/31.

London was that co-operation could not be expected of the United States.[1] Of the three remaining powers, Belgium was regarded as being in the Dual Alliance camp, Spain was equally suspect, and the Netherlands would vote according to her own interests.

Since November 1900 the various ways in which this unfavourable position could be bettered had been explored by Great Britain and Germany. Germany suggested that, in voting, the majority principle should be adopted and that, to secure this majority, Spain, Belgium, and the Netherlands should be excluded from the conference on the ground that they had not participated in the relief of the legations.[2] Lord Salisbury was reluctant to abandon the principle of unanimity as a general rule and he felt that the exclusion of the non-expeditionary powers should only be considered if Great Britain found herself in the minority.[3] Subsequent negotiation over the Joint Note indicated that Great Britain did stand in a minority and also that some of the other powers, particularly the United States, showed a tendency to follow majority opinion. The issue was important; the conclusions arrived at in the peace settlement at Peking could affect Great Britain's future position in China. As it was felt that an open demand for the exclusion of the non-expeditionary powers would drive them over to the side of Russia and France, a compromise solution was attempted on 17 December and Satow was instructed to press that they should be denied a casting vote in the negotiations.[4] However, the other representatives at Peking thought the matter too delicate to discuss and in the face of this reluctance, shown also by Germany, Satow was instructed to drop the matter.[5]

In a review of the position at the end of December 1900, Bertie observed that the participation of Spain, Belgium, and the Netherlands would be 'an element of obstruction if not

[1] On the general feeling of reserve between Great Britain and the United States at this time see L. M. Gelber, *The Rise of Anglo-American Friendship. A study in world politics, 1898–1906* (London, 1938), 80; C. S. Campbell, *Anglo-American Understanding, 1898–1903* (Baltimore, 1957), 204.

[2] Memoranda by Bertie of 7 and 9 Nov. 1900, F.O. 17/1449; memorandum by Bertie of 31 Dec. 1900, F.O. 17/1451.

[3] Memorandum by Salisbury of 8 Nov. 1900; memorandum by Bertie of 9 Nov. 1900, F.O. 17/1449.

[4] Lansdowne to Satow, tel. 233 of 17 Dec. 1900, F.O. 17/1418.

[5] Lansdowne to Satow, tels. 1 and 2 of 1 and 3 Jan. 1901, F.O. 17/1482.

opposition to England' and that, while without them Great
Britain, Germany, Austria, and Italy could have balanced the
votes of France, Russia, Japan, and the United States, with
them the position was changed. Japan became 'the important
but uncertain factor'; for if she were content to be led by Great
Britain and the Triple Alliance powers her adhesion would help
to draw the United States to the British side as 'a sleeping
partner'.[1] The analysis was based on the attitudes which had
been adopted by the powers on the various issues raised in the
Joint Note; it was also made during the brief period of co-
operation between Great Britain and Germany which followed
the negotiation of the Anglo-German Agreement. Actually, in
the conference which was to be held at Peking, Great Britain
was to get valuable support from the United States and Japan,
while all too frequently her bitterest critic was to be Germany.
Nevertheless, Bertie's assessment, which Lansdowne shared,
indicates the feeling of disadvantage with which the Government approached the opening of peace negotiations with the
Chinese.[2]

However, for a time it appeared that the conference would
not be held. Six weeks of arduous negotiation had dissipated
the enthusiasm of the assembled representatives, who were
supposed to have plenipotentiary powers and were yet not empowered to speak without first referring to their governments.
No one had a clear idea of the nature of the meetings which
were being held. Discussions over the Joint Note had been carried
out at the residence of Cologan, the Spanish doyen of the
diplomatic body, but with the forthcoming participation of the
Chinese the question of prestige became all-important. Cologan
naturally argued that the representatives were a meeting of the
diplomatic body and that the question of seating should be
decided by seniority of credentials. This was violently opposed
by Satow who argued that as plenipotentiaries the representatives were no longer the diplomatic body but should take their
seating alphabetically under an elected chairman. Satow had
in mind a gathering along the lines of the Conference of Berlin

[1] Memorandum by Bertie of 27 Dec. 1900, F.O. 17/1451.

[2] Bertie thought Great Britain's voting position so disadvantageous he suggested
that Portugal be invited to send her minister (the Governor of Macao). Lansdowne approved the suggestion, but hesitated to make the move. Memorandum
by Bertie of 3 Jan. 1901, F.O. 17/1499.

of 1884.[1] He was driven to this stand largely by the absolute confusion which had reigned in the meetings presided over by the Spanish minister, where subjects were begun without notice, two or three representatives spoke at once and interrupted one another continually. The meetings, Satow reported, resembled 'a conversation at a round dinner table where every one cares more to make himself heard than to listen to the others'.[2] Cologan's inefficiency was admitted by the other representatives but the matter, as with the participation of the non-expeditionary powers, was considered too delicate to be raised and when the representatives finally assembled they did so as a meeting of the diplomatic body, both expeditionary and non-expeditionary powers participating.

The difficulty of negotiating under these conditions weighed so heavily on Satow that on 23 December, the day after the signing of the Joint Note, he reported home that discussion on everything but the posting of the punishment and prohibition decrees (Art. 10 of the Joint Note) would have to be referred to a European Conference.[3] The suggestion was hurriedly rejected by the Foreign Office. Salisbury was strongly of the opinion that every effort should be made to settle as many questions as possible on the spot.[4] Lansdowne, who was new to the Foreign Office and who had no experience of the mountain of work which had been raised by the Hague Peace Conference, thought that while as many questions as possible should be settled locally, ultimately a new agency would have to be called in to take over the work of the assembled representatives at Peking.[5] This view was not shared by the Foreign Office staff; Sanderson later revealed that Satow's suggestion had 'made the blood freeze in the veins of some of us'. European conferences, he lectured Satow, were useful for putting on record, or sometimes for bringing into shape, conclusions already arrived at by a majority of the powers, but were 'very

[1] S.J., 10 Dec. 1900.

[2] Satow to Lansdowne, 25 Dec. 1900, Lansdowne Papers. A second factor influencing Satow's attitude was that he had not formally presented his credentials at the Court.

[3] Satow to Lansdowne, tel. 242, secret, of 23 Dec. 1900, F.O. 17/1418.

[4] Minute on above. The report had been forwarded immediately to the Prime Minister by Bertie.

[5] Lansdowne to Satow, 16 Jan. 1901, P.R.O. 30/33/7/1.

bad machinery' for arriving at conclusions. If Satow's suggestion were taken up, he stressed, a secondary conference would
still have to sit at Peking, each would constantly be referring to
the other and 'Doomsday would find both still sitting'.[1]

Consequently, it was with profound discouragement that the
Foreign Office received, on 4 January, so soon after rejecting
Satow's suggestion, an American proposal put forward as a
personal suggestion to the powers by the President of the United
States. This suggested that all discussion on the indemnity and
on treaty and commercial revision (Arts. 6 and 11) should be
referred to Washington or some European capital. It was
difficult to find an answer which could keep the conference at
Peking without alienating the American vote. Not until it was
known that Japan and Germany had rejected the proposal did
Lansdowne reply to Washington, on 10 January, that while it
was probable that the two questions would have to be dealt
with separately in their final stages, it was advisable that they
should be advanced as much as possible in the initial stages
by the representatives at Peking.[2] The next day, 11 January,
Choate, the American Ambassador at London, informed Lansdowne that 'owing to the decided opposition offered by the
German and Japanese Governments' the President's proposal
had been withdrawn.[3]

The Punishment Issue

After the withdrawal of the American proposal there was some
confusion among the assembled representatives at Peking on
how the peace conference was to begin. Preliminary discussion
on the indemnity was begun in January, but it was realized that
this aspect of the settlement would require considerable prepara-
tory work before being taken up at the conference table. An
opening was provided on 16 January when the Chinese plenipotentiaries, Prince Ching and Li Hung-chang, submitted a
memorandum on the Joint Note. The memorandum made

[1] Sanderson to Satow, 1 Mar. 1901, P.R.O. 30/33/7/1.
[2] Memoranda by Bertie of 7 and 10 Jan. 1901, F.O. 17/1499; memorandum by
Campbell of 19 Jan. 1901, F.O. 17/1499; Lansdowne to Lord Pauncefote (British
Ambassador to U.S.), tel. 4 of 10 Jan. 1901, F.O. 5/2459.
[3] Memorandum by Lansdowne of 11 Jan. 1901, F.O. 17/1499; Lansdowne to
Satow, tel. 11 of 11 Jan. 1901, F.O. 17/1486. The move was suggested to Washington
by Conger. Cf. memorandum by Tower of 5 Jan. 1901, F.O. 17/1469.

various observations on the terms which had been laid down by the powers and also put forward the argument that, as the Joint Note had been accepted by China, the forces in Peking, Paotingfu, and all places other than those which were to be occupied to ensure open communication to the sea, should be withdrawn.[1]

The initiative was taken by Satow, who immediately observed to Lansdowne that

The whole tone of the observations of the Chinese plenipotentiaries is objectionable and almost arrogant. The contents of the Chinese memorandum instead of being a supplication that the severity of the terms imposed by the Powers be lessened, are rather advice and recommendations to the Powers how they should consult among themselves and then at once inform China of the result.[2]

Satow proposed that he should suggest to his colleagues that the Chinese should be told that they had completely misunderstood the last paragraph of the Joint Note and that, before replying to the Chinese memorandum, the powers would insist on the punishment of the guilty officials.

Satow then suggested to the assembled representatives that, before a reply was sent to the Chinese, definite proof of Chinese sincerity should be shown, and that for this Article 2a of the Joint Note should be taken as a test case. Article 2a was the punishment clause which provided for the severest punishment in proportion to their crimes for the persons named in the Imperial decree of 25 September 1900, and for those whom the representatives should subsequently designate. Most of the representatives approved the idea of a test case, but the majority were against making the death penalty a prior condition of future negotiation. The Russian and Japanese ministers suggested that a selection should be made, possibly providing the death penalty for Prince Chuang and Yu Hsien, and banishment or degradation for Tung Fu-Hsiang. Satow's proposal was formally considered at meetings held on 22 and 24 January and approved by all the representatives, with reservations by Russia and Japan. On 26 January a reply was given to the Chinese memorandum of 16 January insisting on the prior

---

[1] Satow to Lansdowne, tel. 17 of 18 Jan. 1901, F.O. 17/1487; the memorandum is given in Satow to Lansdowne, No. 24 of 19 Jan. 1901, F.O. 17/1469.
[2] Satow to Lansdowne, tel. 19 of 18 Jan. 1901, F.O. 17/1487.

fulfilment of Articles 2 and 10 of the Joint Note as a necessary condition before there could be any talk of withdrawal.[1]

Satow's move was approved by the Foreign Office. While Lansdowne felt that some of the points raised in the Chinese memorandum were worthy of consideration, especially the restriction on the number of legation guards, he approved Satow's suggestion for making the punishment clauses a test case, emphasized that the persons named in the Imperial decree of 25 September deserved death, left the exact choice of names to Satow's discretion, and then added, significantly, that it was premature to fix a date for the evacuation of Chihli.[2]

The British attitude on punishment requires closer attention. It will be remembered that the paragraph referred to by Satow stated that the evacuation of Peking and the province of Chihli would not be considered until after the Chinese had complied with the conditions laid down by the powers in the Joint Note. It had been inserted by the Cabinet when it was realized that the inclusion of the word 'irrevocable' could commit Great Britain to ulterior measures entailing possible expeditions into the interior, beyond the boundaries of Chihli. It will also be remembered that on 9 December the Cabinet determined to persist in the demand for the death penalty against the guilty officials after the other powers had shown a willingness to take a more moderate stand, and that Satow had been instructed to press this demand in the negotiations with the Chinese plenipotentiaries.[3]

British insistence on this point sprang partly from the desire to exact due punishment for the outrages which had been committed; 112 of the 240 foreigners who lost their lives in the rising were British nationals.[4] Nevertheless, the stand on the death penalty cannot wholly be explained by this reason. In general, a surprising degree of tolerance and even sympathy was shown for the Chinese. The attitude to missionary activity has been noted; it will also be seen that Great Britain was

---

[1] Satow to Lansdowne, tel. 20 of 18 Jan. 1901, F.O. 17/1487; text of reply given in Satow to Lansdowne, encl. 2 in No. 62 of 13 Feb. 1901, F.O. 17/1470.

[2] Lansdowne to Satow, tel. 13 of 22 Jan. 1901, F.O. 17/1482.

[3] Lansdowne to Satow, tel. 179 of 9 Dec. 1900, F.O. 17/1417.

[4] The number of foreigners killed during the outbreak totalled 240: British 112; American and Swedish 79; French 26; Belgian and Dutch 11; Italians 10; German 1; Swiss 1. Cf. No. 100 of 13 Mar. 1901, F.O. 17/1471.

opposed to an indemnity for military casualties. During the negotiation of the Joint Note a stand on the death penalty was taken because the ignominious retreat by the other powers in November was resented. In January 1901 the demand was persisted in because it became linked with the question of the withdrawal of the military forces from north China, over which a change of view had occurred since the previous autumn. After the presentation of the Joint Note, which made it unlikely that the partition of China would occur, and after the negotiation of the Anglo-German Agreement, which at once hampered Germany's opportunistic inclinations and apparently removed Great Britain from an isolated position, Great Britain was in no anxiety to secure a rapid withdrawal from north China. This was a pertinent consideration both for her over-all imperial policy and for her position in China.

If she could be assured that the activities of the powers would not lead to the partition of China, it was to Great Britain's advantage that they should be tied up in the Chinese peace settlement. The attention of the European powers, who had shown themselves to be hostile, would be deflected from the South African war. Again, while Great Britain was occupied in South Africa, she could not take a vigorous stand in China. Thus it was to her advantage that north China should stay under international occupation, which would preclude individual action by any one power. The Government worked on the assumption that as soon as the European powers withdrew Russian influence would become paramount in north China. At the beginning of 1901 there were sufficient signs of Russia's territorial ambitions. On 3 January it was revealed that she was negotiating for the control of Manchuria; arrangements were also being made, against British protests, for a Russo-German convention for the transfer of the Northern railways; and Russia had acquired a hugh concession of territory in Tientsin.[1] Although these issues were negotiated independently of the Chinese peace settlement, it was nevertheless true that Russian activity was hampered while the combined attention of the powers was centred on Peking and while the powers could dictate the attitude of China through the terms of the

[1] Satow to Lansdowne, tel. 13 of 9 Jan. 1901, F.O. 17/1487. Manchuria and the Northern railways are discussed in separate chapters.

peace settlement. It will be seen that Lansdowne was in no hurry to bring the negotiations at Peking to a rapid conclusion.

Another reason leading Great Britain to press for the death penalty was to secure Chinese compliance over the implementation of the Joint Note. Just as it was assumed that Russia would take advantage of a general withdrawal, so was it assumed that China would prove obstructive over the terms of the settlement. Thus in an estimate of the policy which should be followed, made on 27 December, Bertie suggested that the question of capital punishments should be kept *in terrorem* over the Chinese plenipotentiaries.[1]

These considerations lay behind the British attitude to the various issues which came up in the peace settlement, just as the determination not to encourage the return of the Court lest it fell under Russian control had influenced decisions on the Joint Note. Consequently, when Satow secured the support of the representatives for his proposal that punishment should precede withdrawal, the Conference turned in a direction which accorded with British policy. The day after he received Satow's report on the general attitude of the representatives on the matter of punishment, Lansdowne felt that the time was opportune to assert the British view that any prominent culprit who was merely exiled would be regarded as liable to execution if he returned at any time.[2] At the same time a stand was made on the death penalty. Discussion centred on the fate of Prince Tuan, Duke Lan, and Tung Fu-hsiang. Russia, Japan, and the United States were formally against the death penalty; France was for it, but Pichon, the French minister, did not feel it could be obtained; Germany was also for it though Mumm felt that the moment to make the demand had passed when the powers began to retreat in November, while the Austrian and Italian ministers had instructions to act with their German colleague, with the maintenance of unanimity their first consideration. On this assessment Lansdowne concluded that a working majority was in favour of the death penalty and Satow was instructed to vote for it.[3]

[1] Memorandum by Bertie of 27 Dec. 1900, F.O. 17/1451.
[2] Lansdowne to Satow, tel. 14 of 22 Jan. 1901, F.O. 17/1482; Satow to Lansdowne, tel. 21 of 23 Jan. 1901, F.O. 17/1484.
[3] Satow to Lansdowne, tel. 24 of 26 Jan. 1901, F.O. 17/1484; Lansdowne to Satow, tel. 17 of 28 Jan. 1901, F.O. 17/1482.

The foreign representatives met on 31 January to discuss the question of punishment. Brief statements were drawn up of the charges against the eight persons named in the decree of 25 September, with the addition of four other ministers who had been judged guilty of instigating attacks on the legations. Arrangements were made to meet the Chinese plenipotentiaries on 5 February, when the doyen was to make a verbal communication stating that the foreign plenipotentiaries demanded for the guilty ministers 'the severest penalty in proportion to their crimes. You will thus understand . . . that these personages deserve death.' The last four words were submitted at the instance of the United States minister in place of the previously agreed reading 'the penalty which would be in proportion to the crimes committed by these personages would be the death penalty'. Satow preferred the original wording, but he gave way to general feeling, and he expressed to the Foreign Office his determination to ensure the death penalty be put on record even though commutation would have to follow.[1] In reply, Lansdowne emphatically agreed that the death penalty be placed on record.[2]

At the conference with the Chinese representatives, held at the British Legation on 5 February, the Chinese attempted to mitigate the demands; they also communicated a secret decree which promised the punishment of Tung Fu-hsiang at some future date.[3] In the discussion which followed among the foreign ministers Satow found it impossible to get his colleagues to agree to the demand for the death penalty for the guilty members of the Imperial family (Tuan and Lan), and so, in the afternoon, he proposed and secured agreement on a demand for a sentence recording the death penalty, but leaving the Emperor liberty immediately to commute this into perpetual exile to Turkestan. He had privately told the

---

[1] Satow to Lansdowne, tel. 27 of 31 Jan. 1901, F.O. 17/1484. The twelve guilty ministers were Prince Chuang, Prince Tuan, Duke Lan (Tsai Lan), Yu Hsien, Tung Fu-hsiang, Li Ping-heng, Ying Nien, Kang I, Chao Shu-chiao, Hsu T'ung, Hsu Ch'eng-yu, and Ch'i Hsiu. The statement of the crimes is given in China No. 6 (1901), 157–8. The Blue Books do not give a clear impression of the British attitude on this issue.

[2] Lansdowne to Satow, tel. 24 of 2 Feb. 1901, F.O. 17/1482.

[3] An account of the meeting and the secret decree against Tung of *Kuang Hsu* 26/12/8 (27 Jan. 1901) is given in Satow to Lansdowne, No. 50 of 6 Feb. 1901, F.O. 17/1470.

Chinese representatives that morning that he would not accept less.[1]

This concession was not acceptable to Lansdowne, who repeated in some detail that the death penalty should merely remain in abeyance, and would be carried out in the event of the return of the condemned men.[2]

The instruction arrived too late to be included in a note on punishments which had been drawn up on 6 February for communication to the Chinese, and so Satow made Lansdowne's wishes known in a special declaration on 8 February, to which he asked the other powers to subscribe. Only Germany and Austria gave their full support with regard to all three of the condemned men. Consequently, in view of lack of unanimity, Satow inserted the British declaration into the procès-verbal. A French resolution for the death of Tung Fu-hsiang was accepted.[3]

The refusal of the powers to demand the death penalty for the guilty members of the Imperial family had gradually driven Satow on to the defensive. His position was relieved in the middle of February, when the Court attempted to secure a mitigation of the sentence against the other condemned men, notably Ying Nien and Chao Shu-chiao. The Chinese made a desperate attempt to save Chao, whom they considered to be unjustly condemned, and approaches were made on his behalf both in London and Peking.[4] Lansdowne left the matter to Satow's discretion, but the sympathy of the British minister, who had been considering the question of mitigation for Chao, was alienated when the Court issued a decree on 13 February detailing the punishments of the guilty with a leniency which appeared to ignore the recommendations presented by the foreign representatives on 6 February.[5] Satow was convinced

---

[1] Satow to Lansdowne, tel. 32A of 5 Feb. 1901, F.O. 17/1484.

[2] Lansdowne to Satow, tel. 26 of 6 Feb. 1901, F.O. 17/1482.

[3] Satow to Lansdowne, tel. 36 of 8 Feb. 1901, F.O. 17/1484.

[4] For the appeal made in London on Chao Shu-chiao's behalf see Chinese Legation, London Despatches: Issued and Received, No. 64, telegram from Liu K'un-i and Chang Chih-tung of 18 Feb. 1901; No. 67 Lansdowne's reply.

[5] Chuang was to commit suicide, the other royal members were banished to Sinkiang; Yu Hsien was to be executed and the others were given lesser sentences. Satow to Lansdowne, No. 68 of 18 Feb. 1901, F.O. 17/1470; T.T.S.L. 477/96, 116. Lansdowne's decision to leave the fate of Chao in Satow's hands is indicated in Lansdowne to Satow, tel. 33 of 12 Feb. 1901, F.O. 17/1482, Sanderson to Satow, 12 May 1901, P.R.O. 30/33/7/1.

that the Court and the Chinese plenipotentiaries were relying on dissension among the powers and he felt strongly that if they gave way on punishments, difficulties over the rest of the negotiations would increase. He thought that a threat to break off negotiations would have an excellent effect.[1]

This militancy was shared by the other representatives. It was unanimously agreed to send a note through the doyen expressing the belief that the note of 6 February could not have reached the Court when the Emperor issued the decree of 13 February.[2] But this diplomatic reproach could not alleviate the sense of outrage at Chinese obstructiveness felt by British and German ministers, and a stronger move involving the military forces was considered. This was partly to satisfy the restlessness which had become noticeable among the troops by the middle of February.

The Question of Military Reprisals

To give the military something to do the ministers had asked the generals of the contingents to formulate a plan to implement Articles 8 and 9 of the Joint Note, which provided for open communication between Peking and the sea. But these arrangements, as with everything else in the peace settlement, became a political matter, out of the hands of the military, to their increasing discontent. Consequently, when the Chinese attitude on punishments was known, the military suggested a solution. On 15 February Waldersee issued an army order which declared:

Although the peace negotiations still continue to be carried on, their course up to the present induces me to point out that a resumption of larger operations may become shortly necessary. I request therefore that as the favourable season is approaching such prompt measures may be taken as to ensure the mobilization of all the troops by the end of the month.[3]

Ostensibly the order was issued to bluff the Chinese into a more pliable frame of mind. But the military were inclined to a real move; orders were given for an eight-day expedition, equipped

[1] Satow to Lansdowne, tel. 43 of 17 Feb. 1901, F.O. 17/1484.
[2] Satow to Lansdowne, tel. 45 of 18 Feb. 1901, F.O. 17/1484.
[3] Satow to Lansdowne, tel. 46 of 19 Feb. 1901, F.O. 17/1484.

for mountain travel. The plan, which originated with Walder-see's chief of staff, was for 8,000 or 9,000 German troops to cross the mountain range into Shansi and so put themselves into a position to menace the Court in its retreat. If the French co-operated they were to move on T'aiyuan; the Italians would march with the Germans; the British would move on the flank of the main force into south-west Chihli; the Japanese and Americans were to remain in Peking. In all, the project would cover a 700-mile front, using about 13,000 men. The object was the extension of the territory occupied in order to facilitate the negotiations.

General Gaselee, who had on his hands the problem of a large force of idle men made restless after the long winter, also had the idea of a 'somewhat ostentatious mobilization of a large force'.[1] He approved Waldersee's plan and telegraphed for permission to participate.[2] General Voyron, the commander of the French, was also enthusiastic and within a few days a movement of French and German troops was noticeable. On 19 February the United States minister declared himself against the project. Satow noted that 'it would be regrettable if notice were taken of the United States Minister's protest'.[3]

In London, Lansdowne could not make up his mind about this development over the punishment issue and decided to wait for Gaselee's report. Sir John Ardagh, the Director of Military Intelligence, was more outspoken and bluntly declared that while it was satisfactory that the Chinese should be alarmed by this mobilization of force, in other respects the news was not satisfactory, because Great Britain was not interested in hurrying on a solution of the Chinese difficulties:

the policy of procrastination has, at the present moment, many advantages—notably that of diverting the attention of the Powers least friendly to us, from other questions and places where advantage might be taken of our entanglements in South Africa to press for solutions of a nature we are not now in a position to strenuously oppose—e.g. Persia, Afghanistan, Yunnan, Newfoundland, Nicaragua, Alaska, etc.[4]

[1] Grierson's diary, No. 10 of 21 Feb. 1901, F.O. 17/1505.
[2] G.-O.-C., China Expedition, to India Office, 18 Feb. 1901, F.O. 17/1501.
[3] Satow to Lansdowne, tel. 46 of 19 Feb. 1901, F.O. 17/1484.
[4] Memorandum by Ardagh, encl. in Satow to Lansdowne, tel. 49, secret, of 19 Feb. 1901, F.O. 17/1484.

Fortunately, it did not prove necessary either to join in an expedition into the interior or to fall back defensively on a partition of territory, for on 21 February, at the prospect of renewed military activity, Chinese resistance collapsed; the only concession she obtained was that Ying Nien and Chao Shu-chiao were allowed to die by suicide instead of strangulation.[1]

The question of the punishment of the provincial officials guilty of outrages was then taken up. It had been decided on 24 January that the representatives with demands respecting the murder of missionaries should confer to draw up a list of the guilty officials. A first meeting was held on 28 January with the French, United States, Italian, Netherlands, Belgian, and British ministers attending.[2] Work on framing the list was continued throughout February. The United States was against further capital punishment; Russia, Japan, Germany, Austria, and Spain, with no missionary dead, were uninterested. Satow felt that if the provincial officials who were guilty of actual massacres were treated leniently while the ministers responsible for the attack on the legations were punished, the contrast would be striking; Lansdowne concurred with this view. The list was presented to the assembled representatives on 28 February. Ten officials were given the death penalty, about ninety-four were named for lesser degrees of punishment.[3] Giers, the Russian minister, opposed the death penalty, but Lansdowne instructed Satow to insist, whether Russia concurred or not. For most of the representatives the question of provincial punishments was of lesser political importance, and Giers was the only one to maintain his opposition. It must be remembered that Russia's advocacy of leniency was at least as much a political move as the demand for severity made by the other powers. The question of punishments was considered against the background of the Sino-Russian negotiations over Manchuria.

On 12 March Giers stated that he had been instructed to say that Russia 'considered the question of punishments exhausted'.[4]

---

[1] Tan, *The Boxer Catastrophe*, 222.

[2] For details of the massacres cf. Satow to Lansdowne, No. 41 of 31 Jan. 1901, F.O. 17/1469.

[3] Satow to Lansdowne, tel. 60 of 28 Feb. 1901, F.O. 17/1484. Additions were made later.

[4] Satow to Lansdowne, tel. 72 of 13 Mar. 1901, F.O. 17/1484.

His instructions caused the Russian minister some embarrassment, for he had acquiesced in all the earlier stages connected with provincial punishments. The other representatives, after expressing their resentment against the refusal of Russia to maintain unanimity on this delicate point, continued the negotiations. Satow was told to continue pressing for the punishment of the provincial offenders, 'in communication with your German colleague who has been instructed to cooperate'.[1] The only noteworthy consequence of the Russian stand was the embarrassment in which it placed the French minister, who had hitherto worked closely with Giers. 'He fears to act apart from the Russian Minister,' Satow reported, 'but on the other hand not to press for punishment of murderers of French missionaries would impair claim of France to protectorate of Catholics.'[2] Finally, this consideration dictated the French stand and when a Joint Note on provincial punishments was presented to the Chinese on 1 April it had been signed by all except the Russian minister.

To Satow, the presentation of the list indicated the end of the punishment issue. He did not anticipate a Chinese refusal to comply. In a note to the Chinese plenipotentiaries on 26 January the foreign representatives had intimated that they would discuss military questions (the occupation of coastal points, the razing of the Taku forts, and the evacuation of Peking and Chihli) when the punishment clauses of the Joint Note had been carried out. On 3 April Satow reported that although the German minister advocated the postponement of all discussion about evacuation until the indemnity proposals had been settled, he, Satow, thought that immediate steps for considering evacuation measures should be begun.[3]

Lansdowne's reply forced the British minister to realize that he had been carrying out British policy without really understanding its aim. For two and a half months he had carried out his instructions of the previous December and pressed for vigorous punishment of the Chinese offenders. Because of the lack of co-operation among the other representatives upon the question of the death penalty, Satow had begun to modify his

[1] Lansdowne to Satow, tel. 73 of 19 Mar. 1901, F.O. 17/1482.
[2] Satow to Lansdowne, tel. 90 of 22 Mar. 1901, F.O. 17/1484.
[3] Satow to Lansdowne, tel. 104 of 3 Apr. 1901, F.O. 17/1484.

stand and to countenance the idea of the immediate commutation of the sentence of death by the Emperor. He had been
corrected repeatedly by Lansdowne and had consequently
been forced to reopen the question with his colleagues, leading to
interminable discussion. Satow found the close attention of the
Foreign Secretary trying. 'This interfering in small details is
sometimes childish', he noted in his Journal on 8 February,
'as if out here one could not be trusted to do a thing properly.'[1]
Thereafter the British minister had carried out his task well
and had the satisfaction of knowing that in the latter stages
of the negotiations on punishment Russia had been placed in
the isolated position in which Great Britain had found herself
during the negotiation of the Joint Note.

Lansdowne, however, thought it remarkable that the British
representative should be 'the man in a hurry' while the German
advocated delay, and added that there was considerable risk
in letting it appear that the British were intent on getting away
by a certain date. Consequently, on 4 April Satow was instructed to act with his German colleague by holding up evacuation
until the indemnity was settled.[2] A few days later he explained
his view in a private letter to Satow: 'What we have to look out
for is a sudden burst of impatience here or elsewhere which
would lead to urgent demands for a precipitate withdrawal.'[3]
Withdrawal was to be linked with the indemnity negotiations,
which were then in the first stages of full-scale discussion.
Lansdowne added that if a total sum could be decided on
among the powers, evacuation would be carried out in relation
to Chinese compliance *au fur et à mesure*.

However, within a month Lansdowne was to change his
mind. Over 60,000 allied troops in the province of Chihli
created a problem diplomacy could not control.[4] The French
concession in Tientsin had been out of bounds to British troops
since November 1900. The French infantry, made up of large
numbers of Parisian apaches, were violent and unruly. At
night the streets of the city resounded with cries of 'à bas les

[1] S.J., 8 Feb. 1901.
[2] Lansdowne to Satow, tel. 98 of 4 Apr. 1901, F.O. 17/1482.
[3] Lansdowne to Satow, 9 Apr. 1901, P.R.O. 30/33/7/1.
[4] Strength of allied contingents in Chihli: Great Britain 11,160; Australia 340;
France 17,800; Germany 18,700; Italy 2,150; Japan 6,270; Russia 2,620; United
States 2,100. India Office to Foreign Office, 15 May 1901, F.O. 17/1504.

Anglais' and 'Fashoda'; German troopers fraternized with them and 'Vive les Boers' was echoed by 'Verdammte Engländer'.[1] Riots were frequent. In mid-March a mutiny broke out in the French contingent. In June a serious clash occurred over the closing of a brothel; over 200 of the French attacked with drawn swords and needle bayonets; a pitched battle ensued with the British and Japanese on one side, the French and Germans on the other; about a score were killed and wounded.[2]

Tension developed between the military and the diplomats. Army circles considered the ministers sitting 'twice a week in Solemn Conclave' slightly ridiculous.[3] A tendency developed among the allied commanders to act on their own. Thus they extended the jurisdiction of the Provisional Government of Tientsin without consulting the ministers.[4] Satow had difficulty even with the British commanders, and the question of consular jurisdiction of military personnel had to be referred home for decision. The decision of the law officers did not help matters: the troops in north China were considered to be on active service and thus not amenable to the jurisdiction of the British consul-general.[5] General Gaselee interested himself in railway politics and pressed for an extension from Tungchow to Tong-shan which would confine Russia to the north and frustrate her declared intention of building a railway from Manchuria into China.[6]

Military restlessness was particularly significant in the crisis over the Russian concession in Tientsin. On 15 March Russian sentries were placed near where the Madras Pioneers were erecting a siding. Neither side would give way and the position became difficult. At midday the Russians began a trench which menaced the British position; the latter then occupied some houses enfilading the Russians. The situation, although ludicrous, was explosive; the Manchurian crisis was at its height. At 2 p.m. a Russian sentry was posted with one foot on the last railway sleeper the British had laid; a British sentry was immediately placed with his foot on the other end. The United

[1] Grierson's Diary, 21 Mar. 1901, F.O. 17/1507.
[2] G.-O.-C. to India Office, tel. 268 of 3 June 1901, F.O. 17/1505.
[3] Powell to Stedman, 20 Feb. 1901, F.O. 17/1503.
[4] Satow to Lansdowne, tel. 50 of 21 Feb. 1901, F.O. 17/1484.
[5] Correspondence given W.O. 32/139/7842/1525/1559, 1583, 1706, 1990.
[6] G.-O.-C. to India Office, 9 May 1901, F.O. 17/1504.

States Commander remembered his history and declared to his British opposite that 'we'll stand by you. Blood's thicker than water.'[1] Orders were given to the British railway officials to prevent Russian troops from arriving, while all the available British marines were gathered to replace the Indian troops on the spot. It was felt the Russians were aggressive because they were dealing with Indians. General Barrow in charge of the British troops, asked whether the Russians were to be ejected by force. The issue was taken up between London and St. Petersburg and on 22 March a simultaneous withdrawal took place.[2] The Russian argument was that the land fell into their concession and they continued work on the siding. General Barrow asked Satow to protest but he was reluctant and observed: 'De minimis would probably be the view of His Majesty's Government.'[3] He wrote to Lansdowne that he thought the action of the military in commencing the siding without coming to a previous understanding with the Russians 'extremely imprudent'.[4]

The issue was political, but aggravated by the vigorous action of the military. The latter were confined by political bonds and restless after a long winter. Waldersee's mid-February expedition might have released the tension, but this had been deemed politically inadvisable. By the spring the Field-Marshal had tired of his role. On 8 April a massive display was given to mark his sixty-ninth birthday; but the shrill of Scottish pipers, Japanese music, and Bersaglieri trumpets could not remove the feeling that such displays had already been held too often. This was Waldersee's opinion and on 6 April he had decided with the other generals that partial reduction of the allied troops was advisable. The diplomatic body phrased a cautious reply to the effect that this was possible, but that proper evacuation could not be begun till the Chinese had complied with the punishment clauses.[5]

---

[1] Grierson's Diary, 21 Mar. 1901, F.O. 17/1507.
[2] Satow to Lansdowne, tels. 74 of 15 Mar., 77 of 16 Mar. 1901, F.O. 17/1484; Lansdowne to Satow, tel. 70 of 16 Mar. 1901, F.O. 17/1482; Barrow to India Office, tel. 167 of 15 Mar. 1901, F.O. 17/1502; Secretary of State to G.-O.-C. China Expedition, tel. 88, secret of 16 Mar. 1901, F.O. 17/1502.
[3] S.J., 1 Apr. 1901.
[4] Satow to Lansdowne, 23 Mar. 1901, Lansdowne Papers.
[5] Satow to Lansdowne, tel. 122 of 19 Apr. 1901, F.O. 17/1484.

The reply did not satisfy the military who had tired of serving as a diplomatic counter, without the power to move on their own initiative. In May they brought the climatic factor into account and argued that unless a reduction were begun immediately, a mass movement would be impossible after the hot rainy summer set in, which would affect the health of the troops.[1]

Lansdowne then agreed to a reduction in the number of troops.[2] Apart from the military consideration, several other factors influenced him in this decision. The indemnity negotiations had revealed that by the beginning of May the aggregate claim of the powers had been set at so large a sum that it was clear that the military expenses of continued occupation could not easily be charged on the Chinese. The cost of the occupation for British forces was £129,000 a month.[3] Moreover, the indemnity negotiations were not conducted with a dispatch likely to bring about a precipitate withdrawal; nor were the troops necessary to coerce the Chinese. The military force were superfluous during the later stages of the peace settlement. Further, by May the Manchurian crisis had passed and, with it, much of the apprehension over Russia's aggressive intentions in north China.

On 25 May Eckardstein communicated a telegram from Baron Richthofen to the effect that the Kaiser thought that Waldersee should be recalled.[4] Early in June the Field-Marshal left for Europe by way of Japan. Military decisions in north China were then made by the Council of the Commanding Officers of the various forces, and the confusion which had preceded Waldersee's arrival recurred.

By agreement, the international forces were to be reduced gradually until the strength of the various contingents accorded with the number of troops allowed for the permanent legation garrisons. Except for the United States, which withdrew its entire contingent, mutual suspicion among the powers made

---

[1] G.-O.-C. China Expedition to India Office, tel. 256 of 19 May 1901, F.O. 17/1505.
[2] Memorandum by Lansdowne in draft to India Office of 17 May 1901, F.O. 17/1504.
[3] W.O. 32/137/7842/996.
[4] Memorandum by Sanderson of 25 May 1901, F.O. 17/1505; W.O. 32/137/7842/1067, 1069.

this difficult. In 1902 an acrimonious exchange of views took place between Great Britain and Germany over the evacuation of Shanghai. To avoid exciting British opinion the Government was forced to edit the correspondence on the subject which was laid before Parliament.[1] By 1906 there were still over 5,000 foreign troops, exclusive of legation guards, in north China.[2] The withdrawal of the international contingents from China after the Boxer rising has a wretched history, entirely lacking in the verve and drama which attended their arrival.

The Indemnity Negotiations

The indemnity negotiations were complicated because the powers, apart from making a claim, had to agree among themselves on the amount of the claim, the form in which it was to be paid, and the resources which were to be utilized. These points were raised and discussed during the siege of the legations and were a matter of intense speculation in the post-relief period.[3] The vast scope of the problem encouraged a leisurely start and the indemnity issue was not brought before the assembled representatives until 16 February 1901. Before that time various schemes were circulated privately by persons who were qualified to speak on the subject and also by many more who believed they were informed enough to do so. In the subsequent negotiation these theoretical solutions to the indemnity problem were discarded.

The meeting of 16 February concerned itself with the general principles on which the indemnity claims were to be made. It was agreed that claims would have to be divided into government claims covering war expenses and compensation for military personnel, to be decided by the home governments, and non-governmental, that is to say private, commercial, and missionary claims, which the representatives agreed to consider. Satow suggested that the principles of assessment in the claims should be agreed on; on the other hand, most of the other powers thought that the amount of each individual claim

[1] This is covered in *B.D.* ii. 138–53.
[2] 'North China: Withdrawal of International troops', W.O. 106/17. The figures for July 1906 were: Germany 450; France 1,400; Japan 800; Italy 100; Russia 40; Austria 40; United States nil; Great Britain 1,900.
[3] Bredon to Bertie, 27 Nov. 1900, F.O. 17/1450.

should be decided, while ways and means could be settled later. Komura, the Japanese minister, proposed that the war indemnity, based on actual expenditure, should be added to the private claims, based on direct loss, and that the aggregate should represent the whole indemnity. Discussion was then deferred until instructions had been received.[1]

In London also the indemnity had been discussed. The British aim was not to claim a large indemnity, which would react on the Chinese Customs and thus on Great Britain. Instead, as moderate an amount as possible was to be claimed, while the remainder of British expenses incurred in the rising were to be waived in return for largely increased trade facilities and commercial reform.[2] On 5 February Bertie suggested the formation of a committee to consider the Chinese indemnity. This was formed with Bertie as chairman. Five meetings were held between 17 February and 13 March, when a report was submitted. Discussion ranged over the whole field of China's resources. The committee concluded that by using all her available resources, such as tariff revision up to the full treaty obligation of 5 per cent, use of the salt gabelle, savings in the transport of tribute rice and the transfer of the native customs to the maritime customs, the most China could find was about £1½ million a year. At 5 per cent this would service a loan of £30 million. As a Chinese loan could only be floated at 80, the money actually received by China, after the cost of issue of the loan, would be about £23 million.[3] Lansdowne thought this estimate of China's resources a 'low one'.[4] Nevertheless, on the most optimistic appraisal, it was impossible to hope that China would be able to find, either by scraping the surplus from her existing revenue, or by reforming her resources, enough money to service a loan large enough to meet the anticipated aggregate claim of all the powers.

Consequently, Great Britain aimed at keeping the claims of the other powers as moderate as possible. Satow was instructed

---

[1] Satow to Lansdowne, tel. 44 of 17 Feb. 1901, F.O. 17/1484; No. 65 of 16 Feb. 1901, F.O. 17/1470.

[2] Memorandum by Bertie, 27 Dec. 1900, F.O. 17/1451.

[3] The report and minutes of the meetings are contained in F.O. 17/1502. The members were Bateman (Board of Trade), Alford (B. and C. Corporation), Hippisley (C.I.M.C.), and Cockburn (H.M. Legation, Peking).

[4] Lansdowne to Satow, 9 Apr. 1901, P.R.O. 30/33/7/1.

to propose the exclusion of indirect claims and to oppose the presentation of separate claims by individual powers.[1] He had already pressed for a principle of assessment to be applied to non-governmental claims.

However, the other powers were not anxious to admit their individual claims to public scrutiny. A committee was formed at Peking on 23 February to consider the principles to be applied in assessing claims, but a reluctance to co-operate was already evident. France declared that indemnities were regulated by 'treaties and conventions and constant usage' and so there was no need to agree on common principles. She also expressed her intention of claiming compensation for native converts. Germany agreed with France.[2]

If the French intention were followed by all the powers each could present a monstrous claim. Satow was instructed to press that all non-governmental claims should be considered by all the representatives. The other ministers thought this impractical and, in view of the excessive amount of work involved, Satow was forced to agree with them.[3] Each power then began to receive its non-governmental claims privately. When the Peking committee met on 13 and 18 March, Russia stated that she would make a separate indemnity claim (the Sino-Russian negotiations over Manchuria were then at their height); the United States stated she would claim a round sum; and the British proposal for the revision of non-governmental claims was rejected 8 to 3, with Italy and Germany supporting Great Britain.[4] Lansdowne observed that if the powers took this attitude Great Britain could retaliate by refusing to facilitate loan arrangements.[5]

Lansdowne's aim in pressing 'revision' was to prevent fraudulent claims. An example of the many which were presented, but by no means the most excessive, was in connection with the French claim for the Peking–Hankow railway. The estimated Belgian claim was £1 million although the estimated construction of the whole line was £5 million and only a small portion had

[1] Lansdowne to Satow, tel. 38 of 18 Feb. 1901, F.O. 17/1482.
[2] Satow to Lansdowne, tel. 53 of 23 Feb. 1901, F.O. 17/1484.
[3] Lansdowne to Satow, tel. 46 of 26 Feb. 1901, F.O. 17/1482; Satow to Lansdowne, tel. 59 of 28 Feb. 1901, F.O. 17/1484.
[4] Satow to Lansdowne, tels. 80 and 81 of 18 Mar. 1901, F.O. 17/1484.
[5] Minute on tel. 80 above.

been completed. When questioned, France retorted that the original estimate of construction had been exceeded by 65 million francs, the bonds had depreciated, it was impossible to raise further capital, and the estimated earnings of the line if the rising had not taken place had to be considered.[1]

As each power was to make up its own claim, which meant a large aggregate indemnity, attention was then concentrated on the Chinese resources available to service a loan. This aspect of the negotiations held the interest of all the powers. While Bertie's committee in London had been hampered in its work by having to find surplus revenue without disturbing Great Britain's trading position, the other powers were not restricted by this consideration. Many suggestions were put forward, but the most aggressive was advanced by Germany.

Chinese import and export duties had originally been fixed in 1858 at 5 per cent *ad valorem*. In many instances this had been accepted as the specific duty. By 1899–1900, mainly in consequence of the depreciation of silver, the ratio of duties to the actual value of goods had become altered, and it was estimated that in many instances the import duty amounted to less than 3 per cent. Mercantile bodies were willing to admit the discrepancy, on condition that likin (provincial transit duty) were abolished.[2] This reciprocal concession was considered essential as tariff revision to 5 per cent imposed a heavy burden on British trade.

On 21 February Germany proposed, in London, that adequate revenue would be obtained to service an indemnity loan if import duties were raised to 10 per cent.[3] On existing figures, the increase, with the abolition of the duty-free list, would provide about £3 million, sufficient to service a loan of £50 million, but the burden would be carried by British trade. The suggestion for an increase to 10 per cent was then made to the Peking committee by Mumm, the German minister, on 23 March.[4] In addition, a few days later Dr. Stuebal, Director of

---

[1] Satow to Lansdowne, tel. 115 of 11 Apr. 1901, F.O. 17/1484.

[2] Cf. China Association to Foreign Office, 6 July 1901; Gundry to Lansdowne, 12 June 1901, F.O. 17/1505; Liverpool Chamber of Commerce to Foreign Office, 5 July 1901; Halifax Chamber of Commerce to Foreign Office, 6 July 1901, F.O. 17/1506.

[3] German proposals communicated by the German Embassy, 21 Feb. 1901, appendix to Report (of Bertie's Committee), pp. 50–4, F.O. 17/1502.

[4] Satow to Lansdowne, tel. 92 of 24 Mar. 1901, F.O. 17/1484.

the Colonial Department of the German Foreign Office, was sent to London to discuss the raising of the tariff. In his report to Lansdowne of his conversations with Stuebal, Bertie observed: 'I believe that apart from the fact that Customs Duties are the most convenient security for a Loan that the German and other Governments desire to upset the present system of the Customs Staff under the British Inspector General and to substitute for it an International Board of Control.'[1] A 10 per cent tariff was pressed by Germany throughout April. She was supported by Russia and France. The United States and Japan were ready to accept a 10 per cent tariff only on condition China agreed to concede likin and other reforms. This was the stand Lansdowne adopted and which he maintained persistently throughout the subsequent negotiations: that an increase in duties beyond the effective 5 per cent tariff would only be considered in connection with a scheme of general reform of the commercial treaties, provided for in Article 11 of the Joint Note.[2]

A second attack on Great Britain's position developed from the discussion on tariff reform. At the meeting of the Peking committee on 23 March, Mumm, the German minister, suggested that if the 10 per cent tariff, the salt gabelle, and the native customs were insufficient then it might be possible for the powers to guarantee a loan. Subsequently he adopted an indeterminate stand, both affirming and denying the suggestion.[3] A joint guarantee by the powers would mean a right to interest themselves in the securities China would offer for the loan, in other words an international board of control over the maritime customs, the surplus revenue of which could be used even if Great Britain resisted a 10 per cent tariff. Understandably, the suggestion was taken up by Russia. When M. Pokotiloff, manager of the Russo-Chinese Bank, was interviewed by the Peking committee on 28 March he admitted he had not considered a loan guaranteed by all the powers. However, when the committee met on 29 April, Giers, the Russian minister, remarked on the advantages of a 4 per cent guaranteed loan. He observed that as China could not borrow on the open

[1] Minutes of Bertie's conversations with Dr. Stuebal (with notes), 27–30 Mar. 1901, F.O. 17/1502.
[2] Lansdowne to Satow, tel. 94 of 30 Mar. 1901, F.O. 17/1482.
[3] Satow to Lansdowne, tels. 92, 107, 136 of 24 Mar. 3 and 24 Apr. 1901, F.O. 17/1484; Satow to Lansdowne, tel. 155 of 7 May 1901, F.O. 17/1487.

market at less than 7 per cent, to obtain £40 million she would have to issue a loan for nearly £52 million, while on a guaranteed loan at 4 per cent she could get £70 million for £73 million.[1]

The argument was difficult to refute because, by this time, an approximation to the individual claims of each of the powers had been received, and it was clear that a large indemnity was to be demanded of China. At a meeting of the representatives at Peking on 7 May, it was agreed that a note should be sent to the Chinese plenipotentiaries giving the aggregate indemnity figure to 1 July as about 450 million taels (about £68 million).[2] It was also stressed that occupation costs after that date would be added. But in fact the powers realized that China could not stand a heavier burden, and that the costs of continued occupation would have to be borne by themselves. It has been seen that this consideration influenced them in favour of beginning a gradual withdrawal of the military forces.

An aggregate indemnity of 450 million taels was larger than Great Britain had anticipated. Satow observed pessimistically, 'It would appear that our choice is between accepting the proposal for a joint guarantee and having to concede 10 per cent tariff.'[3] Alternatively, Great Britain had to find a solution which would keep the maritime customs out of the control of the powers. Four methods were discussed: (1) an unguaranteed Chinese loan, which was not feasible in view of the large indemnity which was being demanded; (2) a loan guaranteed by all or some of the powers, which it was against British interests to support; (3) payment of the claims by means of bonds; and (4) the promise of an annuity.

Discussion in London centred on either bonds or an annuity. On 3 and 4 May Sir Thomas Sanderson and Sir Francis Mowatt (Treasury) discussed the relative merits of the two methods.[4] Although annuities were favoured it was thought the powers would demand a marketable security. Consequently, after Lansdowne and Bertie had reviewed the Mowatt–Sanderson correspondence, Bertie drew up a plan suggesting that

---

[1] Satow to Lansdowne, tel. 149 of 1 May 1901, F.O. 17/1484.
[2] Satow to Lansdowne, tel. 156 of 7 May 1901, F.O. 17/1487.
[3] Satow to Lansdowne, tel. 155 of 7 May 1901, F.O. 17/1487.
[4] Mowatt to Sanderson, 3 May 1901; Sanderson to Mowatt, 4 May 1901, F.O. 17/1504.

China should issue bonds at 4 per cent interest with $\frac{1}{2}$ per cent sinking fund.[1] The position was then reviewed by Lansdowne and circulated to the Cabinet on 8 May. Then, in reply to Satow's report of the meeting of 7 May, the Government laid down the cardinal points of British policy for Satow's instruction.

1. To avoid making China bankrupt.
2. To make no addition beyond 5% to the Maritime Customs; except in consideration of satisfactory settlement of questions dealt with in Article XI of joint note to the Chinese Plenipotentiaries.
3. Not to take part in a joint international guarantee of a Chinese loan.

The Government favoured reduction, admitted the unfeasibility of an unguaranteed loan, and then suggested:

The issue by China to each of the creditor Powers bonds which at face value will represent the share of indemnity which it has been decided is payable to that Power. These bonds to bear interest at say 4% with $\frac{1}{2}$% for amortization.

The service of the bonds was to be effected by revenue from the surplus of the maritime customs (with the tariff raised to 5 per cent), the native customs, the taxation of certain duty free articles, and the salt gabelle. These revenues were to be received and distributed by a board or committee approved by the powers. The board was to have no right to direct interference in the Chinese administration or the right to collect taxes. To give China time, the bonds were to be issued in instalments; any power could guarantee its own bonds.[2]

Throughout May and June Great Britain fought for the bonds scheme. Attention was concentrated on Germany and Japan. German support was secured by concessions on the interest of the bonds. Germany put forward several schemes all designed to bring about a progressive improvement in the position of German bondholders in proportion to the anticipated improvement in the financial position of the Chinese Government.

---

[1] Memorandum by Lansdowne of 5 May 1901; draft of project (by Bertie) of 5 May 1901; Lansdowne's minute on Mowatt to Sanderson of 4 May 1901, F.O. 17/1504.
[2] Lansdowne to Satow, tel. 148 of 11 May 1901, F.O. 17/1486.

Lansdowne finally accepted a proposal, made by Mumm on 1 July, for the amortization of the indemnity by a sinking fund.[1]

With Japan the position was more delicate. Although Komura, the Japanese minister in Peking, was in favour of the bonds scheme, he had instructions to support a guaranteed loan. Japan stood to lose by supporting the bonds scheme because she could not hope to borrow at 4 per cent. On 23 May Satow reported that unless Great Britain offered to help Japan by guaranteeing her share of the bonds there was a possibility of Japan supporting a guaranteed loan. Lansdowne, who was then concentrating on Germany, thought that 'Unless Germany plays us false the proposal for an international guarantee is not likely to be carried' and that Great Britain could not agree to guarantee the Japanese bonds 'at this stage of the proceedings'.[2] However, it will be seen, in relation to the Anglo-Japanese alliance negotiations, that from the end of May Lansdowne became increasingly concerned with the need to hold Japan's goodwill. The bonds issue became involved with the political relations of the two powers. On 15 June Komura declared in Peking that 4 per cent bonds at par would result in a loss for Japan as she could not borrow at a lower rate than 5 per cent. Komura then proposed that additional bonds, at 4 per cent, to cover this difference should be granted to Japan. Russia too declared that Russian 4 per cent rentes stood at 96 or 97, so that she would also stand a loss with the bonds at par.[3] Russia's difficulties did not occasion much concern, but on 19 June Lansdowne drew up a memorandum for the use of the Cabinet on the next day, in which he stressed the political importance of satisfying Japan.[4] Lansdowne suggested that Great Britain could either (1) support an increased Japanese claim, (2) guarantee the Japanese bonds, (3) give her part of the British bonds, or (4) buy Japan's bonds from her at face value.

---

[1] Satow to Lansdowne, tels. 220, 223, 232 of 1, 3, 6 July 1901, F.O. 17/1485; Lansdowne to Satow, tel. 221 of 8 July 1901, F.O. 17/1483. The background of negotiation is given in memoranda by Bertie of 30 May, 3 June 1901; Lord Rothschild's memorandum on a conversation with Lansdowne, 6 June 1901; memorandum by Lansdowne of 10 June 1901 (encl. tels. to and from Lascelles); memorandum by Bertie of 10 June 1901, F.O. 17/1505.

[2] Satow to Lansdowne, tel. 177 of 23 May 1901, minuted F.O. 17/1484.

[3] Satow to Lansdowne, tel. 202 of 15 June 1901, F.O. 17/1484.

[4] Memorandum by Lansdowne of 19 June 1901, S.P. Cabinet General 1901, unclassified.

He was in favour of the fourth solution. The next day the Cabinet chose the third alternative and offered to transfer about £500,000 worth of British bonds to Japan. This was refused by Japan, who stated that the loss she was suffering entitled her to compensation, and that the powers would support this contention. Komura in Peking told Satow that the Japanese 'appreciated the generous offer although a natural pride prevented them from accepting it'.[1] Japan's refusal led to some confusion in London and some apprehension was felt that she would drift into support of Russia. This led, on the one hand, to a definite move towards a political understanding with Japan; on the other, an effort was made to see the Japanese point of view over the bonds.

Japan maintained that while 450 million taels had been asked of the Chinese, the actual total claim only came to 416 million taels, leaving a surplus of 34 millions, part of which could be used to meet the Japanese claim. Although Lansdowne was doubtful whether there would be a surplus he instructed Satow to propose that Japan should have first claim on any surplus available.[2]

This intention was blocked by Russia. Since the beginning of June there had been a relaxation of the Russian stand over the guaranteed loan and on the 10 per cent tariff; partly through a general withdrawal in Russian policy after the failure of the Manchurian negotiations, partly because of her financial difficulties. On 13 June Giers was instructed to agree to any scheme for the indemnities whether by loan, bonds, or obligations, provided the claims were covered.[3] On 3 July Giers stated that Russia would accept the bonds at par but that if any power put in an extra claim Russia would do likewise. Komura then agreed privately with Satow only to advance Japan's claim if any surplus proved to be available.[4]

The acceptance of the British bonds scheme by the powers

[1] Lansdowne to Satow, tel. 205, secret, of 28 June 1901, F.O. 17/1483; Satow to Lansdowne, tel. 218, secret, of 29 June 1901, F.O. 17/1484. The Cabinet's offer was illegal. The Chancellor of the Exchequer pointed out that once the bonds were handed over they became British property. Sir E. Hamilton to Bertie, 22 June 1901, F.O. 17/1506.

[2] Lansdowne to Satow, tels. 203, 213 of 27 June, 2 July 1901, F.O. 17/1483.

[3] Lansdowne to Satow, tel. 191 of 13 June 1901, F.O. 17/1482.

[4] Satow to Lansdowne, tel. 225 of 4 July 1901, F.O. 17/1485.

allowed negotiations to proceed more rapidly. China was to meet the indemnity claims by payment in 4 per cent bonds, which were to be accepted at face value. Various plans of amortization were discussed, and it was finally decided that the principal was to be divided into five series. Amortization of these was to be graded over the years so that, after commencing in 1902, the whole debt would be extinguished in 1940.[1]

On 18 July Satow drew up a draft protocol. This was circulated for amendment by the powers and a final protocol was drafted on 2 August.[2] British policy during these closing stages of the negotiations for a peace settlement with the Chinese is illustrated by two objections which Lansdowne made to the amendments which had been returned.

The first concerned China's ability to pay off the bonds before the appointed time. Japan had added a clause to Satow's first draft to the effect that the bonds were to be redeemed by China only by action of the sinking fund. The effect of this proposal was that no power could use its share of the bonds to secure territorial acquisitions from China. It will be seen that Japan made this move after misunderstanding a British inquiry about Manchuria during the course of the Anglo-Japanese alliance negotiations. When she realized the true direction of the British inquiry, Japan dropped this proposal.[3] However, it was acceptable to Lansdowne, who saw its value in preventing Russia from coming to any separate arrangements with China. Consequently when the final draft protocol was received in London, and it was seen that France, Russia, and Germany had voted for the excision of the clause precluding private arrange-

---

[1] The correspondence on the various amortization schemes is given in Satow to Lansdowne, tels. 179, 186 of 28 May, 4 June 1901, F.O. 17/1484; Satow to Lansdowne, tel. 220 of 1 July 1901, F.O. 17/1405; Lansdowne to Satow, tels. 210, 216 of 2 and 5 July 1901, F.O. 17/1483. It should be noted that, with the interest involved, China's total obligation by 1940 would have amounted to over 980 million Haikuan taels (£147·7 million). However, a remission of the unpaid portions of the indemnity was made at the Treaty of Versailles by Germany and Austria-Hungary. Thereafter, during the 1920s, most of the other powers remitted the outstanding amounts of their indemnities, while stipulating that the money was to be used for educational and other beneficial purposes. See Hou, *Foreign Capital in China's Economic Development*, 44; Wang Chin-chun, 'The Work of the British Indemnity Advisory Commission', *CSPSR*, 11 (1927), 361–72.

[2] Satow to Lansdowne, tel. 246 of 18 July 1901; Satow to Lansdowne, tel. 261 of 2 Aug. 1901 and enclosures, F.O. 17/1485.

[3] See below, pp. 298–303.

ments between China and the powers for the payment of the debt, Lansdowne instructed Satow to vote for its retention.[1]

On 6 August Giers called on Satow and stated that Russia could not limit China's liberty to pay off the debt earlier if she could. On hearing this, Lansdowne, who had always assumed that Russia was working for a surreptitious arrangement, began to wonder whether the two powers had laboured under a misunderstanding throughout the peace settlement, and he allowed the clause to be dropped.[2] It has been noticed that Lansdowne had pursued a policy of procrastination over the implementation of the Joint Note, primarily to keep the powers in China to oppose Russian territorial acquisitions. It will be seen in the next section, when this Anglo-Russian struggle is discussed, that Lansdowne adopted a franker approach to Russia from the autumn of 1901.

Lansdowne's second objection was concerned with the measures put forward for a revision of the commercial position. In the draft protocol for a peace settlement with China, provision was made for an international committee for the conversion of duties to an effective 5 per cent tariff. This was resented by Lansdowne, who felt that it would be contrary to British interests to have commercial policy in the hands of the less concerned powers. Lansdowne preferred a small group, which should be invited by Great Britain to join in the negotiations for commercial revision. Consequently, when he saw that provision had been made for an international committee to discuss the raising of foreign import duties to an effective 5 per cent, he instructed Satow to oppose the measure and to place on record, if outvoted, the view that Great Britain neither approved nor accepted the provision and that she could not undertake to submit to such a commission the conversion of any duties imposed under the treaty arrangements between China and Great Britain.[3]

Satow was considerably embarrassed by this instruction, for no objection had been raised when he reported plans for the formation of the commission.[4] Many of the representatives

[1] Annotations on Satow's draft, Satow to Lansdowne, tel. 261 of 2 Aug. 1901 and enclosures, F.O. 17/1485.
[2] Satow to Lansdowne, tel. 269 of 6 Aug. 1901, F.O. 17/1485; Lansdowne to Satow, tel. 258 of 7 Aug. 1901, F.O. 17/1483.
[3] Lansdowne to Satow, tel. 263 of 9 Aug. 1901, F.O. 17/1483.
[4] Satow to Lansdowne, tels. 197 of 12 June, 258 of 31 July 1901, F.O. 17/1485.

showed impatience at the delay and the strain of nine months of arduous negotiation was noticeable. Satow pressed that the protocol should be accepted without alteration. On 27 August he reported that the Chinese plenipotentiaries were ready to sign. Lansdowne stood firm. Moreover, to the apprehension of the representatives he raised the question of punishments again and ordered Satow not to sign until the edicts on provincial punishments had been received.[1] The edicts were rushed through by the Chinese, and the final protocol was signed on 7 September. But in it all reference to the international commission for the conversion of duties was dropped.[2]

After six months of arduous negotiation over the Indemnity, Great Britain had resisted successfully both the 10 per cent tariff and the guaranteed loan. Acceptance of either of these would have been sufficient to impair her control over the China trade. Further, Great Britain kept the negotiations for a revision of the tariff in her own hands. By 17 September Sir James Mackay had been named as Commissioner to carry out the revision of the commercial treaties.[3] By December he was in Shanghai. He was instructed to keep on good terms with the other representatives 'but not to tack them officially on to his skirts'. Lansdowne added: 'We must keep a free hand for ourselves, and the others must keep step with us.'[4] The Mackay treaty was then successfully concluded on 5 September 1902.[5] It must be admitted that British diplomacy in the peace settlement with China was notably successful, particularly when it is remembered that these negotiations were carried out during a period of political tension over the Northern railway and Manchuria.

[1] Lansdowne to Satow, tel. 277 of 28 Aug. 1901, F.O. 17/1483.
[2] The Final Protocol is given in Steiger, *China and the Occident*, 306–15.
[3] Lansdowne to Satow, tel. 295, confidential, of 17 Sept. 1901, F.O. 17/1483.
[4] Lansdowne to Satow, 20 Jan. 1902, Lansdowne Papers.
[5] For an account of the negotiations, see S. F. Wright, *China's Struggle for Tariff Autonomy, 1843–1938* (Shanghai, 1938), 353–91.

XI

MANCHURIA

ON the outbreak of the Boxer rising Russia's first concern was for her position in Manchuria. In the three years following the Sino-Russian agreements of 1896 over 1½ billion roubles had been committed to the general development of the area and to the construction of the Chinese Eastern Railway, which was regarded as an integral part of the Siberian railway project. Consequently Witte's aim was to keep the area neutral through an understanding with China. The best hope of achieving this appeared to be by directly negotiating with Li Hung-chang, who had informed Witte that he had been summoned from his post in the south to advise the Court at Peking. To avoid delay Prince Ukhtomsky was sent as Witte's personal representative to confer with the Chinese statesman before he left Canton. However, Russian apprehensions over the safety of her possessions were too strong for her to wait on the outcome of these negotiations and troops were ordered to Manchuria to protect the Chinese Eastern Railway. This show of military force stirred up an already restive populace and Boxer activity spread rapidly through the three eastern provinces.

At first the unrest was confined to the province of Feng t'ien, from where it spread to the other two provinces, Heilungkiang and Kirin. On 17 July the whole Amur district was proclaimed to be in a state of war. By 21 July orders were given for the mobilization of all Russian forces in Siberia, Semirechia, and Turkestan. Until Aigun was taken on 4 August the Russian forces were on the defensive, and tended to be grouped in the north; after that date an offensive was begun, of which the general plan was the convergence of seven columns of troops on Harbin. These operations continued throughout September; on 2 October General Subotich entered Mukden. By the middle of October approximately 3,900 officers and 173,000 men had been accumulated in Chihli, Manchuria, and Siberia; of these, since the outbreak, 54,410 men and 11,407 horses had been transported to the east by the Siberian railway, and approximately 20,000 men to Vladivostok and Port Arthur by sea.[1]

The long-drawn-out nature of these operations in Manchuria provides a key to Russia's attitude to the general rising in north China. Until the three eastern provinces had been subdued, and Ukhtomsky had time to make separate arrangements with Li, Russia's aim was to delay events in north China.

By the time Ukhtomsky reached Shanghai on 29 September he was too late to carry out his original intention of arranging a separate peace for Manchuria. Consequently his mission was changed and he was directed to see what privileges he could obtain in lieu of direct monetary compensation for the damage done in Manchuria. However, Ukhtomsky missed Li, who had by then moved up to Tientsin, and preliminary negotiations were opened with Li Ching-fang, Li's nephew and adopted son, who had remained in Shanghai for the purpose. Li Ching-fang proposed that China should pay Russia a substantial indemnity in a form which would not enhance the cupidity of the other powers. The suggestion was that Russia should occupy the Chinese Eastern Railway *manu militari* and declare in principle her magnanimous refusal to appropriate the whole region. In return, China would agree to the unconditional exploitation of Mongolia and Kashgar '. . . masking concessions to the Russian Government itself under the patent of sundry sham private companies'.[2]

It was obvious to Witte that Li Hung-chang's aim was to draw Russia away from Manchuria, and as Li Ching-fang had accompanied his suggestion with a pressing demand for a second instalment of the bribe promised to his uncle during the

[1] Captain E. R. H. Chapman (Intelligence, War Office), *The Russian Operations in Manchuria, June–October 1900* (1901), 16 f., forwarded to Foreign Office, 11 Mar. 1901, F.O. 17/1501. During the first or 'defensive' phase both the Chinese and the Russians acted under considerable excitement and mutual fear. The outstanding incident occurred on 17 July when the Russians were reported to have driven several thousands of Chinese into the river at Blagoveshchensk and then massacred them by gun-fire. However, an independent British observer gives the version that the rafts crowded with refugees were fired on by the Chinese not the Russians. Cf. Report of Captain Dorrien, R.N., of 26 Dec. 1900, S.P. Chronological Series, Imperial and Foreign, II.

[2] Ukhtomsky to Witte, tel. of 1 Oct. 1900, quoted in Romanov, *Russia in Manchuria*, 188.

Sino-Russian negotiations of 1896, the negotiations in Shanghai were allowed to drop. When they were resumed a month later by Li Hung-chang, Giers, and Pokotiloff in Peking, the basis of discussion had altered.

By late October Russia was in control of the whole of Manchuria. The temptation to prolong the occupation was practically irresistible. Among the Russian ministers there was no clear idea of the conditions of withdrawal which should be demanded. Witte was inclined to the view that the evacuation of the Russian forces should be linked with the total construction of the Siberian railroad; Lamsdorff and Kuropatkin made it contingent upon the establishment of a tranquil state of affairs and the satisfaction of Russia's economic demands.[1]

The Tseng–Alexieff Agreement

As direct negotiation with the Chinese Government after the flight of the Court was impossible, it was decided to negotiate limited regional agreements with the Tartar generals of the three eastern provinces, and to incorporate these at a later date into a general treaty with the Chinese Government. Admiral Alexieff was enthusiastic when approached by Kuropatkin and he went ahead to arrange an agreement on this basis with Tsent Ch'i, Tartar general of Fengt'ien. The treaty was negotiated under pressure by the Russians. Tseng Ch'i, who was forced to act through a dismissed *taotai* named Chou Mien, only signed with reservations on 10 November. The treaty gave Russia full military control of the province; the Chinese troops were disbanded and an unarmed police guard was substituted to maintain civil order.[2]

Following this, a conference was held in St. Petersburg on 13 November, on Witte's initiative, between the Ministers of Foreign Affairs, Finance, and War to decide on the 'fundamentals of Russian Governmental control in Manchuria'. Kuropatkin presented a plan embodied in fifteen articles which, after referring to the preservation of the existing civil government in Manchuria as 'a component part of the Chinese empire' and to the temporary nature of the Russian occupation,

[1] Romanov, *Russia in Manchuria*, 187, 197–8, 213.
[2] Tan, *The Boxer Catastrophe*, 165–6. The full text of nine articles is given in Romanov, *Russia in Manchuria*, 427–8.

envisaged a scheme whereby Russian troops were to be concentrated along the railway line, unarmed Chinese police were to control the areas beyond the line, while the Chinese administration was to function under Russian military supervision. To this obviously military approach, Witte added four articles which confirmed the independence, of the military, of the Chinese Eastern Railway. By these articles the railway administration was placed under the ultimate supervision of the Ministry of Finance. It was given the right to deal directly with the local military and civil Chinese authorities, or even diplomatically with Peking, and it was allowed an independent railway guard subject to the army only in the event of war. The primacy of the railroad, and consequently of Witte, was emphasized by the fourth article which imposed on the Russian military authorities the duty of rendering all possible assistance to the railway administration. Although Lamsdorff expressed some doubt on the categorical nature of the demands and believed that negotiations should only be carried out with a responsible Chinese Government, under Witte's forceful advocacy the three departments agreed on this programme.[1]

Consequently, when Li Hung-chang took up discussions again with Ukhtomsky in Peking he worked at a great disadvantage. While in September Ukhtomsky had been anxious to secure a settlement, by November Li was making feverish efforts to keep control of the negotiations. To this end he endeavoured to divert Russian attention to Mongolia and Kashgar, to secure control of the local negotiations started in Manchuria, and to arouse Russian diplomacy to a formal move in the Manchurian question. He was unsuccessful. The programme of separate regional agreements with the Manchurian Tartar generals was approved by the Tsar on 27 December. On 22 December Giers was told to arrange full powers for Yang Ju, the Chinese minister in St. Petersburg, so that discussion could be carried on away from Peking, where secrecy might prove impossible. On 3 January 1901 the Court confirmed Yang Ju as plenipotentiary to negotiate a Manchurian agreement.[2]

[1] Kuropatkin's fifteen articles with Witte's additions are paraphrased in Romanov, *Russia in Manchuria*, 191–3. Tan's account (*The Boxer Catastrophe*, 171), based on Gapanovich's summary of Romanov, given in *CSPSR*, 17 (1933), 459–60, gives the dates according to the Julian calendar.

[2] Tan, *The Boxer Catastrophe*, 170–1; Romanov, *Russia in Manchuria*, 200.

At this point the negotiations came to the notice of the powers through the publication of the Tseng–Alexieff agreement in *The Times* of 3 January 1901. The report was telegraphed from Peking on 31 December 1900 by G. E. Morrison, *The Times* correspondent. Morrison's skill in obtaining information excited in Satow a feeling of 'admiration and surprise' and he suspected that the leakage had come through Squiers, the Secretary of the United States Legation, who was in the habit of shopping for curios with Pethick, a well-known confidant of Li Hung-chang, who received political information from Squiers 'in return for expert advice as to the merits of cloisonne, porcelain and lacquer'.[1] It is highly probable that the information was deliberately released by Li. For two months he had carried out secret discussions with Giers, Pokotiloff, and Ukhtomsky in Peking without arousing the suspicions of the assembled diplomats. However, Russia's insistence on moving the negotiations to St. Petersburg had taken control out of Li's hands, and the possibility arose of a permanent treaty for Manchuria, on the pattern of the Tseng–Alexieff agreement, being forced on the fugitive Court. Li's only resource was to force Russia to a formal move, and in China's weak state the only way to do this was to bring the matter to the notice of the other powers. However, the revelation had to be finely balanced because of the Joint Note then under discussion in Peking. A premature disclosure could have led to an abandonment of international concert and a general territorial scramble. This possibility became more remote after the Joint Note had been presented to and accepted by the Court on 27 December. In the few days which intervened between this date and the date when Yang Ju informed St. Petersburg that he held plenipotentiary powers (3 January), the Tseng–Alexieff agreement came into Morrison's hands. More significantly, it came to him in a form which compounded the development in Russia's ideas in the many interdepartmental conferences subsequent to the agreement, the tenor of which had been indicated to Li by the Russian representatives in Peking. Alexieff's agreement with Tseng Ch'i was essentially a military document outlining the terms under which Tseng Ch'i could resume office under Russian occupation. As it stood, little objection could be raised by the

[1] Satow to Bertie, private letter in No. 21 of 17 Jan. 1901, F.O. 17/1469.

powers. From the military point of view, as Ardagh pointed out later when the terms became known, it was moderate and reasonable.[1] A more rigid control was being exercised then by the allies themselves in north China. Therefore it was perhaps not by mistake that the copy that reached *The Times* carried a significant change in one of the articles, emphasizing the establishment of Russian control in a civil rather than a military sense. Whereas the actual text (Article 7) read 'The chiang-chun (military governor) shall be provided with a Russian commissar for convenience of communication with the central authority of Kwantung province . . .', *The Times* rendering gave 'A Russian political Resident with general powers of Control shall be stationed at Mukden . . .'. Consequently, as a civil and therefore permanent, as distinct from a military and thus temporary, agreement, it concerned the other powers.

The British Attitude toward Manchuria and the Northern Railway

Throughout the Boxer rising Lord Salisbury had adopted a policy of restraint over Russian activity in China. Although he was aware of the aggressive attitude of the Russian military forces in north China, he refused to take official notice of their claims except in those instances where British rights were infringed, when he indicated to Russia that these rights would revert to Great Britain when the situation returned to normal. Similarly, he did not approve the policy of anticipatory seizures which had been suggested by MacDonald in September 1900. His aim, he told MacDonald, was to keep to the spirit of the Anglo-Russian agreement of 1899.[2] Consequently, he did not intervene in Manchurian affairs. This was the view adopted by all the powers and, throughout the rising, Manchuria was regarded as a separate area which was Russia's sole concern. In fact, in July 1900 Major-General Ardagh had even welcomed the spread of the rising to Manchuria, for the possible relief which it brought to Great Britain's political position elsewhere.[3] Then in the period after the relief of the legations it

[1] D.M.I. Memorandum respecting the strategical effects of the Russo-Chinese Agreement, encl., Intelligence Division to Foreign Office, 23 Mar. 1901, F.O. 17/1502.

[2] Salisbury to MacDonald, tel. 87 of 7 Sept. 1900, F.O. 17/1417.

[3] Memorandum 60 of 19 July 1900, Ardagh's Memoranda, P.R.O. 30/40/14, Pt. 2, pp. 222–3.

was hoped that Russia's preoccupation with Manchuria would lead to an improved situation in north China. When Lansdowne moved to the Foreign Office in November 1900 he maintained this attitude. Thus when the report of a separate Sino-Russian agreement over Manchuria was published, it was received without excitement in London. Lansdowne instructed Scott, the British Ambassador at St. Petersburg, to find out what he could, but not to make an official inquiry.[1]

At the time of Morrison's disclosure two issues were before the Government relating to Anglo-Russian relations. The first was concerned with the British right of anchorage at the Elliot-Blonde Islands, the second with the Northern railway. Lansdowne's handling of each of these issues illustrates the British attitude toward the Manchurian question before Japan turned Manchuria into a diplomatic issue in the latter part of February.

At the end of November 1900 H.M.S. *Plover*, in expedition against pirates, anchored at Wumantao and Thornton Haven off the Bourchier group which formed part of the Elliot Islands, stretching thirty-five miles off the coast of the Liaotung peninsula. On 16 December Admiral Alexieff protested to Admiral Seymour that the islands were in Russian territorial waters. Alexieff based this claim on a supplementary protocol to the Port Arthur Agreement which leased the islands to Russia.[2] The Foreign Office rejected this contention on the grounds that (1) islands thirty-five miles off the coast did not fall into territorial waters, (2) even if the islands were leased to Russia they remained Chinese territory and, by Article 52 of the Treaty of Tientsin, British men-of-war had the right of visit, and (3) as the Russian arrangement with China was secret, Great Britain could have no cognizance of it. Seymour was instructed to ignore the protest and to continue using the anchorage.[3]

The Northern railway was a more serious issue in Anglo-Russian relations. It has been seen that during the military activity connected with the relief of the legations the Russian

---

[1] Lansdowne to Scott, tel. of 3 Jan. 1901, F.O. 65/1624.
[2] Correspondence given in Admiralty to Foreign Office, 21 Feb. 1901, F.O. 17/1501. Full file given S 323/1901, Adm. 1/1711.
[3] Admiralty to Foreign Office, 8 Jan. 1901, F.O. 17/1499; Foreign Office to Admiralty, 12 Feb. 1901, F.O. 17/1500. The text of the Sino-Russian protocol was revealed to Satow by Li; Satow to Lansdowne, tel. 34 of 7 Feb. 1901, F.O. 17/1484.

military forces had begun to appropriate this British-owned line, and that further seizures were made during August and September 1900. Then, after his arrival, Waldersee confirmed Russian possession of the entire stretch of the line from Shan-haikuan, through Taku and Tientsin, to Yangts'un while the remaining short stretch, from Yangts'un to Peking, was placed under German direction. Salisbury had displayed a restrained attitude over the earlier Russian seizures and had merely notified St. Petersburg of British rights to the line. However, in view of Waldersee's action, in October he took a more definite stand and protests were made at Berlin and St. Petersburg.[1]

Lascelles, the British Ambassador at Berlin, then spoke to Baron Richthofen, the German Under-Secretary of State for Foreign Affairs, and followed this up with a note to Count Bülow, the Foreign Minister. Although no official reply was given by Germany, Bülow did suggest to the Kaiser that Waldersee should show more sympathy for the British point of view. Subsequently an inquiry was made through the German Embassy in London as to what arrangement would be satis-factory to Great Britain. Salisbury replied that the construction and management of the whole line should be handed over to Kinder, the British manager of the railway, subject to such military control by Waldersee as would be necessary to ensure the line being available to all the allied forces.[2] This reasonable demand could not easily be opposed and on 30 October the Kaiser explained to Lascelles that Waldersee's action had been dictated by purely military considerations, the Russians having available a large number of military engineers, and that Waldersee would return to Great Britain such portions of the line as were evacuated by Russia.[3]

German reluctance to take positive action to correct Walder-see's appropriations was considered unsatisfactory, particularly as Russia and Germany appeared to be consolidating their hold on the line. On 31 October Satow reported that the chief engineer of the Peking–Hankow line had applied directly to the Russian and German representatives for permission to trans-

[1] Salisbury to Lascelles, tel. 188 of 7 Oct. 1900, F.O. 64/1496.
[2] Salisbury to Lascelles, tels. 188, 222 of 7, 25 Oct. 1900, F.O. 64/1496; *Große Politik*, xvi. 239–40; memorandum by Bertie of 18 Oct. 1900 (recording Eckard-stein's visit), F.O. 17/1448.
[3] Lascelles to Salisbury, tel. 37 of Oct. 1900, F.O. 64/1496.

port railway material over the Northern line without bothering to approach the British authorities. Lascelles was told to adopt a stiffer tone in Berlin. The British Ambassador then told Richthofen that if Waldersee continued to favour Russia an impression would be created in England which might imperil good relations. This was more effective. On 6 November Richthofen replied that Waldersee had published a further army order stating that all arrangements concerning the line were for military considerations without prejudice to existing rights.[1]

Salisbury's stronger stand also proved effective in St. Petersburg. At first Russia tried to deflect the British protests by maintaining that the British military authorities in China had raised no objection when Russia began restoring the Tientsin–Yangts'un section of the line. Salisbury rejected this oblique reply and instructed Hardinge, the British chargé d'affaires, to lodge a formal and earnest protest and to press that the whole line should be handed over to Kinder and his staff.[2]

These representations coincided with the Tseng–Alexieff negotiations, by which Russia hoped to consolidate her hold on Manchuria. To further this aim, and in the hope of meeting British objections, Russia suggested an arrangement with Great Britain over the extra-mural, or Manchurian, section of the Northern railway, which stretched from Shanhaikuan to Newchwang.

On 8 November Lamsdorff addressed a note to Hardinge stating that with the retirement of Russian troops from Pechili, the line from Yangts'un to Shanhaikuan would be handed to Waldersee on repayment of the money expended on the repair and working of the Peking–Shanhaikuan line, and also that the Shanhaikuan–Newchwang section could not be restored until the outlay for the repair and working of the whole line from Peking to Newchwang had been repaid in full.[3] Lamsdorff's aim was to distinguish between the extra-mural and the intra-mural sections of the line, to restore the intra-mural line by a

---

[1] Satow to Salisbury, tel. 188 of 31 Oct. 1900, F.O. 17/1418; Salisbury to Lascelles, tel. 244 of 2 Nov. 1900, F.O. 64/1496; Lascelles to Salisbury, tels. 39, 40 of 3, 6 Nov. 1900, F.O. 64/1496.

[2] Hardinge to Salisbury, tel. 123 of 29 Oct. 1900, F.O. 65/1604; Salisbury to Hardinge, tel. 222 of 31 Oct. 1900, F.O. 65/1605.

[3] Hardinge to Lansdowne, No. 386 of 14 Nov. 1900, F.O. 65/1602.

process of indirect transfer, thereby avoiding the appearance of a direct surrender and gratifying Waldersee's sense of prestige, and to make the extra-mural line a matter for further negotiation on conditions likely to deter the British.

The Russian intention was not immediately perceived in London. On 21 November Bertie drew up a memorandum to focus attention on the railway issue. 'The question', he stated, '. . . has reached a point when it is necessary to consider how much, if any, further we should go, whether for parliamentary or foreign policy reasons, in remonstrances and protests to the Russian Government.'[1] Lansdowne followed this with a memorandum the next day which declared that Great Britain could not afford to leave unchallenged Count Lamsdorff's attempt to apply to the western, or intra-mural, section of the line an international arrangement into which Great Britain had only entered with regard to the eastern, or extra-mural, line.[2] Lansdowne took the view that Russia, in order to interfere in north China, was attempting to reverse the advantage held by Great Britain through the Anglo-Russian Agreement of 1899. Consequently instructions were sent to Hardinge reaffirming the British stand.[3]

Russia then tried to overcome the opposition of the British Government by negotiating directly with the Hongkong and Shanghai Bank which had advanced the 1898 loan on which the British right to the line was based. On 10 December Pokotiloff, manager of the Russo-Chinese Bank in Peking, approached Hillier, who acted for the Hongkong and Shanghai Bank in Peking, and made him a firm offer to redeem the railway loan with regard to the extra-mural section at 20 per cent premium (£120) less the expenses of occupation and repair. The arrangement was to be negotiated privately by the two banks, preferably at Peking with the approval of the two governments. Hillier emphasized that he could not speak for the Bank and promised to lay the proposal before the directors. At the same time he notified the Foreign Office through Satow.[4]

---

[1] Memorandum by Bertie of 21 Nov. 1900, F.O. 17/1450.
[2] Memorandum by Lansdowne of 22 Nov. 1900, S.P. Cabinet, confidential, unclassified.
[3] Lansdowne to Hardinge, No. 284 of 23 Nov. 1900, F.O. 65/1597.
[4] Hillier's Report to Sir Ewan Cameron of 15 Dec. 1900, encl. Keswick to Bertie, private, of 6 Feb. 1901, F.O. 17/1500. The £100 bonds were issued at 97 at

A similar approach was made by the Russians through Panmure, Gordon, Hill & Company, a firm of stockbrokers in London. One of the partners of the firm was a Belgian, M. W. Koch, brother-in-law of M. Rothstein, a financial adviser to Witte, the Russian Minister of Finance. On 12 December Rothstein communicated with the firm, which approached the British and Chinese Corporation, and tentative negotiations were then started. The Corporation kept the Foreign Office informed.

By the beginning of January the Government began to have a clearer idea of Russia's intentions. On 3 January the separate Sino-Russian Manchurian treaty was published in *The Times*. At the same time Satow reported from Peking on a Russo-German convention for the transfer of the Shanhaikuan–Yangts'un line to Waldersee's army headquarters. This was the policy of indirect transfer of the intra-mural section indicated by Lamsdorff in his note of 8 November. It was also noticed that the convention reserved to Russia 'that part of the line and working material of the station of Shanhaikuan, which is necessary to maintain the line Shanhaikuan–Newchwang in working order'.[1]

Lansdowne's immediate impression was that the terms of the transfer left Britain as 'caretaker' and were unsatisfactory, but as it was important not to leave the intra-mural section in Russian hands and as Waldersee was not prepared to adopt a bolder policy, there was

. . . nothing for it but to take all we can get, and to treat what is given us merely as a payment on account, surrendering nothing, placing our whole claim on record, and making it perfectly clear that the convention is regarded by us as provisional and made for purely military purposes, without prejudice to political and territorial rights or financial obligations. . . .[2]

He told Satow to send the full text and to advise General Gaselee to delay the signing of the convention. At the same time

5 per cent for 45 years; redeemable at 100 by 40 annual drawings, commencing 1905. Extra bonds were to be redeemed at 120.

[1] Satow to Lansdowne, tels. 2, 10 of 2, 6 Jan. 1901, F.O. 17/1484; Satow to Lansdowne, No. 12 of 8 Jan. 1901; Satow to Lansdowne, No. 30 of 24 Jan. 1901 (giving final German text), F.O. 17/1469.

[2] Memorandum by Lansdowne of 3 Jan. 1901, F.O. 17/1499.

he called in the British and Chinese Corporation and the India Office for consultation. The discussion took place on 8 January.[1]

At the meeting Lord George Hamilton, Secretary of State for India, declared himself opposed to any division of the line, except as a temporary measure, or to any surrender of the rolling stock. He then submitted a draft telegram to be sent to Gaselee to say that if it were clearly understood that the division of the line was temporary, Gaselee could concur in the convention. This draft was amended by Lansdowne, Sir E. Stedman (War Office), and Bertie in conference on 10 January to a more explicit reservation of all existing British political and financial rights and the restoration of the whole line (Peking–Newchwang) on conclusion of military operations.[2]

The British were similarly determined about the Russian attempts to buy the line. On 8 January the Foreign Office wrote to the British and Chinese Corporation that

... if the Corporation resolve to negotiate such an arrangement, the course is one which they must take on their own responsibility, and is not a matter on which Her Majesty's Government can properly offer advice. At the same time, I am to observe that when Her Majesty's Government allowed it to be stated in the loan prospectus that the loan had been arranged with their knowledge . . . (they) did so in the belief that under British management the line could not fail to prove of great advantage to the trade of this country, a condition which is not likely to be secured if the line should pass into foreign hands. . . .[3]

In reply, the Corporation agreed to follow the wishes of the Government.[4]

However, this determination could not be maintained. On 12 January General Gaselee reported that Waldersee was only prepared to take notice of the British stand in respect of the Peking–Shanhaikuan line, and that with regard to the extension beyond the borders of Chihli Great Britain would have to negotiate directly with Russia. Gaselee thought that any

---

[1] Foreign Office to India Office, 8 Jan. 1901, F.O. 17/1499.

[2] India Office to Foreign Office, confidential, of 9 Jan. 1901, and amendments, F.O. 17/1499.

[3] Foreign Office to B. & C. Corporation, 8 Jan. 1901, F.O. 17/1499. The more explicit statement that H.M. Government would 'regret any such action' was struck from the draft.

[4] B. & C. Corporation to Bertie, 11 Jan. 1901, F.O. 17/1499.

further attempt to delay the signing of the convention would result in Russia retaining the whole line.[1] On 15 January Gaselee was instructed to withdraw his objections to the convention.[2]

The Russo-German Convention over the Northern railway was signed on 18 January. On the 25th the Peking–Shanhaikuan section was handed over to Army Headquarters. Russia retained such portions of the station at Shanhaikuan as were necessary to work the Shanhaikuan–Newchwang railway; she also kept the workshops and the railway material accumulated at Shanhaikuan. The rolling stock of the whole line (Peking–Newchwang) was divided, three-fifths going to Waldersee's Headquarters, two-fifths to Russia. Much had already been plundered. Gaselee had to ask for an immediate credit of £90,000 to restore the intra-mural line to working order; as the British and Chinese Corporation had no funds, application was made to the Treasury for an advance, to be refunded from the Chinese indemnity.[3] The line was transferred to the British by the Germans on 22 February.

Russia's success in dividing so neatly the extra-mural and the intra-mural sections of the line had an immediate effect in London. On 17 January the British and Chinese Corporation wrote a letter to Panmure, Gordon, Hill & Company which led the Company to believe that the Corporation would lay the matter of the sale of the Shanhaikuan–Newchwang line to Russia before the Foreign Office if satisfactory conditions were proposed. Consequently on 30 January the Company replied that if the bondholders would give up their rights on the extra-mural section, Russia would agree (paraphrased):

(1) by way of compensation, to make good any deficiency towards the service of the loan which the receipts of the line within the wall might show;

(2) not to 'oppose or hamper' any English negotiations with China by which she might seek to strengthen her control of the intra-mural line;

[1] Gaselee to India Office, tel. 124 of 12 Jan. 1901, F.O. 17/1499.
[2] Secretary of State to G.-O.-C. China Expedition, tel. 65 of 15 Jan. 1901, F.O. 17/1499.
[3] B. & C. Corporation to Foreign Office, 8 Feb. 1901; Foreign Office to Treasury, 11 Feb. 1901, F.O. 17/1500; the Treasury replied that the only justification for the expenditure of the money was that of military necessity and it was advanced on condition that it would be repaid from Army Funds. Treasury to Foreign Office, 20 Feb. 1901, F.O. 17/1501.

(3) not to put any differential tariffs on English merchandize on the Manchurian railways; and

(4) to withdraw her claim for a direct line to Peking.

It was also indicated that further understandings were possible, such as the maintenance of a railway service with Newchwang, and the protection of British rights with regard to the coal-mines at Nanpiao. Panmure, Gordon, Hill & Company, who maintained the attitude that they were disinterested brokers in the bargain, nevertheless hinted darkly that should an amicable arrangement prove impossible Russia would be forced to take measures extremely detrimental to British interests.[1]

These negotiations and the full report of Pokotiloff's overture to Hillier in December were known to the Foreign Office by 6 February. By then further evidence of Russia's determination to obtain the extra-mural line, possibly with Chinese backing, had been received. On 1 February the 5 per cent coupon for the half-yearly service of the loan of 1898, by which the British and Chinese Corporation held their rights on the Northern railway, had become due. Besides being unconditionally guaranteed by the Chinese Government the loan was secured as a first charge on the earnings of the railway. In the event of default, the line and property of the Peking–Shanhaikuan section was to be handed over to the British and Chinese Corporation to manage until the principal and interest of the loan had been redeemed in full. The allied occupation of the line left no revenue to pay the interest due in February, which amounted to £57,643. 15s. 0d. (£57,500 plus ¼ per cent distribution charges). By Clause 4 of the Loan Agreement, China was responsible. On 25 January Li Hung-chang told Satow that China could not pay; he admitted with 'brutal frankness'[2] that his aim was to force the bondholders to foreclose and so interpose a British interest between Peking and the Russians. However, in view of Li's Russian leanings, an alternative explanation of his action was current; that at the end of January Li had agreed to an abso-lute transfer of the Newchwang extension to Russia and that, at Russia's suggestion, he sought to bring about the British seizure of the intra-mural section so that a subsequent Russian

---

[1] Panmure, Gordon, Hill & Company to B. & C. Corporation of 30 Jan. 1901, encl. F.O. 17/1500; memorandum by Lansdowne, 15 Feb. 1901, F.O. 17/1500.

[2] Satow to Lansdowne, 30 Jan. 1901, Lansdowne Papers.

seizure of the extra-mural line as a *quid pro quo* could not be opposed.[1]

The coincidence of these various factors led Lansdowne to re-examine the matter. On 12 February, with the British and Chinese Corporation negotiations before him, Bertie wrote a memorandum which posed the question:

> Should His Majesty's Government hold China and Russia to their written undertakings so recently given, or should the bond-holders be encouraged to make terms with the agents acting in the interest of the Russian Government, and so relieve His Majesty's Government of any further responsibility in the matter.[2]

Three days later (15 February) Lansdowne followed this with a memorandum. 'The time has come', he stated, 'when we must consider what line we shall take in regard to these railways. . . .' Lansdowne then referred to the conditions of the 'bargain' proposed by the Russians through Panmure, Gordon, Hill & Company in their letter of 30 January, and then concluded that if Great Britain were to declare that she regarded the Anglo-Russian agreement of 1899 as still in force, he believed that the *status quo* could be maintained for a time, but that the Russian offer was 'a tolerable solution if we were compelled by circumstances to recognize the right of Russia to remain in occupation of Manchuria'.[3] Both memoranda were distributed to the Cabinet on 18 February but no evidence has been traced of any Cabinet meeting. Within a few days the problem of the Northern railway was overshadowed by the Manchurian issue, and the question of the sale of the extra-mural line was resolved by the outcome of that struggle.

The Manchurian Crisis

In the latter part of February, the tendency toward accepting a separate Sino-Russian agreement, which has been noticed in the British Government's handling of the Northern railway issue, was arrested by the attitude adopted by Japan over

---

[1] Satow to Lansdowne, tel. 31 of 3 Feb. 1901, F.O. 17/1484; Satow to Lansdowne, No. 55 of 7 Feb. 1901, F.O. 17/1470; S.J., 25 Jan. 1901.

[2] Memorandum by Bertie on Question with Russia in regard to Northern Railways of China of 12 Feb. 1901, F.O. 17/1500.

[3] Memorandum by Lansdowne of 15 Feb. 1901, F.O. 17/1500.

Manchuria. At the onset of the Russian negotiations with China, Witte, the Russian Finance Minister, had realized the likely strength of Japanese objections. He feared that Japan would take Korea if Russia moved in Manchuria.[1] To counter this he tried to gain Japanese support for the neutralization of Korea under the joint guarantee of the powers. Japan rejected this. Instead, she revealed the project to Great Britain and suggested on 12 January that Great Britain should join with Germany in direct representations to Russia.[2] Japan's intention was clearly to test the effectiveness of the Anglo-German Agreement of October 1900, to which she had also subscribed.

Lansdowne, who had just received news of Waldersee's discouraging attitude over the Northern railway, was 'not much enamoured of the idea'.[3] In December Lascelles, the British Ambassador at Berlin, had observed that Great Britain could work with Germany to advantage in China, 'so long as we do not expect her to ram her head against the Manchurian Wall'.[4] Lansdowne's approach to the Manchurian question indicates that he shared this belief. In reporting the Japanese suggestion to the Prime Minister, he observed that no satisfactory reply could be expected from St. Petersburg, and that if Germany were approached and she would not support the move, then Great Britain's stand would become known to Russia. 'My general feeling', he concluded, 'is that for the present we must show as few signs as possible of being "fussy" about small matters in China—on the other hand we must not, for Parliamentary and other reasons, acquiesce too much.' He then suggested that Scott should mention to Lamsdorff that questions would be asked in the House, but that in doing so he was 'to avoid the appearance of demanding an explanation' of Russian proceedings in Manchuria.[5]

[1] Romanov, *Russia in Manchuria*, 207–8, 432 note 104.
[2] Lansdowne to MacDonald, Nos. 6, 8 of 12, 15 Jan. 1901, F.O. 46/538. The Japanese answer to St. Petersburg, on 21 Jan. 1901, reveals a bitterness not shown in the draft handed to Lansdowne. Direct reference is made to the 'arguments brought forward by the powers when they advised Japan to evacuate the Liaotung province'. The text of the reply, translated from the *Krasnyi Arkhiv*, is given in *CSPSR*, 18 (1934), 574–5.
[3] Lansdowne to Salisbury, memorandum of 15 Jan. 1901, F.O. 17/1499.
[4] Lansdowne to Bertie of 29 Dec. 1900, F.O. 17/1451.
[5] Lansdowne to Salisbury, memorandum of 15 Jan. 1901, F.O. 17/1499. The instruction was sent to Scott on 22 Jan.

Lamsdorff replied on 6 February denying the existence of any negotiations for a convention giving Russia new rights in southern Manchuria. The only ground for the rumour, he stressed, was that the Russian military authorities were arranging with the local Chinese authorities the terms of a *modus vivendi* for the duration of the simultaneous presence of Russia and China in south Manchuria, and that evacuation would take place as soon as arrangements had been negotiated, as in northern China, and a central government restored.[1]

Lamsdorff's position was untenable. The assurance concerned itself with the Tseng–Alexieff agreement, which by this time had been expanded by Russia to an extent which justified representations by the powers. To the clauses extending the power of the Chinese Eastern Railway, decided on in St. Petersburg after the signing of the Tseng–Alexieff agreement, Witte had added a further list of demands. If granted by China, these would have led to the 'consolidation of the economic and political power of the Chinese Eastern Railway on principles of monopoly and restriction of the Peking Government's "sovereign" rights in Manchuria, and, secondly, to a formal broadening of Russia's "sphere of interests" to take in all China beyond the Wall'.[2] Witte drew up these extensive demands in two projects: a separate political agreement between Russia and China and an agreement between China and the Chinese Eastern Railway. These were forwarded to Lamsdorff on 22 and 24 January. Although Lamsdorff modified these demands drastically before presenting them to Yang Ju on 16 February, the remaining conditions nevertheless invalidated the assurance given to Great Britain through Scott on 6 February.

By the beginning of February some indication of Russia's impending demands had come into Japanese hands. On 5 February Hayashi informed Lansdowne that the Russians had formulated and were insisting on the immediate ratification of a permanent treaty. Similar information was sent by Satow on the same day, his informant being the Japanese minister in Peking.[3] Through Baron Hayashi, the Japanese Ambassador

[1] Scott to Lansdowne, No. 41 of 6 Feb. 1901 (received 11 Feb.), given F.O. 17/1501; Scott to Lansdowne, No. 66 of 6 Mar. 1901, F.O. 65/1620.
[2] Romanov, *Russia in Manchuria*, 205–6.
[3] Satow to Lansdowne, tel. 33 of 5 Feb. 1901, F.O. 17/1484.

at London, Japan suggested that an immediate warning should be given to China against ratification of any separate treaty.[1]

Lansdowne was not opposed to this measure, but he would only consider taking it in concert with Germany. Lansdowne contemplated a warning to China not to conclude 'backstairs bargains' with individual powers. A memorandum in this sense was handed to Eckardstein on 7 February suggesting an admonition to China '. . . that the conclusion of any such Agreement would be a source of danger to the Chinese Government, and that no arrangement affecting territorial rights in the Chinese Empire ought to be concluded between the Chinese Government and any one of the Powers'.[2] At the same time, he gave instructions that no reply should be given to Hayashi until a reply had been received from Germany.[3]

Germany's consent was received on 12 February; Satow was instructed to make the communication the next day,[4] Lansdowne's handling of the warning to China reveals that he was only prepared to take a stronger stand over Manchuria if he could be assured of support on this from Germany, and further, that he was not confident that this support could be obtained. Thus in his memorandum on the Northern railway of 15 February, he was encouraged by Germany's approval of the warning to China against 'backstairs bargains', to wonder whether it would not be possible to go further and obtain the 'concurrence of the whole of the Powers to a Self-denying Ordinance'.[5] At the same time, it has been noted, he was contemplating the sale of the extra-mural section of the line if it proved necessary to recognize the right of Russia to remain in occupation of Manchuria. This hesitation was justified the next day when Eckardstein admitted that Germany's consent had been given 'not without serious misgivings'.[6] Also, when the text of the German warning to China was received it was seen that Germany's communication was qualitatively hedged to meet Russian approval and possibly in anticipation of her

[1] Memorandum by Bertie of 5 Feb. 1901, F.O. 46/547.
[2] B.D. ii. 35–6.
[3] Minute on memorandum by Bertie of 5 Feb. 1901, F.O. 46/547.
[4] Lansdowne to Satow, tel. 35 of 13 Feb. 1901, F.O. 17/1482. The warning was given to the Chinese Ambassador in London on the 15th.
[5] Memorandum by Lansdowne of 15 Feb. 1901, F.O. 17/1500.
[6] Lansdowne to Salisbury, memorandum of 16 Feb. 1901, F.O. 17/1500.

own future demands. China was exhorted not to conclude individual treaties 'before they can estimate their obligations towards all the Powers as a whole and before the compliance with such obligations is accepted'.[1]

The idea of a mere warning to China was unsatisfactory to the Japanese. Through MacDonald at Tokyo and Hayashi in London they renewed their efforts and pressed that Great Britain should immediately take the 'longer step' of promising 'material support' to the Chinese in the event of Russian insistence.[2] This proposal was brushed aside by Lansdowne, who, in reporting the suggestion to Salisbury, maintained that it would be unwise for Great Britain to pledge herself in the 'elastic language' suggested by Japan. Great Britain, he maintained, should state that her policy was indicated by the Anglo-German Agreement and that she should reserve for discussion action by any power inconsistent with the principles of that agreement, and 'that we assume that after the warning we have addressed to China she will not conclude any arrangement with a single Power without previous reference to us and to the other two Powers which were parties to the admonition'.[3]

Salisbury, however, was less intent on nursing the delicate Anglo-German alignment and so he gave the Japanese proposal closer appraisal. 'It might suit us to defend the littoral of North China,' he replied, 'though the task would be heavy—say the Gulfs of Liaochung [sic] of Pechili and of Corea—but we have no interests that we need value, or at least that we can defend on the vast inland frontier which separates the Chinese from the Russian Empire.' While to Lansdowne Japan's language was elastic because it raised the question of military action, to Salisbury it was elastic because concurrence would commit Great Britain to defending a vast land-locked frontier which even Japan had no reason to defend. 'I am not opposed in principle to an engagement with Japan', Salisbury concluded, 'to join in defending the coasts which we think we base serious interests in preserving from the Russian grasp, but we must define the extent of our responsibilities very carefully.' This

---

[1] Given in 'Correspondence respecting the Russian Occupation of Manchuria and Newchwang', *Accounts and Papers, 1904* (Cd. 1936), cx. 138.
[2] MacDonald to Lansdowne, tel. 4, secret, of 15 Feb. 1901, F.O. 46/542.
[3] Lansdowne to Salisbury, memorandum of 16 Feb. 1901, F.O. 17/1500.

was the basis of the Anglo-Japanese alliance, overtures towards which were to begin in mid-April. Salisbury thought the matter sufficiently important to be referred to the Cabinet.[1]

To Lansdowne, still preoccupied with the task of working with Germany, the concept was strange and imperfectly understood. Salisbury's mention of a cabinet, he conjectured with Bertie, must be with 'reference to his own suggestion as to a possible pledge to guarantee a part of the Chinese littoral'.[2] Germany, he knew, would not contemplate force and the idea of a bilateral understanding which excluded Germany did not occur to him. Consequently, with Bertie's help, he applied himself to the task of preventing ratification of a Russo-Chinese treaty by stiffening the admonition to China, the only approach on which Germany had shown any willingness to co-operate. Bertie suggested a joint Anglo-German-Japanese warning that in the event of any form of concession to Russia the powers would 'have to consider how the balance of advantages redressed and the result might be to gravely injure the integrity of the Chinese Empire'.[3] Lansdowne agreed to this and laid down the argument as follows:

(1) China must not make separate agreements.
(2) If she is pressed to enter such agreements we expect her to come to us.
(3) If she *doesn't* come to us, we shall have to raise the question of compensations.[4]

Thus tabulated, the proposed warning was revealed as an empty threat. Lansdowne was merely asking China to force into his hand the nettle he was reluctant to grasp; for if China did formally announce a separate agreement, which she was powerless to resist without active aid by the powers, the powers were back where they started. This was realized by Bertie.

Short of giving to China such a guarantee as is suggested by Japan and which it would be dangerous and unpolitic for us to give in the general terms proposed there is nothing that will give actual security against further Russian encroachment; but I think that

[1] Salisbury to Lansdowne, memorandum of 16 Feb. 1901, F.O. 17/1500.
[2] Lansdowne to Bertie, memorandum of 17 Feb. 1901, F.O. 17/1500.
[3] Memorandum by Bertie of 17 Feb. 1901, F.O. 17/1500.
[4] Lansdowne's minute on memorandum by Bertie of 17 Feb. 1901, F.O. 17/1500.

threats mixed with assurances to China might assist her in resisting the pressure of Russia and encourage her to disclose to us Russian proposals.[1]

This was the best that could be done within the limits they allowed themselves, and a telegram containing a suggestion of compensatory reprisal was sent to Tokyo for Japanese opinion.[2]

On 27 February Hayashi informed Lansdowne that the Japanese Government saw disadvantages in such a warning. China would regard it as analogous to the Anglo-German Agreement; she had already been warned, and powers not party to the proposed declaration might construe it as giving them a free hand in their own spheres. Japan therefore suggested that the three powers should join in advising China to present all claims and demands arising out of the Boxer complications for examination and adjustment to the joint conference then sitting at Peking.[3] This suggestion was accepted by Lansdowne, as it offered an alternative whereby Germany could be involved without a direct request being made for German support.

By the end of February the Russian proposals handed to Yang Ju on 16 February had become generally known. In twelve concise articles the Russians asked for exclusive economic, territorial, and political control in Manchuria, Mongolia, and the border regions of Sinkiang. In Manchuria Chinese troops were to be disbanded; the whole province was to remain under Russian military control until Russia's total indemnity claim had been met and, more significantly, until the railway in the direction of Peking, for which Witte had pressed so ardently, had been granted.

The substance of these demands was revealed to the powers by Chang Chih-tung, Liu K'un-i, and Yüan Shih-k'ai, who came out in immediate opposition to the Russian treaty.[4] Through their insistence the Court issued an Imperial Decree requesting the mediation of the powers, which was handed in at the Foreign Office by Lofenglu, the Chinese minister, on 1 March.[5]

---

[1] Bertie to Lansdowne, memorandum of 17 Feb. 1901, F.O. 17/1500.
[2] Lansdowne to MacDonald, tel. 13, secret, of 18 Feb. 1901, F.O. 46/542; cf. B.D. ii. 36.   [3] Memorandum of 27 Feb. 1901, F.O. 17/1500.
[4] Satow to Lansdowne, tel. 56 of 27 Feb. 1901, F.O. 17/1484; Tan, *The Boxer Catastrophe*, 182–3.
[5] Lansdowne to Satow, tel. 49 of 1 Mar. 1901, F.O. 17/1482; Lansdowne to Satow, No. 48 of 1 Mar. 1901, F.O. 17/1467.

Of the influential Chinese concerned, Li Hung-chang alone argued for ratification; the bribe which had been promised him may have played a part, but he was also sincere in his belief that the most China could hope for was the nominal return of Manchuria, and he did use the objections of the powers to persuade the Russians that amendment was necessary.[1] He did his best to retract the mediation request; Lofenglu returned in a panic to the Foreign Office and informed Bertie that he had misunderstood the telegram and had delivered it wrongly. The intention of the viceroys, he explained, was to express their hope that the powers would not oppose the agreement, which was not detrimental to Chinese interests, and which, if opposed, might cause a rupture in relations between China and Russia.[2]

Germany's reply to the request for mediation was that all affairs should be settled by the Conference of Representatives at Peking and not by Cabinet to Cabinet arrangement. Lansdowne urged Satow to support this.[3] Japan, however, displayed a militant mood. Izvolsky, the Russian minister at Tokyo, reported that Japan had announced to Peking that she was 'prepared to support China under any circumstances'.[4] By mid-March the excitement in Japan had grown: 'Practically the whole of the Japanese fleet', Izvolsky reported, 'is being concentrated in the ports nearest to us.'[5] Sir Claude MacDonald now British minister at Tokyo, confirmed these preparations. 'Practically no further mobilization of the Japanese fleet is necessary', he noted, 'to enable it to undertake immediate hostilities.'[6]

The Japanese attitude was partly bluster. The negotiations which were carried out between the powers during the next few days reveal that, over Korea, Japan would have fought with or

[1] Romanov, *Russia in Manchuria*, 214 and 434 note 126.
[2] Lansdowne to Satow, tel. 53 of 2 Mar. 1901, memorandum by Bertie encl., F.O. 17/1482. Later Lo presented a third explanation that Li's telegram meant that China should only accept if absolutely necessary. Lansdowne to Satow, No. 59 of 13 Mar. 1901, F.O. 17/1467.
[3] Memorandum by Bertie of 4 Mar. 1901, F.O. 17/1501.
[4] Izvolsky to Lamsdorff, tel. of 18 Feb. 1901 o.s. (3 Mar.), quoted in Romanov, *Russia in Manchuria*, 214.
[5] Izvolsky to Lamsdorff, report of 1 Mar. 1901 o.s. (14 Mar.), *Krasnyi Arkhiv*, trans. *CSPSR*, 18 (1934), 585. The Kokumin Domei Kai (People's League) and the Kokuryukai (Black Dragon Society) originated at this time with the purpose of expelling Russia from Manchuria and extending Japanese control to the Amur.
[6] MacDonald to Lansdowne, tel. 9 of 18 Mar. 1901, F.O. 46/542.

without support, while over Manchuria she was prepared to fight only if she could be assured of French and German neutrality and of active British support.

On 6 March the Japanese minister at Berlin asked for a statement of Germany's attitude. In reply, Baron von Muhlberg, the German Under-Secretary of State for Foreign Affairs, denied any secret Russo-German understanding. He outlined Germany's position as one of 'benevolent neutrality', and observed that this would keep the French fleet in check and that Great Britain would probably support Japan. This announcement, which implied previous Anglo-German consultation on a vigorous policy, was heartening to the Japanese. Negotiation was then taken a stage further by Japan, and Count Hayashi, the Japanese minister in London, was instructed to ask Lansdowne on 9 March, 'How far may Japan rely upon the support of Great Britain in case Japan finds it necessary to approach Russia?'[1]

Great Britain had not been consulted by Germany. Thus the Japanese query and the report of Muhlberg's announcement, submitted by the Japanese, were examined simultaneously and in relation to each other. The initial question was one of terminology. If the word 'approach' in the Japanese communication were used correctly, it only implied diplomatic support, but if it meant 'resist', as Hayashi admitted he thought it did, it would, as Salisbury pointed out, involve the possibility of war.[2] However, it was first necessary to define clearly the German attitude. The terms of the Franco-Russian alliance were unknown, and it was also not known whether they were limited to European complications.[3] The attitude of the French was a matter of urgent conjecture.[4] Strict German neutrality could encourage rather than restrain the French fleet. On the other hand, a declaration of benevolent neutrality when linked directly with an observation on the French fleet radically altered the situation. As Lansdowne noted later, 'an attitude which would keep the fleet of another Power in check could scarcely be described as neutral'.[5] On 12 March a draft was drawn up to elicit from

[1] B.D. ii. 41.   [2] Minute on B.D. ii. 41.
[3] Sanderson to Lansdowne, 10 Mar. 1901, Lansdowne Papers.
[4] Lansdowne to Monson, tel. 27, very secret, of 8 Mar. 1901, B.D. ii. 40.
[5] Lansdowne to MacDonald, No. 27, confidential, of 16 Mar. 1901, F.O. 46/538.

Germany a distinct statement of her intentions. This stressed that, in the event of war between Japan and Russia, Great Britain and Germany would have as their object the limitation of the war and

to that end they would remain neutral, reserving to themselves absolute freedom of action should the course of events require them in their own interests to intervene on behalf of Japan. In the event, however, of any Power joining Russia in hostilities against Japan, the British and German governments will give naval assistance to Japan to defend herself against such attack.[1]

Lansdowne added that if Germany refused to be a party to this arrangement a reconsideration of the position would be necessary.[2] On the next day the Cabinet debated the matter for an hour and a half and then had to defer a decision until further information was received.[3]

The caution of the British was vindicated when this information was received. By neutrality, Germany had meant a 'correct and strict neutrality'. Further, on 15 March, in the Reichstag, Count Bülow openly defined Germany's attitude to the Anglo-German Agreement of October 1900. According to the German Chancellor, the ambitions of the powers in China could be divided into those who pursued commercial and those who pursued political aims. Germany belonged to the former category and the agreement had been concluded in that spirit and 'was in no sense concerned with Manchuria'. He added, 'There were no German interests of importance in Manchuria, and the fate of that province was a matter of absolute indifference to Germany.'[4]

[1] Memorandum Foreign Office drafts appended 12 Mar. 1901, F.O. 46/547. J. A. S. Grenville, 'Lansdowne's Abortive Project of 12 March 1901 for a Secret Agreement with Germany', *Bulletin of the Institute of Historical Research*, 27 (1954), 201–13. Lansdowne's whole approach to the Manchurian issue indicated his realization of the impossibility of material co-operation between Great Britain and Germany in China.

[2] Memorandum by Lansdowne of 12 Mar. 1901, F.O. 46/547.

[3] Salisbury's report to the King is quoted. Goudswaard, *Some Aspects of the End of Britain's 'Splendid Isolation'*, 72–3.

[4] Extract given in *B.D.* ii. 26. Germany may have used the term 'benevolent' loosely. The Kaiser maintained that while in England at the end of January he had made it clear he would maintain 'a benevolent but strict neutrality' (cf. Lascelles to Lansdowne, No. 94, very confidential, of 11 Apr. 1901, *B.D.* ii. 54), while in conversation with Eckardstein in February Hayashi maintained Japan would fight if she could count on the active support of Great Britain and if she were confident

Bülow's statement aroused perturbation in London. It has been seen that Lansdowne was sufficiently aware of Germany's attitude to cause him to ensure, before acting, that Germany would participate even over the matter of issuing a warning to China. Then, when the approach was made by Japan, the Government had hesitated over, and had even suspected, Germany's motives in declaring her neutrality in ambiguous terms. It appeared, as Sanderson noted on 10 March, as if they were ready to incite Japan to war, and were spuriously indicating British support, while 'their own attitude is apparently to be that of Mr. Bax Allen and Mr. Bob Sawyer, dancing round the combatants and ready to bleed whichever is first stunned'.[1] To clear the situation, Lansdowne had asked Germany to define her attitude more precisely. In reply, Germany had not only defined her use of the term 'benevolent neutrality' but also had categorically limited the application of the Anglo-German Agreement. Lansdowne's view was that the Agreement did apply to Manchuria, at least in so far as the ports were concerned, under Clause 1, which pledged the two countries to maintain that the ports on the rivers and littoral of China should remain free and open to trade, and under Clause 2, which pledged them to maintain undiminished the territorial condition of the Chinese Empire. 'It would be unfortunate if any discrepancy should arise between the German interpretation of the agreement and ours', Lansdowne told Lascelles.[2]

There was urgent activity at the Foreign Office to uncover evidence to prove that Germany was committed to the defence of Manchuria. Lord Cranborne, in the House of Commons on 19 March, quoted Article 2 of the Agreement and stated no qualification was attached. This was true in that no specific qualification had been written into the clause, but it was not true in intention, fully aired in the *pourparlers*, as has been noted during the negotiation of the Agreement. Moreover, the Russian demands, extensive as they were, still left the province nominally in Chinese hands, thus territorially intact. The only pertinent clause in the Agreement was Clause 1, and when this

of the benevolent neutrality of Germany (cf. Eckardstein's report of 16 Feb. 1901, *Grosse Politik*, xvi. 324).

[1] Sanderson to Lansdowne, 10 Mar. 1901, Lansdowne Papers.
[2] Lansdowne to Lascelles, tel. 79 of 16 Mar. 1901, *B.D.* ii. 27.

was closely examined it was found to be hopelessly vague. The two powers had pledged themselves to maintain the open door 'as far as they can exercise influence'. No statement could be found which alleged that the maintenance of the territorial integrity of China was a principle of German policy. Campbell, of the Foreign Office, who was asked to unearth what he could, concluded, 'We cannot find that she ever did say so directly.'[1] Great Britain had no ground for protest. On 28 March Lansdowne announced in the House of Lords: 'I have made enquiries with regard to what took place when this Agreement was under negotiation, and I am told that the German Government did give us to understand that in their view Manchuria was not a place within which they consider they had any influence.'[2]

By then the diplomatic crisis over the Manchurian agreement had passed. On 17 March Satow reported modifications in the Russian demands. The information was also given through the Japanese minister in London, and the new terms, Hayashi was forced to admit, were 'less objectionable'.[3] This was a final effort by the Russians to push their treaty through, the demands being handed to the Chinese on 12 March with a time limit of fourteen days for acceptance. The stratagem failed in its object. The Chinese, strengthened by the force of international interest, rejected the demands and on 5 April Russia stated her intention of abandoning the attempt.[4]

Further efforts towards a Sino-Russian agreement for the evacuation of Manchuria were reported throughout 1901, but these could not arouse the earlier alarm. The Foreign Office worked in the knowledge that the Chinese, acting in the spirit of Lansdowne's advice to Lofenglu that 'the strength of the Chinese Government is to sit still',[5] were being offered more moderate terms with each successive overture. Linked with this was the awareness of the financial strain of the occupation

[1] Campbell to Lansdowne, memorandum of 26 Mar. 1901, F.O. 17/1502.

[2] Lansdowne to Lascelles, No. 136 of 7 Apr. 1901, B.D. ii. 28.

[3] Lansdowne to Satow, tels. 71, 74 of 16, 20 Mar. 1901, F.O. 17/1482; Satow to Lansdowne, tel. 73, secret, of 17 Mar. 1901, F.O. 17/1484.

[4] Lansdowne to Satow, tel. 101, confidential, of 5 Apr. 1901, F.O. 17/1482. Lamsdorff's opinion was that if Russia had not done so there would have been war with Japan. Romanov, *Russia in Manchuria*, 217.

[5] Lansdowne to Satow, tel. 103 of 5 Apr. 1901, F.O. 17/1482.

on Russia. 'The longer the Russians have to stay in force in Manchuria,' Bertie observed, 'the more they will be pinched for money and consequently the more pliable they will become.'[1] When agreement was finally reached between Russia and China on 26 March 1902, Bertie believed it unlikely that better terms would be obtained.[2] Nor was Lansdowne inclined to object on matters of detail, although he felt that 'after having protested so loudly we ought not to climb down out of sheer weariness in too great a hurry'.[3]

The British approach to the Manchurian issue subsequent to Russia's first attempt in the spring of 1901 reflected the true attitude of the Government to the question of Russia in Manchuria. It had always been recognized that Russia had a 'predominating influence' in the area.[4] In January 1901, although Lansdowne recognized the 'inwardness' of the proposed Russo-Chinese convention,[5] he had not protested to Russia, and by February was even contemplating the sale of the extra-mural line if necessary. On 9 April, just after the height of the crisis, he wrote to Satow that although the Russian right to build a railway to Peking was doubtful, 'they may be able to show that they can build as far as the Great Wall'.[6] Throughout, his chief concern was not that Russian appropriations in Manchuria should be resisted, but that, through the vigorous insistence of Japan, the Anglo-German Agreement should not be called to the fore and put to a strain which the alignment could not stand. This was the real significance of the Manchurian crisis in British policy. In 1901 Chamberlain made his third and final effort towards a comprehensive Anglo-German alliance. The distinguishing characteristic of this attempt was his suggestion, made to Eckardstein in January,

[1] Bertie to Lansdowne, memorandum of 6 Dec. 1901, F.O. 17/1511; memorandum by Sanderson of 28 Apr. 1902, F.O. 17/1548. In Apr. 1901 Rothschild had reported Russia's serious financial embarrassment. Instead of the usual credit of £1,000,000 in London she was overdrawn to £80,000; memorandum by MacDonnell, private, of 4 Apr. 1901, S.P. Chronological Series 1901, Imperial and Foreign. Russian commitments in the Far East in 1901 were between 800 and 1,000 million roubles. Romanov, *Russia in Manchuria*, 32.

[2] Memorandum by Bertie of 27 Mar. 1902, F.O. 17/1548.

[3] Lansdowne to MacDonald, 31 Mar. 1902, Lansdowne Papers.

[4] Memorandum by Sanderson, minuted by Lansdowne, of 28 Apr. 1902, F.O. 17/1548.

[5] Lansdowne to Satow, 16 Jan. 1901, P.R.O. 30/33/7/1.

[6] Lansdowne to Satow, 9 Apr. 1901, P.R.O. 30/33/7/1.

for the successful establishment of limited and regional agreements on which a larger alliance could then be based.[1] Lansdowne, who favoured the idea, was forced to the Manchurian
issue just as the overture was being made. This explains his
dogged insistence on a policy of admonition to China and his
reluctance to approach Russia directly during the latter part
of February, when he turned uncomfortably within the limits of
Anglo-German co-operation. Despite this restraint he was led
in March into a position where the Manchurian issue became
a test of the value of German support. Germany's vigorous
and public rejection was not without an effect. Years later
when Lansdowne was asked why he had abandoned the Anglo-
German cause he replied, 'It was something to do with Manchuria. I found I couldn't trust them.'[2] Although overtures for
an Anglo-German Alliance continued into 1901 they were
conducted in a desultory manner, and by their side ran the
growing idea of a bilateral agreement with Japan.

[1] The particular example brought forward was Morocco but 'there is no doubt
that China was uppermost in his mind'. Amery, *Chamberlain*, iv. 145.
[2] A. L. Kennedy, *Salisbury, 1830–1903* (London, 1953), 393.

XII

THE ANGLO-JAPANESE ALLIANCE

AMICABLE relations between Great Britain and Japan were established in 1895, when Great Britain refused to intervene in the Sino-Japanese war. This bond was strengthened over the succeeding years and at the time of the Port Arthur crisis of 1898 the need for an agreement with Japan was frequently mentioned in Parliament and in the British Press.[1] The Boxer rising brought further evidence of the value of Japanese support. In the advance on Peking and during the post-relief period, the British and Japanese contingents co-operated closely, and from this contact there arose an appreciation of Japanese military efficiency. But until 1901 on the level of great power alignments Japan was regarded as a secondary power, whose support in the Far East was welcomed to strengthen the Anglo-German alignment against Russia and France.

Japan's vigorous stand over Manchuria in the early spring of 1901 introduced a new element into the Far Eastern situation. Her suggestion in February that material support could be offered by the powers to China to resist the Russian demands cut sharply through the precarious diplomatic situation. It has been noticed that Lord Salisbury had immediately grasped the implications of this suggestion on British policy. The Prime Minister had then voiced the surprising opinion that he was not opposed in principle to the idea of a limited engagement with Japan.[2] Lord Lansdowne, who had yet to be disillusioned about the realities of Anglo-German co-operation, failed to follow the direction of Salisbury's thought. His aim was still that of a common front with Germany, which merely envisaged a

[1] *The Times*, 23 and 31 Dec. 1897, 1 Feb., 26 Mar., 4 Apr., 30 July 1898; *Parliamentary Debates*, 4th Series, liii. 129–31, 302–6, liv. 307–9. . . . Chamberlain's suggestion to Takaakira Kato, then Japanese minister in London, is noted in A. M. Pooley (ed.), *The Secret Memoirs of Count Tadasu Hayashi* (New York and London, 1915), 83; Viscount Ishii, *Diplomatic Commentaries* (Baltimore, 1936), 36.

[2] Salisbury to Lansdowne, memorandum of 16 Feb. 1901, F.O. 17/1500. See above, pp. 285–6.

warning to China against 'backstairs agreements'. A month later, when Japan made a second attempt to obtain British support by trying to arrange for German neutrality in the event of a Russo-Japanese war, again Lansdowne failed to respond. At no time during the Manchurian crisis did Lansdowne assume that Great Britain would take anything other than a neutral stand. The most he anticipated, after being misled by Germany's ambiguous language, was that the two powers could possibly combine in 'keeping a ring' for Russia and Japan.[1] Lansdowne persisted in this policy even after Germany had revealed her attitude over Manchuria. On 16 March, in reply to a guarded suggestion by Count Hayashi, the Japanese Ambassador in London, for joint action between Great Britain and Japan, Lansdowne stated that British policy was still governed by the earlier warning which had been delivered to China in concert with Germany.[2] In view of Lansdowne's attitude, Hayashi directed his efforts to repairing the Anglo-German diplomatic front against Russia in the east. In this he was encouraged by Eckardstein. During the latter part of March and early April the two diplomats exchanged views on how the situation could be improved.[3] On 16 April Eckardstein put a personal scheme of Hayashi's before the Foreign Office for 'an agreement between Japan, Germany and Great Britain based on the Anglo-German Agreement of October last, but going further and pledging the three Governments to support the integrity of China and the maintenance of the "open door" at existing Treaty Ports'.[4] On the next day, encouraged possibly by Eckardstein's opening, Hayashi made the same suggestion directly to Lansdowne. In reply, the Foreign Secretary merely indicated that 'without some substantive proposal for giving effect to such a policy' he could not pass an opinion.[5]

Lansdowne was understandably reluctant to join in a further declaration on Chinese territorial integrity when Germany had already shown that she was not prepared to uphold those

[1] Lansdowne to Lascelles, 18 Mar. 1901, B.D. ii. 60.
[2] Lansdowne to Satow, tel. 74 of 20 Mar. 1901, F.O. 17/1482.
[3] Hayashi, *Memoirs*, 114 f.
[4] Memorandum by Sanderson of 16 Apr. 1901, Lansdowne Papers.
[5] Lansdowne to MacDonald, No. 44 of 17 Apr. 1901, F.O. 46/538; Hayashi, *Memoirs*, 116.

principles under the innocuous terms of the existing Agreement. From the spring of 1901 the British Government lost their faith in repetitive declarations. Instead, as a result of the Manchurian crisis, they turned to a more realistic appraisal of the Far Eastern situation and, in particular, of the position and possible political ambitions of Japan.

It was realized in March that while Manchuria was the immediate issue, Korea was Japan's main preoccupation and that if the latter area were involved she 'would fight with or without support and independently of whether France and Germany would remain neutral'.[1] On 23 March Ardagh, the Director General of Military Intelligence, focused further attention on the area when he observed that the Russian occupation of Manchuria intensified the possibility of a Russo-Japanese war over Korea.[2] Although it was assumed that in the event of such a war Great Britain would remain neutral, by the beginning of July Bertie had posed the question whether a Russian occupation of Korea were important to British interests and that if Great Britain could not admit this, it were 'not much of a sacrifice to promise aid to and get co-operation from Japan'.[3]

The extent of Japan's interest in Korea raised a second consideration. At the height of the Manchurian crisis, Sanderson observed that it would be unwise for Japan to go to war 'if they can get even a tolerable arrangement by showing their teeth'.[4] The observation was made with the Nichi–Rosen Agreement of 1898 in mind. At the time of the occupation of Port Arthur, to placate Japan Russia had negotiated this understanding which, while maintaining the full independence of Korea, stipulated (in Article 3) that Russia would not hinder Japanese economic interests in Korea. With Russia's move into southern Manchuria a further understanding was not impossible on the basis of allowing Japan a strengthened hold on Korea.[5] Or, as Bertie put it, if no assistance were offered to Japan there was a

---

[1] Memorandum by Bertie of 11 Mar. 1901, F.O. 17/1501.

[2] D.M.I. memorandum respecting the Strategical Effects of the Russo-Chinese Agreement, encl. 1 in Intelligence Division to Foreign Office of 23 Mar. 1901, F.O. 17/1502.

[3] Bertie to Lansdowne, 2 July 1901, F.O. 17/1506.

[4] Sanderson to Lansdowne, 10 Mar. 1901, Lansdowne Papers.

[5] Hayashi had just reported Witte's suggestion of a joint neutralization pact. The text of the Agreement is given in MacMurray, *Treaties and Agreements*, i. 126.

danger of her coming to terms with Russia to the detriment of British interests.[1] The Manchurian question had raised Japan to a level on which her co-operation, or rather the failure to secure her co-operation, was a matter of consequence.

Speculation in this direction did not assume real form until May, when a difference of opinion arose between Great Britain and Japan in relation to the indemnity negotiations at Peking. After considerable discussion on the method of payment of the indemnity, a British proposal for the payment of claims in 4 per cent bonds at face value was accepted by the powers. As Japan's credit was low she could not hope to borrow at less than 5 per cent and she put forward several counter-proposals designed to compensate this disadvantage. Great Britain resisted these alternatives and a strained relationship resulted. The issue of the indemnity bonds, which was not resolved until July, and which came up in the period following the breakdown of the Anglo-German alliance overtures which had been revived that spring, was the second stage (the Manchurian question being the first) through which British opinion moved towards the Anglo-Japanese alliance.

Early in the discussion Satow suggested that to help the Japanese Great Britain should join in guaranteeing the Japanese share of the bonds.[2] When MacDonald, the British minister at Tokyo, was asked for his opinion he replied that the move would bring Japan over to the bonds scheme, and that the 'feeling of gratitude throughout this country [Japan] would be a very deep and lasting one, and might at some future time be well worth the financial risk at present incurred'.[3] Bertie, who had just returned from a month's holiday, observed with some truth that the 'gratitude of a nation is an ephemeral product...' and questioned the advisability of securing Japanese favour by this means.[4] Lansdowne was also of the opinion that it was impossible to guarantee the Japanese share of the bonds 'at this stage of the proceedings',[5] and the scheme was allowed to drop. A week later Japanese annoyance over the British bonds proposal had become more marked and Lansdowne advised Satow at

[1] Memorandum by Bertie of 11 Mar. 1901, F.O. 17/1501.
[2] Satow to Lansdowne, tel. 166 of 15 May 1901, F.O. 17/1487.
[3] MacDonald to Lansdowne, tel. 34 of 20 May 1901, F.O. 46/542.
[4] Memorandum by Bertie of 21 May 1901, F.O. 17/1505.
[5] Minute on Satow to Lansdowne, tel. 177 of 23 May 1901, F.O. 17/1484.

Peking to humour them over other aspects of the negotiations. 'They are, I am afraid, a little sore,' he noted, 'and perhaps not unnaturally.'[1]

The next move was made by Japan two weeks later. On 15 June Komura, the Japanese minister at Peking, claimed additional bonds to cover the difference in Japan's credit.[2] This hitch to the British bonds scheme was discussed by the Cabinet on 20 June on the basis of a memorandum drawn up by Lansdowne the previous day exploring the various ways of making 'the bargain a better one for the Japanese'. Lansdowne observed:

> It is of the utmost importance that we should stand well with her in the Far East, and I do not think I am wrong in saying that she is a little sore with us, and inclined to think that we have not supported her sufficiently against Russia.[3]

The warning was timely. On 2 July Eckardstein came forward with the information that negotiations were in progress at Paris to raise a loan at 4 per cent for Japan on the security of her share of the bonds. This, Eckardstein stressed, would be the first step in a Far Eastern arrangement between Russia, France, and Japan. Bertie expressed some doubt on whether even French finance could prevail on Russia to forgo any intention of occupying Korea, which Bertie thought would be the indispensable condition of Japanese cohesion. Nevertheless, the news was disturbing, especially when Hayashi confirmed the possibility of Japan seeking a French loan.[4]

This situation which arose out of Japan's objections to the bonds scheme during the latter part of June led Bertie to make a constructive suggestion for a closer understanding with Japan. In a memorandum of 20 June in support of Lansdowne's view, he pointed out that any financial gesture by Great Britain towards Japan would require some satisfaction in Parliament. To meet this demand Bertie suggested a mutual understanding or even

---

[1] Lansdowne to Satow, 31 May 1901, Lansdowne Papers.

[2] Satow to Lansdowne, tel. 202 of 15 June 1901, F.O. 17/1484.

[3] Memorandum by Lansdowne of 19 June 1901, S.P. Cabinet General 1901, unclassified.

[4] Bertie to Lansdowne, 2 July 1901, F.O. 17/1506; Lansdowne to Whitehead, No. 82, secret, of 18 July 1901, F.O. 46/538. At this time Witte made a second attempt to settle with Japan over Korea (cf. Romanov, *Russia in Manchuria*, 224).

a secret agreement between the two countries.[1] A fortnight later, in reporting Eckardstein's information Bertie once again emphasized the political issue. 'Until we have attached Japan to us by something more substantial than general expressions of goodwill towards her,' he observed, 'we shall run a risk of her making some arrangement which might be disadvantageous to us.' He then raised the problem of Korea, the recognized focus of Japan's ambitions, and suggested that if it were a condition of British policy that Korea should not fall under Russian occupation then it would not be much of a sacrifice to make a definite promise of co-operation to Japan for its defence. If the Government were not disposed 'to go so far at the moment', Bertie concluded, then it would be advisable to address inquiries to the Japanese Government on their views with regard to China and the Far East, 'so as to make them believe that later on we shall be willing to come to an understanding with them and so keep them from gravitating towards our rivals'.[2]

At the same time, Bertie drew up a draft under the heading 'Suggestions for Agreement with Japan' which he forwarded to Lansdowne under cover of his memorandum of 2 July:

Mutual undertaking not, without consultation with each other, to enter into a separate agreement with any other Power in regard to China.

A Declaration that the policy of the two countries is to maintain the independence and integrity of the Chinese Empire; the observance of those of its Treaties which are known to and have not been protested against by both Powers, particularly the stipulations in 'open door' and 'equal opportunity'.

An agreement that the two Powers will whenever any of these principles are endangered confer together for protecting China by sea against any Power that may proceed to coercive measures in order to obtain engagements or concessions at variance with the objects in the Agreement between England and Japan.

Or a *secret* agreement with Japan that we will assist her by sea in resisting Russian occupation of Corea and that she will assist us by sea in resisting any encroachment by any Foreign Power on the Yangtze region and the South of China.[3]

---

[1] Memorandum by Bertie of 20 June 1901, F.O. 46/547.
[2] Bertie to Lansdowne, 2 July 1901, F.O. 17/1506.
[3] Memorandum by Bertie, 'Suggestions for Agreement with Japan', encl. in Bertie to Lansdowne of 2 July 1901, F.O. 17/1506.

The draft was the first tentative outline for a political agreement with Japan. It appropriated to Great Britain and Japan, on a basis of naval co-operation, the maintenance of the principles contained in the Anglo-German Agreement. It was more than a declaration of principle, but it also paid careful heed to Salisbury's warning that, in any co-operation with Japan, Great Britain should carefully limit the extent of her responsibility to naval matters. Finally, in the alternative secret agreement, Bertie correlated the protection of British interests in the Yangtze region with the maintenance of Japanese interests in Korea, without making provision for Manchuria, which from the Japanese point of view required positive action before there could be a return to a normal state of affairs. These considerations were eventually incorporated in the Anglo-Japanese Alliance of 30 January 1902, and Bertie's reasons for advancing them at this time need to be examined in greater detail.

British anxiety over German activity at the time of the occupation of Shanghai in August 1900 had led to the negotiation of the Anglo-German Agreement. Over the winter of 1900–1 the attention of the powers had been centred on the events in the north of China. In the spring of 1901, however, disturbing reports were again received of renewed activity, particularly by France, in the centre and south. On 11 April the *China Mail* reported the laying of a direct telegraph cable by France between Saigon and Amoy and the landing of French troops at the latter port. Then French activity on the West river raised the concern of the Admiralty, and two gunboats were sent to augment the British force in those waters.[1] When Sir Henry Blake, the Governor of Hong Kong, confirmed these reports of French activity, Lansdowne declared the matter to be 'one of serious moment'.[2] To all intents, it appeared that with the return of a more stable situation in north China the powers were to revert to the practice of concession hunting which had occupied them before the rising. On 8 April Sir Ernest Satow wrote from Peking: 'Recent events seem to have shown that the political centre of gravity is not here, but on the Yangtze and down South.'[3]

[1] 'French Activity in the Region of the West River', S 86/1901, Adm. 1/7511.
[2] Lansdowne's minute on Blake to Chamberlain, 22 June 1901, in Colonial Office to Foreign Office, 25 July 1901, F.O. 17/1507.
[3] Satow to Lansdowne, 8 Apr. 1901, Lansdowne Papers.

The letter was received by Lansdowne on 31 May, just after Salisbury had issued his well-known memorandum on isolation which exposed the consequences of joining the Triple Alliance and effectively terminated the Anglo-German alliance overtures. Thereafter there was a rising distrust of German cooperation. In a memorandum of 22 July, in which he again called for agreement with Japan on the basis of the protection of each other's interests in the Yangtze and Korea, Bertie stated categorically, 'A reliable arrangement with Germany is not to be had.'[1] The mood called into question the validity of the Anglo-German Agreement of October 1900, not specifically with regard to possible German encroachment, although her ambitions in the Yangtze area were to be revealed before the end of the year over the evacuation of Shanghai, but as a comprehensive safeguard to restrain the ambitious tendencies of all the powers.

However, it would be impossible for Lansdowne to act on Bertie's suggestion and to turn to an agreement with Japan if Japan were intent on securing Russia's withdrawal from Manchuria. Great Britain's aim was not an anti-Russian alignment over Manchuria but an effective agreement to preserve British interests in the Far East *in statu quo*. Since the spring Lansdowne had been anxious to break down the assumption that Great Britain was aligned behind China to oppose the Russian demands. In July he observed, in relation to a further Chinese overture for support, 'we must be careful not to admit that we are pledged to obtain withdrawal of Russians'.[2] A few days later, as a necessary preliminary for an approach to Japan, he suggested to Hayashi that as long as Russia did not take advantage of her exceptional position to interfere with the integrity of China or to injure the interests of other powers there would be no reason to object to Russia making her own arrangements with the Chinese as to the conditions of her withdrawal from Manchuria.[3]

The Japanese were given no indication of the direction of Lansdowne's suggestion. Consequently, a cautious reply was

[1] Memorandum by Bertie of 22 July 1901, F.O. 17/1507.
[2] Satow to Lansdowne, tel. 238 of 13 July 1901, minuted by Lansdowne, F.O. 17/1485.
[3] Memorandum by Bertie of 22 July 1901, F.O. 17/1507.

returned on 18 July which attempted to tie the future of Manchuria to China's indemnity obligations, then under negotiation at Peking. Japan made the extreme suggestion that China should be denied the right of redeeming the indemnity bonds except by action of the sinking fund, and that as long as the bonds remained unpaid China was not to grant to any power any separate or exclusive territorial advantages. The sinking fund was not due to start for three years and it had been estimated that the huge indemnity would take forty years to settle. The Japanese reply was plainly designed to stem a retreat by Great Britain before Russia in Manchuria, which was an alternative interpretation of Lansdowne's suggestion. Hayashi admitted that although this arrangement was not all that was to be desired, the Japanese idea was that it would keep any advantages granted to Russia in Manchuria open to the other powers.[1]

The absence of Japanese belligerence over Manchuria was satisfactory to Great Britain, and a meeting was arranged between Lansdowne and Hayashi on 31 July. At this meeting Hayashi confirmed that while Japan had a sentimental distaste for Russia's retention of Manchuria, her real concern was Korea. Lansdowne then stated that there was so much resemblance between the policies of the two powers that it was worth considering 'what line of conduct we might follow supposing the balance of power in the waters of the Far East to be threatened with serious disturbance'.[2] The Japanese reply of 14 August was cautious and merely asked the conditions Great Britain would require for an understanding, to which Lansdowne replied that as Japan was the more interested power she had to formulate a proposal.[3] Negotiations were then not resumed until mid-October.

This reserve was maintained only at an official level. Privately the question of closer co-operation between the two powers had already become a matter of thorough discussion. These background conversations gave the understanding a form not initially contemplated by either Lansdowne or Bertie. The

[1] Memorandum by Bertie of 22 July 1901, F.O. 17/1507; memorandum of Japanese reply of 18 July 1901, F.O. 46/545.
[2] Lansdowne to Whitehead, No. 89, secret, of 31 July 1901, B.D. ii. 90–1.
[3] Lansdowne to Whitehead, No. 91, secret, of 14 Aug. 1901, B.D. ii. 91–2.

original intention was agreement on the basis of the Anglo-German Agreement, with two further provisions: (1) that there should be naval co-operation, and (2) that special notice should be taken of the Yangtze and Korea. When Hayashi declared on 14 August that the aim of any agreement would be the maintenance of the open door and the integrity of China and that 'he did not for a moment suppose that there could be any question of an offensive or defensive alliance',[1] he was merely stating the official position. Since mid-July he had been seeing MacDonald, who had been recalled from Tokyo,[2] and through him he knew that King Edward favoured an agreement, while Salisbury approved an alliance.[3] On 16 August, just before the summer vacation, Lansdowne brought the matter before the Cabinet and before he went on holiday he asked Hayashi to get plenipotentiary powers to open discussion on an official basis.[4] By the end of August Lansdowne wrote Satow that there had been 'some interesting conversations with Hayashi as to the possibility of a closer understanding between us and I think it not at all improbable that we may succeed in arriving at this'.[5]

The initiative came from Hayashi, who concentrated his efforts on making the most of the favourable climate of opinion in London. Everything was put forward as his own personal view, which Baron Komura, now the Japanese Minister for Foreign Affairs, later declared had found favour with the Japanese Government.[6] By 3 September MacDonald was writing to Lansdowne with reference to an 'understanding' the main lines of which were, 'If A and B fall out they are to settle the matter themselves, but if C interferes then D will have a word to say.'[7] To this Lansdowne replied the next day,

Your formula is clear enough so far as it goes, but if the undertaking is ever to take shape we shall have to clothe it in more precise language, and to consider what are the eventualities in which A is to come to the rescue of C, or B to the rescue of D, and whether

---

[1] B.D. ii. 92.
[2] Lansdowne to MacDonald, tel. 75 of 20 May 1901, F.O. 46/542. MacDonald left Tokyo on 28 May and returned to his post on 22 Oct.
[3] Hayashi, *Memoirs*, 121–3.
[4] Goudswaard, *Some Aspects of the End of Britain's 'Splendid Isolation'*, 77, gives Salisbury's report of the Cabinet meeting to the King.
[5] Lansdowne to Satow, 25 Aug. 1901, Lansdowne Papers.
[6] MacDonald to Lansdowne, 31 Oct. 1901, Lansdowne Papers.
[7] MacDonald to Lansdowne, 3 Sept. 1901, Lansdowne Papers.

anything is to be said as to the form in which assistance might be given. But I am sincerely desirous to make something of the idea.[1]

The evolution of a formula which could be applied to both Russia and France aroused an immediate interest in naval circles. Since 1895 Great Britain's disadvantageous position in respect of the Dual Alliance powers had occasioned concern, particularly when considered in relation to the country's naval self-sufficiency, the first and only real line of national defence. At that time British naval policy was based on the two-power standard laid down by Lord George Hamilton in 1889. This envisaged a British Navy on a scale which would at least equal the naval strength of any two other powers. Thus the ship-building programme of 1889–94 anticipated, in first- and second-class battleships, a margin of six against France and Italy combined, of eight against France and Germany, and of fourteen against France and Russia.[2] At that time the next greatest naval power to France was Italy, and as relations with Italy were amicable an ample margin of superiority existed against any probable combination. Between 1895 and 1901, however, the naval position of the powers was radically changed, and by the latter year the formula of 1889 was no longer applicable. During these years Russia, Germany, and the United States became great naval powers, Japan an important one. From 1895 an increased Russian ship-building programme aroused the anxiety of the Cabinet; recurrent reports of additional Russian naval expenditure led to corresponding supplementary programmes for the British fleet, to the extent that the Navy Estimates rose from £18,700,000 in 1895–6 to £30,876,000 in 1901.[3] By 1899 Russia's extraordinary programme had excited sufficient alarm for Lord Goschen, First Lord of the Admiralty, to propose a mutual halt to new construction; but this was rejected by Russia on the ground that

[1] Lansdowne to MacDonald, 4 Sept. 1901, Lansdowne Papers.
[2] Memorandum by Lord Selborne, First Lord of the Admiralty, of 16 Nov. 1901, 'The Navy Estimates and the Chancellor of the Exchequer's Memorandum on the Growth of Expenditures', confidential, S.P. Cabinet General, 1901; A. J. Marder, *British Naval Policy, 1880–1905* (London, 1940), 105 f.
[3] 'Naval Estimates and Remarks on Naval Progress of the Principal European Countries, the United States and Japan', Admiralty, Intelligence Division, No. 585 of Aug. 1900, S.P. Confidential Prints, 1900; memorandum by Sir Michael Hicks Beach, Chancellor of the Exchequer, confidential, of Oct. 1901, S.P. Cabinet General, 1901.

she could not allow her navy to be inferior to Japan's.[1] In 1901 Lord Selborne, who succeeded Goschen at the Admiralty, placed a memorandum before the Cabinet which assessed the significance of this naval development on British policy. If the naval formula of 1889 were to be maintained, Selborne argued, it would have to take into account the rise of Russia, Germany, and the United States to great naval power standing. A three-power or a four-power standard was impossible, and the two-power standard could not be discarded without being misunderstood. In view of the Dual Alliance the conclusion was inevitable; the two-power standard had to be applied in political terms. Selborne concluded:

> The standard which I believe now to be the true one for us is not one which could be publicly stated. In Parliament I would always speak, in general terms, of not falling below the two-Power Standard. To the Cabinet I would suggest that if we make such provision as will offer us the reasonable certainty of success in a war with France and Russia, we shall have fully provided for all contingencies.[2]

In other words, it was necessary to assume that Germany would not be hostile when the Dual Alliance was considered in relation to British naval defence. Consequently, as Great Britain's interests overseas were increasingly encroached upon by Russia and France during these years, a group of the Cabinet led by Joseph Chamberlain, the Colonial Secretary, turned to a possibility of an understanding with Germany. The failure of the three overtures made in this direction between 1898 and 1901 did little to bolster British confidence.

Moreover, with the growth in importance of the Far East after 1895 the struggle for naval superiority had been extended to those waters. Great Britain, with her naval expenditure already under strain, was forced either to carry this extra burden to the disadvantage of her Home and Mediterranean fleets or to concede the position in the Far East. On 4 September Lord Selborne, First Lord of the Admiralty, drew up a memorandum on the balance of naval power in the Far East in

---

[1] Goschen to Salisbury, confidential, of 1 Mar. 1899, S.P. 93/47; Sir Charles Scott, British Ambassador at St. Petersburg, to Goschen, tel., private, of 10 Mar. 1899, S.P. 129/63; A. R. D. Elliot, *The Life of George Joachim Goschen, first Viscount Goschen*, 2 vols. (London, 1911), ii. 215–16.

[2] Memorandum by Selborne of 16 Nov. 1901, S.P. Cabinet General, 1901.

relation to a possible alliance with Japan. By 1901, in the Far East, Russia had 5 battleships with 3 under construction; Japan 6 with 1 under construction; France 1; Germany 4; and Great Britain 4. If Japan should come to an arrangement with Russia the position would be critical, while if she aligned herself with Great Britain the ratio would be 11 : 9 against the Dual Alliance powers. This was the first reaction of the Admiralty and it brought them out in favour of the alliance.[1]

When Parliament reassembled after the summer recess, the Government displayed a greater confidence in their handling of foreign affairs. In respect of Russia the policy of indirect diplomacy, adopted during the Manchurian crisis in the spring, was abandoned. Reports had been received, on 9 October, of a renewed effort by Russia to negotiate a treaty over Manchuria which apparently included the right to construct a railway to Peking.[2] Lansdowne decided on a direct approach to Russia. On 22 October he had an informal conversation with Baron de Staal, the Russian Ambassador at London, and he followed this up, on the 25th, by suggesting to the Cabinet that it would be better to make an overture to Russia in an attitude of 'absolute frankness'.[3] On the same day Chamberlain lashed out, in reply to German criticism of Kitchener's guerrilla-war policy in South Africa, by citing German atrocities during the Franco-Prussian war. On 25 October, also, Lansdowne drew up a draft treaty of alliance with Japan.[4] This draft was approved by the Cabinet on the 28th.

On 29 October Hayashi presented a clause for British acceptance. This read: 'In view of the preponderating interests of Japan in Corea, His Britannic Majesty's Government shall acquiesce in the adoption by Japan of suitable measures for the maintenance of those interests.'[5] In effect, this meant a free

[1] Memorandum by Selborne of 4 Sept. 1901, F.O. 46/547.
[2] Major-General Creagh to Hamilton, tel. 405 of 9 Oct. 1901; Lansdowne to Bertie, 10 (?) Oct. 1901, F.O. 17/1510; Intelligence Division to Foreign Office, 21 Oct. 1901, F.O. 17/1510.
[3] Memorandum by Lansdowne, confidential, of 25 Oct. 1901, S.P. Cabinet General, 1901; memorandum by Lansdowne of 25 Oct. 1901, F.O. 17/1510. The overture was rejected, and the information, on which Lansdowne based his move, incomplete. The Times of 9 Nov. 1901 gives notice of the Russian terms. Langer, The Diplomacy of Imperialism, 754 f., links this Manchurian move with an 'approach' to Russia. [4] The draft is contained in F.O. 46/547.
[5] Memorandum submitted by Baron Hayashi, 29 Oct. 1901, F.O. 46/563.

hand for Japan in Korea. Lansdowne remarked immediately to Hayashi that he did not like the form in which the clause had been drafted, but that he would find some means of meeting Japanese wishes.[1] On 5 November the Cabinet agreed on the conclusion of an alliance with Japan. On 6 November the preliminary draft of an agreement was handed to Hayashi.

The draft contained a preamble, four formal articles and a separate one. The preamble declared the intention of the two powers to maintain the *status quo* and the independence and territorial integrity of China and the right of equal opportunity. Korea was specifically mentioned in connection with these principles, to allow for the Japanese clause of 29 October. The four articles laid out the formula on which the treaty was based: strict neutrality by either power in the event of hostile action by any other single power (Art. 1); the duty of participation should either power be engaged by more than one other power (Art. 2); an undertaking that neither power would enter without previous consultation into separate arrangements prejudicial to the interests outlined in the preamble (Art. 3); and mutual communication should those interests be in jeopardy (Art. 4). The separate article provided for co-operation between the two navies, with mutual docking and coaling facilities.[2]

When Lansdowne handed the draft to the Japanese minister he observed that the proposed agreement, limited as it was to the Far East, seemed an 'incomplete solution of the question' and that the disappearance of Great Britain as a sea power would be a calamity for Japan regardless of whether the calamity were brought about by a quarrel in the Far East or in some other part of the world.[3] The observation was apparently prompted by the discussion which had taken place in the Cabinet meeting of the previous day. At that meeting, the Cabinet had also considered Selborne's memorandum of 4 September on the balance of naval power in the Far East. The report on the meeting has not been traced, but from the trend of the negotiations which followed it seems that the Cabinet wished to extend the application of the alliance beyond the

[1] Lansdowne to MacDonald, No. 113, secret, of 29 Oct. 1901, *B.D.* ii. 98.
[2] Contained in F.O. 46/563. The various stages of negotiation of the treaty are admirably set out in *B.D.* ii. 116–20.
[3] Lansdowne to MacDonald, No. 115, secret, of 6 Nov. 1901, *B.D.* ii. 99.

waters of the Far East, possibly to include India and south-east Asia. At the same time, some disquiet was voiced on the possible nature of Japan's ambitions in Korea. For his part, in accepting the British draft on 6 November, Hayashi remarked that the treatment of Korea in that draft did not sufficiently meet the requirements of Japan.[1]

An amended draft was not returned by Japan until 12 December. The reason for this display of reticence lay in the way Korea had been handled in the British draft. In turn, this brought out a division of opinion which existed in the Japanese Government over the question of an alliance with Great Britain. On the one hand, a group of ministers led by the Elder Statesman, Prince Ito Hirobumi, were inclined toward the view that Japan's best interests were served by an arrangement with Russia over Korea and Manchuria. Ito had come to office in September 1900 after the abortive Amoy incident, and throughout the negotiation of the Joint Note, Japan's advocacy of moderation and rapid withdrawal from north China, which accorded with Russia's policy, had been a matter of concern to Great Britain. At the beginning of May 1901 the Ito Cabinet fell. Viscount (later Prince) Katsura, the new Prime Minister, did not hold Ito's views and was more disposed to come to an arrangement with Great Britain. In this he was supported by Baron Komura, the Foreign Minister, and by Hayashi in London.[2]

The aim of both these groups was the extension of Japanese control over Korea. However, the Anglophile group was at a disadvantage in that an arrangement with Great Britain which was designed to maintain Japanese interests in Korea could not compare with an agreement which Ito could possibly arrange with Russia, allowing for the extension of those interests. By the summer of 1901 it was generally known that the occupation of Manchuria had become a burden on Russia. The Russian Government, in fact, were inclined toward an unconditional withdrawal from southern Manchuria and at this time Witte apparently made a further attempt to placate Japan by offering her advantages in Korea.[3] Moreover, in September Ito left

---

[1] Lansdowne to MacDonald, No. 115, secret, of 6 Nov. 1901, *B.D.* ii. 94.
[2] Ishii, *Diplomatic Commentaries*, 48–9.
[3] Romanov, *Russia in Manchuria*, 222–4, 227. Lamsdorff's inter-departmental

Japan for Europe to arrange a foreign loan, and with the further intention of visiting St. Petersburg. In mid-November he was met in Paris by Hayashi who showed him the British draft agreement. Ito, apparently surprised by the advanced state of the negotiations, appears to have pressed the Japanese Ambassador to hold the British proposals in abeyance until any Russian proposals could be examined.[1] Ito then travelled to St. Petersburg, where some minor and unsatisfactory concessions were offered by the Russians during informal conversations held at the beginning of December.[2] The results of these conversations were not known in Tokyo until 13 December, by which time the Japanese Government had already applied to Great Britain. Nevertheless, this meant that in examining the British proposals the Anglophile ministers were aware they could not afford to weaken over Korea.

In London there was some disillusion over the delay. When MacDonald was asked for an explanation, the British minister replied that it was because the Japanese Emperor, the Prime Minister, and the Cabinet had gone to attend the grand manoeuvres, and that the Foreign Minister had been laid up with pneumonia since 10 November.[3] These reasons had already been advanced by Hayashi and, apart from Komura's illness, did not carry conviction. More pertinently, MacDonald observed on 27 November that the Japanese were alarmed 'at the magnitude of this new departure' and were not quite comfortable about the way Korea had been handled in the British draft.[4] Lansdowne, who thought Japanese tardiness was to be explained by Ito's tour, was not reassured when MacDonald reported that although the Prince had no authority from the Japanese Government to undertake any negotiations, he was powerful enough to authorize himself to do so.[5]

letter of 18 June 1901 o.s. (1 July) from the *Krasnyi Arkhiv* is given in *CSPSR*, 19 (1935) 136 f.
   [1] Ishii, *Diplomatic Commentaries*, 44–6; Hayashi, *Memoirs*, 137–44.
   [2] Malozemoff, *Russian Far Eastern Policy*, 171–3. Ito's conversations with the Tsar, Lamsdorff, Witte, and others, translated from the official Japanese text which was published as an appendix to vol. i of Ito's secret memoirs, *Ito Hirobumi Hiroku*, 2 vols. (Tokyo, 1929–30), are given in K. Hamada, *Prince Ito* (London, 1936), 135 f.
   [3] MacDonald to Lansdowne, tel., private, of 22 Nov. 1901, Lansdowne Papers.
   [4] MacDonald to Lansdowne, tel. of 27 Nov. 1901, Lansdowne Papers.
   [5] MacDonald to Lansdowne, tel. 62 of 3 Dec. 1901, F.O. 46/542.

When the Japanese amendments were returned on 12 December, it was seen that Korea had been their concern.[1] In the preamble, where the British had suggested that the two powers were 'specially interested in preventing the absorption of Corea by any foreign Power', the Japanese had subtly amended this to read 'any other power' and then had added a separate clause which confirmed her own freedom of action in Korea:

(Separate) Article III: Great Britain recognizes that Japan may take such suitable measures as she deems necessary to safeguard and promote the preponderating interests which she actually possesses in Corea.

A further separate article, added by Japan, stipulated:

(Separate) Article II: Each of the High Contracting Parties shall endeavour to maintain in the Far East at all times naval forces superior in efficiency to the naval strength of any other Power which has the largest naval forces in the Far East.

The final important amendment suggested by Japan, in the main body of the treaty, was that the alliance should be restricted to five years, subject to renewal. Moreover, on returning the Japanese amendments Hayashi stated that Japan would prefer that the agreement should not be extended beyond the limits contemplated in the draft as it stood, and added, 'If India, the Straits Settlements, and Siam were to be brought within its scope, the liability would be one which the Japanese Government could not venture to assume.'[2]

Japan thus wanted a free hand in Korea and wished to dictate Great Britain's naval commitments in the Far East. She refused to extend the scope of the alliance, and preferred to restrict it to a term of five years, subject to renewal.

At the time Lansdowne observed to Hayashi that Great Britain would not be likely to agree to the new separate Article II

---

[1] In this section no attempt is made at a comprehensive analysis of either the terms or the negotiation of the treaty and attention is confined to those points which caught the attention of the Cabinet. References are drawn from the British Draft of 28 Oct. (i.e. Lansdowne's draft of 25 Oct.) containing the Japanese amendments, printed for the use of the Cabinet on 16 Dec. Memorandum by Lansdowne, most secret, of 16 Dec. 1901, S.P. Cabinet General, 1901.

[2] Memorandum by Lansdowne of 16 Dec. 1901, S.P. Cabinet General, 1901. The substance of this conversation was given to MacDonald, cf. B.D. ii. 102–3.

which specified the strength of naval forces to be maintained by each power. Great Britain's naval commitment in the Far East he explained, 'would have to be determined by Imperial considerations rather than with reference to purely local conditions'. Lansdowne also stressed that the new separate Article III indicating a free hand for Japan in Korea could be criticized. He added, 'it might have the effect of entangling us in war with two great European Powers all over the world on account of some comparatively trivial quarrel between Russia and Japan over matters of purely local interest'.[1]

On 16 December Lansdowne drew up a Cabinet memorandum in which he stated that the naval commitment was unacceptable. He thought, however, that this objection could be overcome if Great Britain accepted the five-year limitation, which would allow her to refuse a renewal if she were 'dissatisfied with the manner in which the other Party has contributed to the defence of common interests'. About the Japanese claim on Korea he remarked, 'What the Japanese evidently desire is to reserve to themselves a free hand to make a casus foederis out of any Russian encroachment in Corea.' As a safeguard he suggested amendments (in Arts. 1 and 4) which would specify the measures to be taken by either power in defence of their interests.[2]

On 17 and 19 December two further memoranda were handed in by Hayashi.[3] The memorandum of the 17th stated that if Great Britain could approve the Japanese amendments Hayashi was empowered to sign. The necessity for both powers to hold preponderating naval forces in the Far East was reaffirmed. So was the Japanese desire to limit the alliance to China and Korea. On Korea, Komura emphasized Japan's attitude more fully. He stated: 'Japan and Corea having peculiar relations on account of their geographical position, their history, commerce and industry, the Imperial Government consider it highly important that they should reserve to themselves a certain degree of liberty of action on the penin-

[1] Memorandum by Lansdowne of 16 Dec. 1901, S.P. Cabinet General, 1901.
[2] Memorandum by Lansdowne, most secret, printed for the use of the Cabinet on 16 Dec. 1901, S.P. Cabinet General, 1901.
[3] Memorandum by Lansdowne, most secret, printed for the use of the Cabinet, 17 Dec. 1901; Japanese communication of 19 Dec. 1901, printed for the use of the Cabinet on 24 Dec. 1901, S.P. Cabinet General, 1901.

sula. . . .' The second memorandum rejected the British suggestion that either power should specify the measures it intended to take in defence of its interests. In explanation, Komura stressed that disturbances tended to arise suddenly in Korea, demanding prompt action and making consultation with Great Britain impossible in most cases. To reassure the British, Komura added that Japanese policy was in strict accordance with the Nishi–Rosen Agreement of 1898. On the naval commitment clause Komura pointed out that although this would be more burdensome to Japan than to Great Britain, who had reserves to call on, Japan was nevertheless prepared to assume that burden.[1] It was then stressed that the balance of advantage could not be said to rest with Japan for, although the Yangtze was quiet at the moment, serious trouble could arise there. Finally, Japan inquired about German participation, but agreed to defer to Great Britain on this.

At the Cabinet meeting of 19 December the idea of a Japanese alliance was generally accepted, and 'the differences of opinion' as Salisbury reported to the King, 'were more with respect to details than to substance . . .'.[2] Discussion centred on the naval clauses and Korea. It was felt that the agreement offered by the Japanese was much too one-sided, and that Japan's gains in Korea should be balanced by extending the alliance to cover India and Siam. The naval commitment clause was rejected. On 16 November Selborne had again reminded the Cabinet of the heavy expenditure involved in Great Britain's need to match foreign naval expansion. 'As long as France and Russia continue their present scale of new construction we cannot lessen ours,' Selborne stressed, 'nor is it possible for us to ignore the growth of naval power all the world over. The real fact is that we have run our margin of naval strength to a finer point than prudence warrants. . . .'[3] The Japanese proposal would have forced Great Britain to match Russia's expanding fleet in

[1] On 11 Dec. Komura explained to MacDonald that the aim was to make the naval strength of the allies in the east strong enough to cope with Russia and France and, in case of need, also with Germany, MacDonald to Lansdowne, No. 151A, secret, of 11 Dec. 1901, F.O. 46/563.

[2] Salisbury's report to the King is quoted in Goudswaard, *Some Aspects of the End of Britain's 'Splendid Isolation'*, 85.

[3] Memorandum by Selborne, 'The Navy Estimates and the Chancellor of the Exchequer's Memorandum on the Growth of Expenditure', confidential, 16 Nov. 1901, pp. 5–6, S.P. Cabinet General, 1901.

the Far East and would have nullified the very purpose which
had led the Admiralty to favour the alliance in the first instance.
Salisbury reported to the King: '... the Cabinet (were) disposed
to reject a proposal that each Power should bind itself always
to keep in Japanese seas a fixed naval force. We could not
sacrifice the free disposal of our ships and the Japanese treaty
would not repay us for the surrender.'[1]

From mid-December until the signing of the treaty on
30 January 1902 discussion continued on the Korean question
and on the naval issue. At a Cabinet meeting, perhaps that of
24 December, it was decided to reject the separate articles
which covered these issues and which Japan wanted to keep
secret while publishing the rest of the treaty.

On 31 December Hayashi submitted a draft Diplomatic
Note to replace them.[2] 'It is an informal proposal which the
Japanese Government will make officially, if it commends itself
to us . . .', Lansdowne observed when forwarding it to Salisbury.[3] In the Note Japan reaffirmed her claim over Korea.
The relevant section (paragraph 3) read '. . . in view of Japan's
preponderating interests in that country, Great Britain recognizes the right of Japan to take such measures as she may find
necessary to safeguard and promote those interests'. Lansdowne
thought the paragraph a little alarming, but added

there is, so far as I can see, no halfway house between such a recognition of Japanese preponderance in Corea, and a stipulation that
Japan is not to be allowed to pick quarrels with Russia except with
our permission and that if she does become involved in such quarrels
without our approval, the casus foederis will not be held by us to
have arisen. To such a stipulation Japan would not, I think I may
say 'could not', agree.[3]

Lansdowne drew Salisbury's attention to the fact that there
was to be no Cabinet meeting for a few days, then concluded
that the other members of the Cabinet were 'content to leave

---

[1] p. 313, n. 2.
[2] Memorandum by Baron Hayashi of 31 Dec. 1901, F.O. 46/563. It was minuted
by Lansdowne and forwarded to Salisbury as Paper A on the same day; accompanied by the views of Selborne, Hicks Beach, James, Balfour of Burleigh, Ritchie,
Chamberlain, and Walter Kerr. Lansdowne to Salisbury, 31 Dec. 1901, encls.,
Lansdowne Papers.
[3] Lansdowne to Salisbury, minute of 31 Dec. 1901, Lansdowne Papers.

the settlement of this matter to your decision. Do you think we may close with the Japanese? Hayashi is very anxious to avoid further delay.'[1]

However, Lansdowne's anxiety to close the matter was not shared by the majority of the Cabinet. Over the next few days Hicks Beach, Chamberlain, Selborne, Ritchie, and Balfour declared themselves against accepting the Diplomatic Note as it stood. The Chancellor of the Exchequer thought strongly that it ought to be considered again in Cabinet. 'The Japanese proposal . . .', he declared, 'seems simply that the provisions which we rejected as "secret articles" should be agreed to in the form of a "Confidential note" which is quite as objectionable.'[2] Balfour and Chamberlain were inclined to the same opinion. Hicks Beach argued further that as 'this apparently harmless treaty' would have to be published it should not be secretly supplemented, particularly in that it was a new departure in foreign policy, '. . . if we are to have a treaty, it must be above board'.[2]

Again it was felt that the treaty was much too one-sided. Japan was to get all she wanted in Korea, while the British proposal to extend the alliance to cover India had been abandoned. Hicks Beach pointed out that there was no reciprocal recognition of British interests in the Yangtze, and that it should be correlated with Korea.[2] In this he was supported by Balfour and Chamberlain. Chamberlain argued that the Yangtze should be written into the treaty, but he was prepared to drop the suggestion if need be.[3] But the Cabinet were fighting a rearguard action; in the final text only the protection of British interests with regard to China generally was correlated with the Korea clause.

The only remaining point on which a stand could be made was the commitment of British naval strength in eastern waters. It was on this issue that the interest of the Admiralty had first been aroused and which had turned the understanding with Japan from an agreement relating to Chinese affairs into an alliance capable of world-wide implications. If Great Britain were committed to matching Russian naval expansion in

---

[1] Ibid.
[2] Hicks Beach to Lansdowne, 2 Jan. 1902, Lansdowne Papers.
[3] Chamberlain to Lansdowne (undated), Lansdowne Papers.

the Far East, she could not look to the alliance for relief of her over-all naval expenditure. The alliance would then be meaningless, except in so far as it prevented Japan from gravitating into the Dual Alliance camp. However, open reliance on external help was a difficult role for the First Sea Power. When the Diplomatic Note of 31 December came up for consideration, on the clause relating to the maintenance of naval superiority over any third power Selborne gave his approval if tonnage were meant, not numerical superiority in any and every class of ship.[1] A few days later Selborne wrote to Lansdowne:

> I hope that in the next five years we shall teach the Japanese 3 things which they do not at present understand and where they have gone quite wrong.
>
> 1. The sea is one. If England were beaten by a quarrel in Europe the Japanese were as fatally affected as if the quarrel were over the Yangtze.
> 2. The proper standard should have been that the combined fleet was superior to the combined fleet of any two powers on the China station.
> 3. The standard should not have been by tonnage but by numbers in the different classes of ships.[2]

A draft treaty was drawn up on 14 January 1902.[3] In the accompanying Diplomatic Note naval commitment in terms of tonnage was implied, though not specifically stated. The Japanese amendments were returned on 18 January. To the general recognition of her special interests in Korea Japan had added specific mention of her 'political as well as commercial and industrial' interests in that country. This was then amended by Salisbury to a special recognition of Japan's political and commercial interests in Korea. Balfour, Hicks Beach, and Chamberlain then gave their approval,[4] and the treaty was handed to Hayashi on the 24th. The latter indicated the acceptance of his Government on the 27th.[5] On the next day

---

[1] Selborne to Lansdowne, secret, of 2 Jan. 1902, Lansdowne Papers.

[2] Selborne to Lansdowne, 7 Jan. 1902, Lansdowne Papers. Selborne's opinion of the Japanese fleet was that it was 'good' but restricted by a lack of funds, 'unfortunately the Russian purse is the longest of the two'. Memorandum by Selborne of 16 Nov. 1901, S.P. Cabinet General, 1901.

[3] Contained in F.O. 46/563.

[4] Lansdowne to Balfour, minuted, 21 Jan. 1902, F.O. 46/563.

[5] Memorandum by Barrington of 27 Jan. 1902, F.O. 46/563.

Hayashi insisted on the recognition of Japan's special industrial interests in Korea, and this was conceded by Great Britain.[1] The Agreement was then signed on 30 January 1902.[2]

The Anglo-Japanese Alliance removed the feeling of diplomatic isolation which had oppressed the British Government since 1898 and which had put them on the defensive in their conduct of Chinese affairs. From that date it had been accepted that the development of communication with the east along the Siberian railway would give Russia an increasing influence in China. It was realized that without a suitable reply to the Dual Alliance Great Britain had to acquiesce in this situation. Salisbury rejected the idea of any Anglo-German alliance to meet this challenge which could involve Great Britain in Europe. Instead, he endeavoured to come to an understanding with Russia in order to maintain British interests in China intact. By 1899 Great Britain admitted the changed situation in China on the basis of a tacit acceptance of a policy of spheres.

However, the Boxer rising of June 1900 indicated a further deterioration in the Chinese situation. It was probable that Russia would take advantage of the unrest to secure a hold on north China and that, in the period after the relief of the legations, Germany would seek to execute a policy of reprisal into the interior and on the Yangtze. To meet these possibilities, Great Britain negotiated the Anglo-German Agreement. At the same time, in respect of the settlement with China, she entered into a period of careful negotiation at Peking.

Throughout the autumn and winter of 1900–1, British policy in China was conducted with an awareness of Great Britain's isolated diplomatic position and of her inability to take a strong stand in defence of her interests because of her commitments in the South African war. Consequently, she sought to discourage any measures which would favour the aggressive tendencies of the other powers. In the negotiations at Peking she opposed the suggestion of punitive expeditions into the interior, which could possibly have led to the partition of China, and she opposed the proposal for a withdrawal from the Chinese capital, which would have encouraged Russian ambitions in the north.

Salisbury's aim, during this period, was to work for the

[1] Memorandum by Hayashi of 28 Jan. 1902, F.O. 46/563.
[2] Text is given in F.O. 46/563.

restoration of the situation which had been established in China before the Boxer rising. He tolerated the attempts which were made to secure German co-operation, but, because it seemed the only possible way, his faith was in a re-establishment of the Anglo-Russian understanding of 1899.

The emergence of Japan at the time of the Manchurian crisis provided an alternative means by which Russian expansion could be opposed and by which British interests in the east could be maintained. Salisbury realized this possibility, and as early as February 1901 he gave it his support.

The Anglo-Japanese Alliance was a practical means of meeting Great Britain's diplomatic needs at the time. It helped to maintain British interests in the east without committing Great Britain in Europe, which appeared to be the only way in which a reliable German arrangement could be secured. It opposed continued Russian expansion, without involving Great Britain in a direct alignment against Russia.[1] Finally, as Sanderson noted, it had 'a steadying effect on Japan'[2] and prevented that power from seeking an alternative arrangement with Russia. These considerations, which emerged as a result of the Boxer rising of 1900, were sufficient to bring about a reorientation of British policy, leading to a new departure in foreign affairs.

---

[1] This was the continental view of the growing Anglo-Japanese *rapprochement*. 'Il faut empêcher l'Angleterre de trouver en Extrême-Orient dans le Japon le soldat qui lui manque.' Beau (the French minister at Peking) to Delcasse, 1 July 1901, *D.D.F.* (2e série), i. 365.

[2] Sanderson to Satow, 9 May 1902, P.R.O. 30/33/7/2.

APPENDIX I

FOREIGN TRADE OF CHINA
1899

(Drawn from Statistical Abstract of the Board of Trade and Imperial Maritime
Customs, Report (1899), p. 9, and Imperial Maritime Customs Returns of Trade
and Trade Reports (1898), Pt. 1; (1899), Pt. 2. These figures were the latest
available to the British Government at the time of the Boxer Rising.)

Trading figures for 1899 were:

Country	Total trade (in pounds sterling)
Great Britain	8,118,549 (direct)
Hong Kong	28,491,264 (including trade of all countries through Hong Kong)
Germany	3,598,200
France	9,292,206 (imports into France 9,074,280; exports from France 217,926)
U.S.A.	6,596,169
Russia	1,286,508 (by sea)
	1,498,155 (by Kiakhta)
Japan	7,972,183

In percentages (for British control of the shipping trade)

	1898	1899
British	65%	61%
Foreign	35%	39%
(for values of goods carried)		
British	54%	53%
Foreign	56%	47%

APPENDIX II

THE JOINT NOTE

(Source: Chinese Legation, London, Despatches, June 1900–February 1901; issued and received by Sir Chihchen Lofenglu.)

During the months of May, June, July and August of the present year serious disorders broke out in the northern provinces of China, and crimes unprecedented in human history, crimes against the law of nations, against the laws of humanity and against civilization, were committed under peculiarly odious circumstances. The principal of these crimes were the following:

1. On 20th June, His Excellency Baron Ketteler, German Minister, proceeding to the Tsungli Yamen, was murdered while in the exercise of his official duties by soldiers of the regular army, acting under the orders of their chiefs.

2. On the same day the foreign Legations were attacked and besieged, and these attacks continued without intermission until 14th August, on which date the arrival of foreign troops put an end to them. The attacks were made by regular troops who joined the Boxers, who obeyed the order of the Court, emanating from the Imperial Palace. At the same time the Chinese Government officially declared by its Representatives abroad that it guaranteed the safety of the Legations.

3. On 11th June M. Sugiyama, Chancellor of the Japanese Legation, in the discharge of an official mission, was killed by regulars at the gates of the city. At Peking and in several provinces, foreigners were murdered, tortured, or attacked by Boxers and regular troops, and only owed their safety to their determined resistance. Their establishments were pillaged and destroyed.

4. Foreign Cemeteries at Peking especially were desecrated, the graves opened, and the remains scattered abroad.

These events led the foreign Powers to send their troops to China in order to protect the lives of their Representatives and to restore order. During their march to Peking the allied forces met with the resistance of the Chinese armies and had to overcome it by force. China, having recognised her responsibility, expressed her regrets, and manifested the desire to see an end put to the situation created by the disturbances referred to, the Powers have decided to accede to her request on the irrevocable conditions enumerated below, which they deem indispensable to expatiate the crimes committed and prevent their recurrence:

Article 1

(a) Prompt despatch to Berlin of an Extraordinary Mission, headed by an Imperial Prince, to express the regrets of His Majesty the Emperor of China and the Chinese Government for the murder of His Excellency the late Baron Ketteler, German Minister.

(b) Erection on the place where the murder was committed of a commemorative monument suitable to the rank of the deceased, bearing an inscription in the Latin, German and Chinese languages, expressing the regret of the Emperor of China for the murder.

Article 2

(a) The severest punishment in proportion to their crimes for the persons named in the Imperial Decree of September 25, 1900, and for those whom the Representatives of the Powers shall subsequently designate.

(b) Suspension of all official examinations for five years in all the towns where foreigners have been massacred or have been subjected to cruel treatment.

Article 3

An honourable reparation shall be accorded by the Chinese Government to that of Japan for the murder of Mr. Sugiyama, Chancellor of the Japanese Legation.

Article 4

An expiatory monument shall be created by the Chinese Government in each of the foreign or international cemeteries which have been desecrated, and in which the graves have been destroyed.

Article 5

Maintenance, under conditions to be settled between the Powers, of the prohibition of the importation of arms, as well as the material serving exclusively for the manufacture of arms and ammunition.

Article 6

An equitable indemnity to Governments, societies, companies, private individuals, as well as for Chinese who have suffered during the recent occurrences in their persons or property, in consequence of their being in the service of foreigners.

The Chinese Government shall adopt financial measures acceptable to the Powers for the purpose of guaranteeing the payment of the said indemnities and the interest and amortisation of the loans.

Article 7

The right of maintaining, by each Power, a permanent guard for its Legation, and of placing the Legation quarters in a condition of defence. Chinese not to have the right of residing there.

Article 8

The Taku and other forts, which might impede free communication between Peking and the coast, are to be razed.

Article 9

The military occupation of certain points to be determined by agreement between the Plenipotentiaries in order to maintain communication between the capital and the sea.

Article 10

The Chinese Government shall cause to be published for two years in all the sub-prefectures an Imperial Decree embodying:

(a) Perpetual prohibition under pain of death of being a member of an anti-foreign society.

(b) Enumeration of the penalties which shall have been inflicted on the guilty persons including the suspension of all official examinations in the towns where foreigners were massacred or subjected to cruel treatment.

(c) For a further guarantee against future trouble an Imperial Edict shall be issued and published everywhere in the Empire de jure, making all Viceroys, provincial and local officials, responsible for order in their respective jurisdictions; and whenever anti-foreign disturbances or any other Treaty infractions occur therein which are not forthwith suppressed and the guilty persons punished.

Article 11

The Chinese Government will undertake to negotiate regarding amendments to the Treaties of commerce and navigation considered useful by the Powers, and also other subjects connected with commercial relations with the object of facilitating them.

Article 12

The Chinese Government shall undertake to reform the office of foreign relations, and modify the Court ceremonial relative to the reception of foreign Representatives in the manner which the Powers shall indicate.

Until the Chinese Government have complied with the above conditions to the satisfaction of the Powers the undersigned can hold out no expectation that the occupation of Peking and the Province of Pechili by the allied forces can be brought to a conclusion.

Received December 21, 1900.

BIBLIOGRAPHY

PRIMARY SOURCES

A. OFFICIAL

Foreign Office General Correspondence (Public Record Office)

To a large extent this study is based on the Foreign Office General Correspondence, China Series, F.O. 17/ . There are 362 volumes, which cover the years 1895–1902. The international nature of the Boxer settlement has made it necessary to refer also to the General Correspondence relating to various other countries. Principally, these are Japan, F.O. 46/ ; Germany (Prussia), F.O. 64/ ; Russia, F.O. 65/ ; France, F.O. 27/ ; and the United States, F.O. 5/ .

In using the Foreign Office Correspondence, reference has been made, in the first instance, to the telegraphic drafts and dispatches between the Foreign Office and the British ambassadors abroad. The Boxer Rising was the first major international incident in which diplomacy was carried out on the basis of these telegraphic reports. The time taken in transmission varied from a few hours to two weeks or more, owing to the disruption in communications at the time. When the numerical sequence of these telegrams is examined it will be seen that a large number of reports have been misplaced, or are missing. Some of these are to be found attached to later dispatches, or are misbound in other volumes. Where these have not been located, or when the decypher is obscure, recourse has been made to the copies which were circulated to other government departments. For the events of the summer of 1900, when serious gaps occur in the sequence of the telegraphic reports located in the General Correspondence, extensive use has been made of the copies found in the Admiralty Papers.

The telegraphic reports are supplemented by the Diplomatic drafts and dispatches, which were transmitted by sea. This meant a delay of about five weeks before they reached Shanghai, and a week to ten days after that before they reached Peking. They had no great influence on the conduct of policy, and are mainly useful for the detail they provide. Extensive use has also been made of the departmental and inter-departmental memoranda and minutes which circulated among the various ministers and the permanent Foreign Office staff. These are to be found scattered throughout the Correspondence and attached to the incoming dispatches. In the China series the Volumes Various provide a rich quarry for this miscellaneous material.

Cabinet Papers (Public Record Office)

Particularly Cabinet 1 and Cabinet 37, which usefully indicated correspondence and memoranda specifically brought to the attention of the Cabinet.

The Embassy and Consular Archives (Public Record Office)

The China series are located under F.O. 228/   . This material provides a detailed picture of the activities of the British minister at Peking and of the British consular officials at the various treaty ports. Instructions from the Foreign Office, the drafts of which are missing from the General Correspondence, may be located in this series. Volumes of particular interest are as follows: F.O. 228/1350, Dispatches to and from Chinese Authorities, 1900; F.O. 230/143, 144, Letter Books, to and from Yamen, 1900; F.O. 233/44, Record Book of Interviews with Chinese Authorities, etc., 30 June 1897–31 October 1899, indexed; F.O. 233/124, Chinese Secretary's Office, Vol. 52, Misc. Papers, Chinese and English.

Colonial Office Correspondence (Public Record Office)

C.O. 521/1, 2, 3 contain the Dispatches for 1898–1902 in relation to the affairs of Weihaiwei (WHW.).

Admiralty Papers (Public Record Office)

These Papers provide valuable material on the measures taken for the relief of the legations, on the safety of the Yangtze, and on the appointment of Waldersee, as well as the routine C.-in-C. reports to the Admiralty on the movement of ships, etc. The relevant files are located under Adm. 1/ and Adm. 116/   .

War Office Papers (Public Record Office)

The material in these Papers is of a more general nature than that which is to be found in the Admiralty Papers. The W.O. 32/   files contain the routine reports relating to the China Expedition. The W.O. 106/   files provide military and intelligence reports, as well as collected material, relating to China, of a military nature.

B. PRIVATE PAPERS

Salisbury Papers (Christ Church Library, Oxford)

Material which has been drawn from this essential source has been cited by (*a*) bound volumes, (*b*) boxes, and (*c*) unclassified material.

A general Index for the bound volumes is available. The following are of particular interest:

Vol. 83—from Queen Victoria.
    84—to Queen Victoria.
    89—Cabinet Memoranda.
    93—Admiralty and War Office.
    95—Under-Secretaries.
    96—Private Secretaries and Memoranda.
    97—Admiral Lord Charles Beresford.
   106—China and Siam.

Vol. 114–19—France.
    120–2—Germany.
    126—Japan.
    129—Russia.
    139–40—United States.

In this study, material which has been cited from the boxes has been given the requisite descriptive legend, (e.g. S.P. Cabinet General 1901). Unclassified material has been so cited.

Personal Papers of Lord Lansdowne and Sir T. Sanderson, 1898–1905 (Foreign Office Library and Public Record Office)

Valuable for the period after November 1900, particularly in connection with the negotiation of the later stages of the Joint Note, the peace settlement with the Chinese from January to September 1901, and the Anglo-Japanese Alliance. The Papers are in bound volumes and are not indexed. They have been cited as the Lansdowne Papers; located, F.O. 277/   ·
The Sanderson Papers, located F.O. 800, are available for the period from 1897.

Chamberlain Papers (University Library, Birmingham)

The papers of Joseph Chamberlain, Secretary of State for the Colonies, 1895–1903, contain very little on the Far East.

Hamilton Papers (India Office Library)

Lord George Hamilton was Secretary of State for India from 1895 to 1903. The Collection, during this period, comprises one printed volume and thirty-four containing printed, typescript, and manuscript material. Cited as the Hamilton Papers, located as follows:

Private Correspondence, India, Hamilton to Curzon:

Vol. 1 (1899) C 126/1.
    2 (1900) C 126/2.
    3 (1901) C 126/3.

Private Correspondence, India, Pt. 2, Curzon to Hamilton:

Vols. 16–18 (1900) D 510/4–6.
    19–21 (1901) D 510/7–9.

Ardagh Papers (Public Record Office)

The Papers of Major-General Ardagh, Director-General of Mobilization and Military Intelligence, are located in the collection P.R.O. 30/40, and are listed under 'Gifts and Deposits'. The following are of particular interest:

P.R.O. 30/40/6 Diaries and Private Memoranda, 1867–1901.

P.R.O. 30/40/14 Memoranda, D.M.I. Misc., 1896–1901 (Military and Political), 2 vols.

Satow Papers (Public Record Office)

Sir Ernest Satow was British Minister at Tokyo, 1895–1900, and at Peking, 1900–6. His Papers are located in the collection P.R.O. 30/33, and are listed under 'Gifts and Deposits'. They are an essential source; the relevant material for this period is located as follows:

P.R.O. 30/33/7/1	Correspondence and Private Papers, Chinese Mission, Aug. 1900–Dec. 1901.
P.R.O. 30/33/7/2	Ibid., 1902–3.
P.R.O. 30/33/7/9	Ibid., Various; including Satow's memoranda.
P.R.O. 30/33/7/11	Ibid., Legation Staff Papers.
P.R.O. 30/33/8/1–24	
/9/1–9	Corr. Consular Staff, Treaty Ports.
P.R.O. 30/33/9/14	Satow's Corr. with MacDonald, etc.
/9/18, 19	Ibid., with Creagh, Gaselee.
/9/23	Ibid., with naval authorities.
/9/24	Ibid., with Chinese authorities.
/10/1	Ibid., with Foreign Representatives.
/10/4–11	Misc., Various.
P.R.O. 30/33/14/11–13	Letter Books.
P.R.O. 30/33/16/3–6	Diary, 11 Oct. 1899–21 Dec. 1903.

Mission Archives

The archives of the various societies provide a detailed picture of the work of the missions in China. The reports and letters home are noticeably of a non-political nature and thus contrast sharply with the reports of the Consular officials which are to be found in the Embassy and Consular Archives. It has been necessary to refer primarily to missionary activity as it was reflected in Consular opinion, for the effect which this had on the formulation of British policy. The following archives have been inspected:

London Missionary Society
North China 5 Boxes (1894–5, 1896–8, 1899–1900, 1901, 1902).
South China 2 Boxes (1898–1900, 1901–3).
Church Missionary Society
Valuable for reports from Central and Southern China:
Fuh-kien Mission (G 1 CH4/P1, 1900–8).
Mid-China Mission (G 1 CH2/P2, 1895–1902).
Society for the Propagation of the Gospel: *S.P.G. Missionary Reports* (Originals) Africa and Asia, 1899, 1900. Copies of this correspondence are also to be found in *China letters received*, Vol. 2.

C. BRITISH PRINTED MATERIAL

The Parliamentary Papers

The Blue Books were edited considerably during this period and they do not provide an adequate account of British diplomacy. The relevant issues, cited by Command number, date of issue, and A & P references are given below:

Treaty Series, No. 7 (1897). Agreement between Great Britain and China, modifying the Convention of 1 March 1894 relative to Burmah and Thibet; Map. Signed at Peking 4 Feb. 1897. C 8654 (1898) CV 129.

China No. 2 (1898). Despatch from H.M. Minister at Peking, forwarding the Notes exchanged with the Chinese Government respecting the Non-alienation of the Yang-Tsze Region. Dated Feb. 1898. C. 8940 (1898). CV 139.

Treaty Series, No. 14 (1898). Convention between the United Kingdom and China respecting WHW. Signed at Peking 1 July 1898. C. 9081 (1899). CIX 635.

Treaty Series, No. 16 (1898). Convention between the United Kingdom and China respecting the extension of Hong Kong Territory. Signed at Peking 9 June 1898. C. 9087 (1899). CIX 639.

China No. 1 (1898). Correspondence respecting the Affairs of China. C. 8814 (1898). CV 53.

China No. 3 (1898). Despatch from H.M. Minister at Peking, forwarding a Report by the Acting British Consul at Ssu-mao on the Trade of Yunnan. C. 9083 (1899). CIX 745.

China No. 1 (1899). Correspondence respecting the Affairs of China. C. 9131 (1899). CIX 251.

Correspondence between H.M. Government and the Russian Government with regard to their respective Railway interests in China. C. 9329 (1899). CIX.

Exchange of Notes between the United Kingdom and Russia with regard to their respective Railway interests in China. C. 9241 (1899). CX.

China No. 1 (1900). Further Correspondence respecting the Affairs of China. Cd. 93. CV 85.

China No. 2 (1900). Correspondence with the United States Government respecting Foreign Trade in China. Cd. 94. CV 731.

China No. 3 (1900). Correspondence respecting the Insurrectionary Movement in China. Cd. 257. CV 523.

China No. 4 (1900). Reports from H.M. Minister in China respecting events in Peking. Cd. 364. CV 655.

China No. 5 (1900). Correspondence respecting the Anglo-German Agreement of 16 Oct. 1900, relating to China. Cd. 365. CV 719.

China No. 1 (1901). Correspondence respecting the disturbances in China. Cd. 436. XCI 1.

China No. 2 (1901). Despatch from H.M. Ambassador at St. Petersburg respecting the Russo-Chinese Agreement as to Manchuria. Cd. 439. XCI 735.

China No. 3 (1901). Further Correspondence respecting events at Peking. Cd. 442. XCI 739.

China No. 4 (1901). Further Correspondence respecting events at Peking. Cd. 443. XCI 775.

China No. 5 (1901). Further Correspondence respecting the disturbances in China. Cd. 589. XCI 225.

China No. 6 (1901). Further Correspondence respecting the disturbances in China. Cd. 675. XCI 403.

China No. 7 (1901). Correspondence respecting the Imperial Railway of north China. Cd. 770. XCI 593.

Correspondence relating to the evacuation of the Summer Palace at

Peking by the British troops. East India, China Expedition (1900–1). Cd. 877. LXX.
China No. 1 (1902). Correspondence respecting the Affairs of China. Cd. 1005. CXXX 61.
China No. 2 (1902). Despatch from H.M. Special Commissioner, inclosing the Treaty between Great Britain and China. Signed at Shanghai 5 Sept. 1902. Cd. 1079. CXXX 375.
China No. 3 (1902). Correspondence respecting the evacuation of Shanghai. Cd. 1369. CXXX 353.
Final Protocol between the Foreign Powers and China for the resumption of friendly relations. Signed at Peking 7 Sept. 1901. Cd. 1390. LXXXVII.
Treaty between the United Kingdom and China respecting Commercial relations, etc. Signed at Shanghai 5 Sept. 1902. Ratifications exchanged 28 July 1903. Cd. 1834 (1904). CX 269.
Correspondence respecting the Russian occupation of Manchuria and Newchwang. Cd. 1936 (1904). CX 121.

The Parliamentary Debates

Cited by series and volumes in the text. For public addresses by ministers and others at semi-official and private functions, reference has been made to the *Extra-Parliamentary Hansard*, 1899–1900, 1900–1.

Great Britain, Foreign Office. Regulations made by H.B.M. Minister at Peking. London, 1902.
Great Britain, Foreign Office. Diplomatic and Consular Reports on Trade and Finance. Annual Series, 1893–1911.
Great Britain, Foreign Office. Diplomatic and Consular Reports on Trade and Finance. Miscellaneous Series, 1894–9.
GOOCH, G. P. and H. TEMPERLEY (eds.). *British documents on the origins of the war, 1898–1914*. Vols. I and II: *From the occupation of Kiao-Chau to the making of the Anglo-French Entente, December 1897–April 1904*. H.M.S.O., 1927.

D. FOREIGN PRINTED MATERIAL

CHINA. Imperial Edicts and related material have been taken from *Ta-ch'ing li-ch'ao shih-lu* (Veritable records of successive reigns of the Ch'ing Dynasty), 4485 chuan, Tokyo, 1937–8. Cited *T.T.S.L.*, by volume. Edicts relating to the Boxer Rising, from the *Ch'ing Shih-lu*, are to be found in Chien Po-tsan (ed.), *I-ho-t'uan (tzu-liao ts'ung-k'an)*, 4 vols., Shanghai, 1951; 3rd ed. 1953, iv. 1 f. Cited *I.H.T.*
—— Chinese Legation, London, Despatches, June 1900–February 1901, issued and received by Sir Chihchen Lofenglu, K.C.V.O. Bound volume, typescript.
FRANCE. Ministère des Affaires Étrangères, *Documents diplomatiques: Chine, 1894–1901*. 5 Parts: *1894–8*, Paris, 1898; *1898–9*, Paris, 1900; *1899–1900*, Paris, 1900; *1900–1*, Paris, 1901; *June–Oct. 1901*, Paris, 1901.

FRANCE. Ministère des Affaires Étrangères, Commission de publication des documents relatifs aux origines de la guerre de 1914, *Documents diplomatiques français, 1871–1914*. 1ʳᵉ série, *1871–1900*: tomes 1–15, *1871–99* (in progress), 15 vols. in 16, Paris, 1929–59. Cited *D.D.F.* Vol. 15, published in 1959, covers the period 2 Jan.–14 Nov. 1899, providing information on foreign rivalries in China and the French attitude to the Anglo-Russian Agreement. 2ᵉ série, *1901–11*: tomes 1–14, 14 vols. in 13, Paris, 1930–55. Vol. 1 provides information on the Boxer settlement, Manchuria, and Japan; Vol. 2, on German policy in China, the evacuation of Shanghai, Manchuria, and the Anglo-Japanese Alliance.

GERMANY. Auswärtiger Amt., J. Lepsius, A. M. Bartholdy, and F. Thimme (eds.), *Die grosse Politik der europäischen Kabinette, 1871–1914* (Sammlung der diplomatischen Akten des Auswärtigen Amtes . . .), 40 vols. in 54, Berlin, 1922–7. See particularly Vol. 14, Pt. 1: *Weltpolitische Rivalitäten*; Vol. 16: *Die Chinawirren und die Mächte, 1900–1902*.

RUSSIA. Russian material from the *Krasnyi Arkhiv* (Red Archives) has only been used in the translation, from the *Chinese Social and Political Science Review*, to which reference has been made in the notes.

UNITED STATES. Congress, Foreign Affairs Committee, *Papers relating to the Foreign Affairs of the United States*, Washington, D.C., 1868– . Annual volumes, cited as *Foreign Relations*.

—— *Foreign relations of the United States, 1901*, Appendix: 'Affairs in China. Report of William W. Rockhill, Late Commissioner to China, with accompanying documents', Washington, 1902.

SECONDARY SOURCES AND MATERIALS

E. COLLECTIONS OF TREATIES AND SEMI-OFFICIAL PUBLICATIONS

MacMurray, J. V. A. *Treaties and agreements with and concerning China, 1894–1919*, 2 vols. New York, 1921.

China, Imperial Maritime Customs, *Treaties, Conventions, etc., between China and foreign states*, 2 vols. 2nd ed., Shanghai, 1917.

—— —— *Returns of trade at the treaty ports and trade reports*. Shanghai, 1882–1912.

—— —— *Decennial reports on the trade navigation, industries, etc., of the ports open to foreign commerce in China and on the condition and development of the treaty port provinces*. Shanghai, 1892–1901, 1902–11.

China Association, The. The Report for 1900 is given in F.O. 17/1449.

F. NEWSPAPERS AND PERIODICAL LITERATURE

Newspapers referred to in this study are cited in the Notes. Contemporary periodical literature is listed in Section G.

G. CONTEMPORARY MATERIAL

This Section contains published and unpublished contemporary material relating to the Boxer Rising and to British policy in China between 1895 and 1902. Anonymous periodical literature is listed under the title of the magazine. Brief notes are appended where necessary.

ALLEN, REVD. R. *The siege of the Peking legations.* London, 1901.

—— 'Of some of the causes which led to the preservation of the foreign legations in Peking', *Cornhill Magazine*, N.S. 54 (Dec. 1900), 754–76.

ALLIER, R. *Les Troubles de Chine et les missions chrétiennes.* Paris, 1901.

ANONYMOUS. 'Note sur la situation des Anglais dans le bassin du Yang-tsé-Kiang.' Paris, 1900.

—— *The rise and progress of the Boxer movement in China.* Extracts from the Reports of the American Bible Society's representative in Tientsin. Yokohama, 1900.

—— 'Further news of the massacres in Shansi.' Shanghai, 1901.

ANSCHUTZ, G. 'The Boxers', *The American Monthly Review of Reviews*, 22 (Sept. 1900), 338–9.

ANTHOUARD, BARON D'. *La Chine contre l'étranger: les Boxeurs.* Paris, 1902. (Anthouard was the First Secretary of the French Legation at Peking.)

'The Author of 1920'. 'Our future empire in the Far East', *Contemp. Rev.* 74 (Aug. 1898), 153–66.

BAINBRIDGE, E. 'China and the Powers', *Contemp. Rev.* 78 (Aug. 1900), 172–82.

BARASCUD, A. C. *Campagne de Chine, 1900–1901.* Vannes, 1903.

BARNES, A. A. S. *On active service with the Chinese regiment: a record of the operations of the First Chinese Regiment in North China from March to October 1900.* London, 1902.

(BARROW, COL.) Intelligence Branch of Q.M.G. Dept. Simla, *Short military report on the province of Chi-li.* Simla, 1900. Also see Sir George de Symons Barrow, *Fire of life*, London, 1942.

BARTON, A. 'The Yang-tsze valley and British commerce', *Imp. and Asiatic Q. Rev.* 3rd Ser. 6 (July 1898), 62–8.

BAZIN, R. *L'Enseigne de vaisseau P. Henry.* Tours, 1905.

BEALS, Z. C. *China and the Boxers.* Toronto, 1901.

'Behind the Scenes'. 'The Far Eastern question', *Imp. and Asiatic Q. Rev.* 3rd Ser. 5 (Apr. 1898), 275–300.

BERESFORD, LORD CHARLES. *The break-up of China* ['With an account of its present commerce, currency, waterways, armies, railways, politics, and future prospects']. New York and London, 1899.

BERTRAND, P. *Les Atrocités de la guerre de Chine.* Paris, 1899.

BIGHAM, C. C. *A year in China, 1899–1900.* London, 1901.

BISMARCK, H. *Die Belagerung von Peking.* Shanghai, 1901.

BLACK, C. E. D. 'The British sphere in Asia', *Nineteenth Cent.* 47 (May 1900), 767–75.

Blackwood's Magazine. 'Chinese imbroglio', 163 (April 1898), 552.

—— 'British interests in the Far East', 163 (May 1898), 718.

—— 'Crisis in China', 163 (Feb. 1898), 295.

—— 'Wei-hai-wei; its value as a naval station', 165 (June 1899), 1069.

—— 'Distracted China', 168 (Aug. 1900), 287.

Board of Trade Journal. 'The commercial importance of the Yang-tze', 24 (June 1898), 651–7.

BOELL, P. *Le Protectorat des missions catholiques en Chine et la politique de la France en Extrême-Orient.* Paris, 1899.

BOULGER, D. C. 'The scramble for China', *Contemp. Rev.* 78 (July 1900), 1–10.

—— 'Peking—and after', *Fort. Rev.* 68 (Aug. 1900), 198–207.

BRENIER, H. *La Mission lyonnaise d'exploration commerciale en Chine, 1895–1897.* Lyons, 1898.

BROOMHALL, M. *Martyred missionaries of the China Inland Mission* ['With a record of the perils and sufferings of some who escaped']. London, 1901.

—— *Last letters and further records of martyred missionaries of the China Inland Mission.* London, 1901.

BROWN, A. J. *New forces in Old China* ['An unwelcome but inevitable awakening']. New York and London, 1904.

BROWN, F. *From Tientsin to Peking with the Allied forces.* London, 1902. Also see *'Boxer' and other China memories.* London, 1936.

BRYSON, MARY. *Cross and crown: stories of the Chinese martyrs.* London, 1904.

BUSHBY, H. N. G. 'The agreement between Great Britain and Japan', *Nineteenth Cent. and After,* 51 (Mar. 1902), 369–82.

BUTTERWORTH, A. E. *Commission of H.M.S. 'Glory', Flag Ship of Commander-in-Chief, China Station, 1900–1904.* London, 1904.

C. G. *From Portsmouth to Peking, via Ladysmith, with a naval brigade.* Hong Kong, 1901.

CASSERLY, G. *The land of the Boxers: or China under the Allies.* New York, Bombay, and London, 1903.

CHʻAI-O. *Keng-hsin chi-shih* (Record of the affair of 1900–1), in *I.H.T.* i. 301 f.

CHAMBERLAIN, W. J. *Ordered to China.* London, 1904.

CHEMINON, J. *Les Événements militaires en Chine.* Paris, 1902.

CHIANG KʻAI. *Pʻing-yüan chʻuan-fei chi-shih* (A record of the Boxers at Pʻing-yuan), in *I.H.T.* i. 351 f.

CHIH PI-HU. *Hsu i ho chʻuan yuan liu kao* (Further research into the source and history of the *I Ho Chʻuan*), in *I.H.T.* iv. 441 f.

CHING-SHAN. *Ching-shan jih-chi* (The diary of Ching-shan), in *I.H.T.* i. 57 f. Annotated and translated by J. J. L. Duyvendak, *The diary of his Excellency Ching-shan.* Leiden, 1924.

CHIROL, V. *The Far Eastern question.* London and New York, 1896.

—— *Our imperial interests in nearer and further Asia.* London, 1905.

CHRISTIE, D. *Thirty years in Moukden, 1883–1913.* London, 1914.

COATES, C. *China and the open door.* Bristol, 1899.

[COISH, W. A. (MCLEISH).] *Tientsin besieged and after the siege from June 15 to July 16, 1900* ['A daily record by the correspondent of the *North China Daily News*']. Shanghai, 1900; 2nd ed. 1901.

COLLIN, V. *Un Reportage belge en Extrême-Orient.* Anvers, 1901.

COLQUHOUN, A. R. *China in transformation.* London and New York, 1898.

—— *Russia against India—the struggle for Asia.* London, 1900.

—— *The 'Overland' to China.* New York and London, 1900.

—— *The problem in China and British policy.* London, 1900.

—— 'The railway connection of India and China', *Imp. and Asiatic Q. Rev.* 3rd Ser. 6 (July 1898), 35–61.

—— 'The Chinese question; how it may affect our imperial interests', *JRUSI* 42 (Apr. 1898), 406–37.

—— 'The Great Trans-Siberian–Manchurian Railway', *JRUSI* 44 (Dec. 1900), 1408–30.

COLTMAN, R. *Beleaguered in Peking; the Boxer's war against the foreigner.* Philadelphia, 1901.

CONANT, C. A. *The United States in the Orient.* Boston and New York, 1900.

CONGER, S. P. *Letters from China.* London and Chicago, 1909.

Contemporary Review. 'Secret history of the Russo-Chinese Treaty', 71 (Feb. 1897), 172–83.

—— 'The problem in the Far East', 73 (Feb. 1898), 193–201.

—— 'The failure of our foreign policy', 73 (Apr. 1898), 457–80.

CORDIER, H. *La Révolution en Chine; les origines.* Leiden, 1900. Reproduced from *Le Temps* of 12 July 1900. Also see *T'oung Pao*, 2nd Ser. i (1900), 407–50.

—— *Conférence sur les relations de la Chine avec l'Europe.* Rouen, 1901.

CORNABY, W. A. *China under the searchlight.* London, 1901.

CROWE, G. *The commission of H.M.S. Terrible, 1898–1902* ['Including an account of the Naval Brigade in the North China wars']. London, 1903.

CURZON, G. N. *Russia in Central Asia in 1889 and the Anglo-Russian question.* London, 1889.

—— *Problems of the Far East: Japan–Korea–China.* London, 1894; new ed. 1896.

DAGGETT, A. S. *America in the China relief expedition.* Kansas City, 1903.

DARCY, E. *La Défense de la Légation de France à Pékin.* Paris, 1901.

DEBROAS, L. *Le drame de Pékin en 1900.* Paris, n.d. (*c.* 1900).

DEUTSCH, L. *Sixteen years in Siberia.* London, 1905. For an account of the Blagoveschensk massacre see pp. 327–43.

DICEY, E. 'Vengeance and afterwards', *Nineteenth Cent.* 48 (Aug. 1900), 339–44.

DILLON, E. L. 'M. Witte and the Russian commercial crisis', *Contemp. Rev.* 79 (Apr. 1901), 472–501.

'DIPLOMATICUS'. 'Breakdown of our Chinese policy', *Fort. Rev.* n.s. 63 (May 1898), 844–54.

—— 'Lord Salisbury's new Chinese policy', ibid. 65 (Apr. 1899), 539–50.

—— 'The crisis in the Far East', ibid. 68 (July 1900), 143–51.

—— 'Have we a policy in China?', ibid. 68 (Aug. 1900), 327–36.

—— 'The coming settlement in China', ibid. 68 (Sept. 1900), 513–22.

—— 'Count Lamsdorff's first failure', ibid. 68 (Oct. 1900), 694–700.

—— 'The concert in China', ibid. 69 (Jan. 1901), 135–46.

DIX, C. C. *The world's navies in the Boxer rebellion, China, 1900.* London, 1905.

DÖISY, A. *The new Far East*, 2nd ed. London, 1900. (About Japan.)

DONNET, G. *En Chine, 1900–1901.* Paris, 1902.

EAMES, J. B. *The English in China* ['Being an account of the intercourse and relations between England and China from the year 1600 to the year 1843 and a summary of later events']. London, 1909. (Eames was legal adviser to the Tientsin Provisional Govt. in 1901 and Professor of Law in the Imperial Tientsin University from 1898 to 1900.)

Edinburgh Review. 'China and international questions', 192 (Oct. 1900), 450–77.

EDWARDS, E. H. *Fire and sword in Shansi.* New York, 1903.

FORSYTH, R. C. *Narrative of massacres in Shansi.* Shanghai, 1900.

—— *The China martyrs.* London, 1904.

Fortnightly Review. 'Lord Salisbury and the Far East', 63 (June 1898), 1029–38.

FREY, H. N. *Français et alliés au Pé-Tchi-Li: campagne de Chine de 1900.* Paris, 1904. (Frey was Commander of the First Brigade of the French Expeditionary Force.)

—— 'The Chinese Army' (from *Revue des Deux Mondes* of Oct. 1903), *JRUSI* 47 (1903), 1270–81, 1427–34; 48 (1904), 56–64.

GAMBIER, J. W. 'A plea for peace—an Anglo-Russian alliance', *Fort. Rev.* N.S. 68 (Dec. 1900), 998–1008.

GILES, H. A. 'Diary of the Boxer riots and the siege of the legation in Peking', *Christ's College* [Camb.] *Mag.* 15. 42–125.

GIPPS, G. *The fighting in North China.* London, 1901.

GLASS, J. G. H. Report on the concessions of the Pekin Syndicate Limited, in the provinces of Shansi and Honan, China, with estimates of cost of railways and other works necessary for their development. Pekin, 1899.

GLOVER, A. E. *A thousand miles of miracle in China; a personal record of God's delivering power from the hands of the Imperial Boxers of Shansi.* London, 1904.

GORST, H. E. *China* ['On the economic resources of China, and the present political and commercial conditions of the country']. London, 1899.

GREEN, C. H. S. *'In deaths oft . . .'.* London, 1901.

GREENWOOD, F. 'The Chinese revolt', *Nineteenth Cent.* 48 (Aug. 1900), 330.

GUENTHER, H. *Die Schreckenstage von Peking.* Hamm, 1902.

GUILLOT, M. J. F. *Pékin pendant l'occupation étrangère 1900–1901.* Paris, 1904.

GUNDRY, R. S. *China, present and past* ['Foreign intercourse, progress, and resources; the missionary question, etc.']. London, 1895.

—— 'China, England and Russia', *Fort. Rev.* N.S. 60 (Oct. 1896), 506–20.

—— 'China: spheres of interest and the open door', ibid. 66 (Jan. 1899), 37–52.

—— 'Last palace intrigues at Peking', ibid. 67 (June 1900), 958–71.

HALLET, H. S. 'France and Russia in China', *Nineteenth Cent.* 41 (Mar. 1897), 487–502.

—— 'British trade and the integrity of China', *Fort. Rev.* N.S. 63 (1898), 664–79.

HAMM, M. A. 'The Boxers and other Chinese secret societies', *The Independent*, 52 (28 June 1900), 1534–7.

HANCOCK, J. G. 'Diary of the siege', London *Graphic*, 6 Oct. 1900. Hancock was a student-interpreter attached to the British Legation at Peking.

HARPER, H. *The handyman in China . . .: the expedition of the British Naval Brigade.* Hong Kong, 1901.

HART, SIR ROBERT. *The Peking legations.* Shanghai, 1900.

—— 'The Peking legations: a national uprising and international episode', *Fort. Rev.* N.S. 68 (Nov. 1900), 713–39; also in *Cosmopolitan*, 30 (Dec. 1900), 121 f.

—— 'China and Reconstruction: November 1900', *Fort Rev.* n.s. 69 (Jan. 1901), 193–206.

—— Articles were then expanded in *These from the land of Sinim*, London, 1901; 2nd ed. 1903, with additional chapter 'China, reform and the powers'.

HEADLAND, I. T. *China heroes; being a record of persecutions endured by native Christians in the Boxer uprising.* New York, 1902.

HEINZE, W. *Die Belagerung der Pekinger Gesandtschaften.* Heidelberg, 1901.

HENRY, L. *Le Siège du Pé-t'ang dans Pékin en 1900.* Peking, 1920.

HEWETT, J. W. *In a Chinese prison.* London, 1901 (in Shansi).

HEWLETT, SIR WILLIAM MEYRICK. *Diary of the siege of the Peking legations, June to August 1900.* London, 1900. Also see *Forty years in China*, London, 1943.

HOLCOMBE, C. *The real Chinese question.* New York, 1900; London, 1901.

Hong Kong Telegraph, The. 'The Kucheng massacre: Telegrams and reports of the massacre of English missionaries at Kucheng, August 1895'. Hong Kong, 1895.

HOOKER, M. *Behind the scenes in Peking; being experiences during the siege of the legations.* London, 1910.

HOSIE, A. *Manchuria: its people, resources, and recent history.* London, 1901; reissue 1904.

JACK, R. LOGAN. *The back blocks of China.* London, 1904.

JANE, F. T. 'Problem in the Far East: another view', *Contemp. Rev.* 73 (Mar. 1898), 387–93.

JEFFERSON, R. L. *China and the present crisis.* London, 1900.

JOHNSTON, J. *China and its future.* London, 1899.

KETLER, I. C. *The tragedy of Paotingfu.* New York, 1902.

KING, P. H. *In the Chinese Customs Service.* Shanghai, 1924.

KOPSCH, H. 'Britain's trade with China', *Empire Rev.* 2 (Sept. 1901), 236–52.

KRAUSSE, A. *China in decay: a handbook to the Far Eastern question.* London, 1898. 3rd ed. by 1900, sub-title changed to 'The story of a disappearing empire', and the account taken to the reported fall of the legations.

—— *Russia in Asia: a record and a study, 1558–1899.* London, 1899.

LAO NAI-HSUAN. *I ho ch'üan chiao-men yuan-liu kao* (Research into the source and history of the *I Ho Ch'uan* sect), in *I.H.T.* iv. 431 f.

—— *Ch'uan-an tsa-ts'un* (Addenda to the Boxer cases), *I.H.T.* iv. 447 f.

—— *Keng-tzu feng-chin i ho ch'uan hui-lu* (Records (kept) on receiving the prohibition against the *I Ho Ch'uan* in 1900–1).

——Lao's postscript *shu-hou* to the 'Research' is found in *Ch'uan-fei chi-lueh* (comp. *Chiao Te-sheng*), ii. 1a–4a.

LAUR, F. *Siège de Pekin* ['Récits authentiques des assiégés: S. Pichon, d'Anthouard, Ct. Darcy, Matignon, Bartholin, Mathieu, Piot, etc.']. Paris, 1904–5.

LEGRANDE-GIRARDE, E. E. *Le Génie en Chine, 1900–1901.* Paris, 1903.

LEROY-BEAULIEU, P. *The awakening of the East: Siberia, Japan, China.* New York, 1900. Trans. by R. Davey of *La Rénovation de l'Asie.* . . . Paris, 1900.

LI HSI-SHENG. *Keng-tzu kuo-pien chi* (The national rising of 1900), in *I.H.T.* i. 9 f.

LIMAGNE, A. *Les Trappistes en Chine*. Paris, 1911. Gives an account of a Trappist monastery at Yang-kia-pin on the Shansi border at the time of the Boxer rising.

LITTLE, A. *The Chinese revenue and the new treaty*. Shanghai, 1902.

LONG, R. E. C. 'Russian railway policy in Asia', *Fort. Rev.* N.S. 66 (Dec. 1899), 914–25.

LOTI, P. See under VIAND, L. M. J.

MACDONALD, SIR CLAUDE. 'The Japanese detachment during the defence of the Peking legations, June–August, 1900', *Transactions and Proceedings of the Japan Society*, 12 (1913–14), 1–20. MacDonald's report on the siege is given in China No. 3 (1901), 1–31.

MACDONALD, LADY ETHEL. 'My visits to the Dowager-Empress of China', *Empire Rev.* 1 (Apr. 1901), 247–55.

MAHAN, A. T. *The problem of Asia and its effect upon international policies*. Boston, 1900.

MARCILLAC, JEAN DE. *La Chine qui s'ouvre*. Paris, 1900.

MARTIN, W. A. P. *The siege in Peking; China against the world*. Edinburgh and New York, 1900. Also see 'Fall of Peking', *Independent*, 52 (Oct. 1900), 2419–21; 'Causes that led up to the siege of Peking', *Nat. Geographic*, 12 (Feb. 1901), 53–63.

—— *The awakening of China*. London, 1907.

MATEER, A. H. *Siege days* ['Personal experiences of American women and children during the Peking siege']. New York, 1903.

MATIGNON, J. J. *La Défense de la légation de France, Pékin, du 13 juin au 15 août 1900*. Paris, 1902. Also given in *Dix Ans au pays du dragon*. Paris, 1910.

MINER, L. *China's book of martyrs, 1900*. New York, 1903.

MITCHIE, A. 'China in commotion', *Imp. and Asiatic Q. Rev.* 3rd Ser. 5 (Apr. 1898), 301–8.

—— *China and Christianity*. Boston, 1900.

—— *The Englishman in China during the Victorian era*, 2 vols. London, 1900. In vol. 2, Ch. XXXIII is a commentary on the Boxers.

MITFORD, A. B. F. *The attaché at Peking*. London, 1900.

MONNIER, M. *Le Drame chinois, juillet–août 1900*. Paris, 1900.

MOREING, C. A. 'Great Britain's opportunity in China', *Nineteenth Cent.* 43 (Feb. 1898), 328–35.

MORRISON, G. E. 'Siege of the Peking legations', in the London *Times*, 13, 15 Oct. 1900.

MUELLER, A. VON. *Die Wirren in China und die Kämpfe der verbündeten Truppen*. Berlin, 1902. (A methodical account of the Seymour Expedition.)

National Review. 'Crisis in the Far East', 30 (Feb. 1898), 817.

—— 'British interests as stated by Mr. Balfour', 31 (May 1898), 340.

NEWMAN, H. *The Indian contingent in China*. Calcutta, 1900.

(NORIE, MAJOR?) 'Official history of the military operations in China, 1900–1901', 350 pp., not published. A draft of this work was submitted to the Foreign Office on 15 Aug. 1902. Lord Lansdowne and Sir Thomas Sanderson decided that the long discourses on political matters and personalities in the work made it unfit for publication without serious editing. See Sanderson to Lansdowne, 2 Oct. 1902 (under 15 Aug. 1902), F.O.

17/1552; Sanderson to Intelligence Division, War Office, 21 Oct. 1902, F.O. 17/1554.

N. C. D. N. *A refugee's experiences at Peking and on the route south.* Shanghai, 1900.

NORTON, LT. R. Report on the Siberian Railway, 11 July 1900, in Admiralty to Foreign Office, 30 July 1900, F.O. 17/1443.

OLIPHANT, N. *Diary of the siege of the legations in Peking during the summer of 1900.* London, 1901.

PALMER, F. 'With the Peking relief column', *Century Illustrated Monthly Mag.* 61 (Dec. 1900), 302–7.

PARKER, E. H. 'Intimate Boxers', *Contemp. Rev.* 78 (Sept. 1900), 318–25.

—— 'The revolt of the "Boxers" in China', *Imp. and Asiatic Q. Rev.* 3rd Ser. 10 (July 1900), 57–62.

—— 'The Chinese imbroglio and how to get out of it', ibid. 10 (Oct. 1900), 252–77.

—— 'The Chinese revenue', *Journal China Br. Royal Asiatic Society*, N.S. 30 (1895–6), 102–41.

PAYEN, C. E. 'Besieged in Peking', *Century Mag.* 61 (Dec. 1900), 453–68.

PELACOT, M. DE. *Expédition de Chine de 1900 jusqu'à l'arrivée du général Voyron.* Paris, 1903. (Pichon's Journal is given on pp. 173 ff.)

PETHICK, W. N. 'The struggle on the Peking wall: an episode of the siege of the legations', *Century Mag.* 61 (Dec. 1900), 308–13.

PIGOTT, C. A. *Steadfast unto death. . . .* London, 1903.

PINON, R. *La Chine qui s'ouvre.* Paris, 1900. (Published before the Boxer rising; presents French and Russian aspirations in the East.)

PONTÈVES, RUFFI DE. *Les Marins en Chine.* Paris, 1903. (Deals with the Seymour Expedition.)

POTT, F. L. H. *The outbreak in China; its causes.* New York, 1900.

Quarterly Review. 'British interests in China', 191 (Jan. 1900), 1–29.

RANSOME, JESSIE. *Story of the siege hospital in Peking, and diary of events from May to August 1900.* London, 1901.

REINSCH, P. S. *World politics at the end of the nineteenth century as influenced by the oriental situation.* New York and London, 1900.

RICHARD, TIMOTHY. *Forty-five years in China.* London, 1916.

ROBERTS, J. H. *A flight for life from Tientsin.* Boston, 1903.

ROSS, J. *The Boxers in Manchuria.* Shanghai, 1901.

—— *Mission methods in Manchuria.* Edinburgh, 1903.

RUSSELL, S. M. *The story of the siege in Peking.* London, 1901.

S. M. *La Chine et les alliés.* Paris, 1903.

SAILLENS, M. M. P. *Campagne de Chine, 1900.* Paris, 1901.

Saturday Review. 'The alleged Russo-Chinese Convention', 12 Dec. 1896.

—— 'Lord Salisbury and China', 16 July 1898.

—— 'The British sphere in China', 6 Jan. 1900.

SAVAGE-LANDOR, A. H. *China and the Allies*, 2 vols. London, 1901.

SCHEIBERT, J. *Der Krieg in China.* Berlin, 1901.

SCHOTT, E. *Die Wirren in China und ihre Ursachen.* Leipzig, 1900.

SEYMOUR, ADMIRAL SIR E. H. Report on the combined naval expedition, in Admiralty to Foreign Office 21 Sept. 1901, F.O. 17/1509.

—— *My naval career.* London, 1911.

Shanghai Mercury, The. The Boxer Rising: a history of the Boxer trouble in China. Shanghai, 1900.

SHOEMAKER, M. M. *The Great Siberian Railway from St. Petersburg to Peking.* New York and London, 1903.

'SINICUS'. 'Chinese reform and British interests', *Imp. and Asiatic Q. Rev.* 3rd Ser. 7 (Apr. 1899), 318–21.

SMITH, A. H. *China in convulsion,* 2 vols. Edinburgh and New York, 1901.

SMITH, S. P. *China from within; or the story of the Chinese crisis.* London, 1901.

SMYTH, G. B., *et. al. The crisis in China.* New York, 1900. (Articles from the *North American Rev.* by Colquhoun, Beresford, Dilke, and others.)

SOWERBY, A. 'The crisis in China', *Contemp. Rev.* 78 (July 1900), 11.

Spectator. 'England and Russia in China', 80 (30 Apr. 1898), 612.

—— 'Great Britain and China', 85 (20 Oct. 1900), 517.

SPEER, R. E. *Missions and politics in China: a record of cause and effect.* New York, 1900.

STEAD, W. T. 'Russia and Mr. Chamberlain's long spoon', *Contemp. Rev.* 73 (June 1898), 761–77.

STEDMAN, MAJOR-GENERAL. Confidential report on the Imperial Railways in China under the British Railway Administration, 21 Jan. 1903, F.O. 17/1757. (Contains a series of $\frac{1}{2}$ in. maps of the Northern Railway, and a collection of twenty-nine photographs.)

STEWART, MAJOR-GENERAL SIR NORMAN R. *My service days.* London, 1908.

'TEAREM, M. P.' 'Our "expert" statesmen', *Contemp. Rev.* 73 (May 1898), 628.

THOMSON, H. C. *China and the powers: a narrative of the outbreak of 1900.* London, 1902. Also see *The case for China.* London, 1933, pp. 28–78.

TISSIER, R. *La Croix-Rouge française et les navires-hôpitaux pendant la campagne de Chine, 1900–1901.* Paris, 1903.

ULAR, A. *Un Empire russo-chinois.* Paris, 1903; Eng. trans. 1904.

VAUGHAN, H. B. *St. George and the Chinese dragon: an account of the relief.* London, 1902.

VIAND, L. M. J. (pseud. Pierre Loti). *Les Derniers Jours de Pékin.* Paris, 1902; trans. by M. L. Jones, *The Last Days of Peking.* Boston, 1902.

VOLPICELLI, Z. (pseud. Vladimir). *Russia on the Pacific and the Siberian Railway.* London, 1899.

WALTON, J. *China and the present crisis.* 2nd ed., London, 1900.

WEALE, B. L. (pseud. Putnam). *Indiscreet letters from Peking,* ed. Simpson, B. L. London, 1907.

WHATES, H. *The third Salisbury administration, 1895–1900.* London, n.d.

—— 'A year of Lord Lansdowne', *Fort. Rev.* N.S. 70 (Oct. 1901), 581.

WHIGHAM, H. J. *Manchuria and Korea.* London, 1904.

WHITEHEAD, T. H. *British interests in China.* Hong Kong, 1897.

—— *Expansion of trade in China.* London, 1901.

WILLIAM, M. *Across the Desert of Gobi: a narrative of an escape during the Boxer rising, June to September 1900.* Ohio, 1901.

WILSON, J. H. *China . . . with an account of the Boxer war.* New York, 1901.

WINGATE, LT.-COL. A. W. S. Military report on the defences of the Yangtzu region (secret). London, 1906, W.O. 106/25.

WRAY, CAPT. Report on the siege of the legations at Peking, in Admiralty to Foreign Office, 5 Dec. 1900, F.O. 17/1450.

'X'. 'The German danger in the Far East', *Nat. Rev.* 36 (1900), 178.

YERBURGH, R. 'China's markets and British apathy', *Empire Rev.* 1 (May 1901), 390–8.

YOUNGHUSBAND, SIR F. E. 'England's destiny in China', *Contemp. Rev.* 74 (Oct. 1898), 457–73.

YUN YU-TING. *Ch'ung ling chuan hsin lu* (The true story of the Kuang-hsu Emperor), in *I.H.T.* i. 45 f.

H. OTHER BOOKS AND ARTICLES

ALLEN, B. M. *The Right Honourable Sir Ernest Satow: a memoir.* London, 1933.

AMERY, L. S. *My political life*; Vol. 1: *England before the storm, 1896–1914.* London, 1953.

ASPINALL-OGLANDER, C. *Roger Keyes.* London, 1951.

Bank of China, Research Department. *Chinese Government foreign loan obligations.* Shanghai, 1935.

BAYLIN, J. R. *Foreign loan obligations of China.* Tientsin, 1925.

BEALE, H. K. *Theodore Roosevelt and the rise of America to world power.* Baltimore, 1956.

BEASLEY, W. G. *Great Britain and the opening of Japan, 1834–58.* London, 1951.

BEE, M. C. 'Origins of German Far Eastern policy', *CSPSR* 21 (1937–8), 65–97.

—— 'The Peterhof Agreement', *CSPSR* 20 (1936–7), 231–50.

BENIANS, E. A. *The Cambridge history of the British Empire*, eds. Sir James Butler and C. E. Carrington; Vol. III: *The Empire-Commonwealth, 1870–1919.* Cambridge, 1959.

BICKFORD, J. D., and JOHNSON, E. N. 'The contemplated Anglo-German alliance, 1890–1901', *PSQ* 13 (Mar. 1927), 1–57.

BLAND, J. O. P., and BACKHOUSE, SIR E. T. *China under the Empress Dowager.* London, 1910.

BRAISTED, W. R. *The United States Navy in the Pacific, 1897–1909.* Austin, 1958.

—— 'The United States and the American China Development Company', *FEQ* 11 (1952), 147–65.

BRANDENBURG, E. *From Bismarck to the World War* (trans. by A. E. Adams of *Von Bismarck zum Weltkrieg.* Berlin, 1924). London, 1927.

BREDON, J. *Sir Robert Hart.* London, 1909.

BRETT, M. V. (ed.). *Journals and letters of Reginald, Viscount Esher,* 4 vols. London, 1934–8.

BUCKLE, G. E. (ed.). *The letters of Queen Victoria*; 3rd Ser.: *1886–1901,* 3 vols. London, 1930–2, vol. 3.

BÜLOW, B. VON. *Memoirs of Prince von Bülow,* Eng. trans., 4 vols. Boston, 1931.

CADY, J. F. *The roots of French imperialism in Eastern Asia.* New York, 1954.

CAMERON, M. E. *The reform movement in China, 1898–1912.* Stanford, 1931.

—— 'The public career of Chang Chih-tung', *PHR* 7 (1938), 187–210.

CAMPBELL, A. E. 'Great Britain and the United States in the Far East, 1895–1903', *Historical Journal,* I (1958), 154–75.

CAMPBELL, A. E. *Great Britain and the United States, 1895–1905.* London, 1960.

CAMPBELL, C. S. *Special business interests and the open-door policy.* Yale, 1951.

—— *Anglo-American understanding, 1898–1903.* Baltimore, 1957.

CARLSON, E. C. *The Kaiping mines, 1877–1912.* Cambridge, Mass., 1957.

CARY-ELWES, C. *China and the Cross: studies in missionary history.* London, 1957.

CECIL, LADY GWENDOLEN. *Life of Robert, Marquis of Salisbury,* 4 vols. London, 1921–2.

CHAN CHUNG SING. *Les Concessions en Chine.* Paris, 1925.

CHANG, C. F. *The Anglo-Japanese alliance.* Baltimore, 1931.

CHANG KIA-NGAU. *China's struggle for railroad development.* New York, 1943.

CH'EN CHIEH. *I-ho-t'uan yun-tung shih* (History of the Boxer movement). Shanghai, 1931.

CH'EN, J. *Yuan Shih-k'ai, 1859–1916.* London, 1961.

CHEN, M. C. *La Presse française et les questions chinoises, 1894–1901: étude sur la rivalité des puissances étrangères en Chine.* Paris, 1941.

CHIANG SIANG-TSEH. *The Nien rebellion.* Seattle, 1954.

CHIEN PO-TSAN (ed. and comp.). *I-ho-t'uan* (The Boxers), 4 vols. Shanghai, 1951; 3rd ed. 1953.

CHRISTIAN, J. L. *Modern Burma.* Berkeley, 1942.

CLEMENTS, P. H. *The Boxer rebellion.* New York, 1915.

CLINARD, O. J. *Japan's influence on American naval power, 1897–1917.* Berkeley, 1947.

COHEN, P. A. *The Hunan-Kiangsi anti-missionary incidents of 1862.* Harvard Univ. Papers on China, 12, 1958.

—— *China and Christianity: the missionary movement and the growth of Chinese antiforeignism, 1860–1870.* Cambridge, Mass., 1963.

CONROY, H. *The Japanese seizure of Korea, 1868–1910: a study of realism and idealism in international relations.* Philadelphia, 1960.

COONS, A. G. *The foreign public debt of China.* Philadelphia, 1930.

CORDIER, H. *Histoire des relations de la Chine avec les puissances occidentales, 1860–1902,* 3 vols. Paris, 1901–2.

COSTIN, W. C. *Great Britain and China, 1833–1860.* Oxford, 1937.

CUNNINGHAM, A. *History of the Szechuan riots, May–June 1895.* Shanghai, 1895.

DAVIES, C. C. *The problem of the North-west Frontier, 1890–1908.* Cambridge, 1932.

DENNETT, T. *Americans in Eastern Asia* ['A critical study of the policy of the United States, with reference to China, Japan, and Korea in the nineteenth century']. New York, 1922.

—— T. *John Hay: from poetry to politics.* New York, 1933.

DENNIS, A. L. P. *Adventures in American diplomacy, 1896–1906.* New York, 1928.

DJANG, F. D. (Chang Feng-chen). *Diplomatic relations between China and Germany since 1898.* Shanghai, 1936.

DUGDALE, B. E. C. *Arthur James Balfour, first Earl of Balfour,* 2 vols. London, 1936.

ECKARDSTEIN, BARON VON. *Lebenserinnerungen,* 3 vols. Leipzig, 1920–1.

EDWARDS, E. W. 'The Japanese alliance and the Anglo-French Agreement of 1904', *History,* 42 (1957), 19–27.

ELKIND, L. *The German Emperor's speeches.* London, 1904.

ELLIOT, A. R. D. *The life of George Joachim Goschen, first Viscount Goschen,* 2 vols. London, 1911.

FAIRBANK, J. K. 'Patterns behind the Tientsin massacre', *HJAS* 20 (1957), 480–511.

FALK, E. A. *Togo and the rise of Japanese sea-power.* New York, 1936.

FAVRE, B. *Les Sociétés secrètes en Chine.* Paris, 1933.

FEIS, H. *Europe, the world's banker, 1870–1914.* New Haven, 1930.

FEUERWERKER, A. *China's early industrialization: Sheng Hsuan-huai (1844–1916) and Mandarin enterprise.* Cambridge, Mass., 1958.

FINDLAY, G. G., and HOLDSWORTH, W. W. *The history of the Wesleyan Methodist Missionary Society,* 5 vols. London, 1924.

FLEMING, P. *The siege at Peking.* London, 1959.

GALLAGHER, J., and ROBINSON, R. 'The imperialism of free trade', *Economic Hist. Rev.* 2nd Ser. 6 (1953), 1–15.

GAPANOVICH, J. J. 'Sino-Russian relations in Manchuria, 1892–1906', *CSPSR* 17 (1933), 283–306, 457–79.

GARDINER, A. G. *Life of Sir William Vernon Harcourt,* 2 vols. London, 1923.

GARVIN, J. L., and AMERY, J. *The life of Joseph Chamberlain,* 4 vols. London, 1932–51.

GELBER, L. M. *The rise of Anglo-American friendship: a study in world politics, 1898–1906.* New York, 1938.

GLANVILLE, J. L. *Italy's relations with England, 1896–1905.* Baltimore, 1934.

GLEASON, J. H. *The genesis of Russophobia in Great Britain.* Harvard, 1950.

GODSHALL, W. L. *Tsingtau under three flags.* Shanghai, 1929.

GOODALL, N. *A history of the London Missionary Society, 1895–1945.* London, 1954.

GOODRICH, L. C. 'American catholic missions in China', *CSPSR* 11 (1927), 414 f., 610 f.; 12 (1928), 59 f.

GOSSES, F. *The management of British foreign policy before the First World War, especially during the period 1880–1914,* trans. by E. C. van der Gaaf. Leiden, 1948.

GOUDSWAARD, J. M. *Some aspects of the end of Britain's 'Splendid Isolation' 1898–1904.* Rotterdam, 1952.

GREENE, R. S. 'Education in China and the Boxer indemnities', *CSPSR* 7 (1923), 199 f.

GRENVILLE, J. A. S. *Lord Salisbury and foreign policy: The close of the nineteenth century.* London, 1964.

GRISWOLD, A. W. *The Far Eastern policy of the United States.* New York, 1938.

GULL, E. M. *British economic interests in the Far East.* London, 1943.

HAMADA, K. *Prince Ito.* London, 1937.

HARGREAVES, J. D. 'Entente Manquée; Anglo-French relations, 1895–1896', *Cambridge Hist. Journal,* 11 (1953), 65–92.

—— 'Lord Salisbury, British isolation and the Yang-tze, June–September, 1900', *Bulletin of the Inst. of Historical Research,* 30 (1957), 62–75.

HICKS BEACH, LADY VICTORIA. *Life of Sir Michael Hicks Beach, Earl St. Aldwyn,* 2 vols. London, 1932.

HINTON, H. C. *The grain tribute system of China (1845–1911)*. Cambridge, Mass., 1956.

HISHIDA, S. *The international position of Japan as a Great Power*. New York, 1905.

HOFFMAN, R. T. S. *Great Britain and the German trade rivalry, 1875–1914*. Philadelphia and London, 1933.

HOLLAND, B. H. *Life of Spencer Compton, eighth Duke of Devonshire*, 2 vols. London, 1911.

HOU CHI-MING. 'Foreign capital in China's economic development, 1895–1937', Columbia Univ., Ph.D., 1954. Univ. Microfilms Publications 10267, Ann Arbor, 1954.

HSIAO I-SHAN (ed.). *Chin-tai pi-mi shi-hui shih-liao* (Historical material on modern secret societies). Peiping, 1935.

HUDSON, G. F. *The Far East in world politics*. 2nd ed., Oxford, 1939.

HUMMEL, A. (ed.). *Eminent Chinese of the Ch'ing period*, 2 vols. Washington, 1943–4.

HYDE, F. E. 'The expansion of Liverpool's carrying trade with the Far East and Australia, 1860–1914', *TRHS* 6 (1956), 139–60.

ISHII, VISCOUNT. *Diplomatic commentaries*, trans and ed. by W. R. Langdon. Baltimore, 1936.

JANSEN, M. B. 'Opportunists in South China during the Boxer Rebellion', 20 *PHR.*, August 1951.

—— *The Japanese and Sun Yat-sen*. Cambridge, Mass., 1954.

JOSEPH, P. *Foreign diplomacy in China, 1894–1900*. London, 1928.

KANN, E. *The history of China's internal loan issues*. Shanghai, 1934.

KAWAI, K. 'Anglo-German rivalry in the Yangtze region', *PHR* 8 (1939), 413 f.

KELLY, J. S. *A forgotten conference: the negotiations at Peking, 1900–1901*. Geneva and Paris, 1963.

KENNEDY, A. L. *Salisbury, 1830–1903*. London, 1953.

KENT, P. H. *Railway enterprise in China*. London, 1907.

KIERNAN, E. V. G. *British diplomacy in China, 1880–1885*. London, 1939.

KUO SUNG-PING. 'Chinese reaction to foreign encroachment; with special reference to the first Sino-Japanese war and its immediate aftermath', Columbia Univ., Ph.D., 1953. Univ. Microfilms Publication 6652, Ann Arbor, 1954.

LANGER, W. L. *The diplomacy of Imperialism, 1890–1902*. 2nd ed., New York, 1951.

LATOURETTE, K. S. *A history of Christian missions in China*. New York, 1929.

LEVENSON, J. R. *Liang Ch'i-ch'ao and the mind of modern China*. 2nd rev. ed., London, 1959.

LEVI, W. *Modern China's foreign policy*. New York, 1953.

LI CHIEN-NUNG. *The political history of China, 1840–1928*, trans. S. Y. Teng and J. Engels. London, 1956.

LI SHIH-YU. *Religions secrètes contemporaines dans le nord de la Chine*. Chengtu, 1948.

LIU LIEN-K'O. *Pang-hui san-pai-nien ko-ming shih* (A history of the revolutionary activities of secret societies during the last three hundred years). Macao, 1940.

MALOZEMOFF, A. *Russian Far-Eastern policy, 1881–1904* ['With special emphasis on the causes of the Russo-Japanese war']. Berkeley and London, 1958.

MARDER, A. J. *British naval policy, 1880–1905*. London, 1940.

McCORDOCK, R. S. *British Far-Eastern policy, 1894–1900*. New York, 1931.

MEYENDORFF, BARON A. *Correspondance diplomatique du baron de Staal*, 2 vols. Paris, 1929.

MONGER, G. *The end of isolation: British foreign policy, 1900–1907*. London and Edinburgh, 1963.

MORSE, H. B. *The international relations of the Chinese Empire*, 3 vols. New York, 1910–18.

—— *The trade and administration of the Chinese Empire*. London, 1908.

MURAMATSU, YUJI. 'The Boxers in 1898–9; the origin of the *I-ho-chuan* uprising, 1900', *Annals of the Hitotsubashi Academy*, 3 (1953), 236–61.

MURPHY, A. *The ideology of French Imperialism*. Washington, 1948.

NEWTON, LORD, *Lord Lansdowne*. London, 1929.

NISH, I. H. *The Anglo-Japanese alliance: the diplomacy of two island empires, 1894–1907*. London, 1966.

NOREM, R. A. 'German Catholic missions in Shantung', *CSPSR* 19 (1935), 45–64.

—— *Kiaochow leased territory*. Berkeley, 1936.

NORMAN, E. H. *Japan's emergence as a modern state*. New York, 1940.

North China Herald Office. *The anti-foreign riots of 1891*. Shanghai, 1892.

OKUMA, SHIGENOBU (comp.). *Fifty years of new Japan*. New York, 1909.

PALMER, A. W. 'Lord Salisbury's approach to Russia, 1898', *Oxford Slavonic Papers*, 6 (1955), 102–14.

PASCOE, C. F. *Two hundred years of the S.P.G.: an historical account of the Society for the Propagation of the Gospel in Foreign Parts, 1701–1900*, 2 vols. London, 1901.

PELCOVITS, N. A. *Old China hands and the Foreign Office*. New York, 1948.

PENSON, DAME LILLIAN. 'The principles and methods of Lord Salisbury's foreign policy', *Cambridge Hist. Journal*, 5 (1935), 87–106.

—— 'The new course in British foreign policy, 1892–1902', *TRHS* 4th Ser. 25 (1943), 121–38.

—— *Foreign affairs under the third Marquess of Salisbury*. London, 1962.

PERGAMENT, M. *The diplomatic quarter in Peking*. Peking, 1927.

POOLEY, A. M. (ed.). *The secret memoirs of Count Tadasu Hayashi*. New York and London, 1915.

PORTER, D. H. 'Secret sects in Shantung', *Chinese Recorder*, 17 (1886), 1–10, 64 f.

POWELL, R. L. *The rise of Chinese military power, 1895–1912*. Princeton, 1955.

RAWLINSON, J. L. *China's struggle for naval development, 1839–1895*. Cambridge, Mass., 1967.

REMER, C. F. *Foreign investments in China*. New York, 1933.

RICH, N. *Friedrich von Holstein: politics and diplomacy in the era of Bismarck and Wilhelm II*, 2 vols. Cambridge, 1965.

ROBERTS, S. H. *History of French colonial policy (1870–1925)*, 2 vols. London, 1929.

ROMANOV, B. A. *Rossia v Manchzhurii, 1892–1906* (with English summary). Leningrad, 1928. trans. S. W. Jones, *Russia in Manchuria, 1892–1906*. Ann Arbor, 1952.

RONALDSHAY, THE EARL OF. *The life of Lord Curzon*, 3 vols. London, 1928.

ROSEN, O. 'German-Japanese relations, 1894–1902: a study of European imperialism in the Far East. Univ. Microfilms Publication 19132. Ann Arbor, 1956.

SARGENT, A. J. *Anglo-Chinese commerce and diplomacy*. Oxford, 1907.

SMITH, C. A. M. *The British in China and Far-Eastern trade*. London, 1920.

SMYTHE, E. J. *The Tzu-li Hui: some Chinese and their rebellion*. Harvard Univ. Papers on China, 12, 1958.

SOULIE, G. *T'seu-Hsi, impératrice des Boxeurs*. Paris, 1911.

SPENDER, J. A. *Fifty years of Europe*. London, 1933.

SPINKS, C. N. 'The background of the Anglo-Japanese alliance', *PHR* 8 (1939), 317–39.

STEIGER, G. N. *China and the Occident: the origin and development of the Boxer movement*. New Haven, 1927.

STEINER, Z. S. 'Great Britain and the creation of the Anglo-Japanese alliance', *Journal of Modern History*, 31 (Mar. 1959), 27–39.

—— 'The last years of the old Foreign Office, 1898–1905', *Historical Journal*, 6 (1963), 59–90.

STOCK, E. *The history of the Church Missionary Society*, 3 vols. and suppl. vol. London, 1899, 1916.

TAN, C. *The Boxer catastrophe*. New York, 1954.

TENG SSU-YU and FAIRBANK, J. K. *China's response to the West: a documentary survey, 1839–1923*. Cambridge, Mass., 1954.

THAYER, W. R. *The life and letters of John Hay*, 2 vols. Boston, 1915.

THOMSON, D. (ed.). *The New Cambridge Modern History*; Vol. xii: *The era of violence, 1898–1945*. Cambridge, 1960.

TILLEY, J. A. C., and GASELEE, S. *The Foreign Office*. London, 1933.

Times, The. The history of 'The Times', 1785–1948, 4 vols. London, 1935–52.

TOWNSEND, M. E. *The rise and fall of Germany's colonial empire, 1884–1918*. New York, 1930.

TYAU, MIN-CH'IEN T. Z. *The legal obligations arising out of treaty relations between China and other states*. Shanghai, 1917.

VARG, P. A. 'The foreign policy of Japan and the Boxer revolt', *PHR* 15 (Sept. 1946), 279–85.

—— 'William Woodville Rockhill's influence on the Boxer negotiations', *PHR* 18 (1949), 369–80.

—— *Open-door diplomat: the life of W. W. Rockhill*. University of Illinois Press, 1952.

—— *Missionaries, Chinese, and diplomats: the American Protestant missionary movement in China, 1890–1952*. Princeton, 1958.

WALDERSEE, A. H. K. L., GRAF VON. *Denkwürdigkeiten des Generalfeldmarschalls Alfred Grafen von Waldersee*, ed. H. O. Meisner, 3 vols. Stuttgart, 1923–5. Cond. and trans. by F. Whyte, *A Field Marshal's memoirs*. London, 1924.

WALSH, W. B. 'The Yunnan myth', *FEQ* 2 (1943), 272–85.

WARD, SIR A. W., and GOOCH, G. P. (eds.). *The Cambridge history of British foreign policy, 1783–1919*, 3 vols. Cambridge, 1923. Vol. iii.

WEHRLE, E. S. *Britain, China, and the antimissionary riots, 1891–1900*. Minneapolis, 1966.

WILDE, R. H. 'The Boxer affair and Australian responsibility for imperial defense', *PHR* 26 (1957), 51–65.

WILLOUGHBY, W. W. *Foreign rights and interests in China*, 2 vols. Baltimore, 1927.

WOODWARD, E. L. *Great Britain and the German Navy*. Oxford, 1935.

WRIGHT, S. F. *China's struggle for tariff autonomy, 1843–1938*. Shanghai, 1938.

—— *Hart and the Chinese customs*. Belfast, 1950.

WU, CHAO-KWANG. *The international aspect of the missionary movement in China*. Baltimore, 1930.

ZEN SUN E-TU. *Chinese railways and British interests, 1898–1911*. New York, 1954.

—— 'The lease of Wei-hai Wei', *PHR* 19 (1950), 277 f.

I. MAPS

At the end of the nineteenth century the growing need for reliable geographical information on the Far East led C. T. Gardiner, of the Foreign Office, to put forward a project (in 1887) for a series of maps to be drawn from Chinese sources. A Roll of Maps for the Far East, which is the probable result of this scheme, may be inspected at the Public Record Office (MR 657). In 1900 the Boxer rising brought about an urgent need for cartographical information on China, particularly in respect of the scene of military operations in the north. Several maps were then drawn up; the more informative of these are listed below.

Map of the scene of operations; in 'Short Military Report on the Province of Chihli', India Office to Foreign Office, 30 July 1900, F.O. 17/1443.

Map of the Western portion of Yunnan, showing Trade Routes, 1897; in India Office to Foreign Office, 3 July 1900, F.O. 17/1441.

Plan of the Defence of the Legations (1 in. to 80 yards); W.O. 32/138/7842/1743.

Series of Maps and Charts concerned with the Northern Railway; in Maj.-Gen. Stedman's report (details given under 'Stedman', Section G, above).

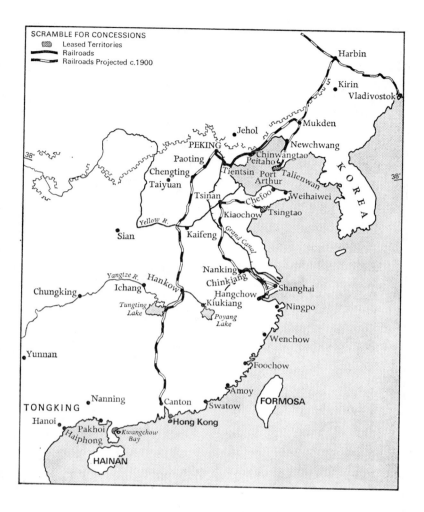

SCRAMBLE FOR CONCESSIONS
  Leased Territories
  Railroads
  Railroads Projected c.1900

Harbin

Kirin
Vladivostok

Mukden

Jehol
Newchwang
PEKING
Chinwangtao
Paoting
Peitaho
Chengting
Tientsin
Port
Talienwan
Taiyuan
Arthur

KOREA

38°
38°

Tsinan
Chefoo
Weihaiwei
Kiaochow
Tsingtao

Yellow R.
Sian
Kaifeng
Grand Canal

Nanking
Yangtze R.
Hankow
Chinkiang
Chungking
Ichang
Hangchow
Shanghai
Kiukiang
Ningpo
Tungting
Lake
Poyang
Lake

Wenchow

Yunnan
Foochow

Amoy
FORMOSA
Nanning
Canton
Swatow
TONGKING
Hanoi
Hong Kong
Pakhoi
Kwangchow
Haiphong
Bay
HAINAN

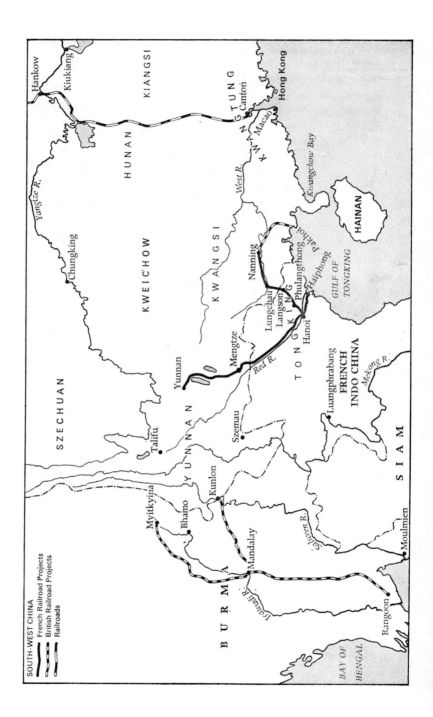

SOUTH-WEST CHINA
━━━ French Railroad Projects
╫╫╫ British Railroad Projects
╍╍╍ Railroads

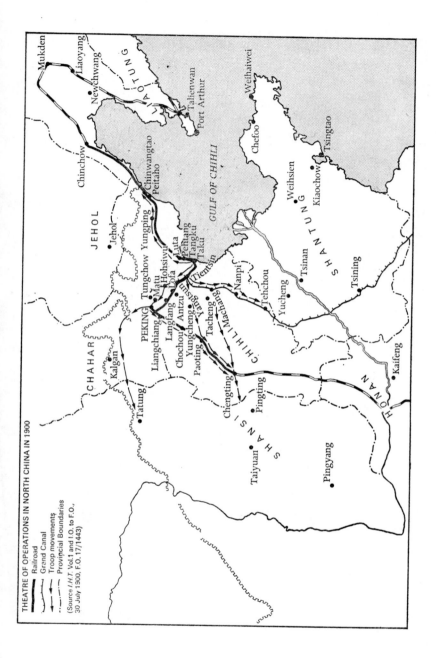

THEATRE OF OPERATIONS IN NORTH CHINA IN 1900

Railroad
Grand Canal
Troop movements
Provincial Boundaries

(Source *I.H.T.* Vol.1 and I.O. to F.O.,
30 July 1900, F.O. 17/1443)

INDEX

Admiralty, British; activity along China coast, 6, 43, 49, 50, 60, 62, 134, 161, 163, 167, 173, 174, 184, 191, 273, 301; and Committee of Defence, 24; and occupation of Weihaiwei, 70, 73–4; and ships at Port Arthur, 75; and Boxer rising, 113, 116, 120; and Anglo-Japanese alliance, 305–7, 313–14, 315–16.

Alexieff, Admiral E. I., 139, 150, 195, 209, 269–72, 273; see also Tseng–Alexieff Agreement.

American Asiatic Association, 98, 174.

American China Development Company, 81, 98.

Amoy, Japanese occupation of, 189–91.

Amur River Society, 189.

Anglo-Chinese Convention (1894), 30.

Anglo-Chinese wars (1839–42, 1856–60), 2–3, 54.

Anglo-French convention concerning Siam and China (1896), 31–3, 93.

Anglo-German (Yangtze) Agreement, 193–213, 282, 293, 296, 302.

Anglo-German banking arrangement, 83, 86, 92.

Anglo-Japanese alliance, 24, 295–318; background of, 137, 285, 295; proposals for, 300, 302; negotiations, 303, 304, 307–13, 314–17.

Anglo-Russian Agreement (1899); Hicks Beach on, 55–6; Salisbury and, 56, 59 f., 93–5, 97, 133, 318; and Northern railway, 196, 276.

Anzer, Bishop, 102.

Aoki Shuzo, Viscount, 136, 137, 143, 151, 182, 272.

Ardagh, Major-General Sir John, 40, 138, 172, 179, 272, 297; on Russian activity in Asia, 41, 248; on Yangtze valley, 80, 186.

Australia, and Boxer rising, 136.

Balfour, Arthur James, 20, 24, 38, 66, 72, 136, 150, 315; and Weihaiwei, 67, 69–71; and Anglo-Russian Agreement, 93–4.

Barrington, E., 152.

Barrow, General Sir George, 253.

Beau, Paul, 318.

Beresford, Admiral Lord Charles, mission to Far East, 95–7.

Bertie, Sir Francis, 20–1, 52, 53, 132, 133, 154, 172, 276, 281, 286, 287, 293, 298, 299–300; on situation in China, 197, 204; and Anglo-Japanese alliance, 300, 302.

Bezaure, Comte de, 182.

Big Swords sect, 104.

Bigge, Sir Arthur, 57.

Blake, Sir Henry, 189, 301.

Boer war, and Far Eastern situation, 97, 117, 170, 232, 242–3, 248, 307, 317.

Boxers, origin of sect, 104, 106–8; attitude of diplomatic body to, 108–10, 115, 117, 128–9; attitude of Manchu Court to, 109–10, 111, 116, 121, 125; attack on Legations, 129, 132; activity in Manchuria, 267.

Brenan, Byron, 170, 171.

British and Chinese Corporation, 83, 86, 91, 93, 95, 277–80.

Brodrick, William St. John, 99, 134, 136, 150, 172.

Brooks, Revd. S. M., 110–11.

Browne, Lieutenant-Colonel G. F., 172.

Bruce, Rear-Admiral, 135, 137, 150.

Buller, Admiral, 49, 62.

Bülow, Prince Bernhard von, 140, 290.

Burma, 14, 34, 35, 79, 81.

Butterfield and Swire, 5.

Cambon, Paul, 92, 146, 215.

Cameron, Sir Ewen, 51, 52, 56, 92.

Canterbury, Archbishop of, 114.

Carles, Consul, 120, 144.

Cassini, Count Arturo, 37, 38.

Chamberlain, Joseph, 20, 32, 136, 200, 315; and understanding with Germany, 65, 72, 97, 203, 293, 306, 307; and Chinese situation, 66, 76; and Weihaiwei, 73.

Chang Chih-tung, 160, 162, 287; request for loan, 180–1.